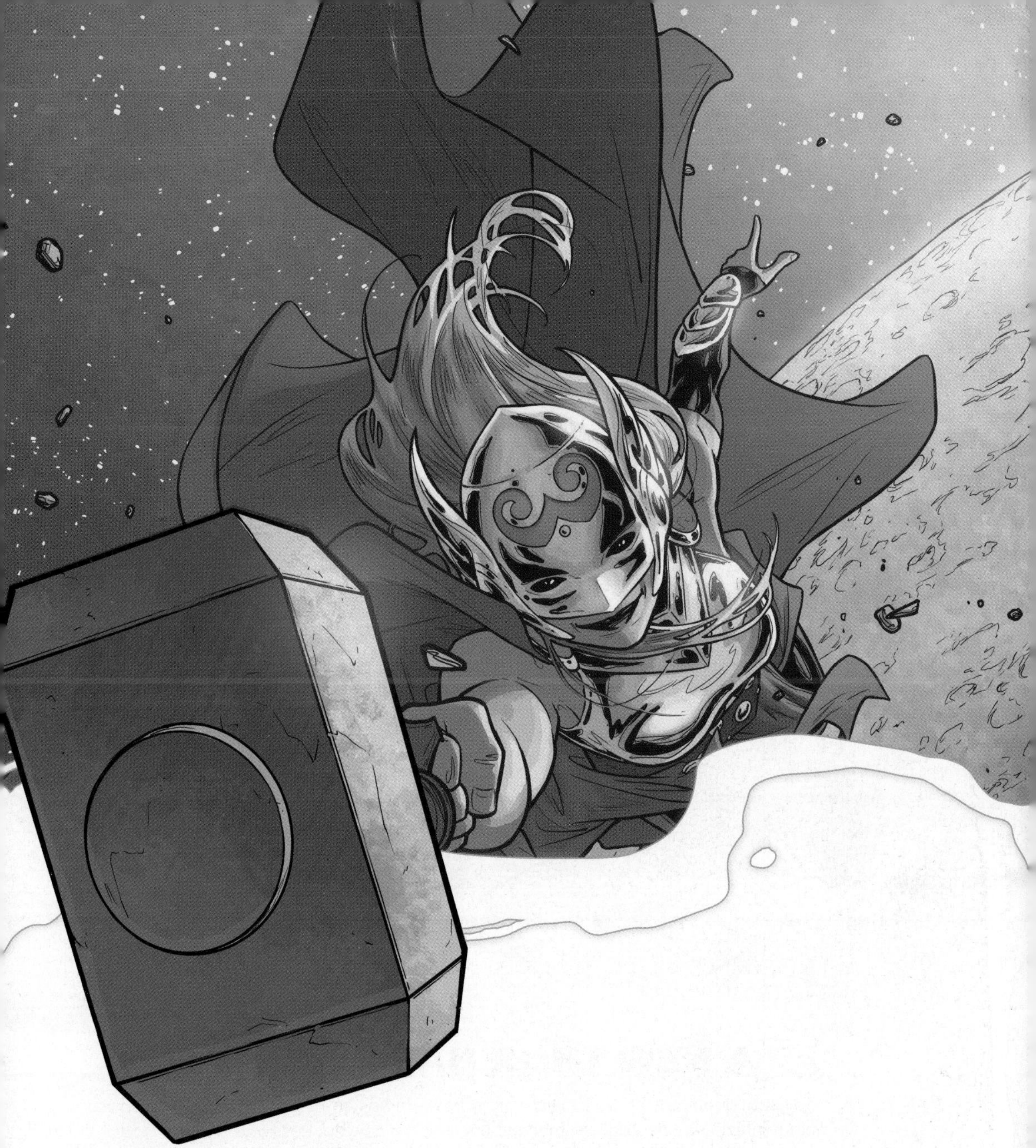

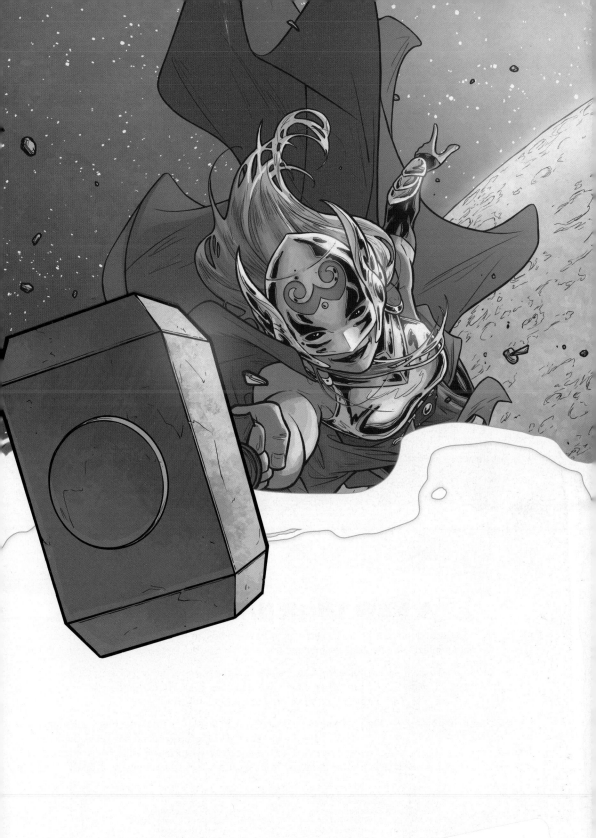

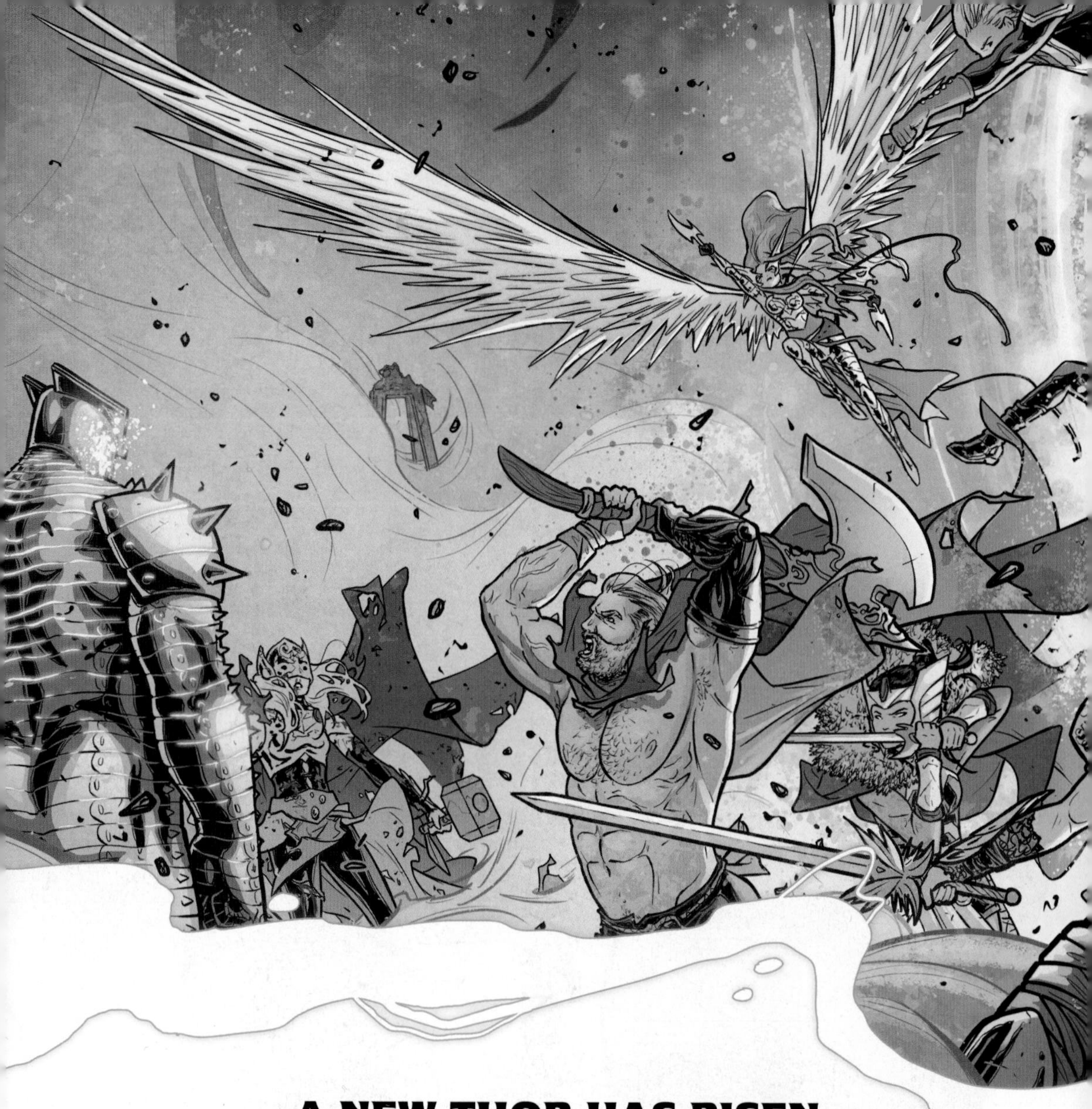

A NEW THOR HAS RISEN.

After Thor Odinson found himself no longer worthy of wielding Mjolnir, a mysterious woman was able to lift the enchanted hammer and became the new goddess of thunder!

So far she has taken down evils great and small, bolstered by the new legitimacy of Thor Odinson officially passing the name of Thor on to her — evils like villainous Roxxon CEO/part-time Minotaur Dario Agger and the Dark Elf sorcerer Malekith.

While Odinson may have given Thor his name, he hasn't given up on discovering what her *true* name is, and Odin the All-Father hasn't either. Offended at this affront to his omnipotence, the All-Father has called into service his brother Cul Borson as well as the Asgardian weapon known as the Destroyer. He is determined to either learn the identity of this new Thor or destroy her in the process.

COLLECTION EDITOR: **JENNIFER GRÜNWALD**
ASSOCIATE EDITOR: **SARAH BRUNSTAD**
ASSOCIATE MANAGING EDITOR: **ALEX STARBUCK**
EDITOR, SPECIAL PROJECTS: **MARK D. BEAZLEY**
VP, PRODUCTION & SPECIAL PROJECTS: **JEFF YOUNGQUIST**
SVP PRINT, SALES & MARKETING: **DAVID GABRIEL**

EDITOR IN CHIEF: **AXEL ALONSO**
CHIEF CREATIVE OFFICER: **JOE QUESADA**
PUBLISHER: **DAN BUCKLEY**
EXECUTIVE PRODUCER: **ALAN FINE**

THOR VOL. 2: WHO HOLDS THE HAMMER? Contains material originally published in magazine form as THOR #6-8 and ANNUAL #1, and WHAT IF? #10. First printing 2016. ISBN# 978-0-7851-9785-0. Published by MARVEL WORLDWIDE, INC., a subsidiary of MARVEL ENTERTAINMENT, LLC. OFFICE OF PUBLICATION: 135 West 50th Street, New York, NY 10020. **Printed in the U.S.A.** ALAN FINE, President, Marvel Entertainment; DAN BUCKLEY, President, TV, Publishing and Brand Management; JOE QUESADA, Chief Creative Officer; TOM BREVOORT, SVP of Publishing; DAVID BOGART, SVP of Operations & Procurement, Publishing; C.B. CEBULSKI, VP of International Development & Brand Management; DAVID GABRIEL, SVP Print, Sales & Marketing; JIM O'KEEFE, VP of Operations & Logistics; DAN CARR, Executive Director of Publishing Technology; SUSAN CRESPI, Editorial Operations Manager; ALEX MORALES, Publishing Operations Manager; STAN LEE, Chairman Emeritus. For information regarding advertising in Marvel Comics or on Marvel.com, please contact Jonathan Rheingold, VP of Custom Solutions & Ad Sales, at jrheingold@marvel.com. For Marvel subscription inquiries, please call 800-217-9158. **Manufactured between 1/15/2016 and 2/22/2016 by R.R. DONNELLEY, INC., SALEM, VA, USA.**

10 9 8 7 6 5 4 3 2 1

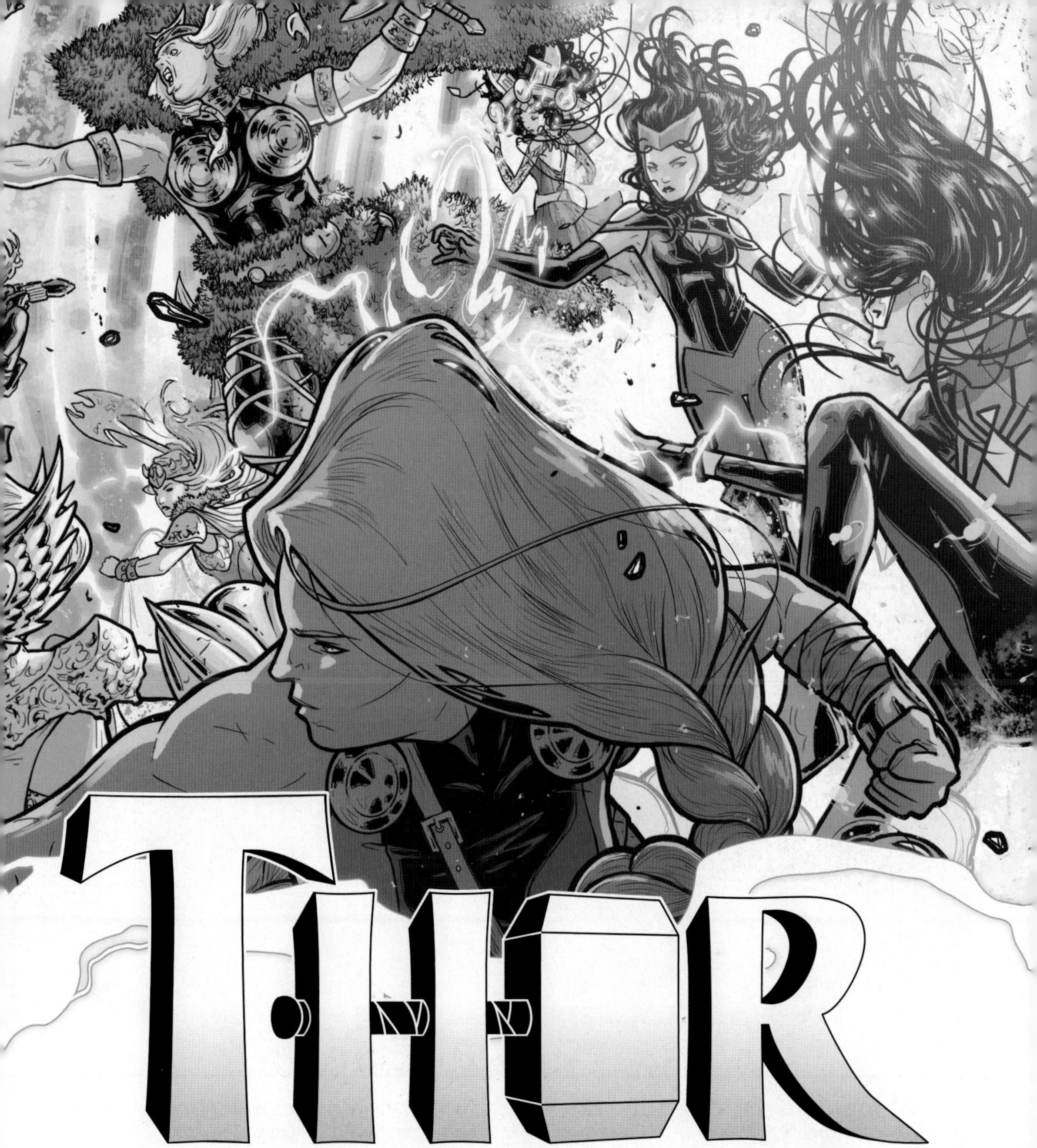

THOR

WHO HOLDS THE HAMMER?

WRITER
JASON AARON

ARTIST
RUSSELL DAUTERMAN

COLOR ARTIST
MATTHEW WILSON

COVER ART
RUSSELL DAUTERMAN & MATTHEW WILSON

ANNUAL #1

WRITERS
JASON AARON, NOELLE STEVENSON & CM PUNK

ARTISTS
TIMOTHY TRUMAN, MARGUERITE SAUVAGE & ROB GUILLORY

COLOR ARTISTS
FRANK MARTIN, MARGUERITE SAUVAGE & ROB GUILLORY

COVER ART **RAFAEL ALBUQUERQUE**

LETTERER
VC'S JOE SABINO

ASSISTANT EDITOR
JON MOISAN

EDITOR
WIL MOSS

THOR CREATED BY STAN LEE, LARRY LIEBER & JACK KIRBY

— 6 —

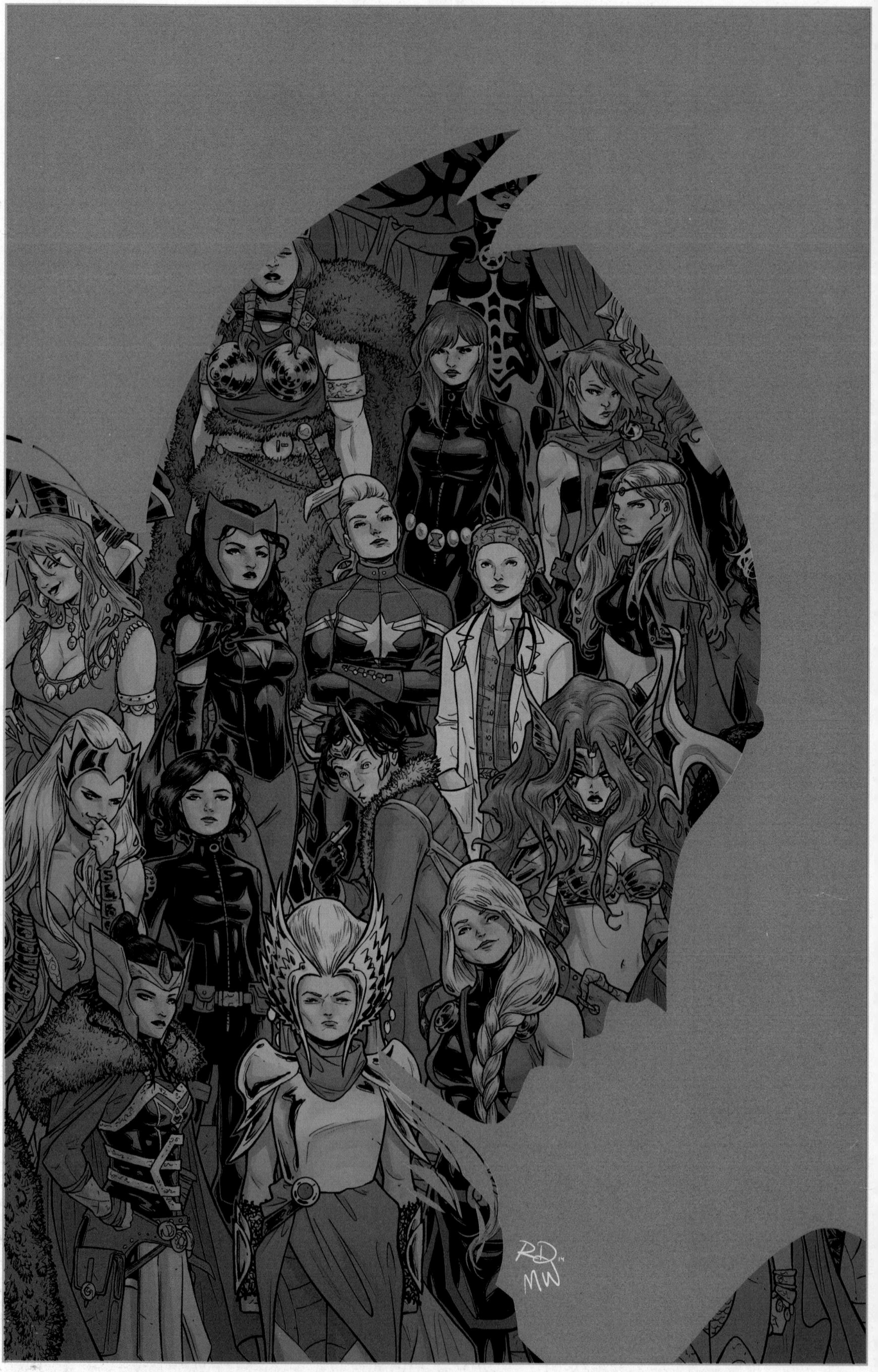
RD
MW

WHO HOLDS THE HAMMER?

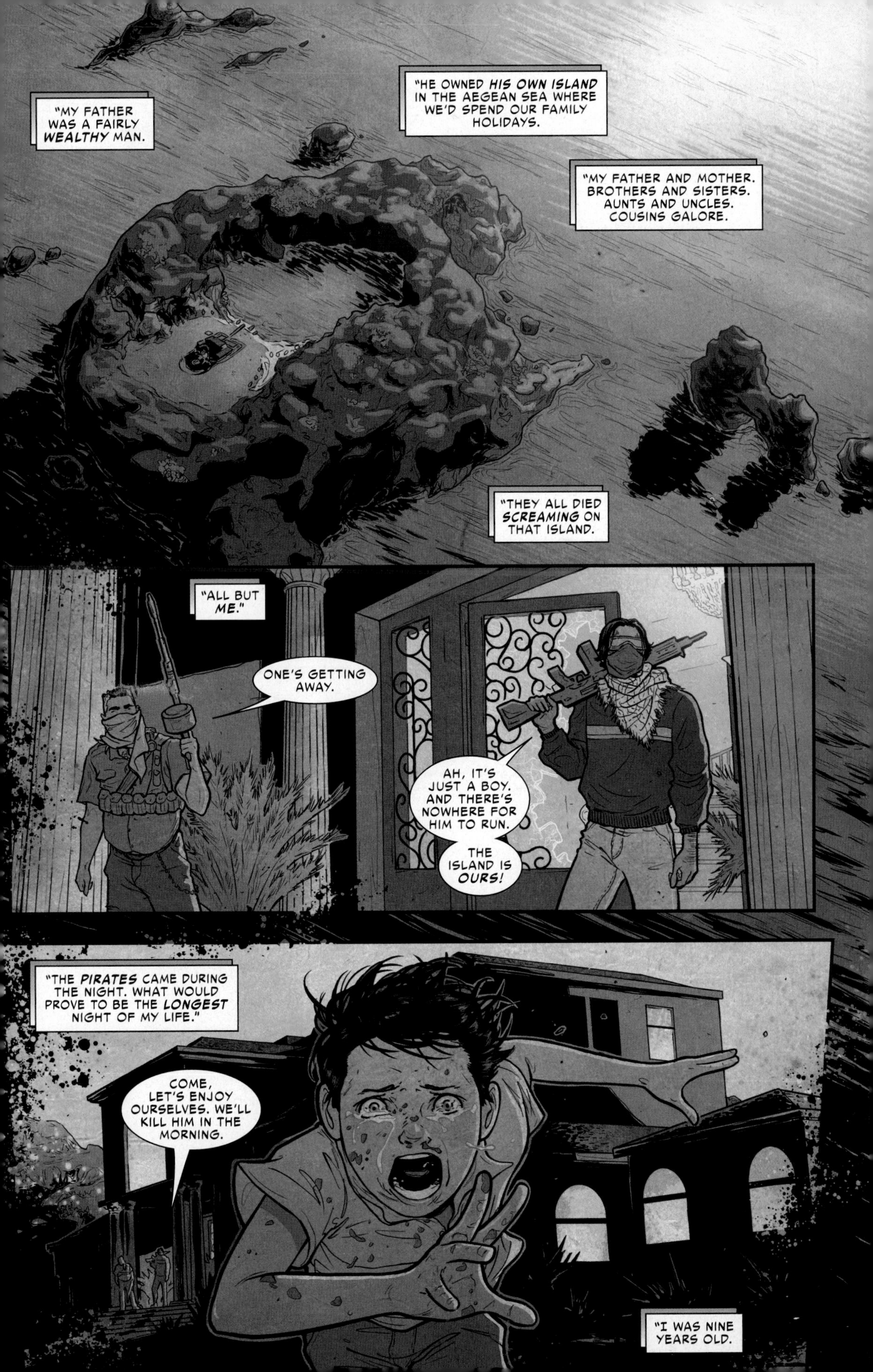
"MY FATHER WAS A FAIRLY *WEALTHY* MAN.
"HE OWNED *HIS OWN ISLAND* IN THE AEGEAN SEA WHERE WE'D SPEND OUR FAMILY HOLIDAYS.
"MY FATHER AND MOTHER. BROTHERS AND SISTERS. AUNTS AND UNCLES. COUSINS GALORE.
"THEY ALL DIED *SCREAMING* ON THAT ISLAND.
"ALL BUT *ME*."
ONE'S GETTING AWAY.
AH, IT'S JUST A BOY. AND THERE'S NOWHERE FOR HIM TO RUN.
THE ISLAND IS *OURS!*
"THE *PIRATES* CAME DURING THE NIGHT. WHAT WOULD PROVE TO BE THE *LONGEST* NIGHT OF MY LIFE."
COME, LET'S ENJOY OURSELVES. WE'LL KILL HIM IN THE MORNING.
"I WAS NINE YEARS OLD.

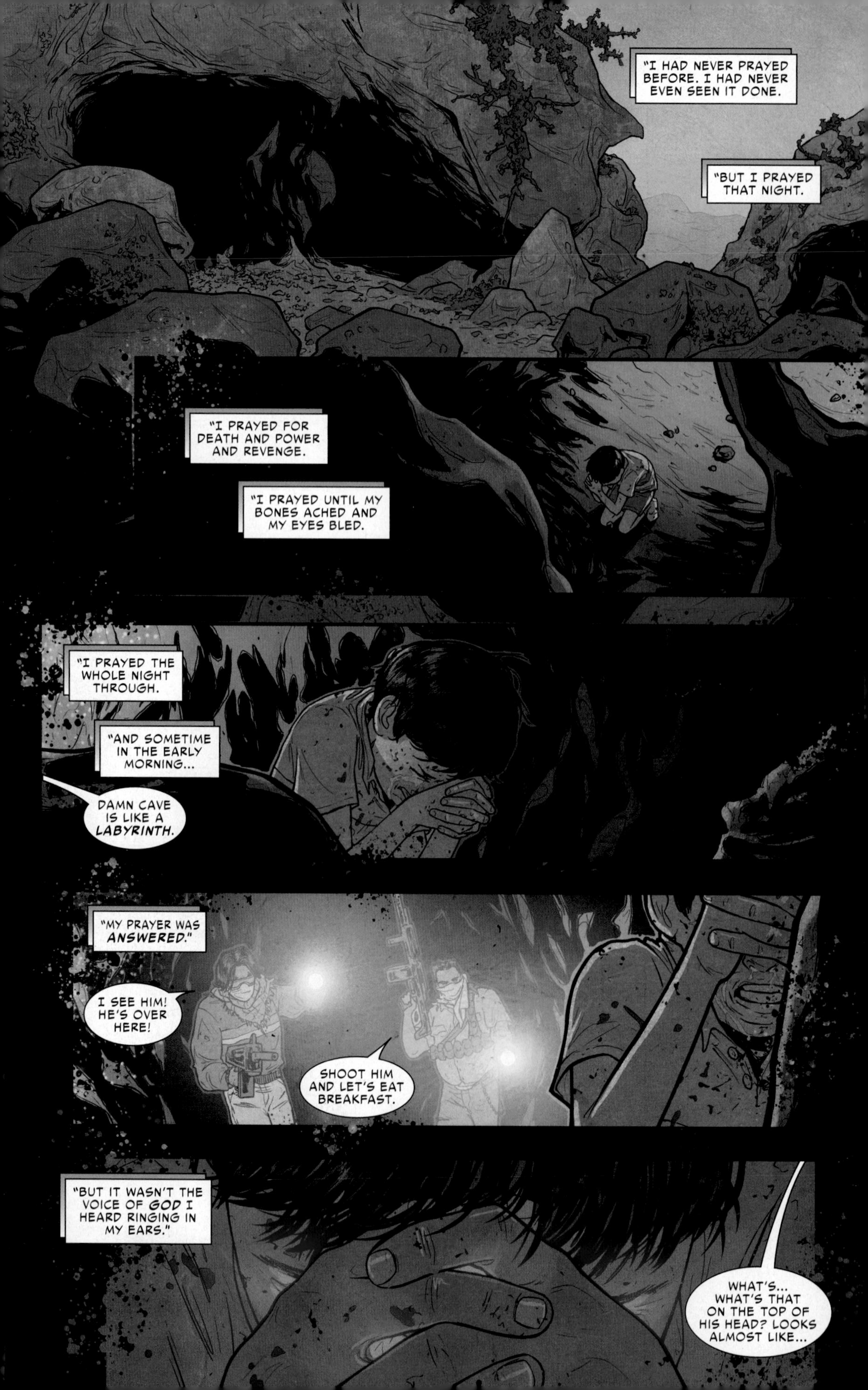
"I HAD NEVER PRAYED BEFORE. I HAD NEVER EVEN SEEN IT DONE.
"BUT I PRAYED THAT NIGHT.
"I PRAYED FOR DEATH AND POWER AND REVENGE.
"I PRAYED UNTIL MY BONES ACHED AND MY EYES BLED.
"I PRAYED THE WHOLE NIGHT THROUGH.
"AND SOMETIME IN THE EARLY MORNING...
DAMN CAVE IS LIKE A LABYRINTH.
"MY PRAYER WAS ANSWERED."
I SEE HIM! HE'S OVER HERE!
SHOOT HIM AND LET'S EAT BREAKFAST.
"BUT IT WASN'T THE VOICE OF GOD I HEARD RINGING IN MY EARS."
WHAT'S... WHAT'S THAT ON THE TOP OF HIS HEAD? LOOKS ALMOST LIKE...

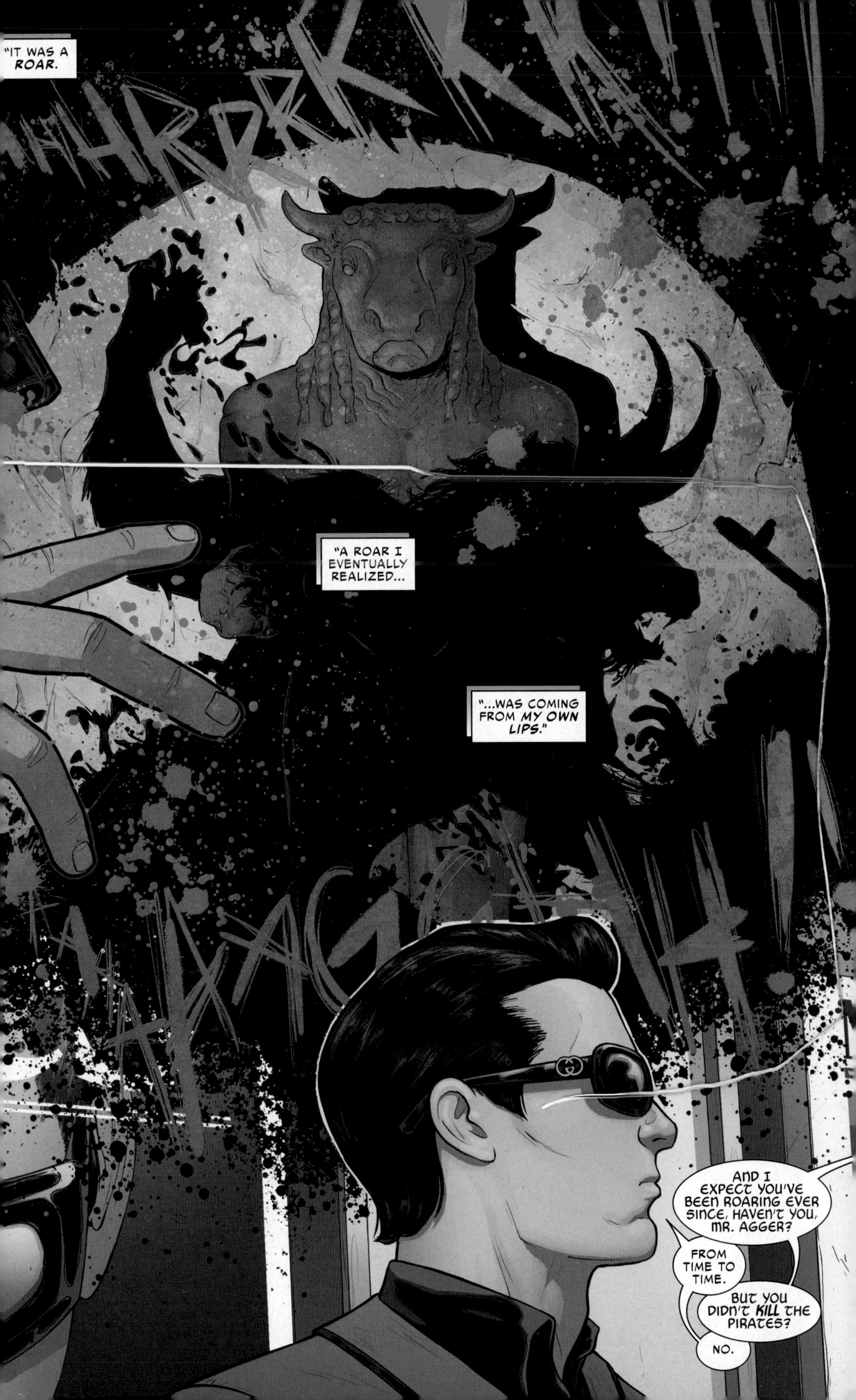
"IT WAS A ROAR.
"A ROAR I EVENTUALLY REALIZED...
"...WAS COMING FROM MY OWN LIPS."
AND I EXPECT YOU'VE BEEN ROARING EVER SINCE, HAVEN'T YOU, MR. AGGER?
FROM TIME TO TIME.
BUT YOU DIDN'T KILL THE PIRATES?
NO.

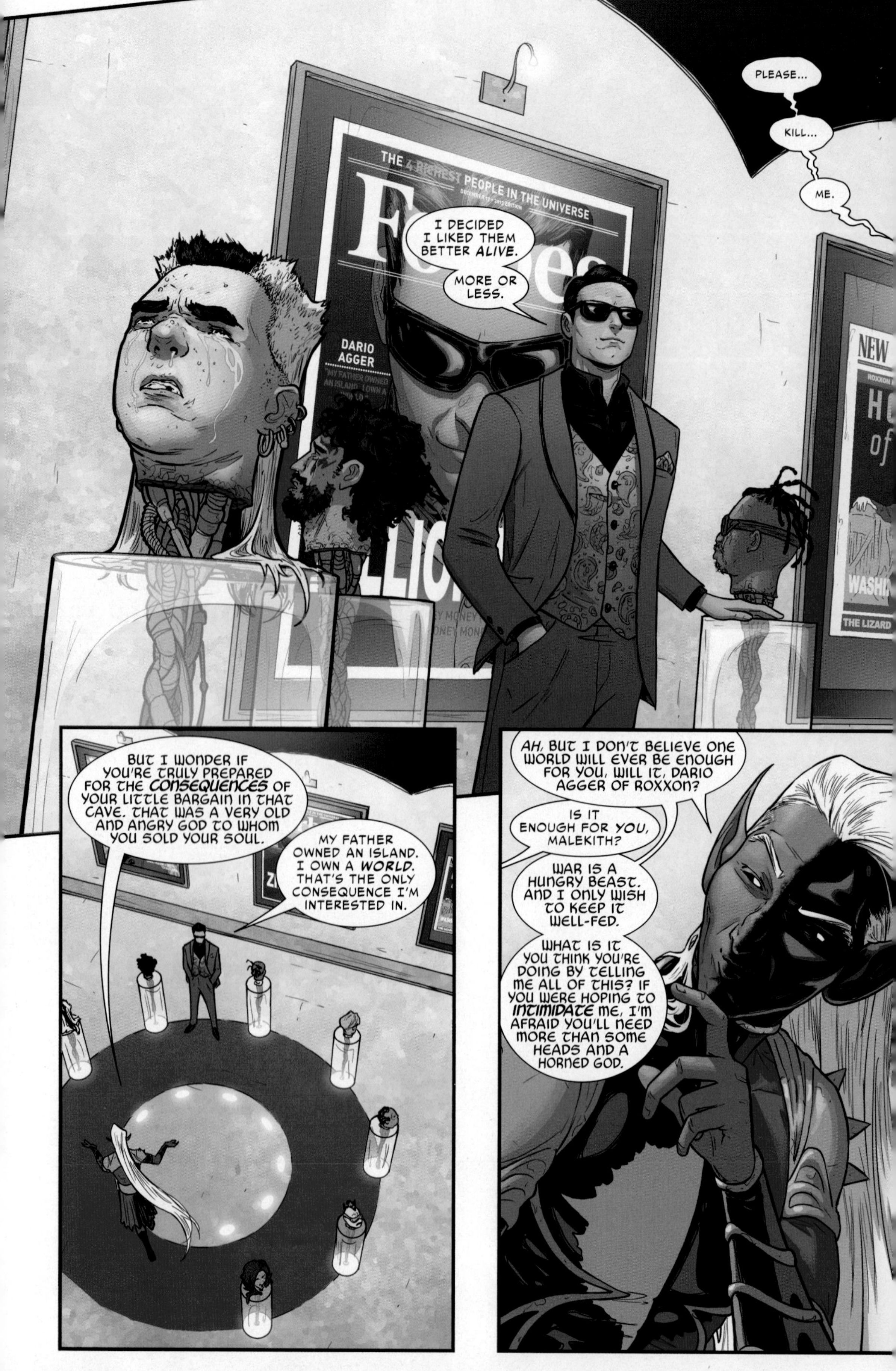
PLEASE...
KILL...
ME.
THE 4 RICHEST PEOPLE IN THE UNIVERSE
Forbes
DARIO AGGER
I DECIDED I LIKED THEM BETTER ALIVE.
MORE OR LESS.
NEW
THE LIZARD
BUT I WONDER IF YOU'RE TRULY PREPARED FOR THE CONSEQUENCES OF YOUR LITTLE BARGAIN IN THAT CAVE. THAT WAS A VERY OLD AND ANGRY GOD TO WHOM YOU SOLD YOUR SOUL.
MY FATHER OWNED AN ISLAND. I OWN A WORLD. THAT'S THE ONLY CONSEQUENCE I'M INTERESTED IN.
AH, BUT I DON'T BELIEVE ONE WORLD WILL EVER BE ENOUGH FOR YOU, WILL IT, DARIO AGGER OF ROXXON?
IS IT ENOUGH FOR YOU, MALEKITH?
WAR IS A HUNGRY BEAST. AND I ONLY WISH TO KEEP IT WELL-FED.
WHAT IS IT YOU THINK YOU'RE DOING BY TELLING ME ALL OF THIS? IF YOU WERE HOPING TO INTIMIDATE ME, I'M AFRAID YOU'LL NEED MORE THAN SOME HEADS AND A HORNED GOD.

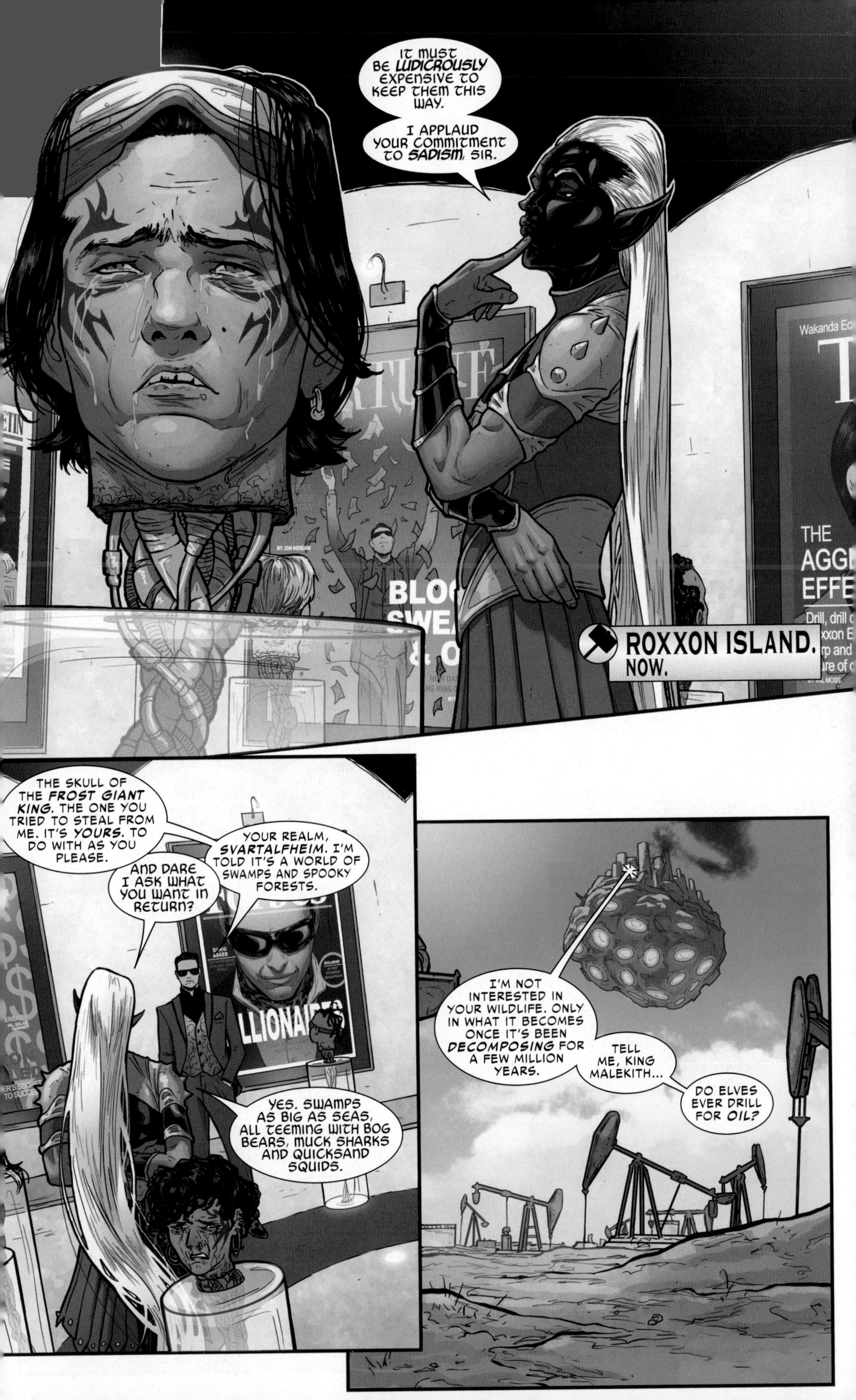

IT MUST BE LUDICROUSLY EXPENSIVE TO KEEP THEM THIS WAY.
I APPLAUD YOUR COMMITMENT TO SADISM, SIR.
ROXXON ISLAND. NOW.
THE SKULL OF THE FROST GIANT KING. THE ONE YOU TRIED TO STEAL FROM ME. IT'S YOURS. TO DO WITH AS YOU PLEASE.
AND DARE I ASK WHAT YOU WANT IN RETURN?
YOUR REALM, SVARTALFHEIM. I'M TOLD IT'S A WORLD OF SWAMPS AND SPOOKY FORESTS.
YES. SWAMPS AS BIG AS SEAS, ALL TEEMING WITH BOG BEARS, MUCK SHARKS AND QUICKSAND SQUIDS.
I'M NOT INTERESTED IN YOUR WILDLIFE. ONLY IN WHAT IT BECOMES ONCE IT'S BEEN DECOMPOSING FOR A FEW MILLION YEARS.
TELL ME, KING MALEKITH...
DO ELVES EVER DRILL FOR OIL?

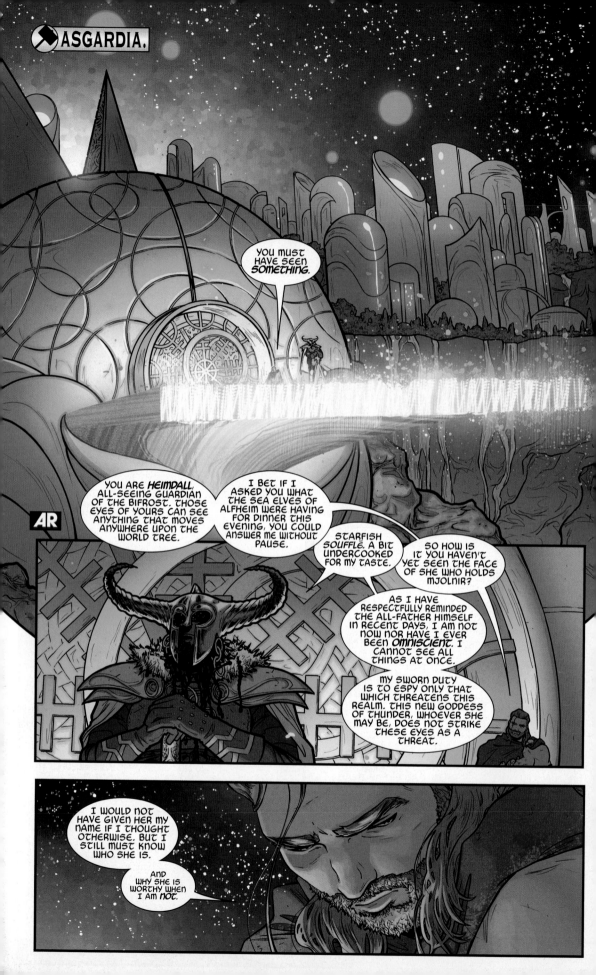

YOU MUST HAVE SEEN *SOMETHING.*

YOU ARE *HEIMDALL,* ALL-SEEING GUARDIAN OF THE BIFROST. THOSE EYES OF YOURS CAN SEE ANYTHING THAT MOVES ANYWHERE UPON THE WORLD TREE.

I BET IF I ASKED YOU WHAT THE SEA ELVES OF ALFHEIM WERE HAVING FOR DINNER THIS EVENING, YOU COULD ANSWER ME WITHOUT PAUSE.

STARFISH SOUFFLE. A BIT UNDERCOOKED FOR MY TASTE.

SO HOW IS IT YOU HAVEN'T YET SEEN THE FACE OF SHE WHO HOLDS MJOLNIR?

AS I HAVE RESPECTFULLY REMINDED THE ALL-FATHER HIMSELF IN RECENT DAYS, I AM NOT NOW NOR HAVE I EVER BEEN *OMNISCIENT.* I CANNOT SEE ALL THINGS AT ONCE.

MY SWORN DUTY IS TO ESPY ONLY THAT WHICH THREATENS THIS REALM. THIS NEW GODDESS OF THUNDER, WHOEVER SHE MAY BE, DOES NOT STRIKE THESE EYES AS A THREAT.

I WOULD NOT HAVE GIVEN HER MY NAME IF I THOUGHT OTHERWISE. BUT I STILL MUST KNOW WHO SHE IS.

AND WHY SHE IS WORTHY WHEN I AM *NOT.*

AR

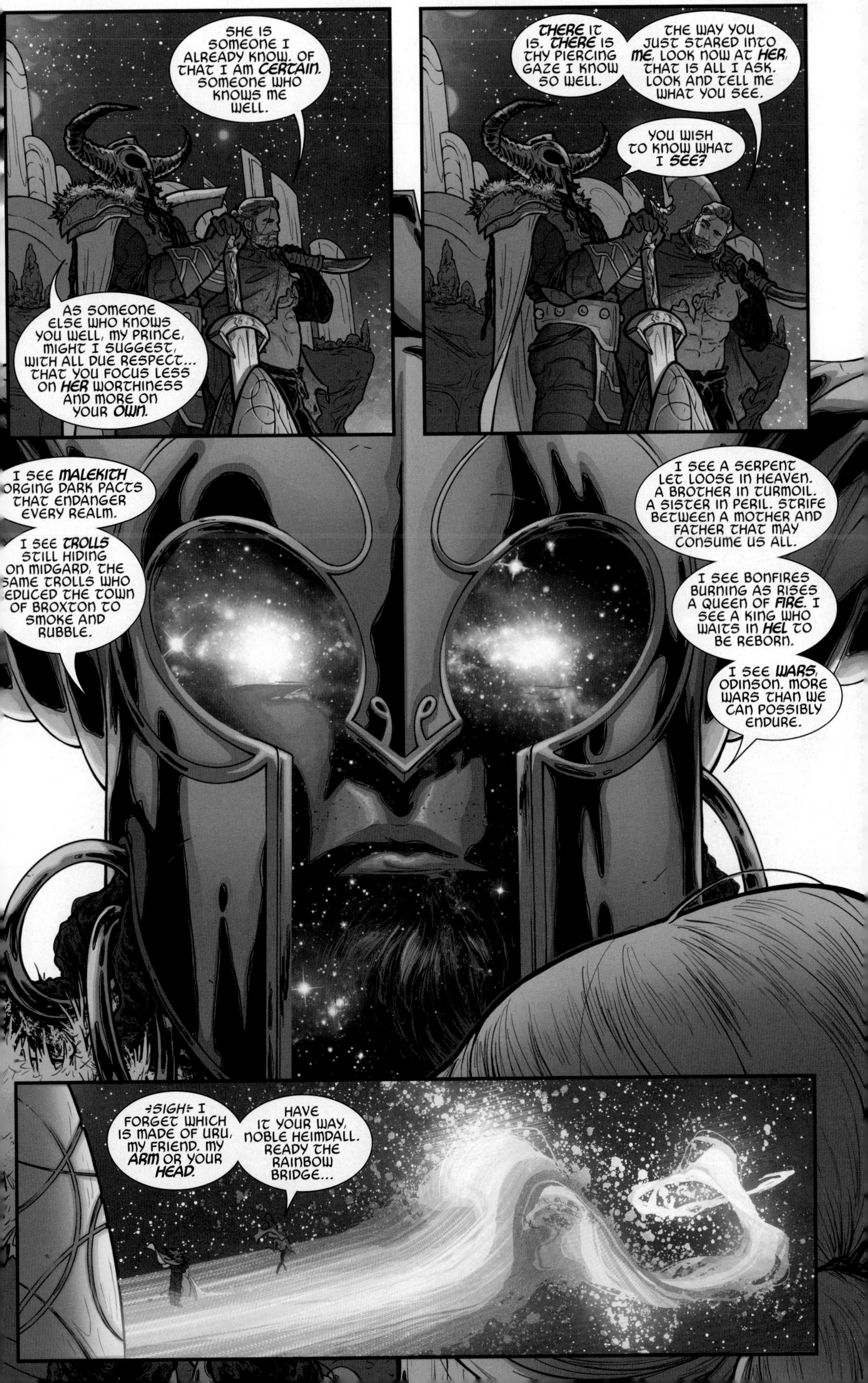
SHE IS SOMEONE I ALREADY KNOW. OF THAT I AM CERTAIN. SOMEONE WHO KNOWS ME WELL.
AS SOMEONE ELSE WHO KNOWS YOU WELL, MY PRINCE, MIGHT I SUGGEST, WITH ALL DUE RESPECT... THAT YOU FOCUS LESS ON HER WORTHINESS AND MORE ON YOUR OWN.
THERE IT IS. THERE IS THY PIERCING GAZE I KNOW SO WELL.
THE WAY YOU JUST STARED INTO ME, LOOK NOW AT HER, THAT IS ALL I ASK. LOOK AND TELL ME WHAT YOU SEE.
YOU WISH TO KNOW WHAT I SEE?
I SEE MALEKITH ORGING DARK PACTS THAT ENDANGER EVERY REALM.
I SEE TROLLS STILL HIDING ON MIDGARD, THE SAME TROLLS WHO EDUCED THE TOWN OF BROXTON TO SMOKE AND RUBBLE.
I SEE A SERPENT LET LOOSE IN HEAVEN. A BROTHER IN TURMOIL. A SISTER IN PERIL. STRIFE BETWEEN A MOTHER AND FATHER THAT MAY CONSUME US ALL.
I SEE BONFIRES BURNING AS RISES A QUEEN OF FIRE. I SEE A KING WHO WAITS IN HEL TO BE REBORN.
I SEE WARS, ODINSON. MORE WARS THAN WE CAN POSSIBLY ENDURE.
SIGH I FORGET WHICH IS MADE OF URU, MY FRIEND. MY ARM OR YOUR HEAD.
HAVE IT YOUR WAY, NOBLE HEIMDALL. READY THE RAINBOW BRIDGE...

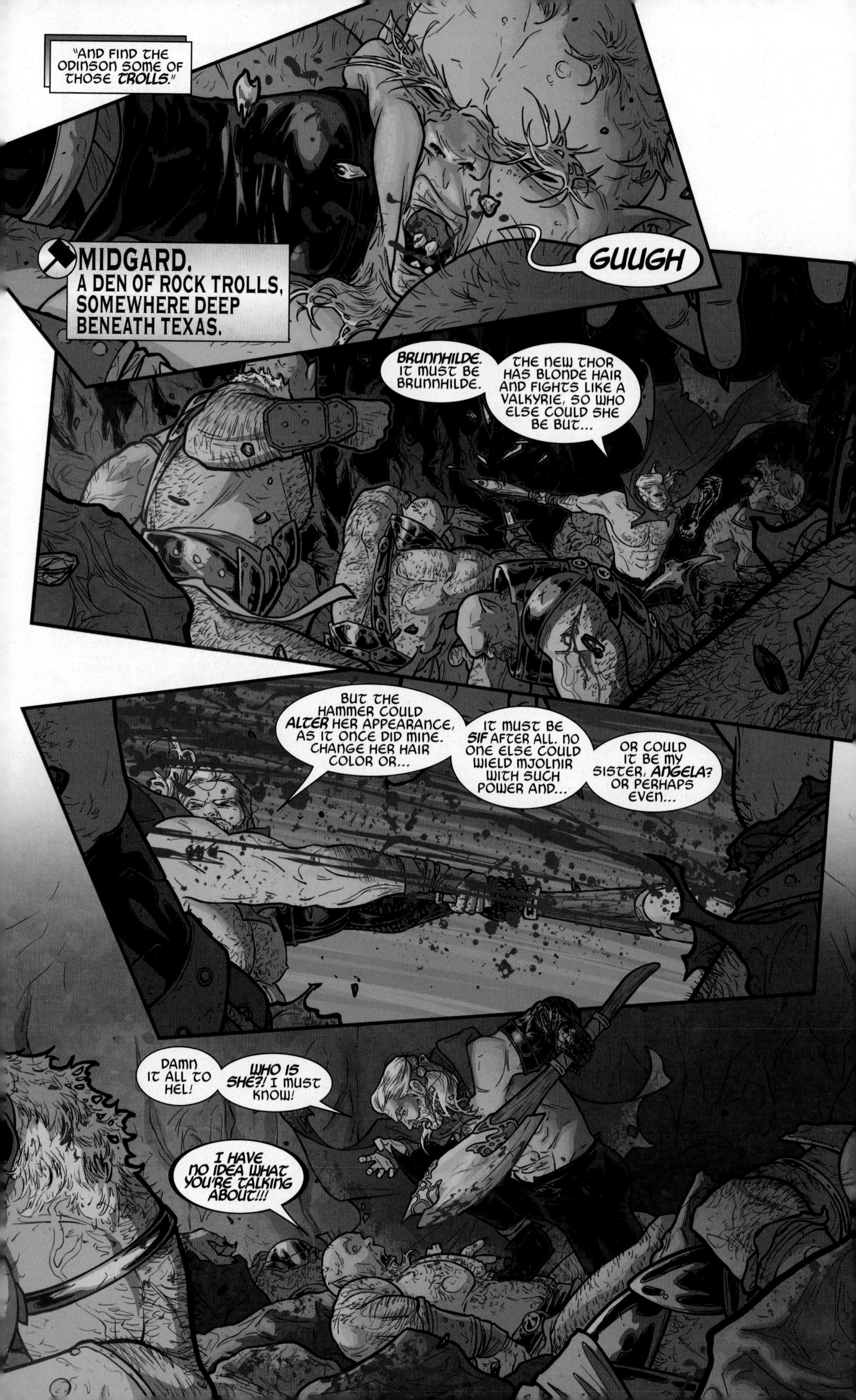
"AND FIND THE ODINSON SOME OF THOSE TROLLS."
GUUGH
MIDGARD. A DEN OF ROCK TROLLS, SOMEWHERE DEEP BENEATH TEXAS.
BRUNNHILDE. IT MUST BE BRUNNHILDE.
THE NEW THOR HAS BLONDE HAIR AND FIGHTS LIKE A VALKYRIE, SO WHO ELSE COULD SHE BE BUT...
BUT THE HAMMER COULD ALTER HER APPEARANCE, AS IT ONCE DID MINE. CHANGE HER HAIR COLOR OR...
IT MUST BE SIF AFTER ALL. NO ONE ELSE COULD WIELD MJOLNIR WITH SUCH POWER AND...
OR COULD IT BE MY SISTER, ANGELA? OR PERHAPS EVEN...
DAMN IT ALL TO HEL!
WHO IS SHE?! I MUST KNOW!
I HAVE NO IDEA WHAT YOU'RE TALKING ABOUT!!!

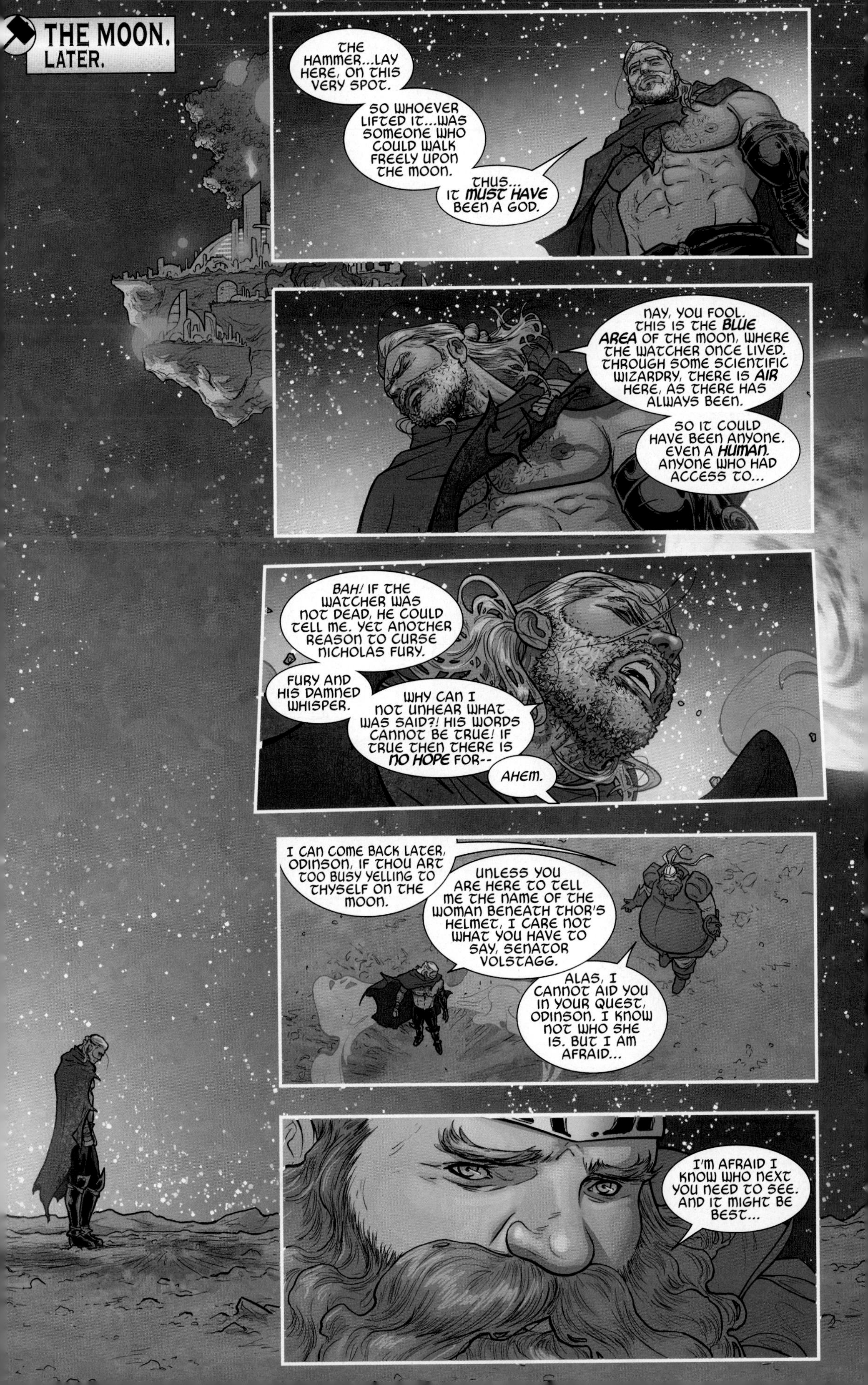
THE MOON. LATER.
THE HAMMER...LAY HERE, ON THIS VERY SPOT.
SO WHOEVER LIFTED IT...WAS SOMEONE WHO COULD WALK FREELY UPON THE MOON.
THUS... IT MUST HAVE BEEN A GOD.
NAY, YOU FOOL. THIS IS THE BLUE AREA OF THE MOON, WHERE THE WATCHER ONCE LIVED. THROUGH SOME SCIENTIFIC WIZARDRY, THERE IS AIR HERE, AS THERE HAS ALWAYS BEEN.
SO IT COULD HAVE BEEN ANYONE. EVEN A HUMAN. ANYONE WHO HAD ACCESS TO...
BAH! IF THE WATCHER WAS NOT DEAD, HE COULD TELL ME. YET ANOTHER REASON TO CURSE NICHOLAS FURY.
FURY AND HIS DAMNED WHISPER.
WHY CAN I NOT UNHEAR WHAT WAS SAID?! HIS WORDS CANNOT BE TRUE! IF TRUE THEN THERE IS NO HOPE FOR--
AHEM.
I CAN COME BACK LATER, ODINSON, IF THOU ART TOO BUSY YELLING TO THYSELF ON THE MOON.
UNLESS YOU ARE HERE TO TELL ME THE NAME OF THE WOMAN BENEATH THOR'S HELMET, I CARE NOT WHAT YOU HAVE TO SAY, SENATOR VOLSTAGG.
ALAS, I CANNOT AID YOU IN YOUR QUEST, ODINSON. I KNOW NOT WHO SHE IS. BUT I AM AFRAID...
I'M AFRAID I KNOW WHO NEXT YOU NEED TO SEE. AND IT MIGHT BE BEST...

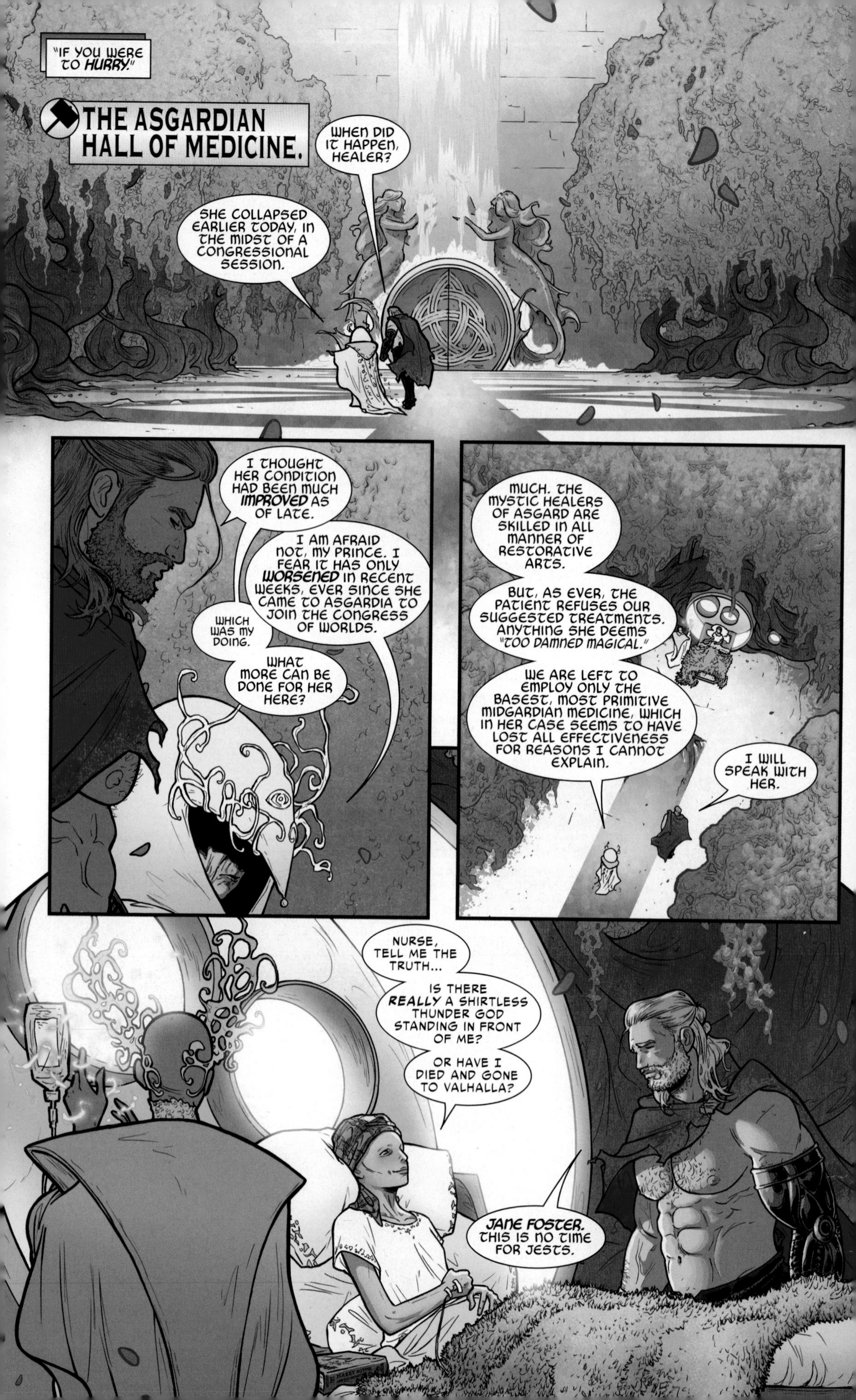

"IF YOU WERE TO HURRY."
THE ASGARDIAN HALL OF MEDICINE.
WHEN DID IT HAPPEN, HEALER?
SHE COLLAPSED EARLIER TODAY, IN THE MIDST OF A CONGRESSIONAL SESSION.
I THOUGHT HER CONDITION HAD BEEN MUCH IMPROVED AS OF LATE.
I AM AFRAID NOT, MY PRINCE. I FEAR IT HAS ONLY WORSENED IN RECENT WEEKS, EVER SINCE SHE CAME TO ASGARDIA TO JOIN THE CONGRESS OF WORLDS.
WHICH WAS MY DOING.
WHAT MORE CAN BE DONE FOR HER HERE?
MUCH. THE MYSTIC HEALERS OF ASGARD ARE SKILLED IN ALL MANNER OF RESTORATIVE ARTS.
BUT, AS EVER, THE PATIENT REFUSES OUR SUGGESTED TREATMENTS. ANYTHING SHE DEEMS "TOO DAMNED MAGICAL."
WE ARE LEFT TO EMPLOY ONLY THE BASEST, MOST PRIMITIVE MIDGARDIAN MEDICINE, WHICH IN HER CASE SEEMS TO HAVE LOST ALL EFFECTIVENESS FOR REASONS I CANNOT EXPLAIN.
I WILL SPEAK WITH HER.
NURSE, TELL ME THE TRUTH...
IS THERE REALLY A SHIRTLESS THUNDER GOD STANDING IN FRONT OF ME?
OR HAVE I DIED AND GONE TO VALHALLA?
JANE FOSTER. THIS IS NO TIME FOR JESTS.

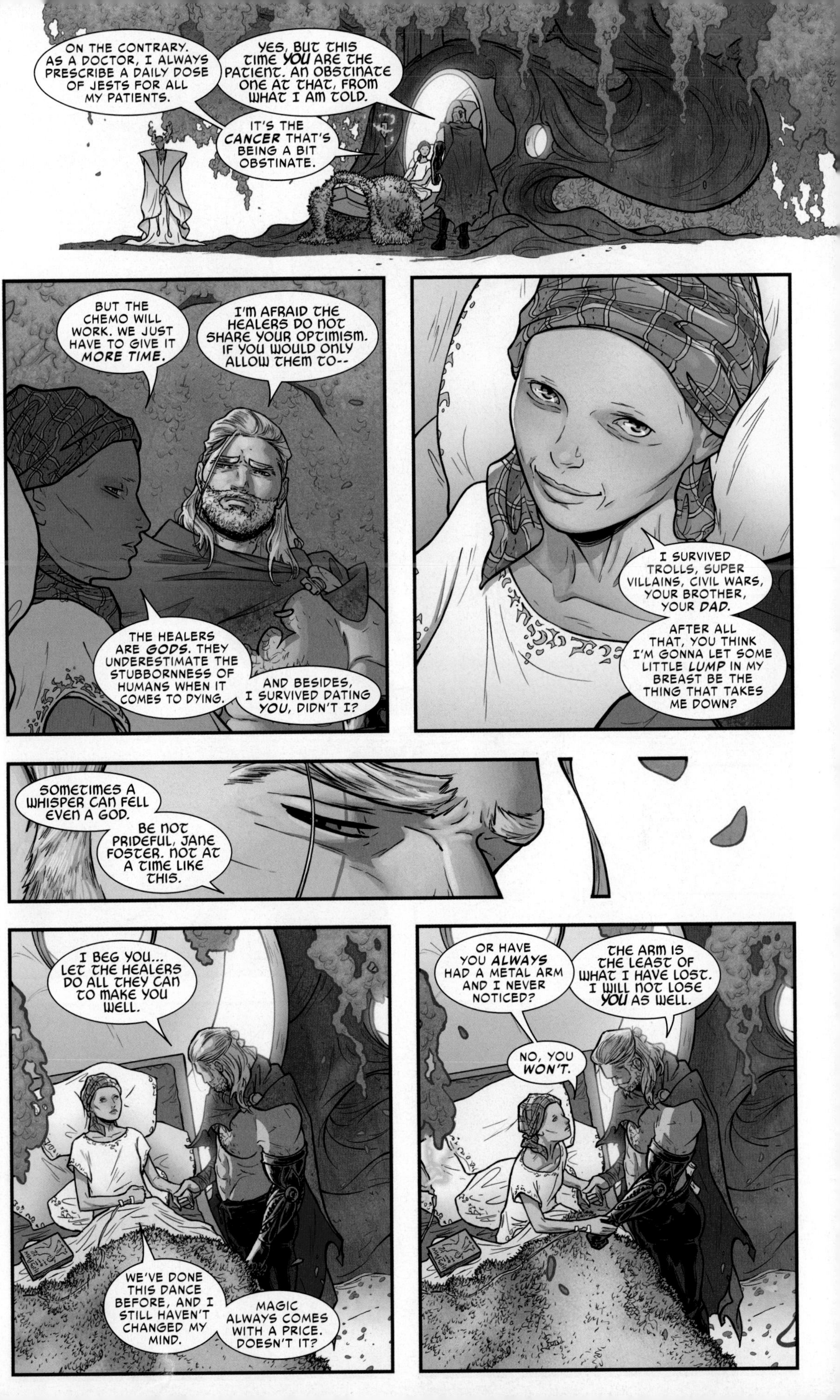
ON THE CONTRARY. AS A DOCTOR, I ALWAYS PRESCRIBE A DAILY DOSE OF JESTS FOR ALL MY PATIENTS.
YES, BUT THIS TIME YOU ARE THE PATIENT. AN OBSTINATE ONE AT THAT, FROM WHAT I AM TOLD.
IT'S THE CANCER THAT'S BEING A BIT OBSTINATE.
BUT THE CHEMO WILL WORK. WE JUST HAVE TO GIVE IT MORE TIME.
I'M AFRAID THE HEALERS DO NOT SHARE YOUR OPTIMISM. IF YOU WOULD ONLY ALLOW THEM TO--
THE HEALERS ARE GODS. THEY UNDERESTIMATE THE STUBBORNNESS OF HUMANS WHEN IT COMES TO DYING.
AND BESIDES, I SURVIVED DATING YOU, DIDN'T I?
I SURVIVED TROLLS, SUPER VILLAINS, CIVIL WARS, YOUR BROTHER, YOUR DAD.
AFTER ALL THAT, YOU THINK I'M GONNA LET SOME LITTLE LUMP IN MY BREAST BE THE THING THAT TAKES ME DOWN?
SOMETIMES A WHISPER CAN FELL EVEN A GOD.
BE NOT PRIDEFUL, JANE FOSTER. NOT AT A TIME LIKE THIS.
I BEG YOU... LET THE HEALERS DO ALL THEY CAN TO MAKE YOU WELL.
WE'VE DONE THIS DANCE BEFORE, AND I STILL HAVEN'T CHANGED MY MIND.
MAGIC ALWAYS COMES WITH A PRICE. DOESN'T IT?
OR HAVE YOU ALWAYS HAD A METAL ARM AND I NEVER NOTICED?
THE ARM IS THE LEAST OF WHAT I HAVE LOST. I WILL NOT LOSE YOU AS WELL.
NO, YOU WON'T.

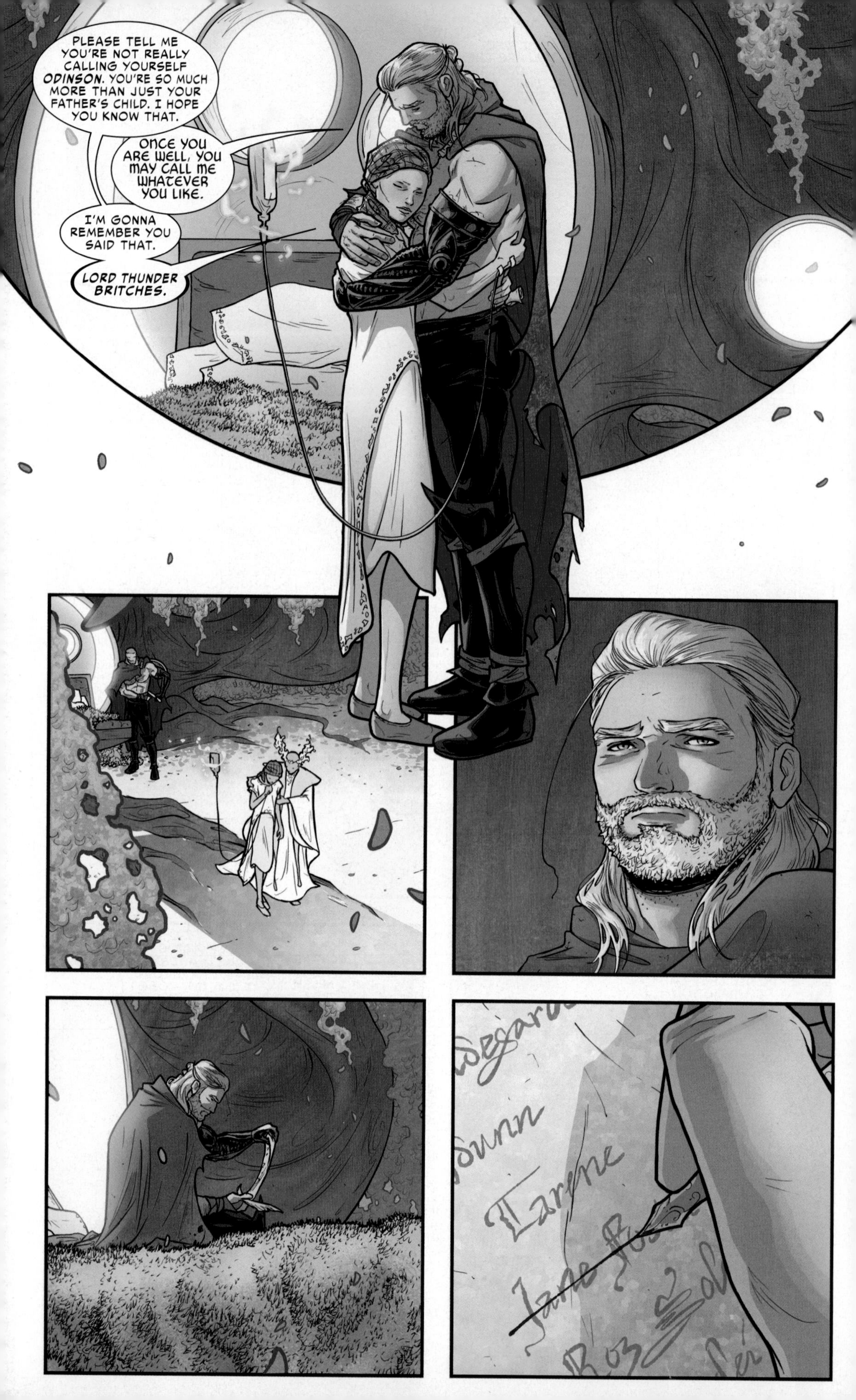
PLEASE TELL ME YOU'RE NOT REALLY CALLING YOURSELF ODINSON. YOU'RE SO MUCH MORE THAN JUST YOUR FATHER'S CHILD. I HOPE YOU KNOW THAT.
ONCE YOU ARE WELL, YOU MAY CALL ME WHATEVER YOU LIKE.
I'M GONNA REMEMBER YOU SAID THAT.
LORD THUNDER BRITCHES.
Tarene

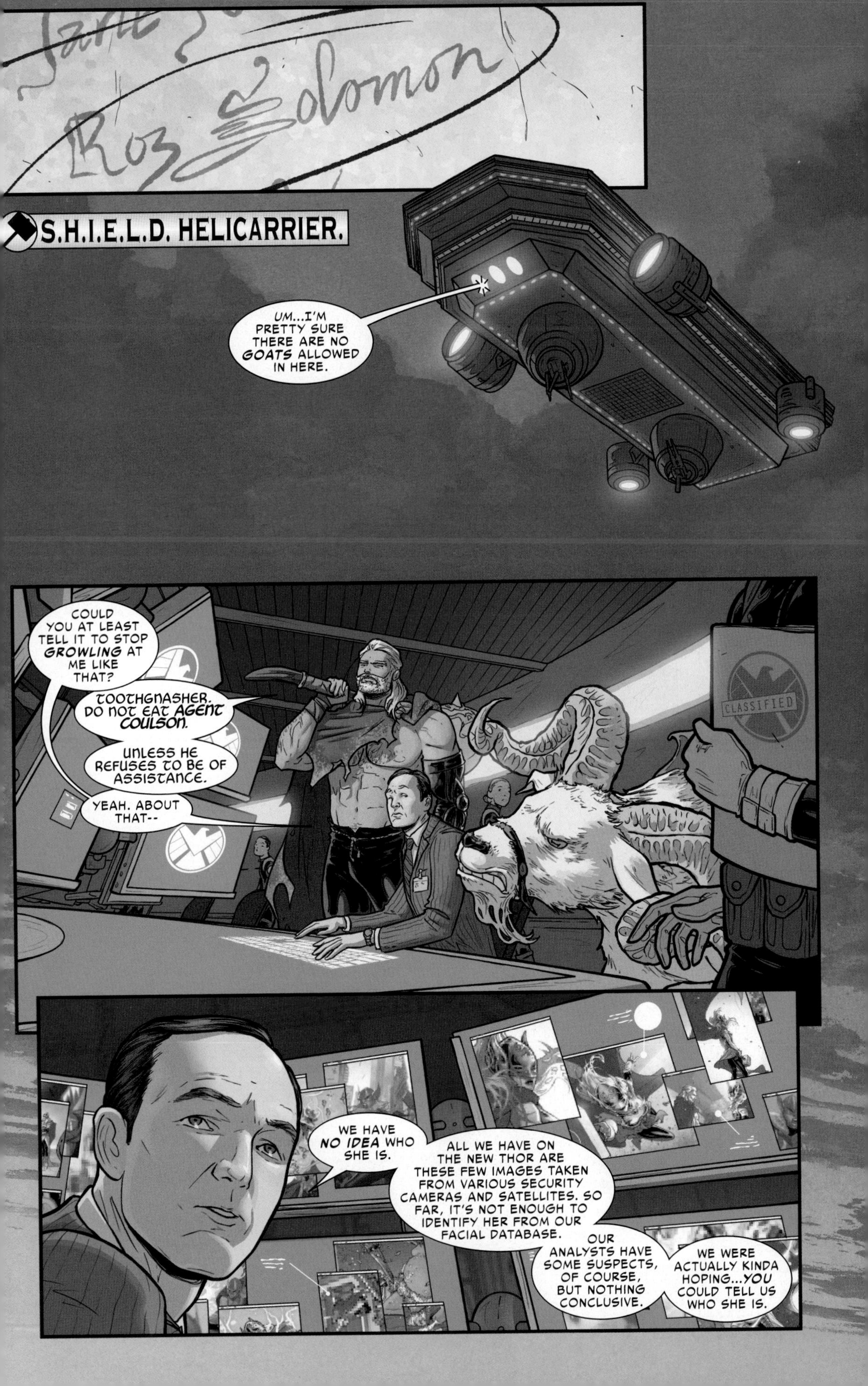

Roz Solomon
S.H.I.E.L.D. HELICARRIER.
UM...I'M PRETTY SURE THERE ARE NO GOATS ALLOWED IN HERE.
COULD YOU AT LEAST TELL IT TO STOP GROWLING AT ME LIKE THAT?
TOOTHGNASHER. DO NOT EAT AGENT COULSON.
UNLESS HE REFUSES TO BE OF ASSISTANCE.
YEAH. ABOUT THAT--
CLASSIFIED
WE HAVE NO IDEA WHO SHE IS.
ALL WE HAVE ON THE NEW THOR ARE THESE FEW IMAGES TAKEN FROM VARIOUS SECURITY CAMERAS AND SATELLITES. SO FAR, IT'S NOT ENOUGH TO IDENTIFY HER FROM OUR FACIAL DATABASE.
OUR ANALYSTS HAVE SOME SUSPECTS, OF COURSE, BUT NOTHING CONCLUSIVE.
WE WERE ACTUALLY KINDA HOPING...YOU COULD TELL US WHO SHE IS.

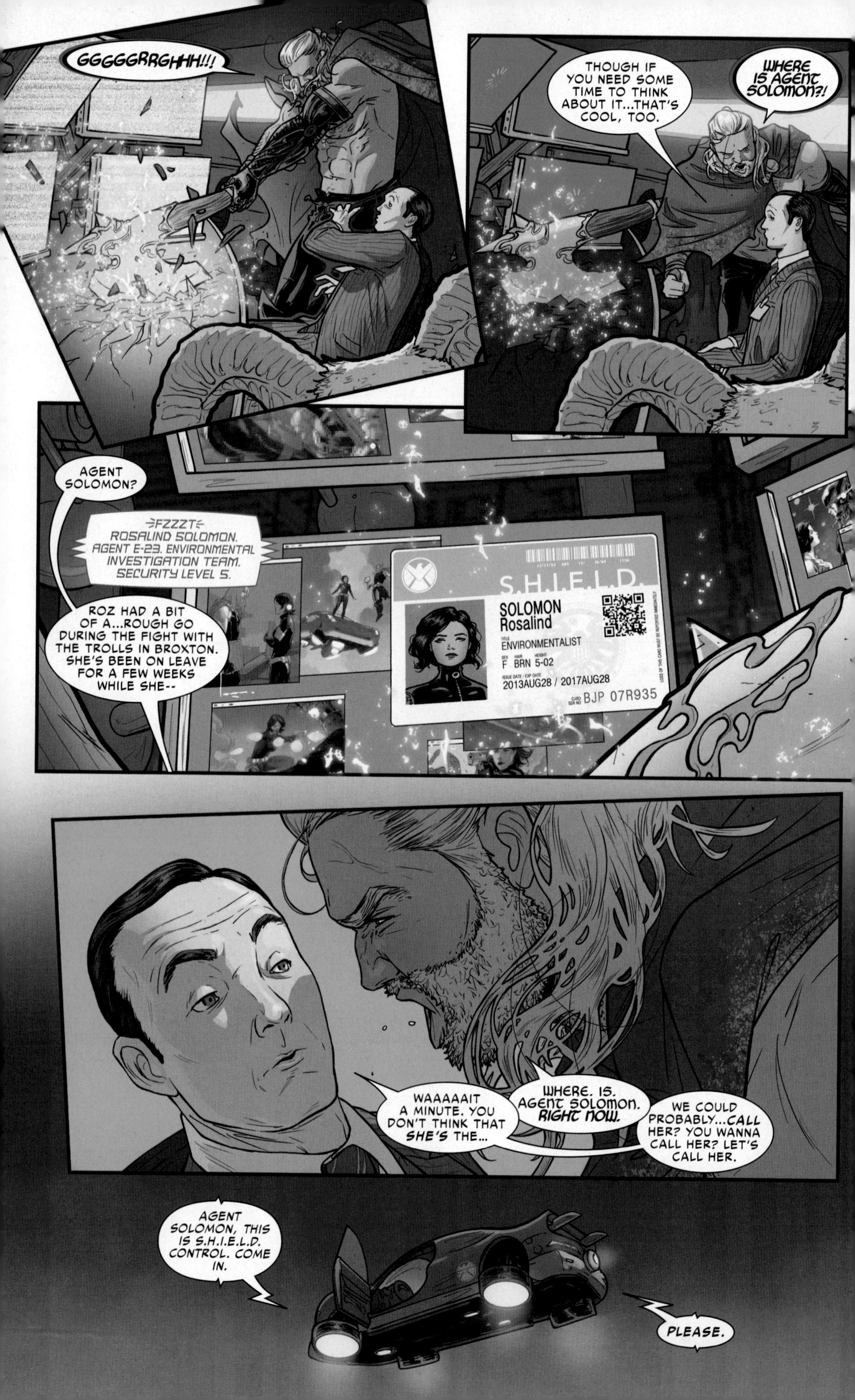
GGGGGRRGHHH!!!
THOUGH IF YOU NEED SOME TIME TO THINK ABOUT IT...THAT'S COOL, TOO.
WHERE IS AGENT SOLOMON?!
AGENT SOLOMON?
FZZZT ROSALIND SOLOMON. AGENT E-23. ENVIRONMENTAL INVESTIGATION TEAM. SECURITY LEVEL 5.
ROZ HAD A BIT OF A...ROUGH GO DURING THE FIGHT WITH THE TROLLS IN BROXTON. SHE'S BEEN ON LEAVE FOR A FEW WEEKS WHILE SHE--
S.H.I.E.L.D.
SOLOMON
Rosalind
ENVIRONMENTALIST
F BRN 5-02
2013AUG28 / 2017AUG28
BJP 07R935
WAAAAAIT A MINUTE. YOU DON'T THINK THAT SHE'S THE...
WHERE. IS. AGENT SOLOMON. RIGHT NOW.
WE COULD PROBABLY...CALL HER? YOU WANNA CALL HER? LET'S CALL HER.
AGENT SOLOMON, THIS IS S.H.I.E.L.D. CONTROL. COME IN.
PLEASE.

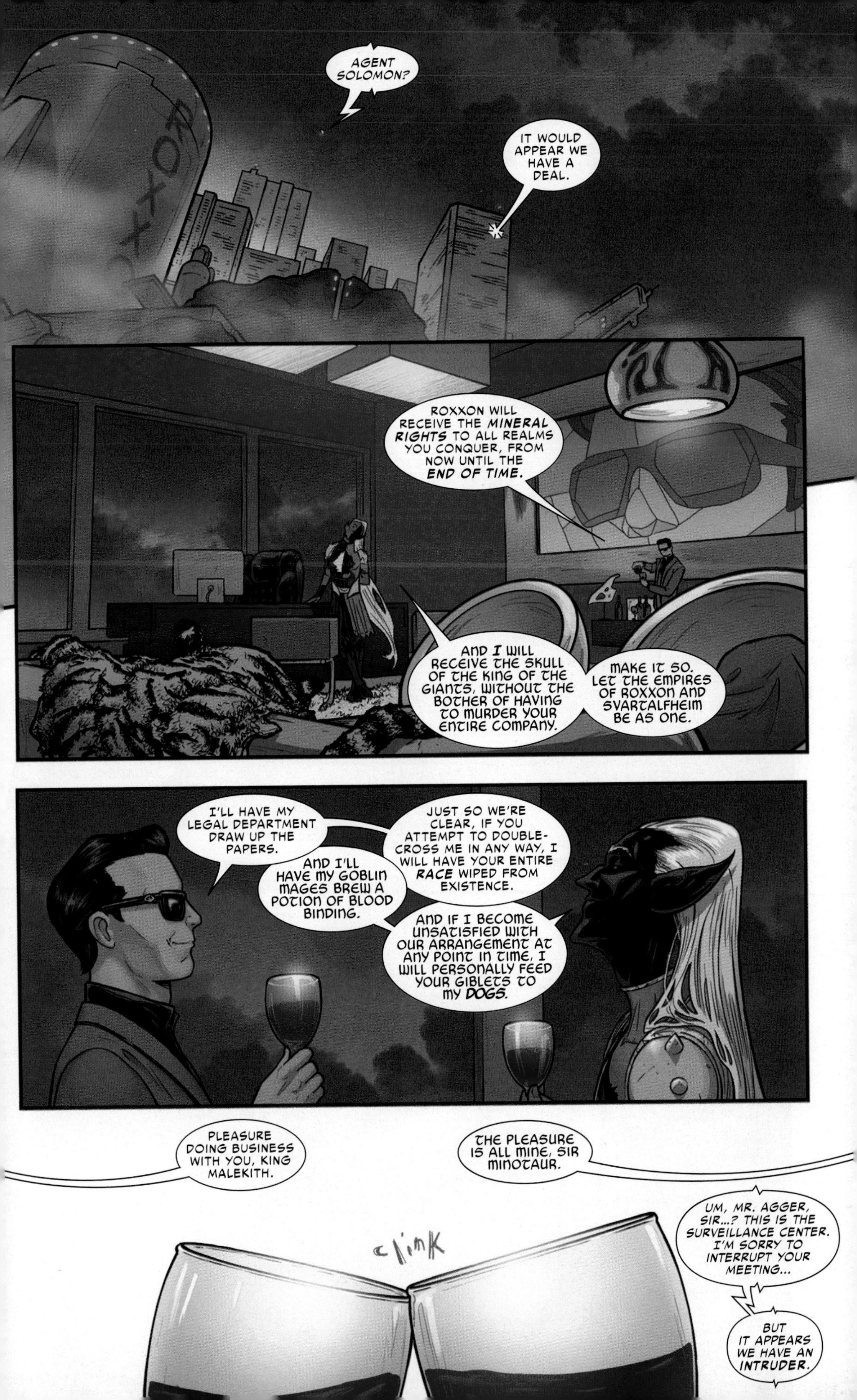
AGENT SOLOMON?
IT WOULD APPEAR WE HAVE A DEAL.
ROXXON WILL RECEIVE THE MINERAL RIGHTS TO ALL REALMS YOU CONQUER, FROM NOW UNTIL THE END OF TIME.
AND I WILL RECEIVE THE SKULL OF THE KING OF THE GIANTS, WITHOUT THE BOTHER OF HAVING TO MURDER YOUR ENTIRE COMPANY.
MAKE IT SO. LET THE EMPIRES OF ROXXON AND SVARTALFHEIM BE AS ONE.
I'LL HAVE MY LEGAL DEPARTMENT DRAW UP THE PAPERS.
JUST SO WE'RE CLEAR, IF YOU ATTEMPT TO DOUBLE-CROSS ME IN ANY WAY, I WILL HAVE YOUR ENTIRE RACE WIPED FROM EXISTENCE.
AND I'LL HAVE MY GOBLIN MAGES BREW A POTION OF BLOOD BINDING.
AND IF I BECOME UNSATISFIED WITH OUR ARRANGEMENT AT ANY POINT IN TIME, I WILL PERSONALLY FEED YOUR GIBLETS TO MY DOGS.
PLEASURE DOING BUSINESS WITH YOU, KING MALEKITH.
THE PLEASURE IS ALL MINE, SIR MINOTAUR.
clink
UM, MR. AGGER, SIR...? THIS IS THE SURVEILLANCE CENTER. I'M SORRY TO INTERRUPT YOUR MEETING...
BUT IT APPEARS WE HAVE AN INTRUDER.

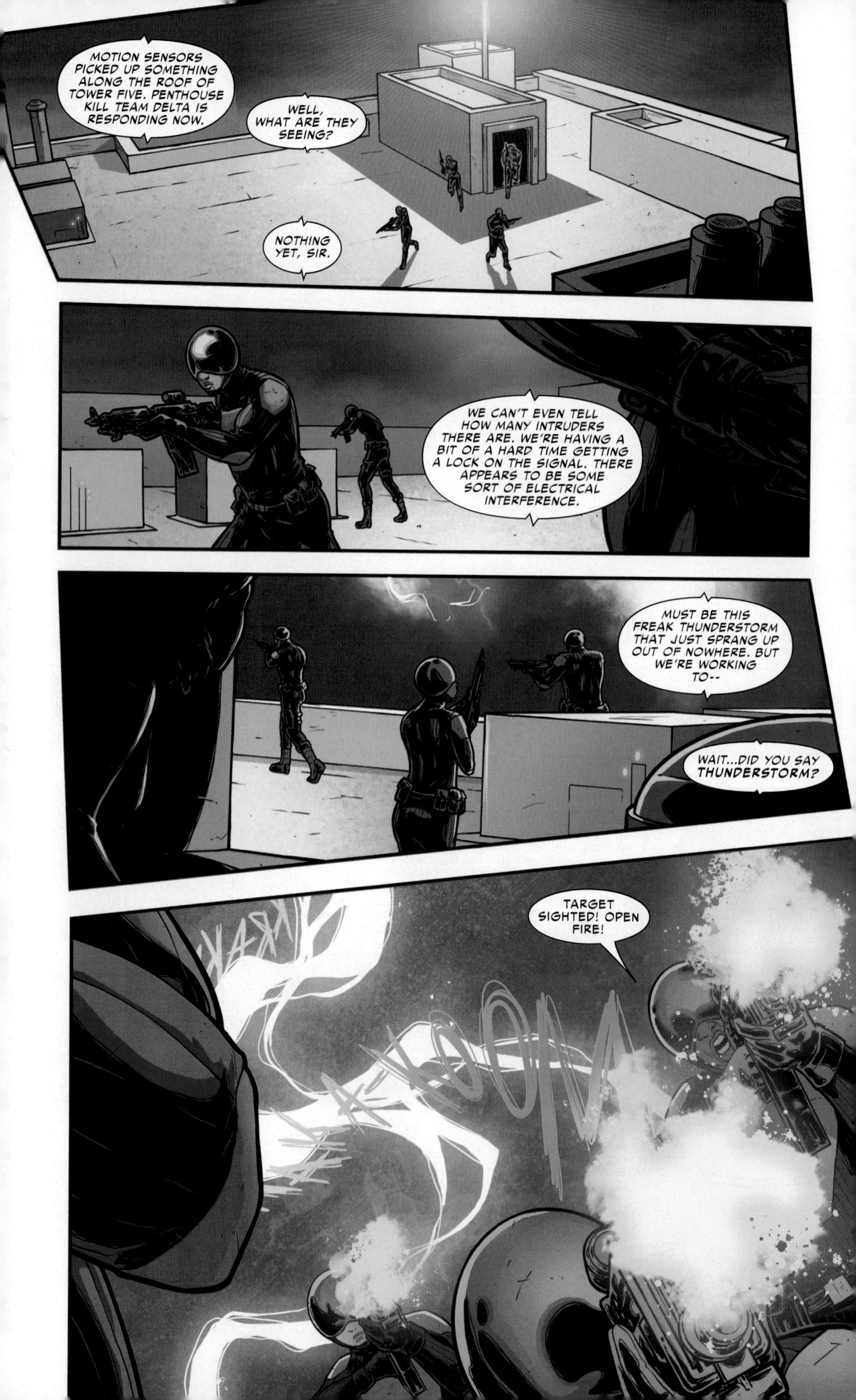
MOTION SENSORS PICKED UP SOMETHING ALONG THE ROOF OF TOWER FIVE. PENTHOUSE KILL TEAM DELTA IS RESPONDING NOW.
WELL, WHAT ARE THEY SEEING?
NOTHING YET, SIR.
WE CAN'T EVEN TELL HOW MANY INTRUDERS THERE ARE. WE'RE HAVING A BIT OF A HARD TIME GETTING A LOCK ON THE SIGNAL. THERE APPEARS TO BE SOME SORT OF ELECTRICAL INTERFERENCE.
MUST BE THIS FREAK THUNDERSTORM THAT JUST SPRANG UP OUT OF NOWHERE. BUT WE'RE WORKING TO--
WAIT...DID YOU SAY THUNDERSTORM?
TARGET SIGHTED! OPEN FIRE!

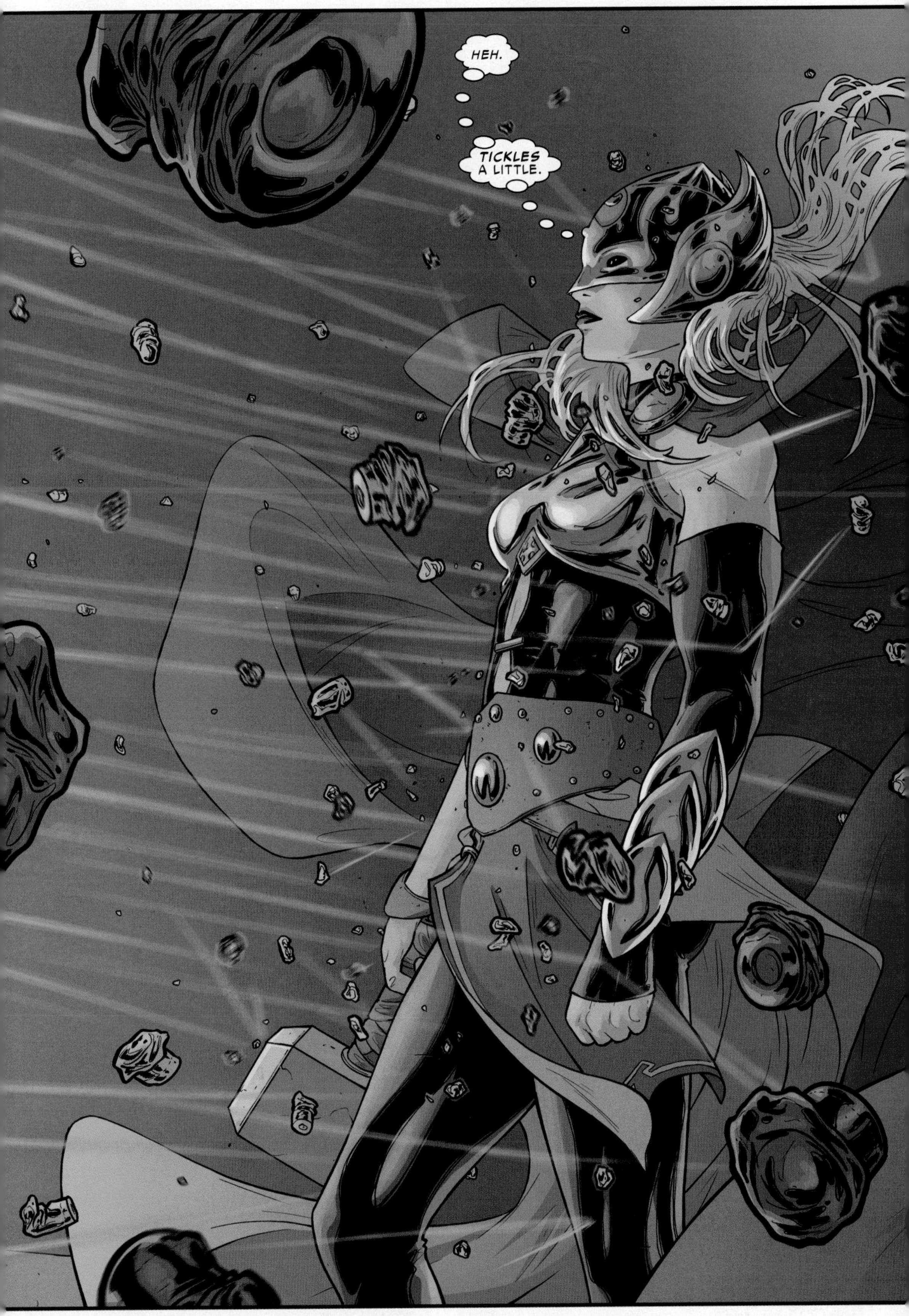
HEH.
TICKLES A LITTLE.

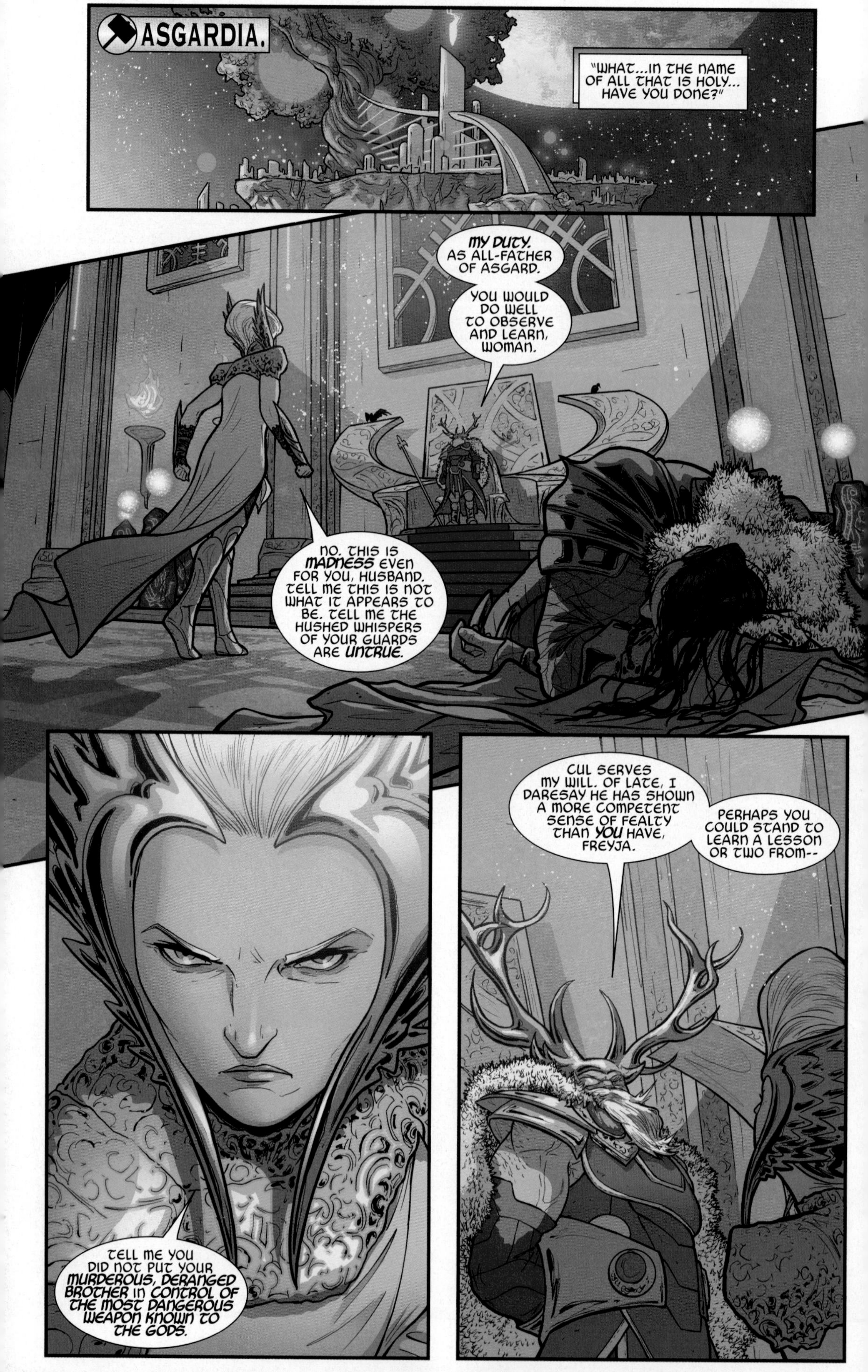
ASGARDIA.
"WHAT...IN THE NAME OF ALL THAT IS HOLY... HAVE YOU DONE?"
MY DUTY. AS ALL-FATHER OF ASGARD.
YOU WOULD DO WELL TO OBSERVE AND LEARN, WOMAN.
NO. THIS IS MADNESS EVEN FOR YOU, HUSBAND. TELL ME THIS IS NOT WHAT IT APPEARS TO BE. TELL ME THE HUSHED WHISPERS OF YOUR GUARDS ARE UNTRUE.
TELL ME YOU DID NOT PUT YOUR MURDEROUS, DERANGED BROTHER IN CONTROL OF THE MOST DANGEROUS WEAPON KNOWN TO THE GODS.
CUL SERVES MY WILL. OF LATE, I DARESAY HE HAS SHOWN A MORE COMPETENT SENSE OF FEALTY THAN YOU HAVE, FREYJA.
PERHAPS YOU COULD STAND TO LEARN A LESSON OR TWO FROM--

YOU SHOULD *NOT* HAVE DONE THAT.

YOU DO NOT GET TO SAY THAT TO ME. NOT AFTER WHAT YOU'VE JUST DONE.

I WILL SEE THAT HAMMER RETURNED TO ASGARD. NO MATTER THE COST.

BE CAREFUL WHAT YOU WISH FOR, YOU ONE-EYED FOOL.

OR YOU MAY COME TO KNOW THAT HAMMER IN WAYS YOU NEVER IMAGINED.

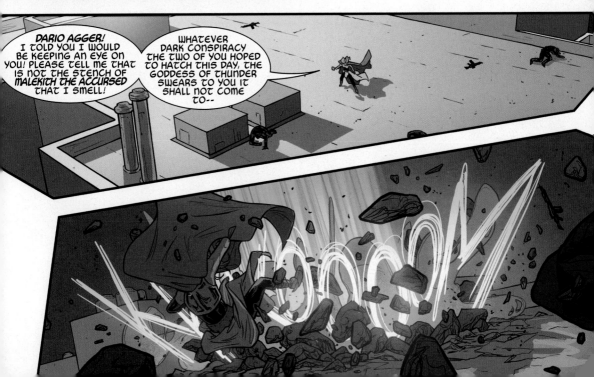

DARIO AGGER! I TOLD YOU I WOULD BE KEEPING AN EYE ON YOU! PLEASE TELL ME THAT IS NOT THE STENCH OF *MALEKITH THE ACCURSED* THAT I SMELL!

WHATEVER DARK CONSPIRACY THE TWO OF YOU HOPED TO HATCH THIS DAY, THE GODDESS OF THUNDER SWEARS TO YOU IT SHALL NOT COME TO--

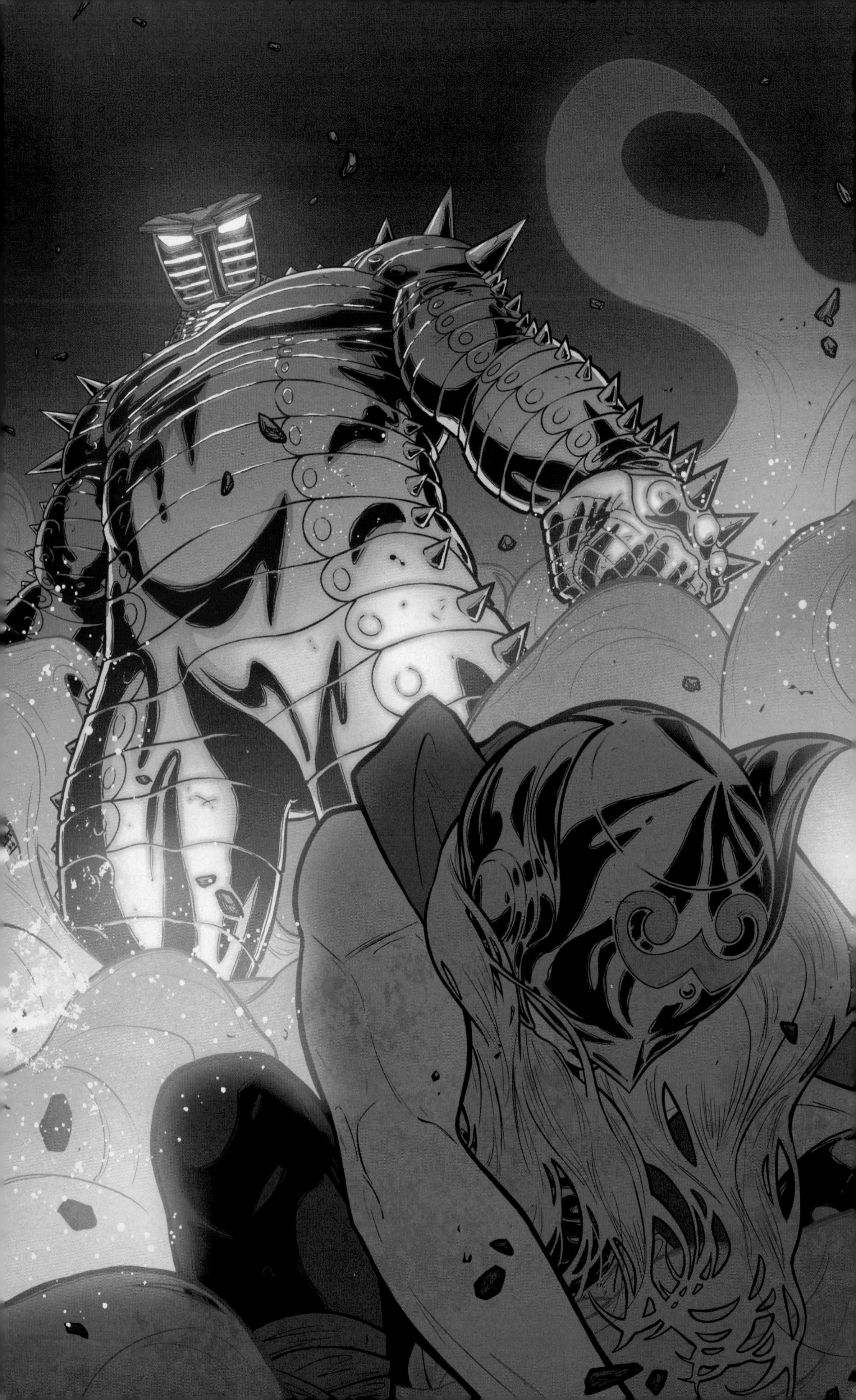

7

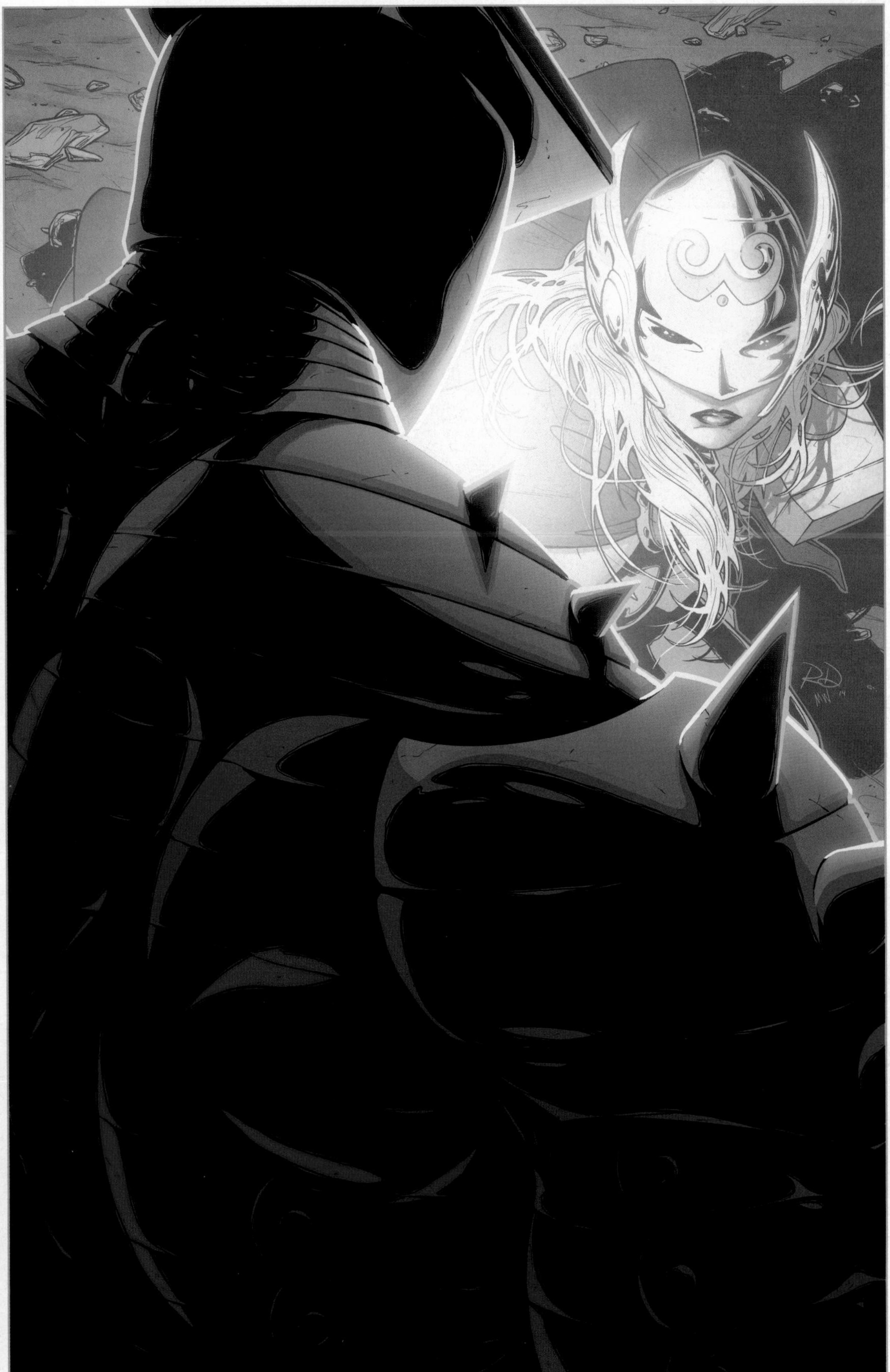

THE BATTLE FOR THE HAMMER

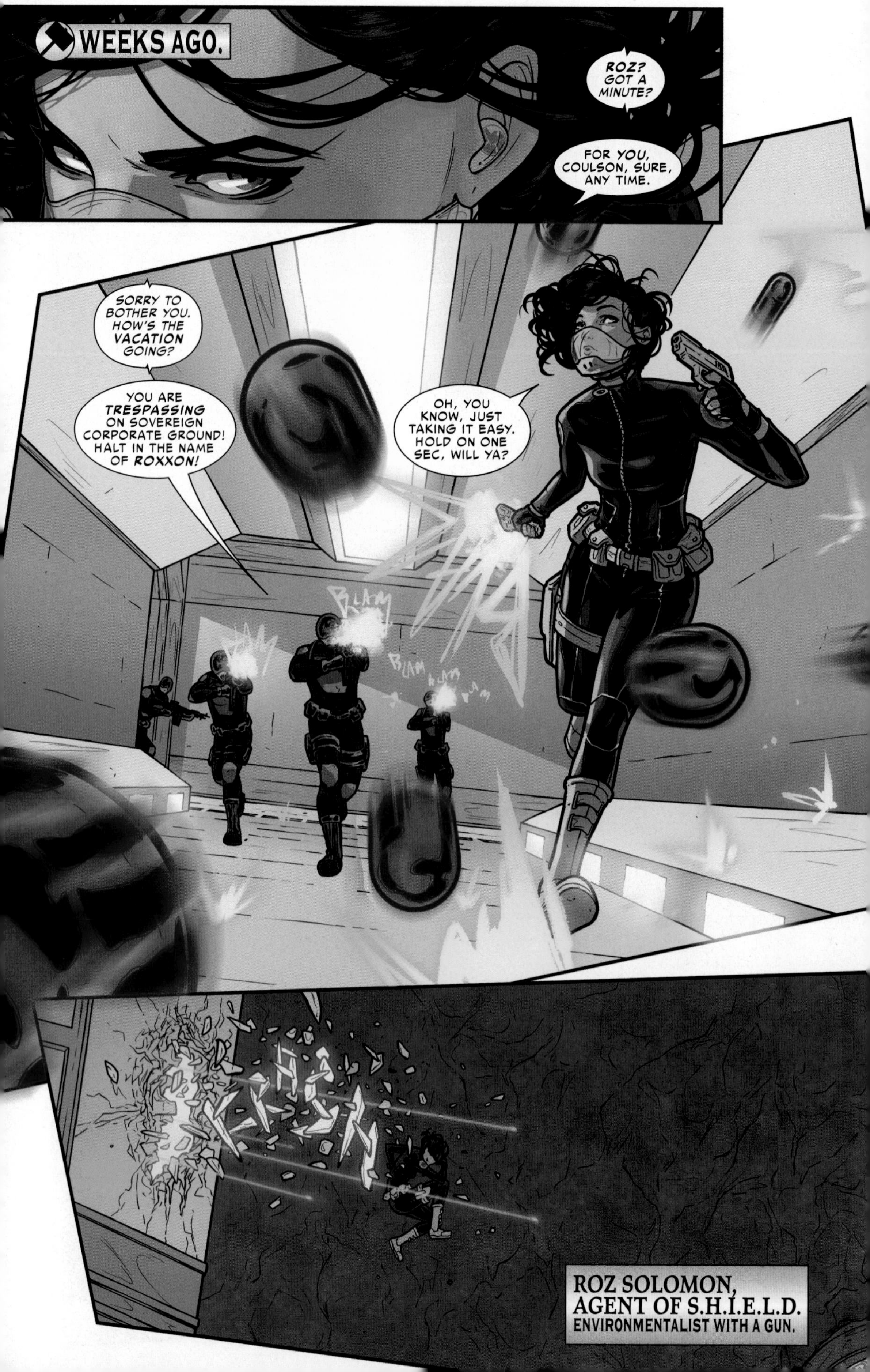
WEEKS AGO.
ROZ? GOT A MINUTE?
FOR YOU, COULSON, SURE, ANY TIME.
SORRY TO BOTHER YOU. HOW'S THE VACATION GOING?
YOU ARE TRESPASSING ON SOVEREIGN CORPORATE GROUND! HALT IN THE NAME OF ROXXON!
OH, YOU KNOW, JUST TAKING IT EASY. HOLD ON ONE SEC, WILL YA?
BLAM
BLAM
BLAM
ROZ SOLOMON, AGENT OF S.H.I.E.L.D.
ENVIRONMENTALIST WITH A GUN.

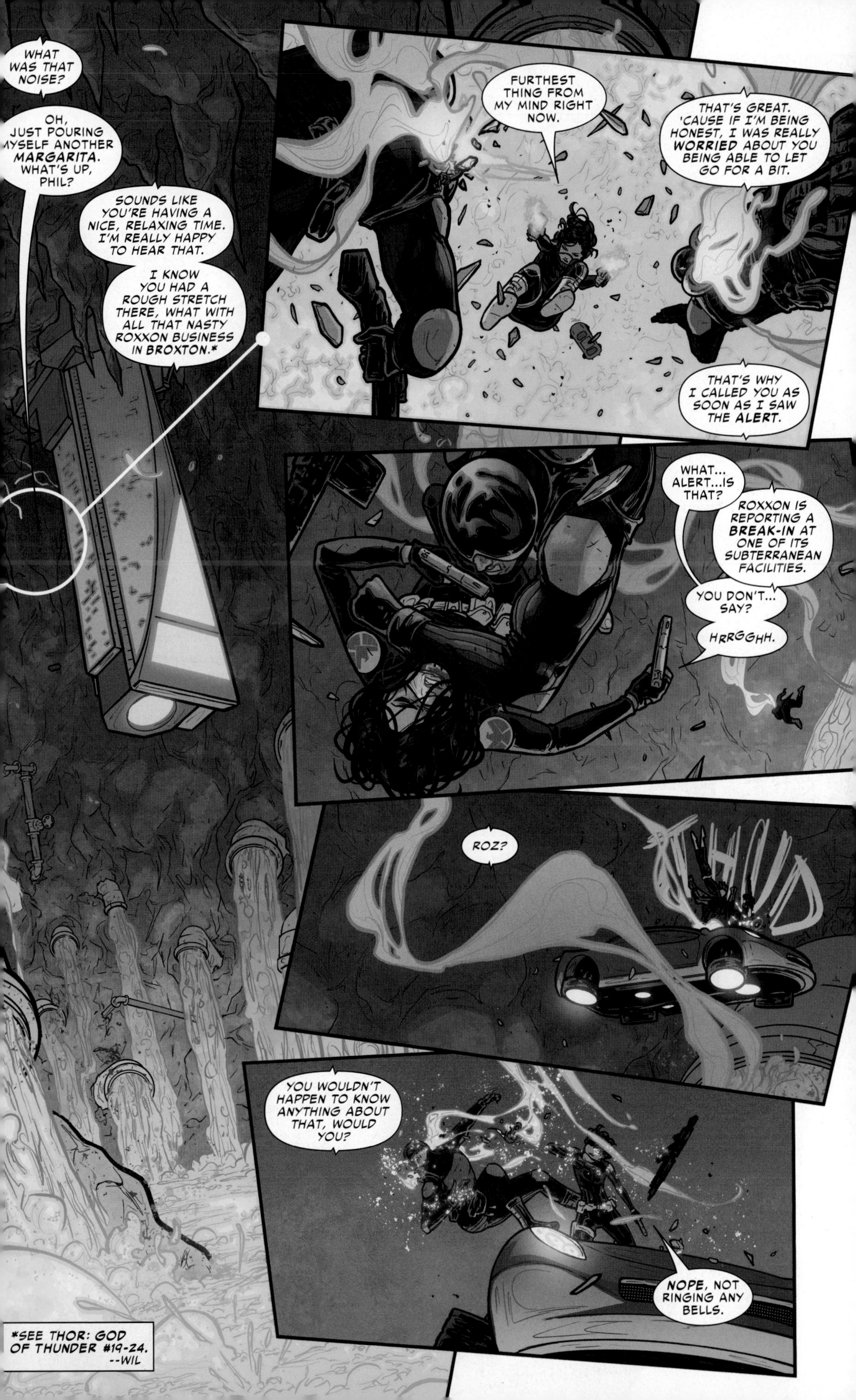
WHAT WAS THAT NOISE?
OH, JUST POURING MYSELF ANOTHER MARGARITA. WHAT'S UP, PHIL?
SOUNDS LIKE YOU'RE HAVING A NICE, RELAXING TIME. I'M REALLY HAPPY TO HEAR THAT.
I KNOW YOU HAD A ROUGH STRETCH THERE, WHAT WITH ALL THAT NASTY ROXXON BUSINESS IN BROXTON.*
FURTHEST THING FROM MY MIND RIGHT NOW.
THAT'S GREAT. 'CAUSE IF I'M BEING HONEST, I WAS REALLY WORRIED ABOUT YOU BEING ABLE TO LET GO FOR A BIT.
THAT'S WHY I CALLED YOU AS SOON AS I SAW THE ALERT.
WHAT... ALERT...IS THAT?
ROXXON IS REPORTING A BREAK-IN AT ONE OF ITS SUBTERRANEAN FACILITIES.
YOU DON'T... SAY?
HRRGGHH.
ROZ?
THUD
YOU WOULDN'T HAPPEN TO KNOW ANYTHING ABOUT THAT, WOULD YOU?
NOPE, NOT RINGING ANY BELLS.
*SEE THOR: GOD OF THUNDER #19-24. --WIL

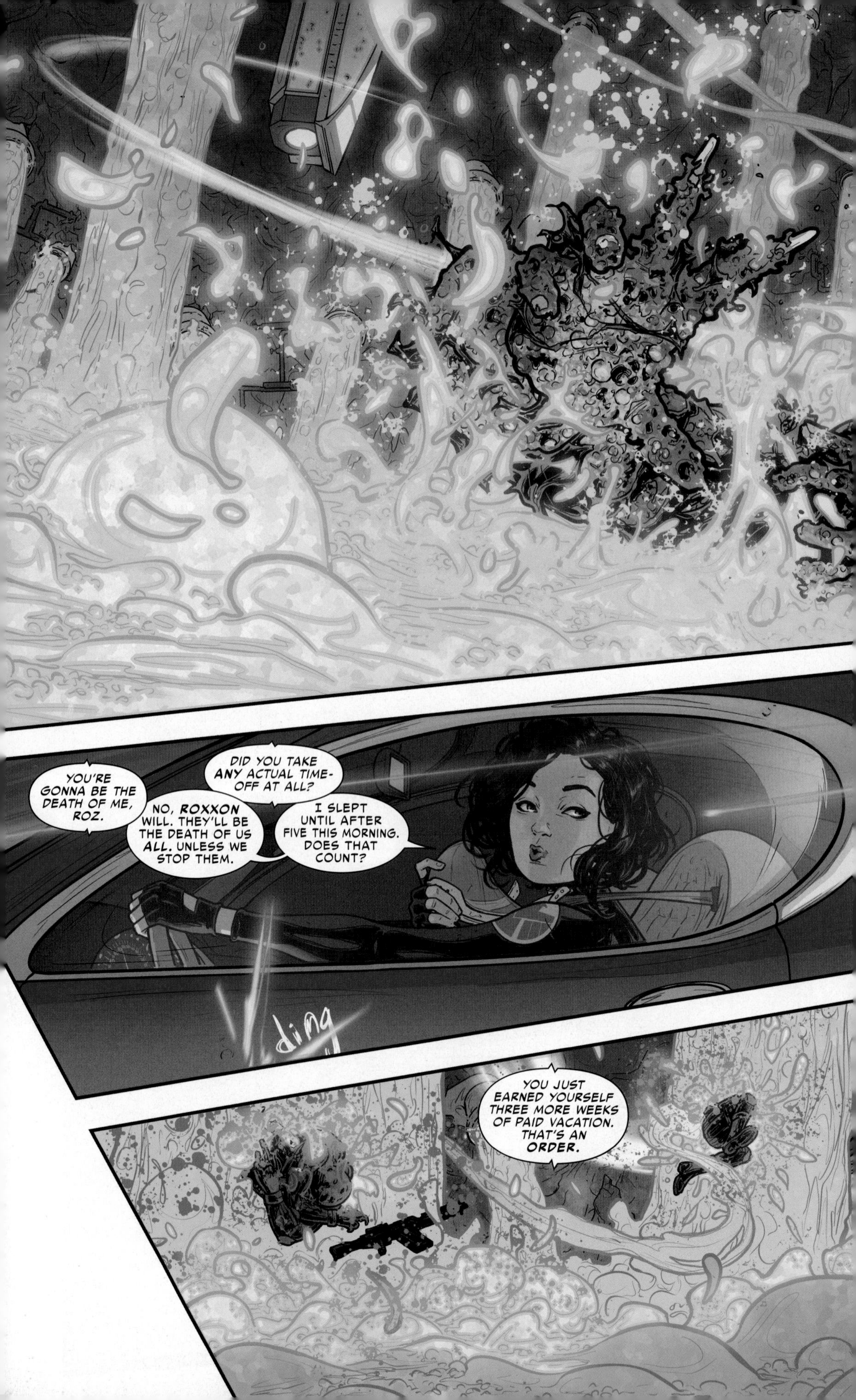
YOU'RE GONNA BE THE DEATH OF ME, ROZ.
NO, ROXXON WILL. THEY'LL BE THE DEATH OF US ALL. UNLESS WE STOP THEM.
DID YOU TAKE ANY ACTUAL TIME-OFF AT ALL?
I SLEPT UNTIL AFTER FIVE THIS MORNING. DOES THAT COUNT?
ding
YOU JUST EARNED YOURSELF THREE MORE WEEKS OF PAID VACATION. THAT'S AN ORDER.

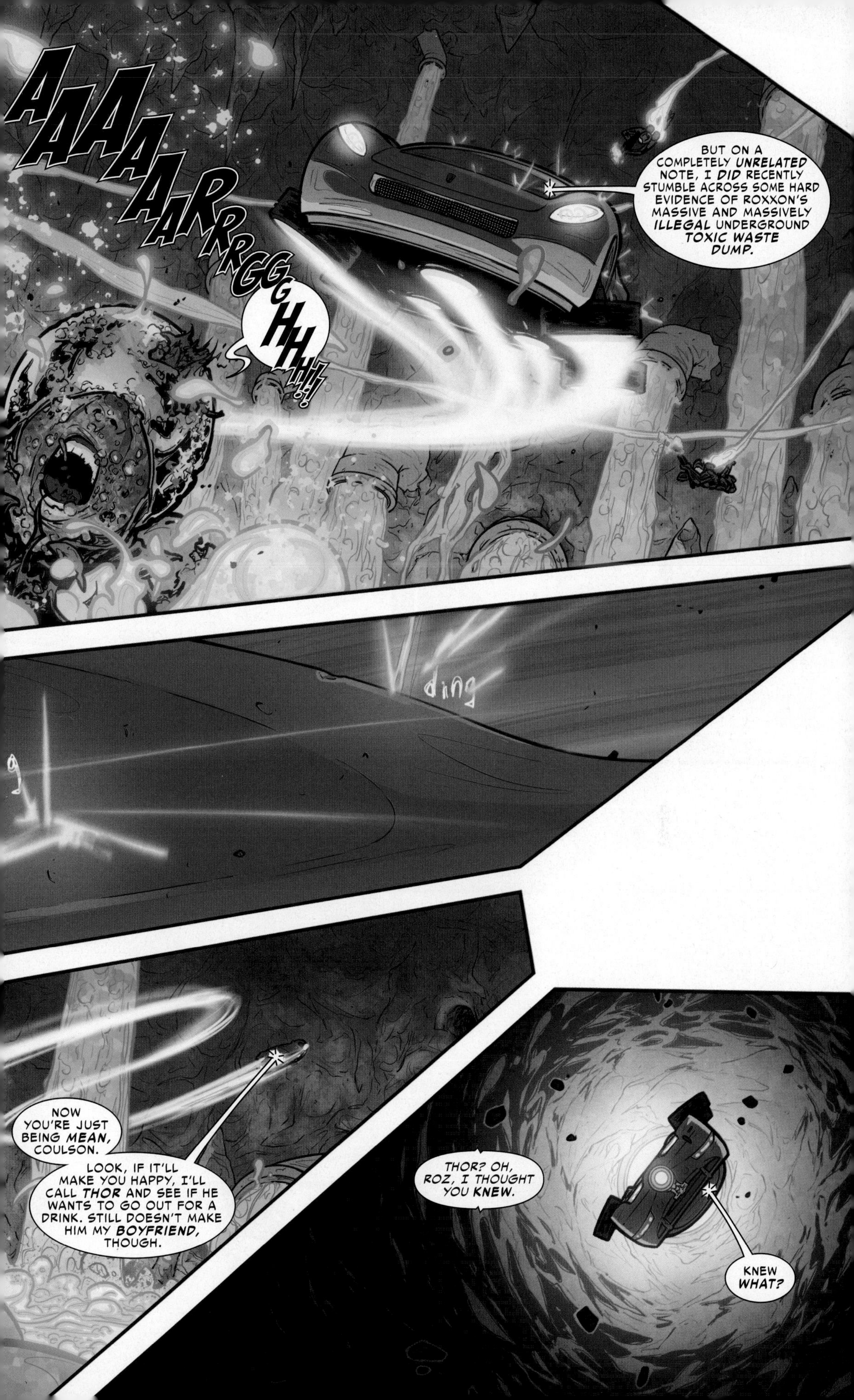
AAAAAARRRGGGHHH!!
BUT ON A COMPLETELY UNRELATED NOTE, I DID RECENTLY STUMBLE ACROSS SOME HARD EVIDENCE OF ROXXON'S MASSIVE AND MASSIVELY ILLEGAL UNDERGROUND TOXIC WASTE DUMP.
ding
NOW YOU'RE JUST BEING MEAN, COULSON.
LOOK, IF IT'LL MAKE YOU HAPPY, I'LL CALL THOR AND SEE IF HE WANTS TO GO OUT FOR A DRINK. STILL DOESN'T MAKE HIM MY BOYFRIEND, THOUGH.
THOR? OH, ROZ, I THOUGHT YOU KNEW.
KNEW WHAT?

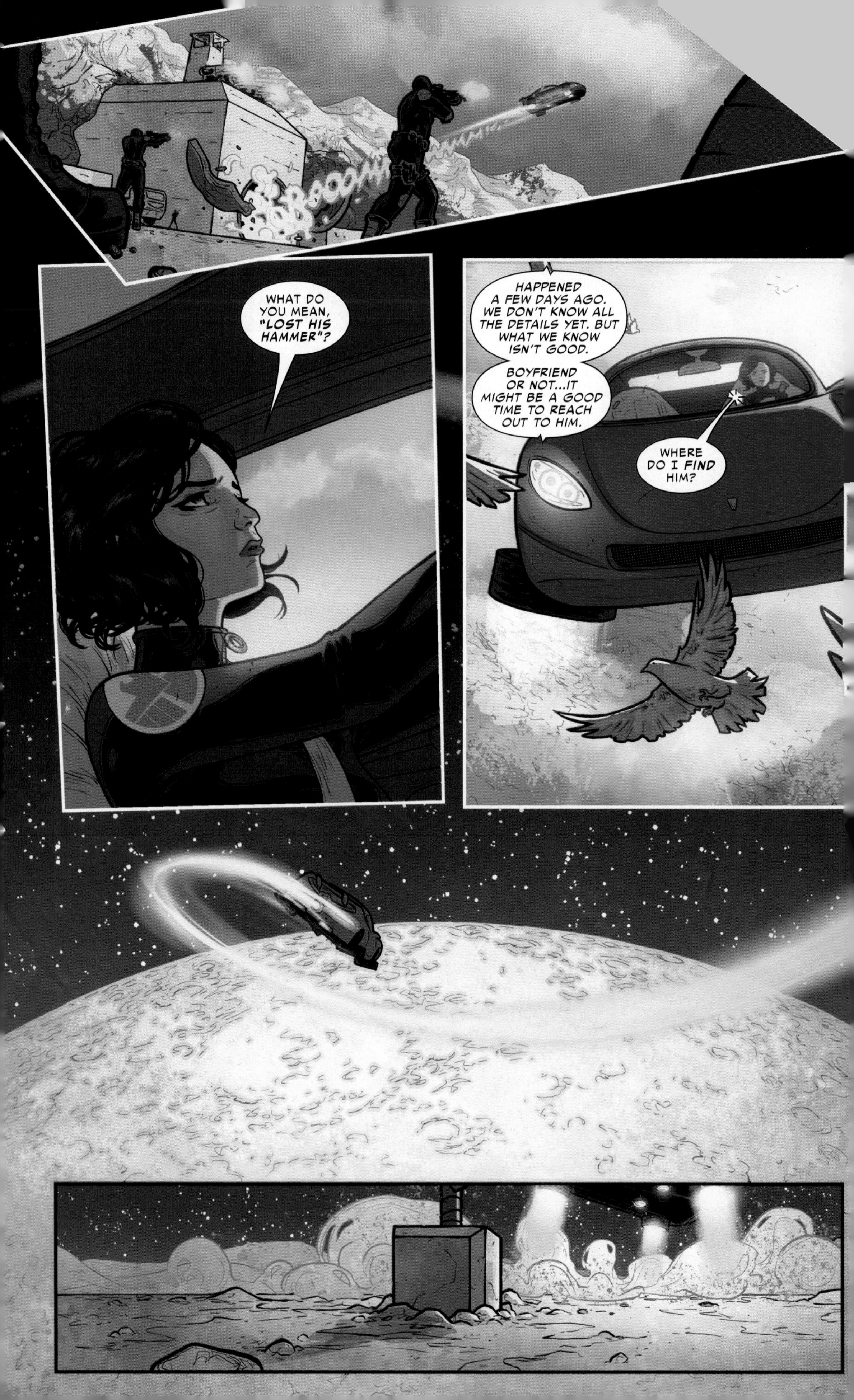
WHAT DO YOU MEAN, "LOST HIS HAMMER"?
HAPPENED A FEW DAYS AGO. WE DON'T KNOW ALL THE DETAILS YET. BUT WHAT WE KNOW ISN'T GOOD.
BOYFRIEND OR NOT...IT MIGHT BE A GOOD TIME TO REACH OUT TO HIM.
WHERE DO I FIND HIM?

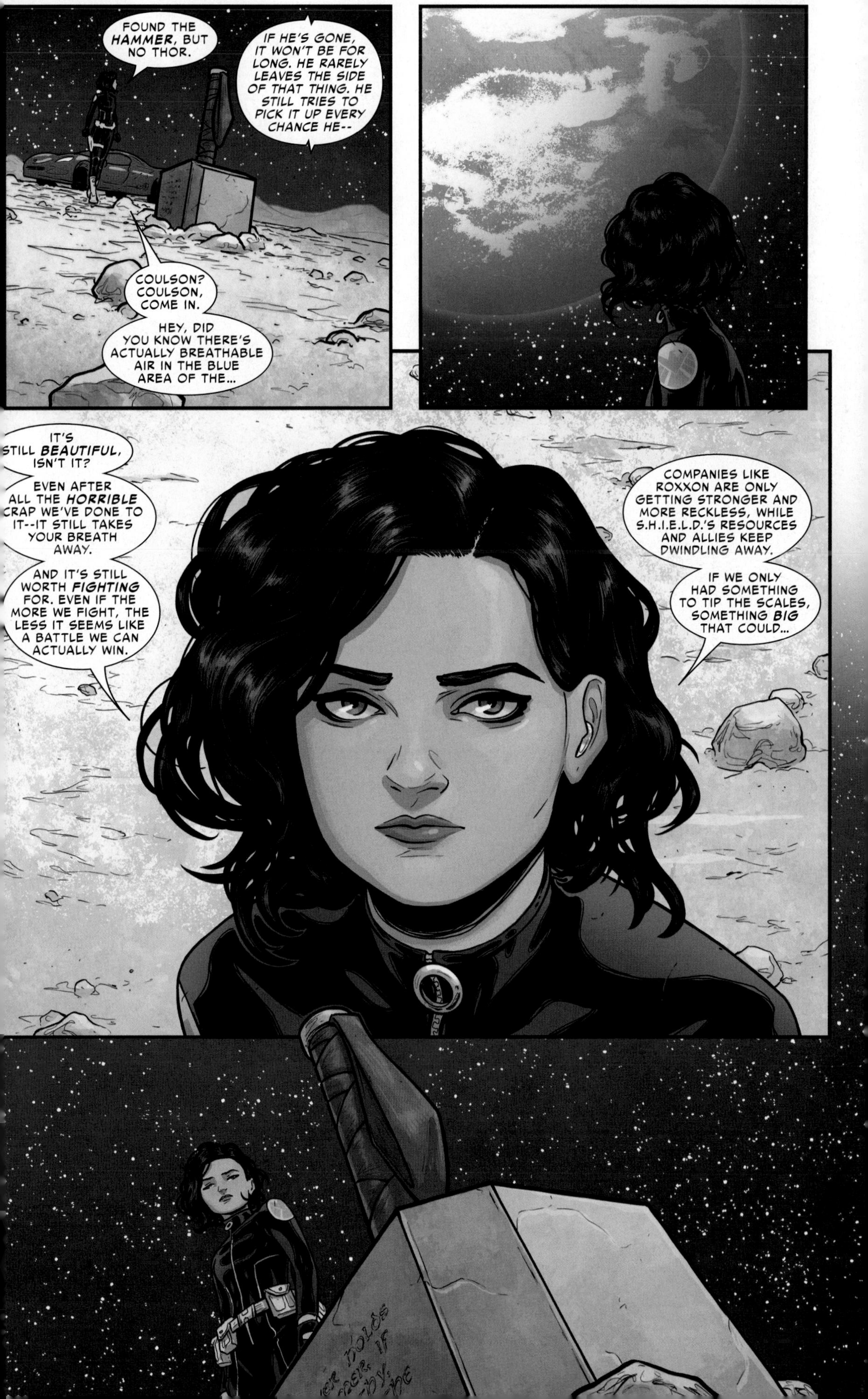
FOUND THE HAMMER, BUT NO THOR.
IF HE'S GONE, IT WON'T BE FOR LONG. HE RARELY LEAVES THE SIDE OF THAT THING. HE STILL TRIES TO PICK IT UP EVERY CHANCE HE--
COULSON? COULSON, COME IN.
HEY, DID YOU KNOW THERE'S ACTUALLY BREATHABLE AIR IN THE BLUE AREA OF THE...
IT'S STILL BEAUTIFUL, ISN'T IT?
EVEN AFTER ALL THE HORRIBLE CRAP WE'VE DONE TO IT--IT STILL TAKES YOUR BREATH AWAY.
AND IT'S STILL WORTH FIGHTING FOR. EVEN IF THE MORE WE FIGHT, THE LESS IT SEEMS LIKE A BATTLE WE CAN ACTUALLY WIN.
COMPANIES LIKE ROXXON ARE ONLY GETTING STRONGER AND MORE RECKLESS, WHILE S.H.I.E.L.D.'S RESOURCES AND ALLIES KEEP DWINDLING AWAY.
IF WE ONLY HAD SOMETHING TO TIP THE SCALES, SOMETHING BIG THAT COULD...

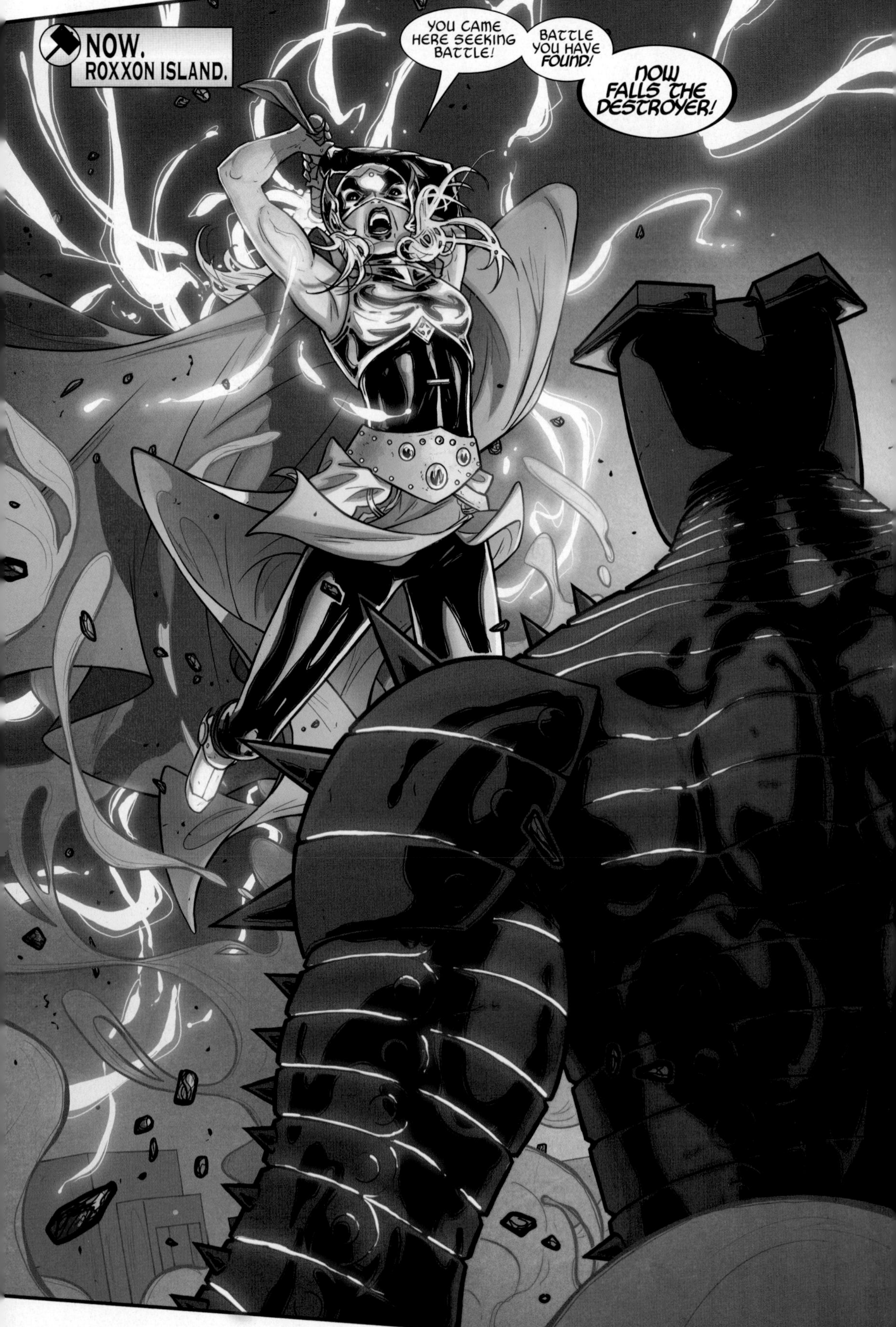
NOW.
ROXXON ISLAND.
YOU CAME HERE SEEKING BATTLE!
BATTLE YOU HAVE FOUND!
NOW FALLS THE DESTROYER!

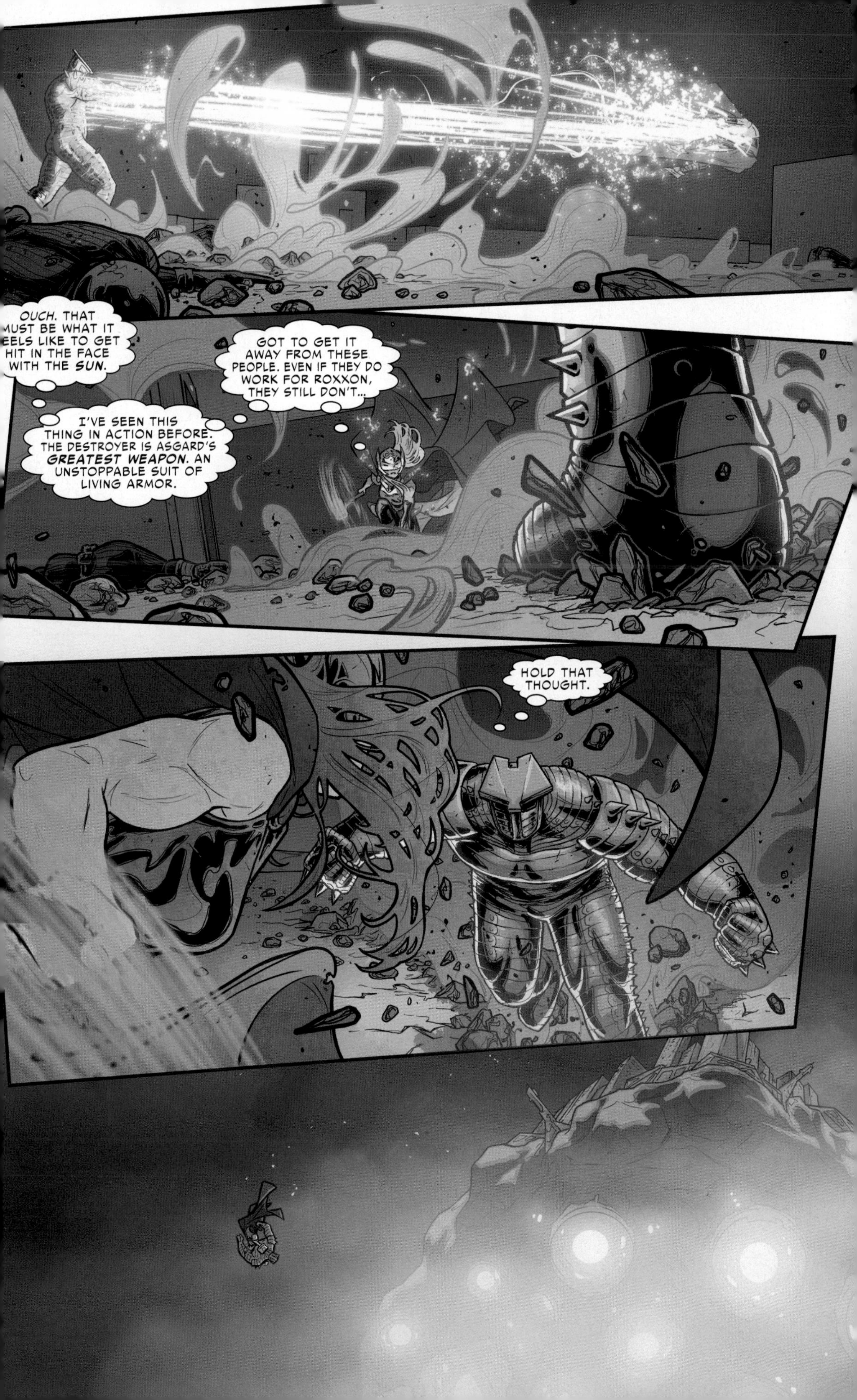
OUCH. THAT MUST BE WHAT IT FEELS LIKE TO GET HIT IN THE FACE WITH THE SUN.
GOT TO GET IT AWAY FROM THESE PEOPLE. EVEN IF THEY DO WORK FOR ROXXON, THEY STILL DON'T...
I'VE SEEN THIS THING IN ACTION BEFORE. THE DESTROYER IS ASGARD'S GREATEST WEAPON. AN UNSTOPPABLE SUIT OF LIVING ARMOR.
HOLD THAT THOUGHT.

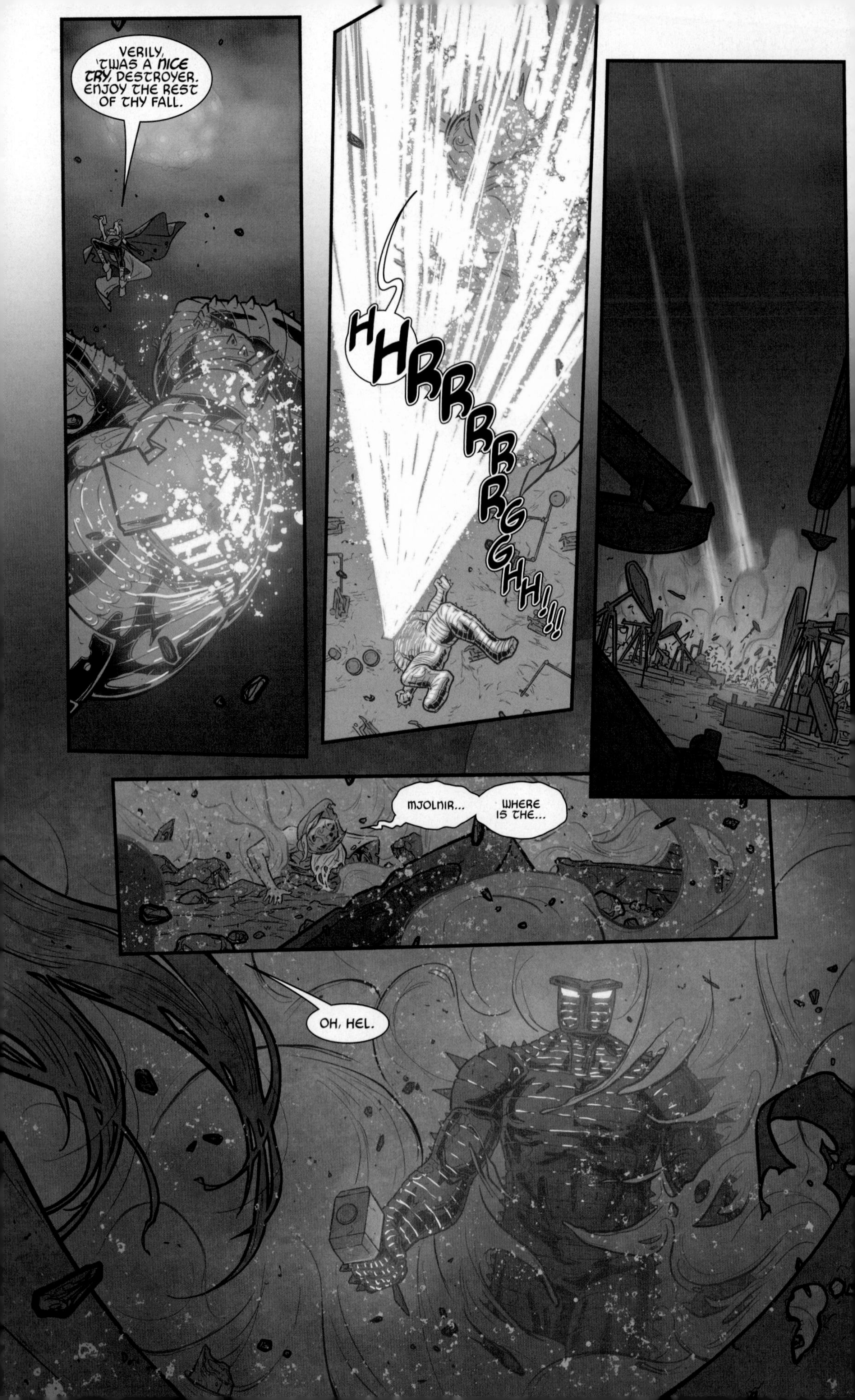
VERILY, 'TWAS A NICE TRY, DESTROYER. ENJOY THE REST OF THY FALL.
HHRRRRRRGGHH!!!
MJOLNIR...
WHERE IS THE...
OH, HEL.

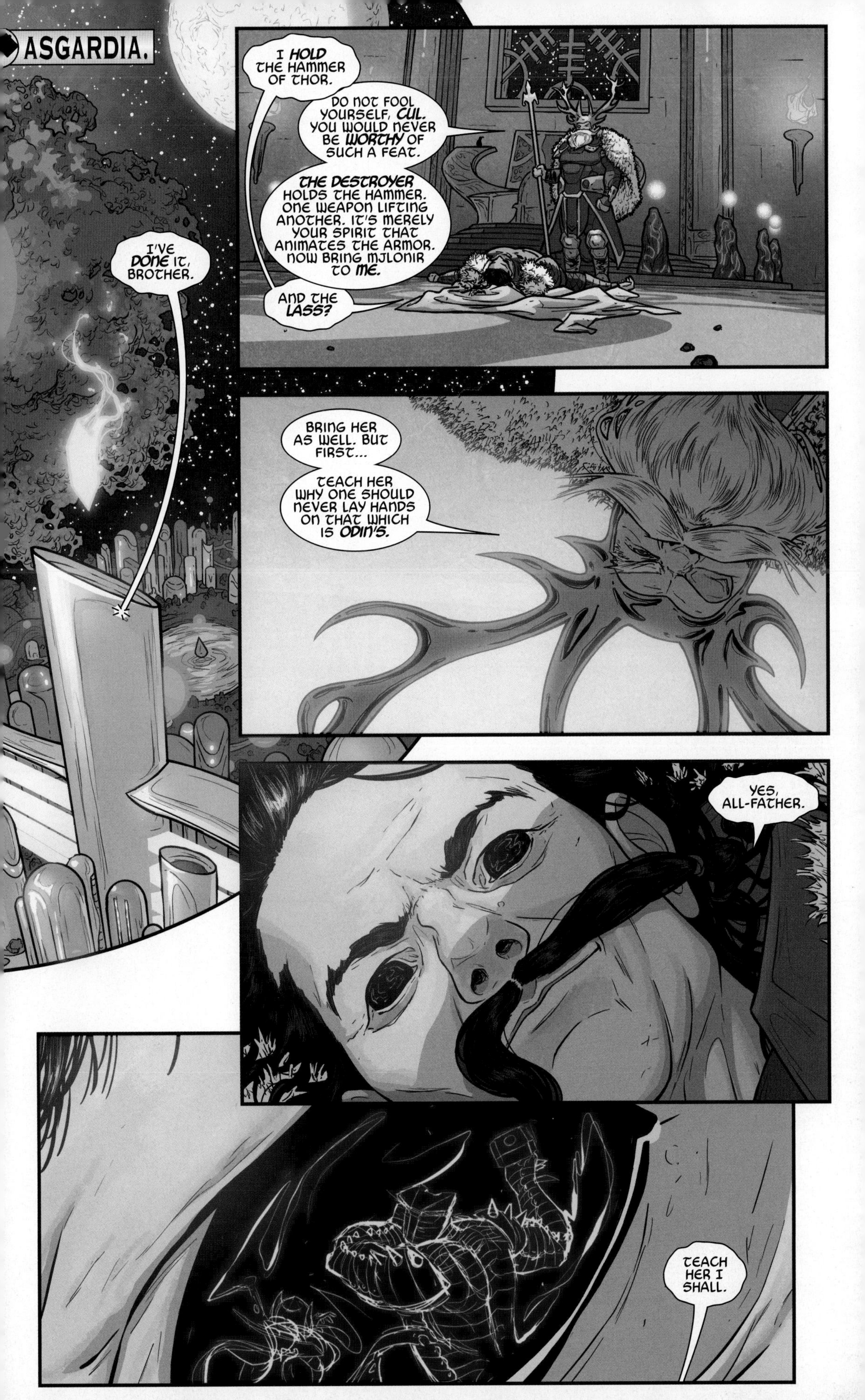
ASGARDIA.
I HOLD THE HAMMER OF THOR.
DO NOT FOOL YOURSELF, CUL. YOU WOULD NEVER BE WORTHY OF SUCH A FEAT.
THE DESTROYER HOLDS THE HAMMER. ONE WEAPON LIFTING ANOTHER. IT'S MERELY YOUR SPIRIT THAT ANIMATES THE ARMOR. NOW BRING MJLONIR TO ME.
AND THE LASS?
I'VE DONE IT, BROTHER.
BRING HER AS WELL. BUT FIRST...
TEACH HER WHY ONE SHOULD NEVER LAY HANDS ON THAT WHICH IS ODIN'S.
YES, ALL-FATHER.
TEACH HER I SHALL.

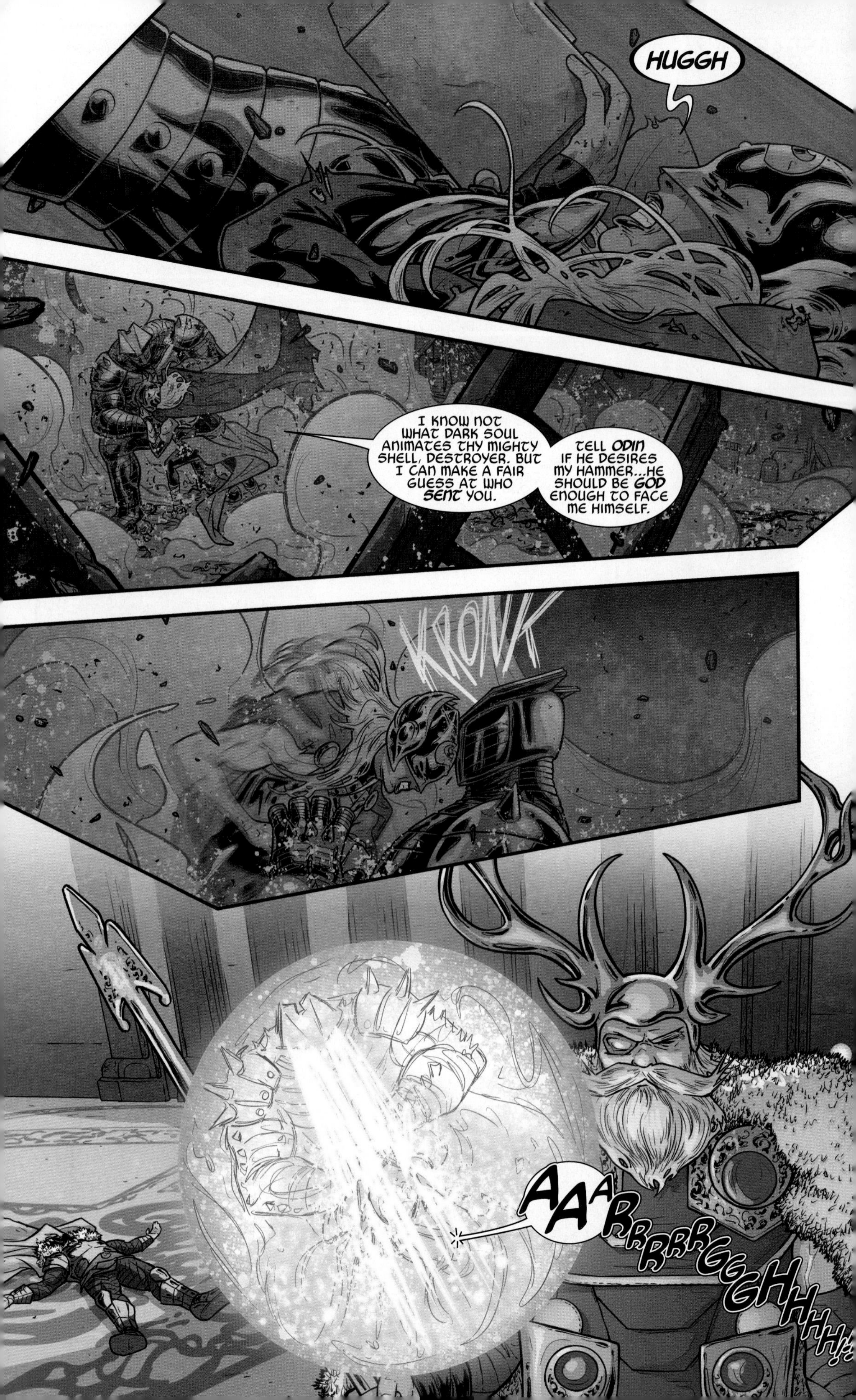
HUGGH
I KNOW NOT WHAT DARK SOUL ANIMATES THY MIGHTY SHELL, DESTROYER, BUT I CAN MAKE A FAIR GUESS AT WHO SENT YOU.
TELL ODIN IF HE DESIRES MY HAMMER...HE SHOULD BE GOD ENOUGH TO FACE ME HIMSELF.
KRONK
AAARRRRRRGGGHHHHH!!

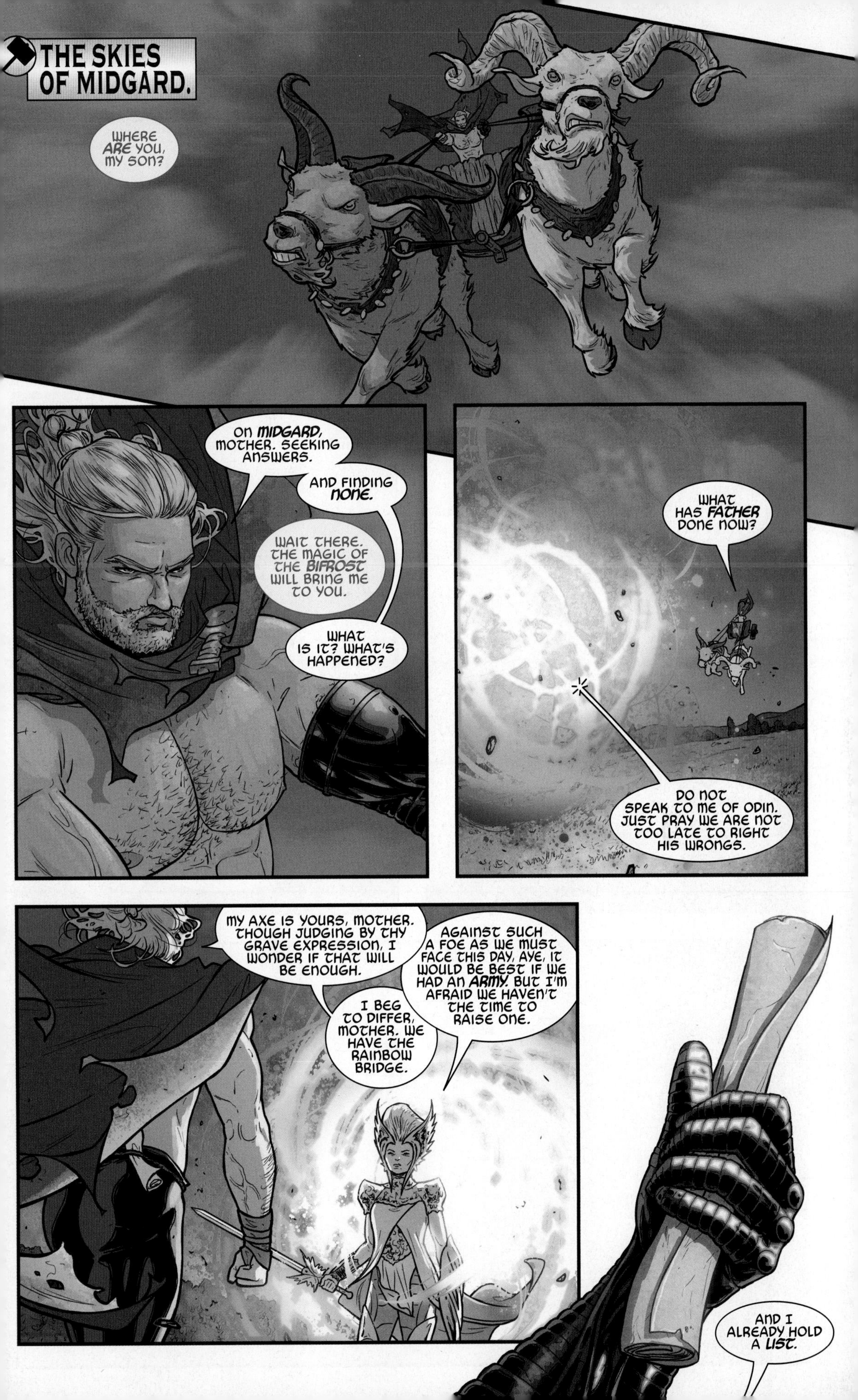
THE SKIES OF MIDGARD.
WHERE ARE YOU, MY SON?
ON MIDGARD, MOTHER. SEEKING ANSWERS.
AND FINDING NONE.
WAIT THERE. THE MAGIC OF THE BIFROST WILL BRING ME TO YOU.
WHAT IS IT? WHAT'S HAPPENED?
WHAT HAS FATHER DONE NOW?
DO NOT SPEAK TO ME OF ODIN. JUST PRAY WE ARE NOT TOO LATE TO RIGHT HIS WRONGS.
MY AXE IS YOURS, MOTHER. THOUGH JUDGING BY THY GRAVE EXPRESSION, I WONDER IF THAT WILL BE ENOUGH.
AGAINST SUCH A FOE AS WE MUST FACE THIS DAY, AYE, IT WOULD BE BEST IF WE HAD AN ARMY. BUT I'M AFRAID WE HAVEN'T THE TIME TO RAISE ONE.
I BEG TO DIFFER, MOTHER. WE HAVE THE RAINBOW BRIDGE.
AND I ALREADY HOLD A LIST.

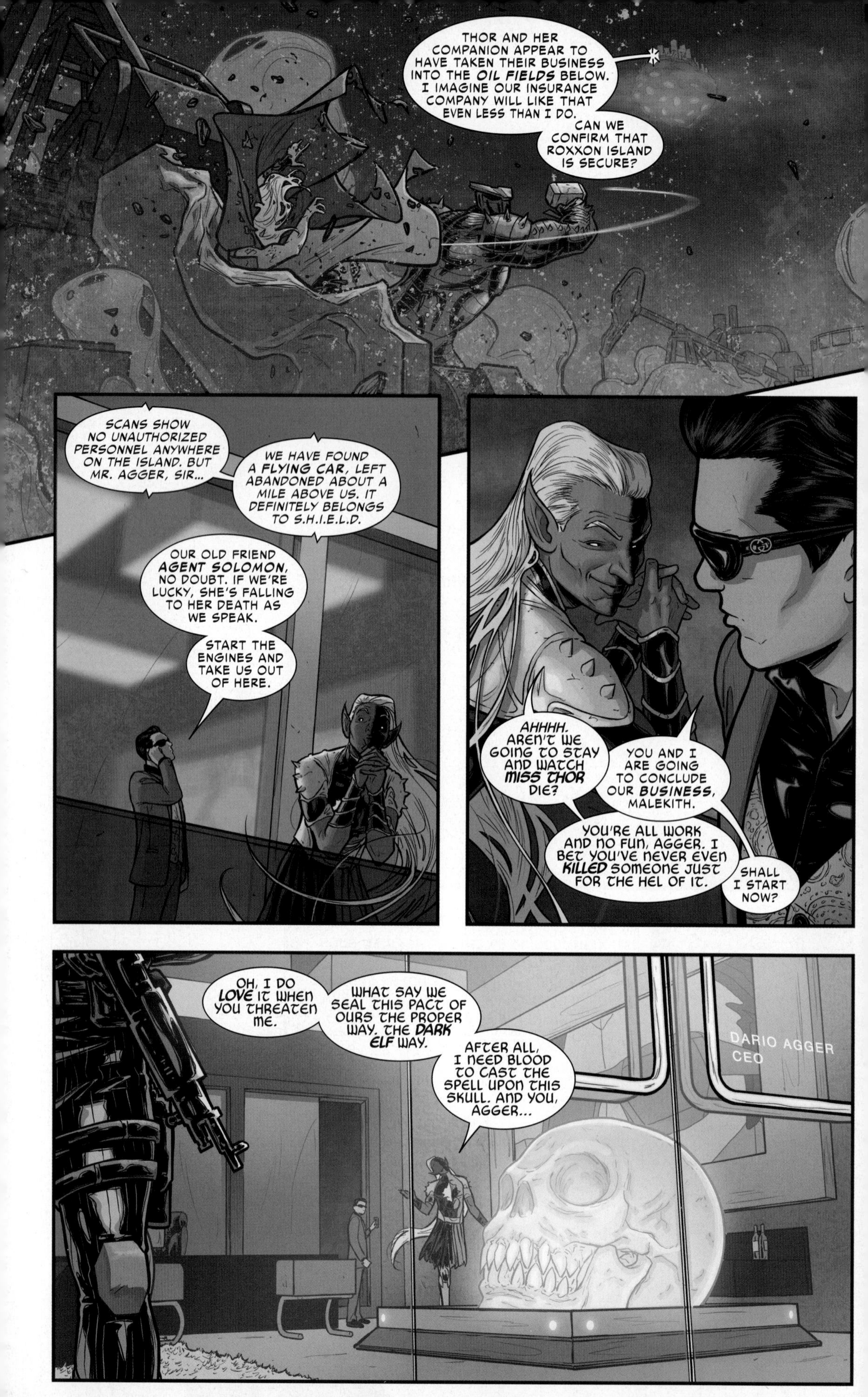
THOR AND HER COMPANION APPEAR TO HAVE TAKEN THEIR BUSINESS INTO THE OIL FIELDS BELOW. I IMAGINE OUR INSURANCE COMPANY WILL LIKE THAT EVEN LESS THAN I DO.
CAN WE CONFIRM THAT ROXXON ISLAND IS SECURE?
SCANS SHOW NO UNAUTHORIZED PERSONNEL ANYWHERE ON THE ISLAND. BUT MR. AGGER, SIR...
WE HAVE FOUND A FLYING CAR, LEFT ABANDONED ABOUT A MILE ABOVE US. IT DEFINITELY BELONGS TO S.H.I.E.L.D.
OUR OLD FRIEND AGENT SOLOMON, NO DOUBT. IF WE'RE LUCKY, SHE'S FALLING TO HER DEATH AS WE SPEAK.
START THE ENGINES AND TAKE US OUT OF HERE.
AHHHH. AREN'T WE GOING TO STAY AND WATCH MISS THOR DIE?
YOU AND I ARE GOING TO CONCLUDE OUR BUSINESS, MALEKITH.
YOU'RE ALL WORK AND NO FUN, AGGER. I BET YOU'VE NEVER EVEN KILLED SOMEONE JUST FOR THE HEL OF IT.
SHALL I START NOW?
OH, I DO LOVE IT WHEN YOU THREATEN ME.
WHAT SAY WE SEAL THIS PACT OF OURS THE PROPER WAY. THE DARK ELF WAY.
AFTER ALL, I NEED BLOOD TO CAST THE SPELL UPON THIS SKULL. AND YOU, AGGER...
DARIO AGGER
CEO

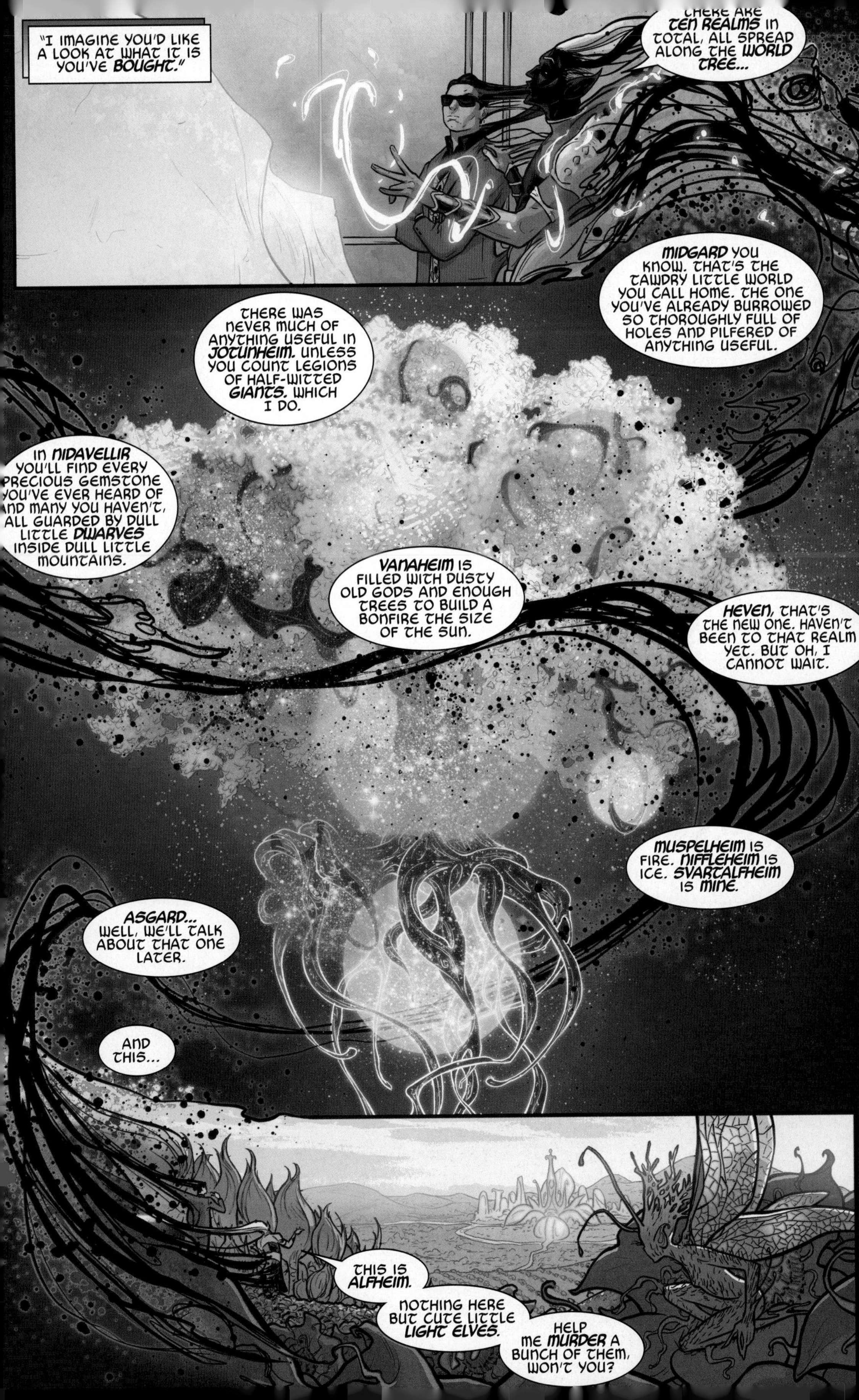
"I IMAGINE YOU'D LIKE A LOOK AT WHAT IT IS YOU'VE BOUGHT."
THERE ARE TEN REALMS IN TOTAL, ALL SPREAD ALONG THE WORLD TREE...
MIDGARD YOU KNOW. THAT'S THE TAWDRY LITTLE WORLD YOU CALL HOME. THE ONE YOU'VE ALREADY BURROWED SO THOROUGHLY FULL OF HOLES AND PILFERED OF ANYTHING USEFUL.
THERE WAS NEVER MUCH OF ANYTHING USEFUL IN JOTUNHEIM. UNLESS YOU COUNT LEGIONS OF HALF-WITTED GIANTS. WHICH I DO.
IN NIDAVELLIR YOU'LL FIND EVERY PRECIOUS GEMSTONE YOU'VE EVER HEARD OF AND MANY YOU HAVEN'T, ALL GUARDED BY DULL LITTLE DWARVES INSIDE DULL LITTLE MOUNTAINS.
VANAHEIM IS FILLED WITH DUSTY OLD GODS AND ENOUGH TREES TO BUILD A BONFIRE THE SIZE OF THE SUN.
HEVEN, THAT'S THE NEW ONE. HAVEN'T BEEN TO THAT REALM YET. BUT OH, I CANNOT WAIT.
MUSPELHEIM IS FIRE. NIFFLEHEIM IS ICE. SVARTALFHEIM IS MINE.
ASGARD... WELL, WE'LL TALK ABOUT THAT ONE LATER.
AND THIS...
THIS IS ALFHEIM.
NOTHING HERE BUT CUTE LITTLE LIGHT ELVES.
HELP ME MURDER A BUNCH OF THEM, WON'T YOU?

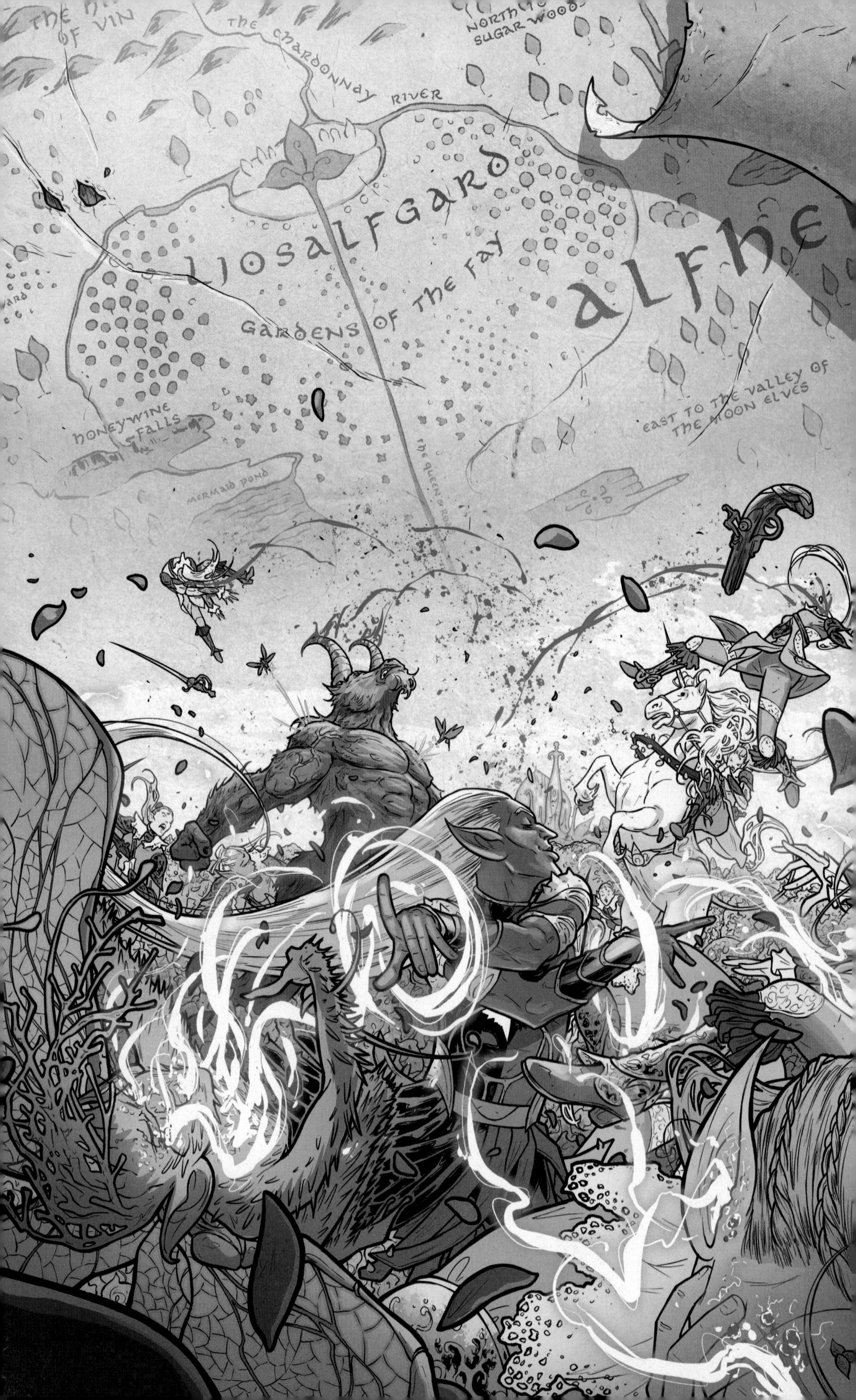
OF VIN
THE CHARDONNAY RIVER
SUGAR WOODS
LIOSALFGARD
GARDENS OF THE FAY
HONEYWINE FALLS
MERMAID POND
EAST TO THE VALLEY OF THE MOON ELVES

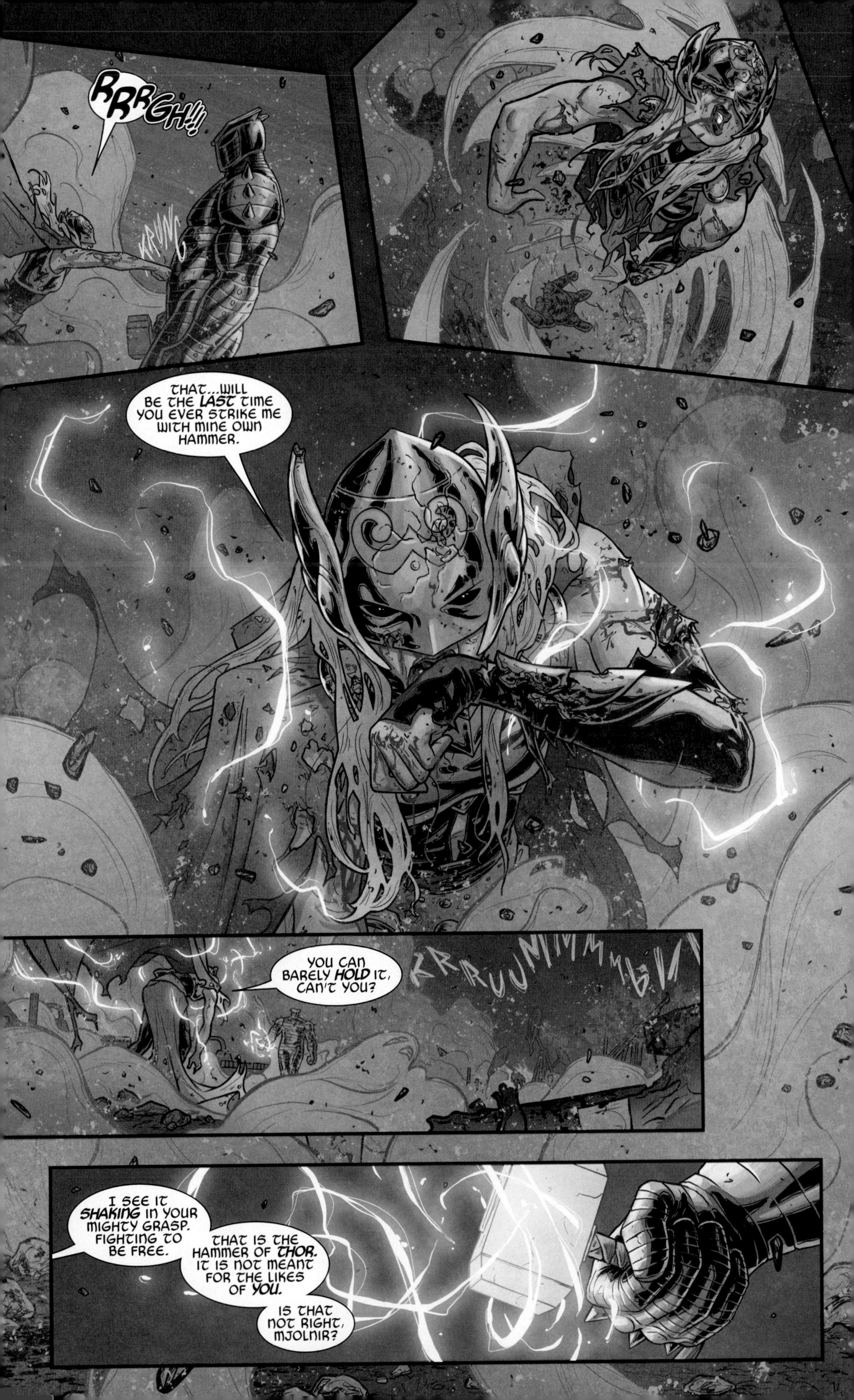

RRRGH!!
KRUNG
THAT...WILL BE THE LAST TIME YOU EVER STRIKE ME WITH MINE OWN HAMMER.
YOU CAN BARELY HOLD IT, CAN'T YOU?
KRRUUMMMMBLLL
I SEE IT SHAKING IN YOUR MIGHTY GRASP. FIGHTING TO BE FREE.
THAT IS THE HAMMER OF THOR. IT IS NOT MEANT FOR THE LIKES OF YOU.
IS THAT NOT RIGHT, MJOLNIR?

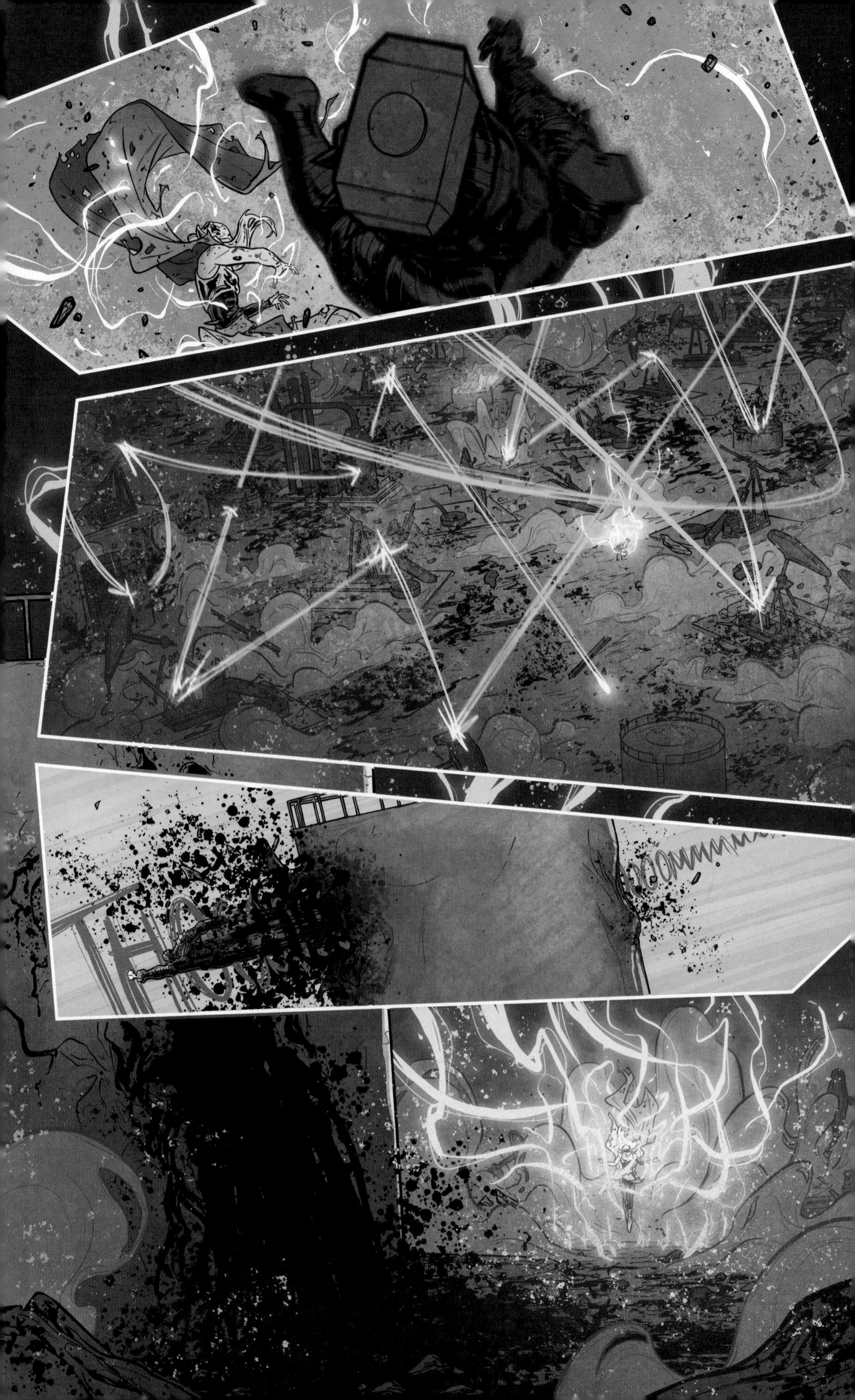

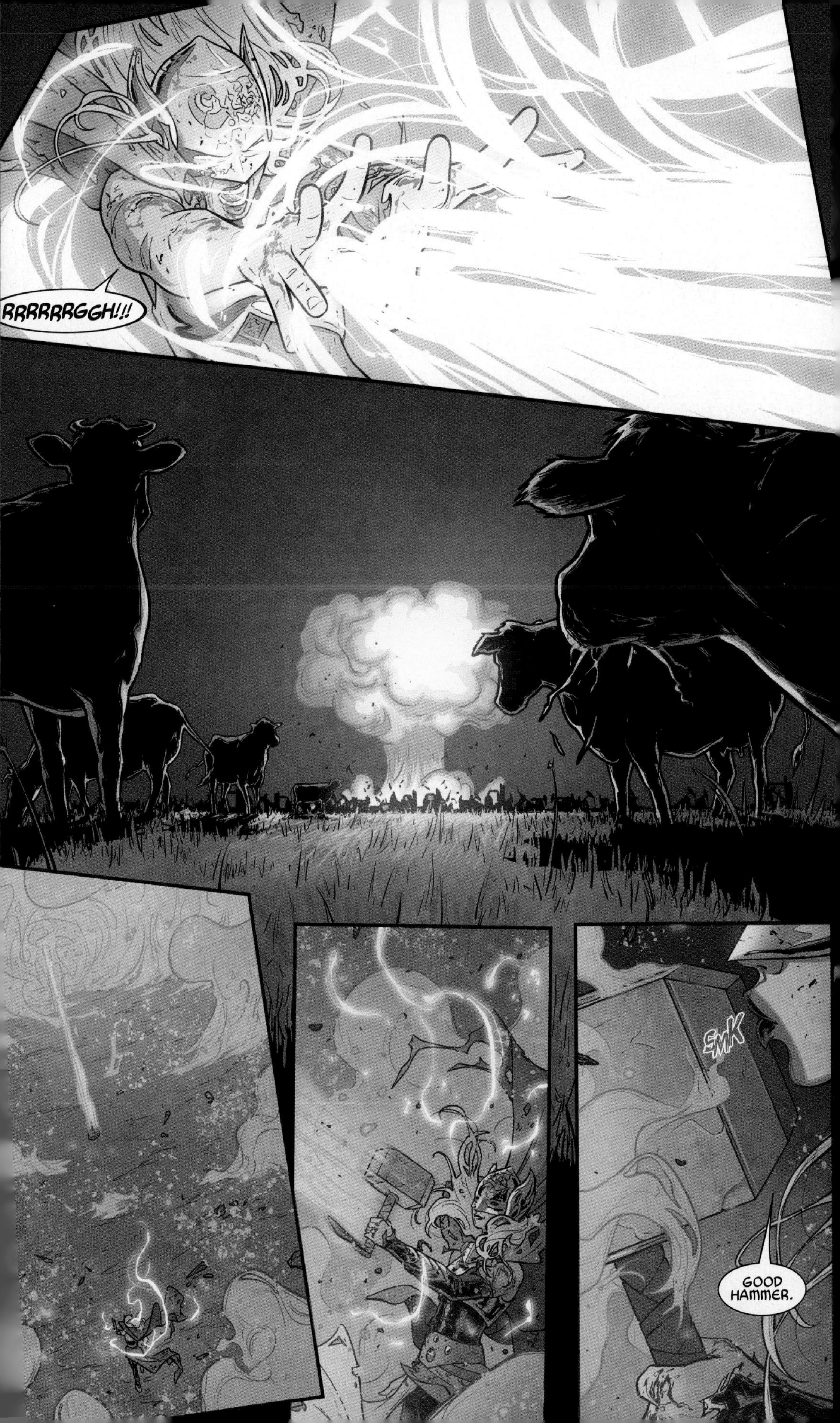
RRRRRRGGH!!!
SMK
GOOD HAMMER.

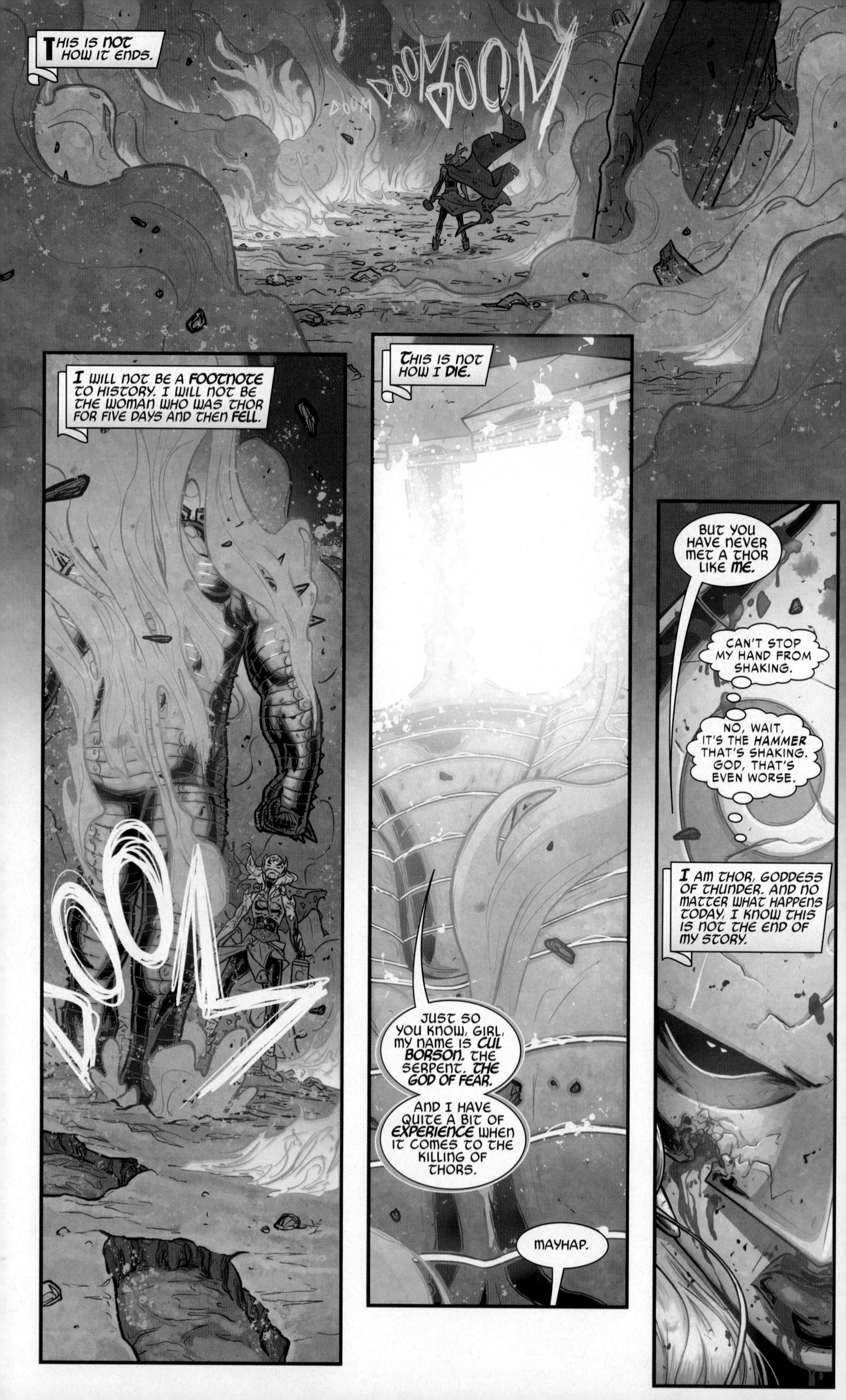

THIS IS NOT HOW IT ENDS.
DOOM DOOM DOOM
I WILL NOT BE A FOOTNOTE TO HISTORY. I WILL NOT BE THE WOMAN WHO WAS THOR FOR FIVE DAYS AND THEN FELL.
DOOM
THIS IS NOT HOW I DIE.
JUST SO YOU KNOW, GIRL, MY NAME IS CUL BORSON. THE SERPENT. THE GOD OF FEAR.
AND I HAVE QUITE A BIT OF EXPERIENCE WHEN IT COMES TO THE KILLING OF THORS.
MAYHAP.
BUT YOU HAVE NEVER MET A THOR LIKE ME.
CAN'T STOP MY HAND FROM SHAKING.
NO, WAIT, IT'S THE HAMMER THAT'S SHAKING. GOD, THAT'S EVEN WORSE.
I AM THOR, GODDESS OF THUNDER. AND NO MATTER WHAT HAPPENS TODAY, I KNOW THIS IS NOT THE END OF MY STORY.

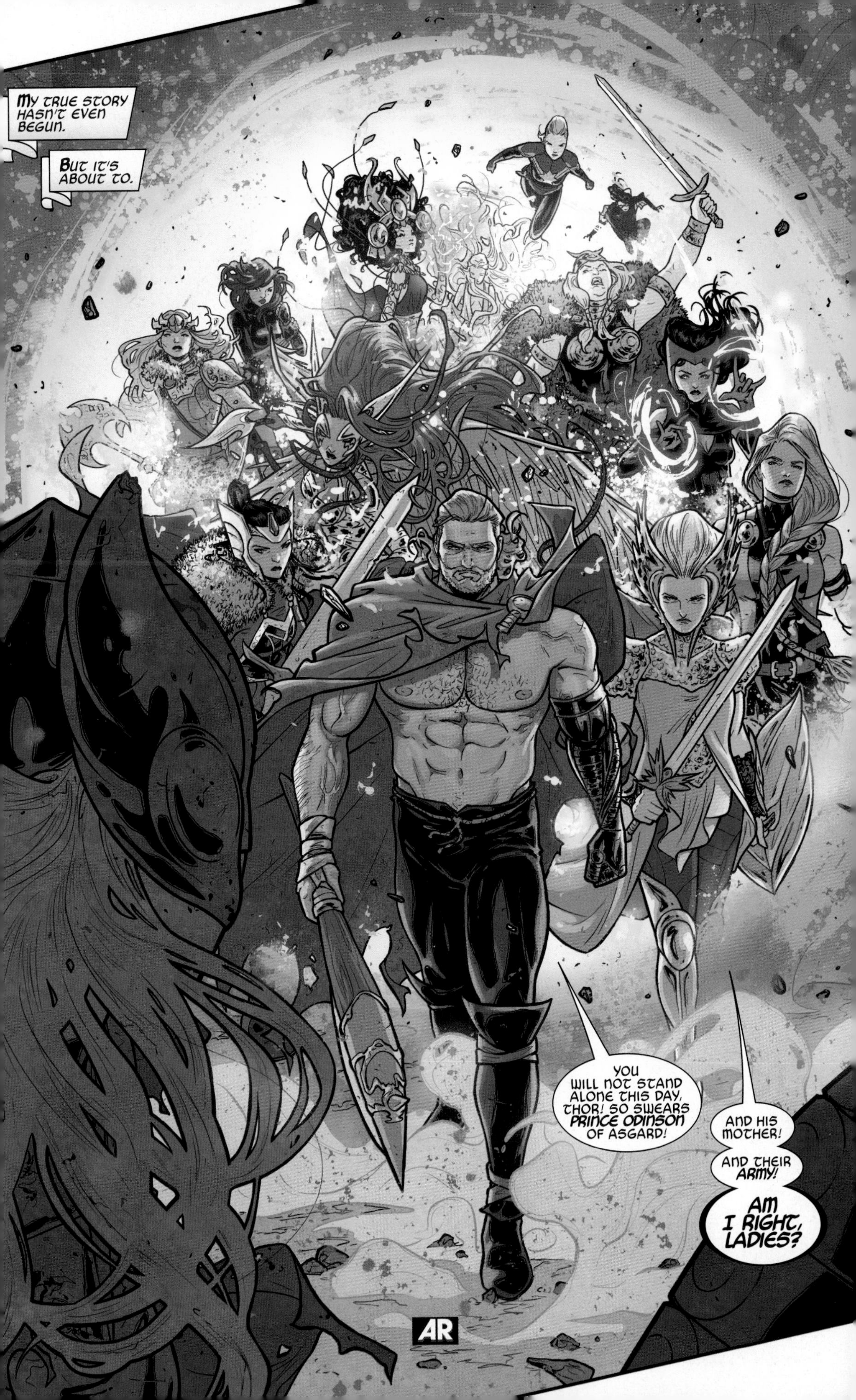

MY TRUE STORY HASN'T EVEN BEGUN.
BUT IT'S ABOUT TO.
YOU WILL NOT STAND ALONE THIS DAY, THOR! SO SWEARS PRINCE ODINSON OF ASGARD!
AND HIS MOTHER!
AND THEIR ARMY!
AM I RIGHT, LADIES?

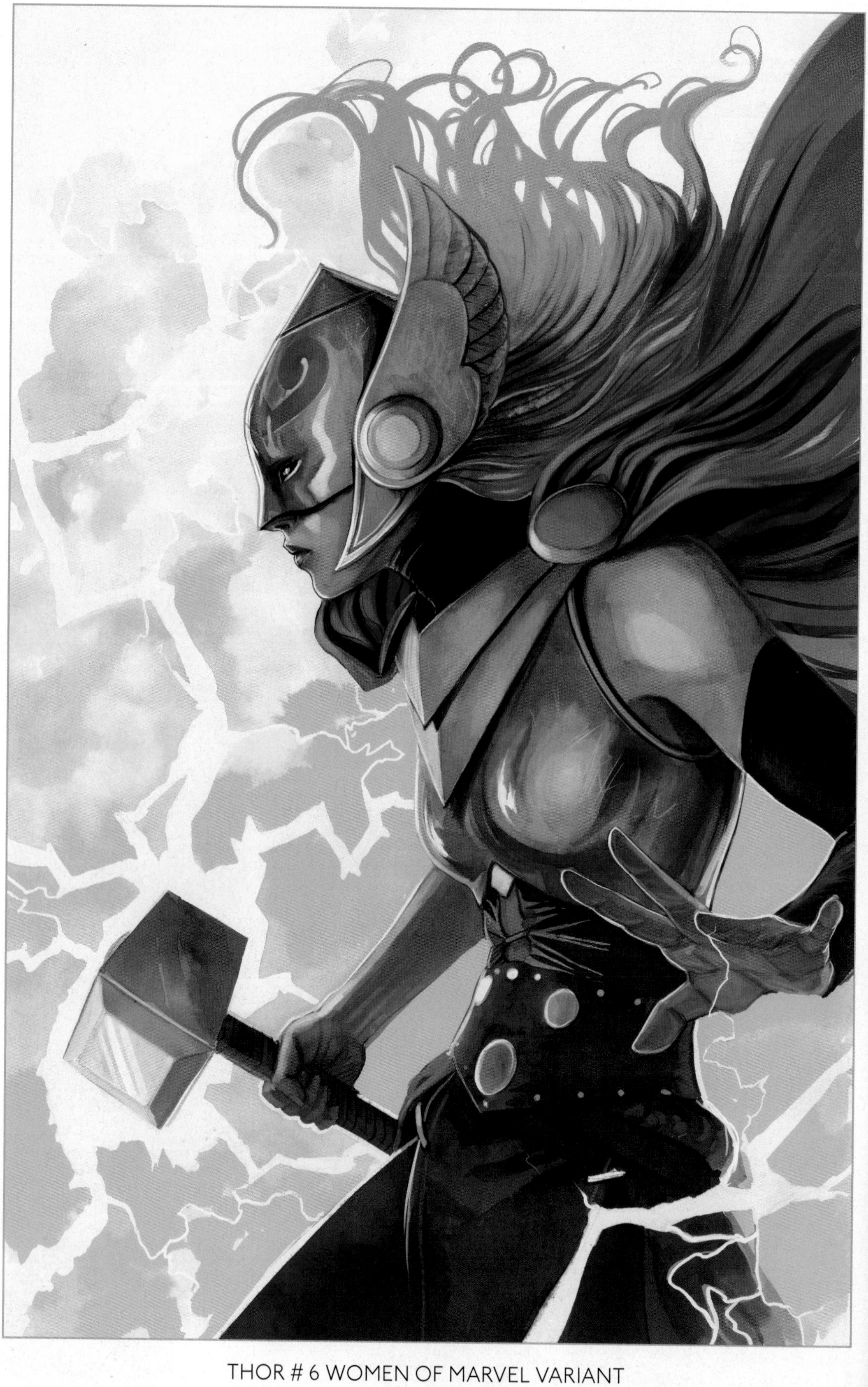

THOR # 6 WOMEN OF MARVEL VARIANT
BY **STEPHANIE HANS**

8

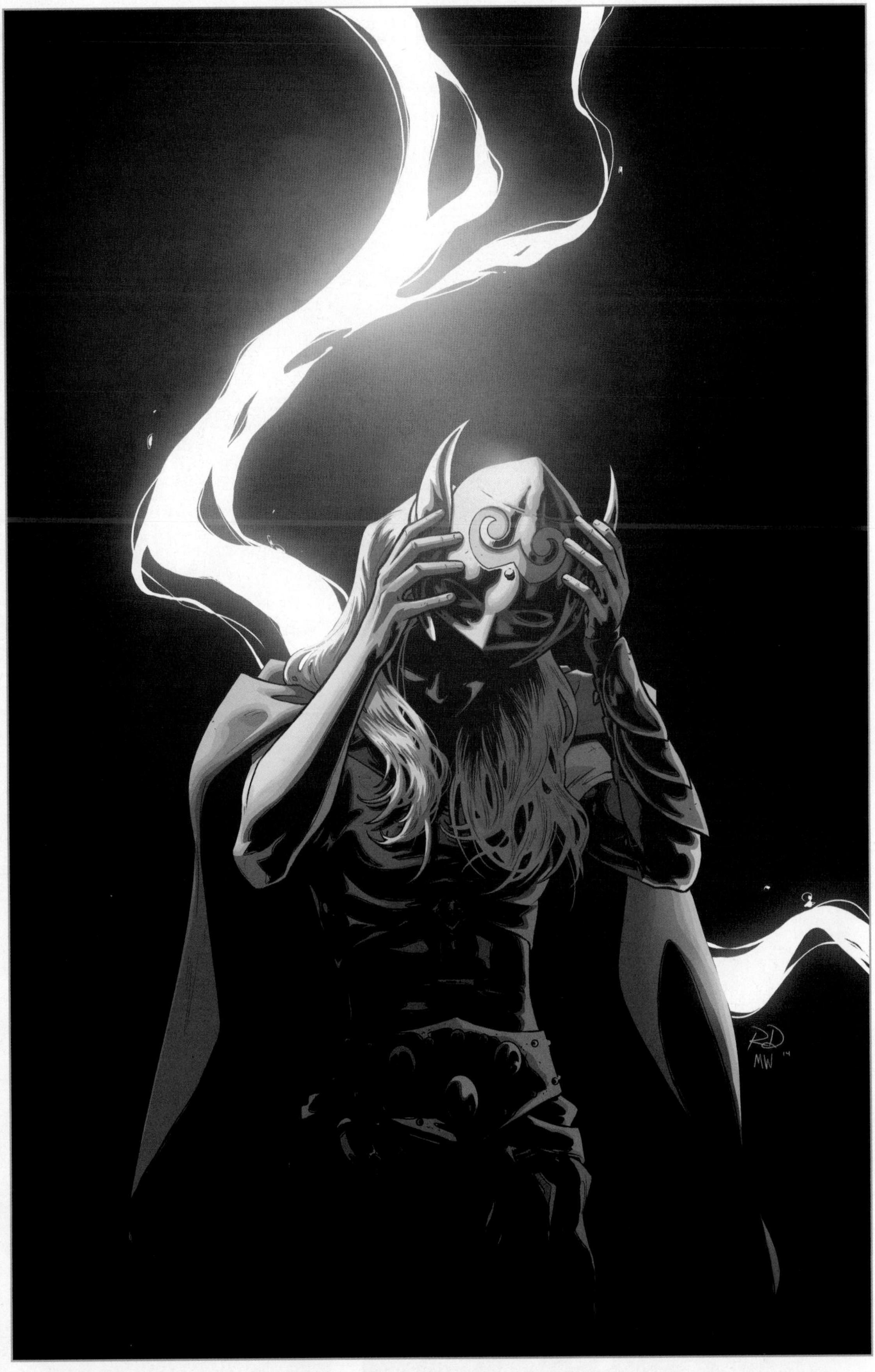

THE WOMAN BENEATH THE MASK

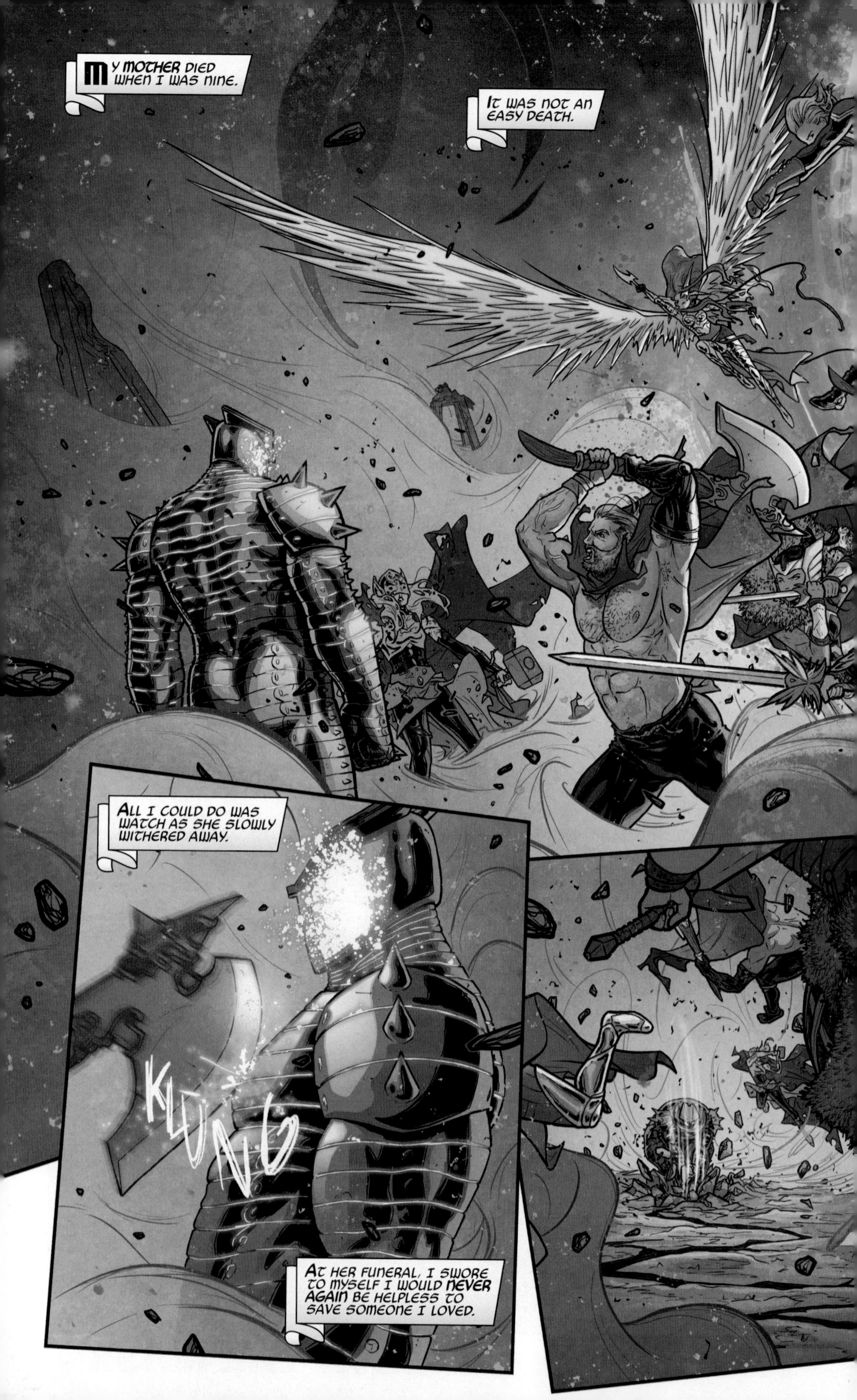
MY MOTHER DIED WHEN I WAS NINE.
IT WAS NOT AN EASY DEATH.
ALL I COULD DO WAS WATCH AS SHE SLOWLY WITHERED AWAY.
KLUNG
AT HER FUNERAL, I SWORE TO MYSELF I WOULD NEVER AGAIN BE HELPLESS TO SAVE SOMEONE I LOVED.

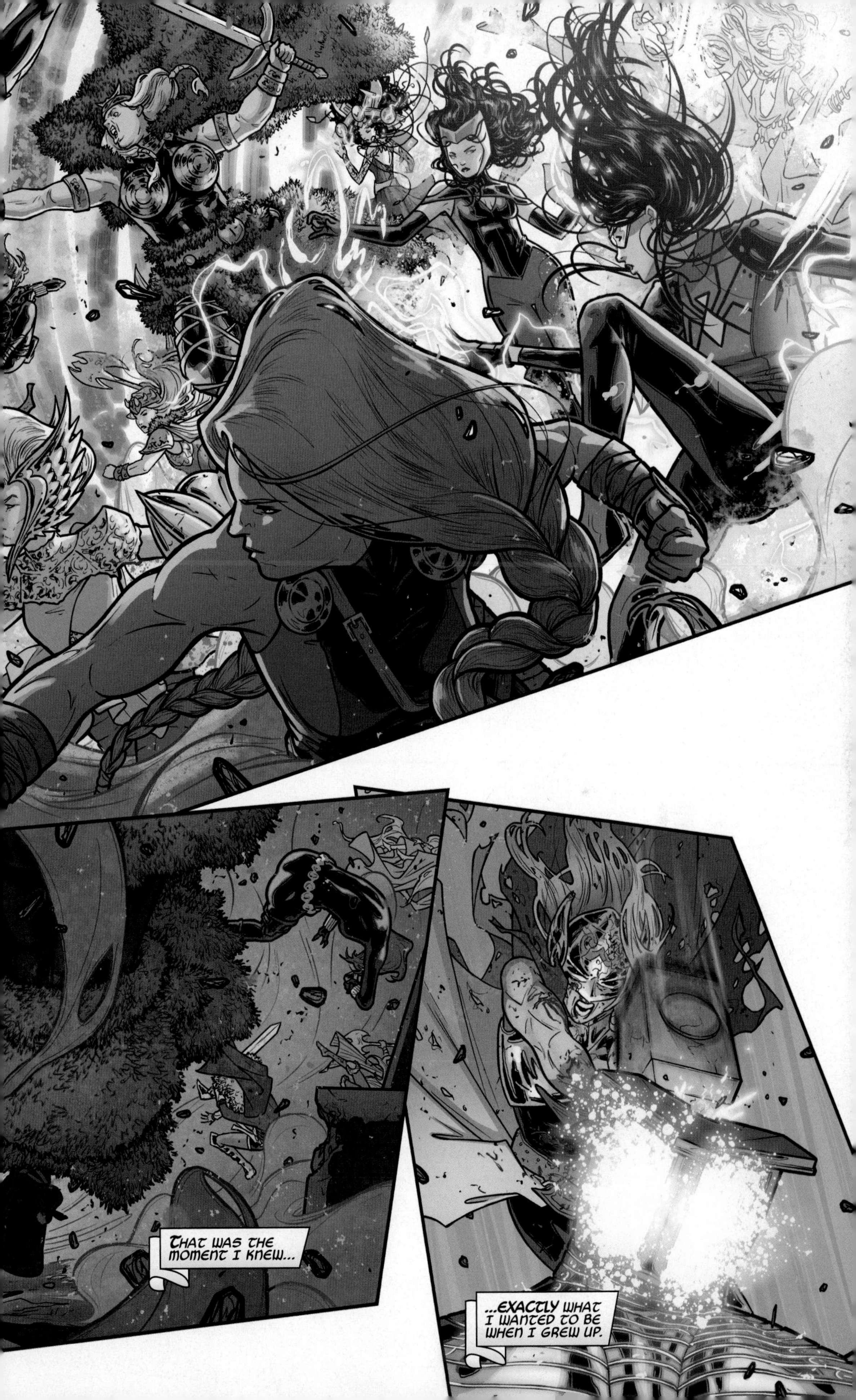
THAT WAS THE MOMENT I KNEW...
...EXACTLY WHAT I WANTED TO BE WHEN I GREW UP.

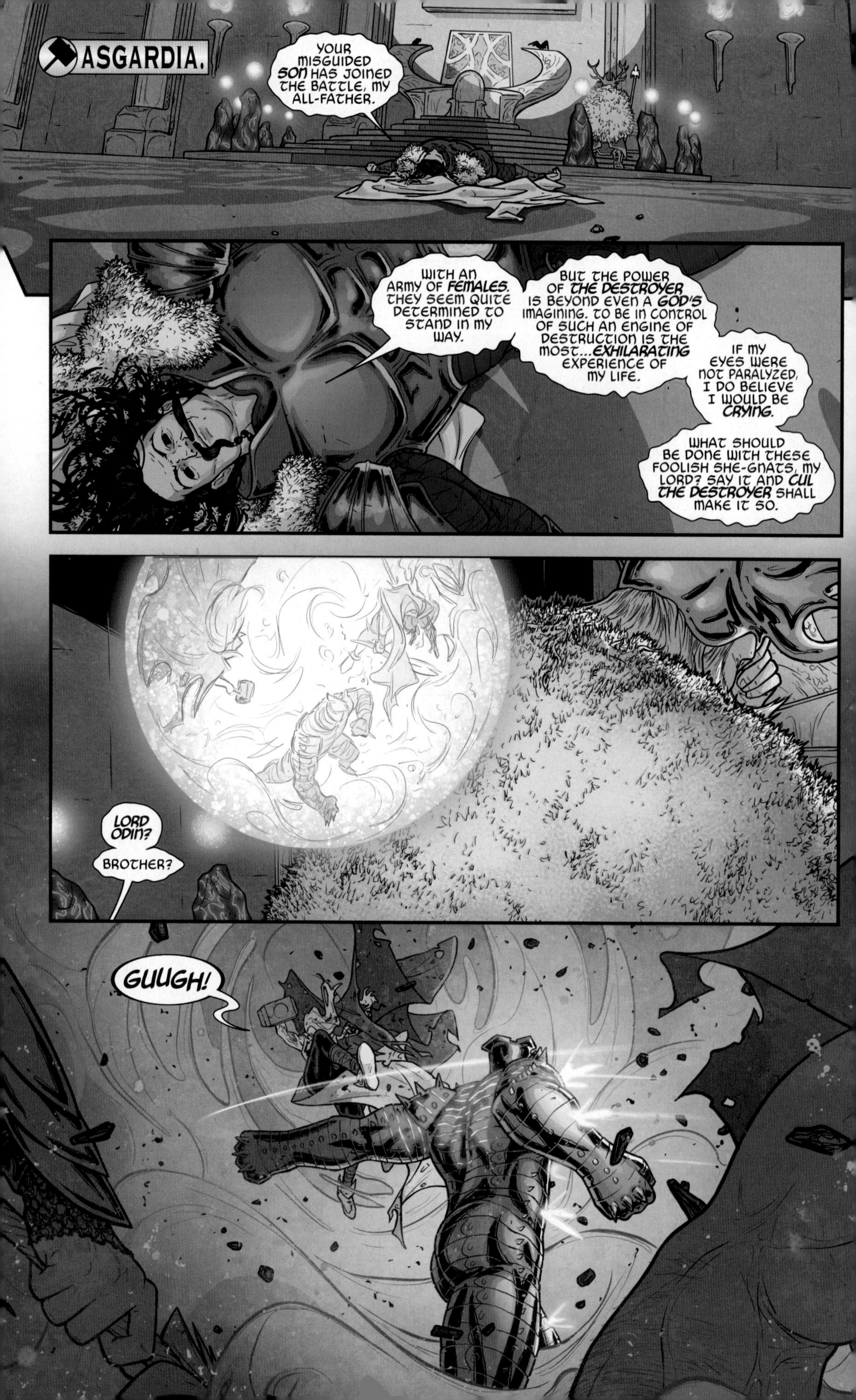
ASGARDIA.
YOUR MISGUIDED SON HAS JOINED THE BATTLE, MY ALL-FATHER.
WITH AN ARMY OF FEMALES. THEY SEEM QUITE DETERMINED TO STAND IN MY WAY.
BUT THE POWER OF THE DESTROYER IS BEYOND EVEN A GOD'S IMAGINING. TO BE IN CONTROL OF SUCH AN ENGINE OF DESTRUCTION IS THE MOST...EXHILARATING EXPERIENCE OF MY LIFE.
IF MY EYES WERE NOT PARALYZED, I DO BELIEVE I WOULD BE CRYING.
WHAT SHOULD BE DONE WITH THESE FOOLISH SHE-GNATS, MY LORD? SAY IT AND CUL THE DESTROYER SHALL MAKE IT SO.
LORD ODIN?
BROTHER?
GUUGH!

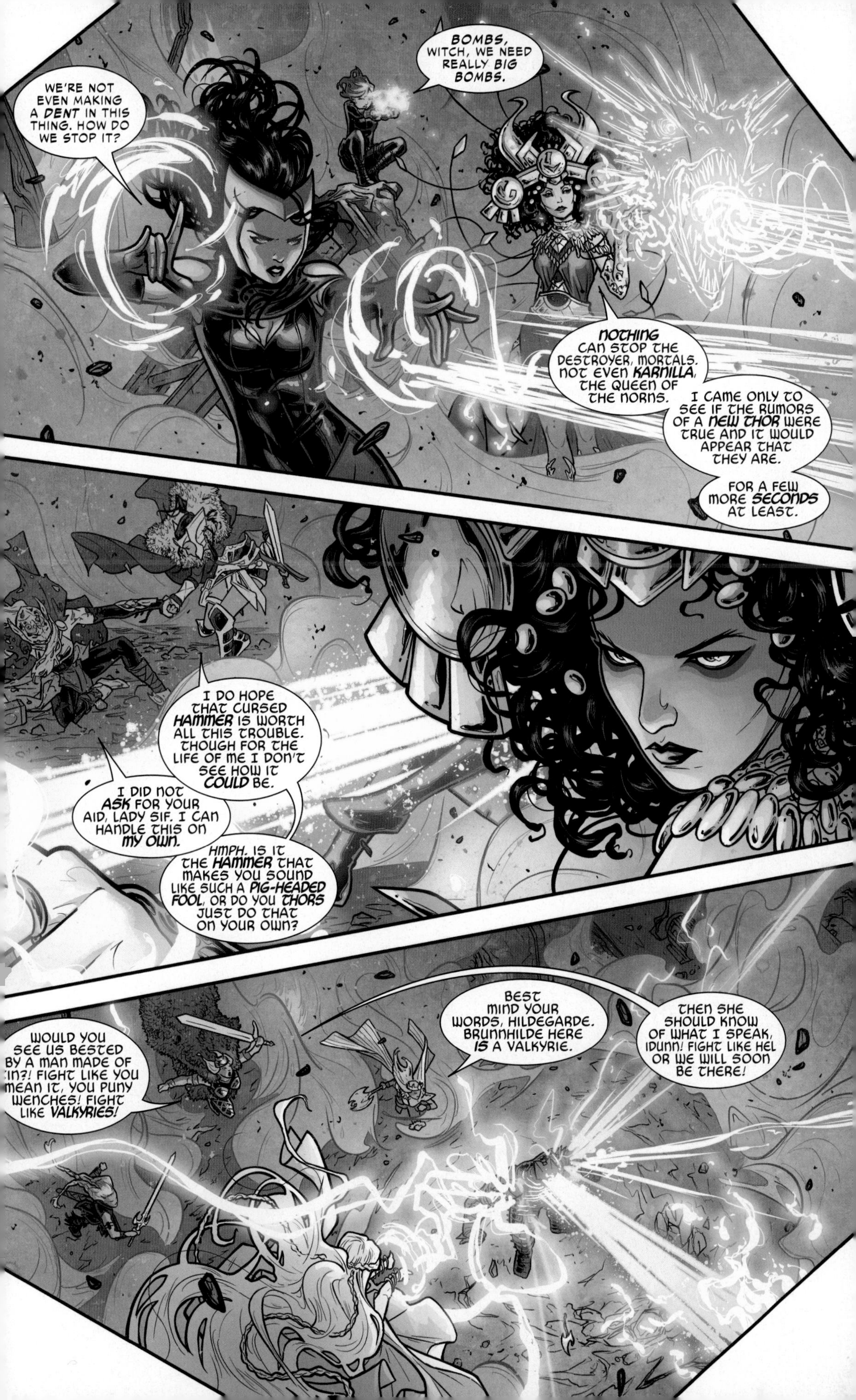
WE'RE NOT EVEN MAKING A DENT IN THIS THING. HOW DO WE STOP IT?
BOMBS, WITCH, WE NEED REALLY BIG BOMBS.
NOTHING CAN STOP THE DESTROYER, MORTALS. NOT EVEN KARNILLA, THE QUEEN OF THE NORNS.
I CAME ONLY TO SEE IF THE RUMORS OF A NEW THOR WERE TRUE AND IT WOULD APPEAR THAT THEY ARE.
FOR A FEW MORE SECONDS AT LEAST.
I DO HOPE THAT CURSED HAMMER IS WORTH ALL THIS TROUBLE. THOUGH FOR THE LIFE OF ME I DON'T SEE HOW IT COULD BE.
I DID NOT ASK FOR YOUR AID, LADY SIF. I CAN HANDLE THIS ON MY OWN.
HMPH. IS IT THE HAMMER THAT MAKES YOU SOUND LIKE SUCH A PIG-HEADED FOOL, OR DO YOU THORS JUST DO THAT ON YOUR OWN?
WOULD YOU SEE US BESTED BY A MAN MADE OF TIN?! FIGHT LIKE YOU MEAN IT, YOU PUNY WENCHES! FIGHT LIKE VALKYRIES!
BEST MIND YOUR WORDS, HILDEGARDE. BRUNNHILDE HERE IS A VALKYRIE.
THEN SHE SHOULD KNOW OF WHAT I SPEAK, IDUNN! FIGHT LIKE HEL OR WE WILL SOON BE THERE!

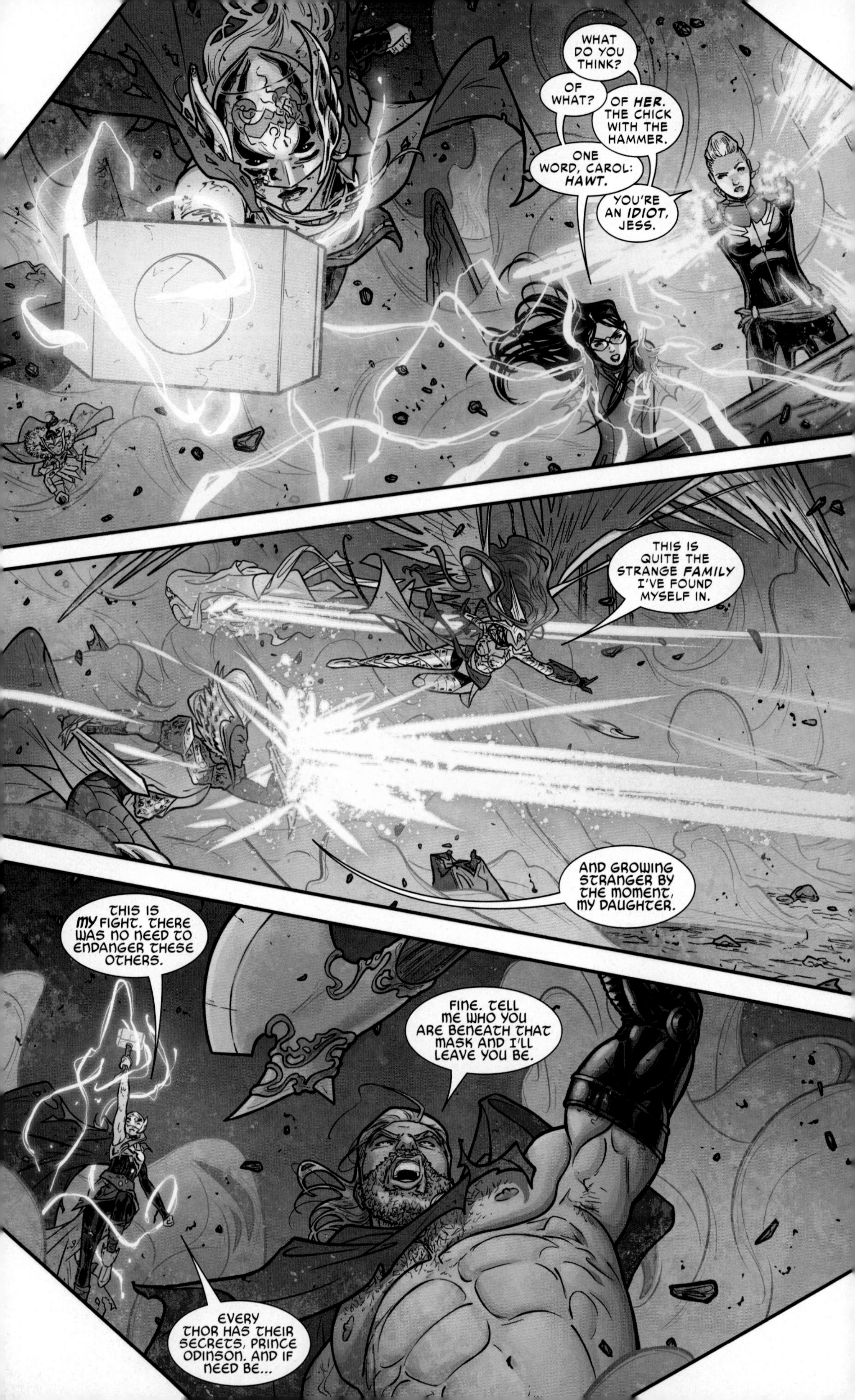
WHAT DO YOU THINK?
OF WHAT?
OF HER. THE CHICK WITH THE HAMMER.
ONE WORD, CAROL: HAWT.
YOU'RE AN IDIOT, JESS.
THIS IS QUITE THE STRANGE FAMILY I'VE FOUND MYSELF IN.
AND GROWING STRANGER BY THE MOMENT, MY DAUGHTER.
THIS IS MY FIGHT. THERE WAS NO NEED TO ENDANGER THESE OTHERS.
FINE. TELL ME WHO YOU ARE BENEATH THAT MASK AND I'LL LEAVE YOU BE.
EVERY THOR HAS THEIR SECRETS, PRINCE ODINSON. AND IF NEED BE...

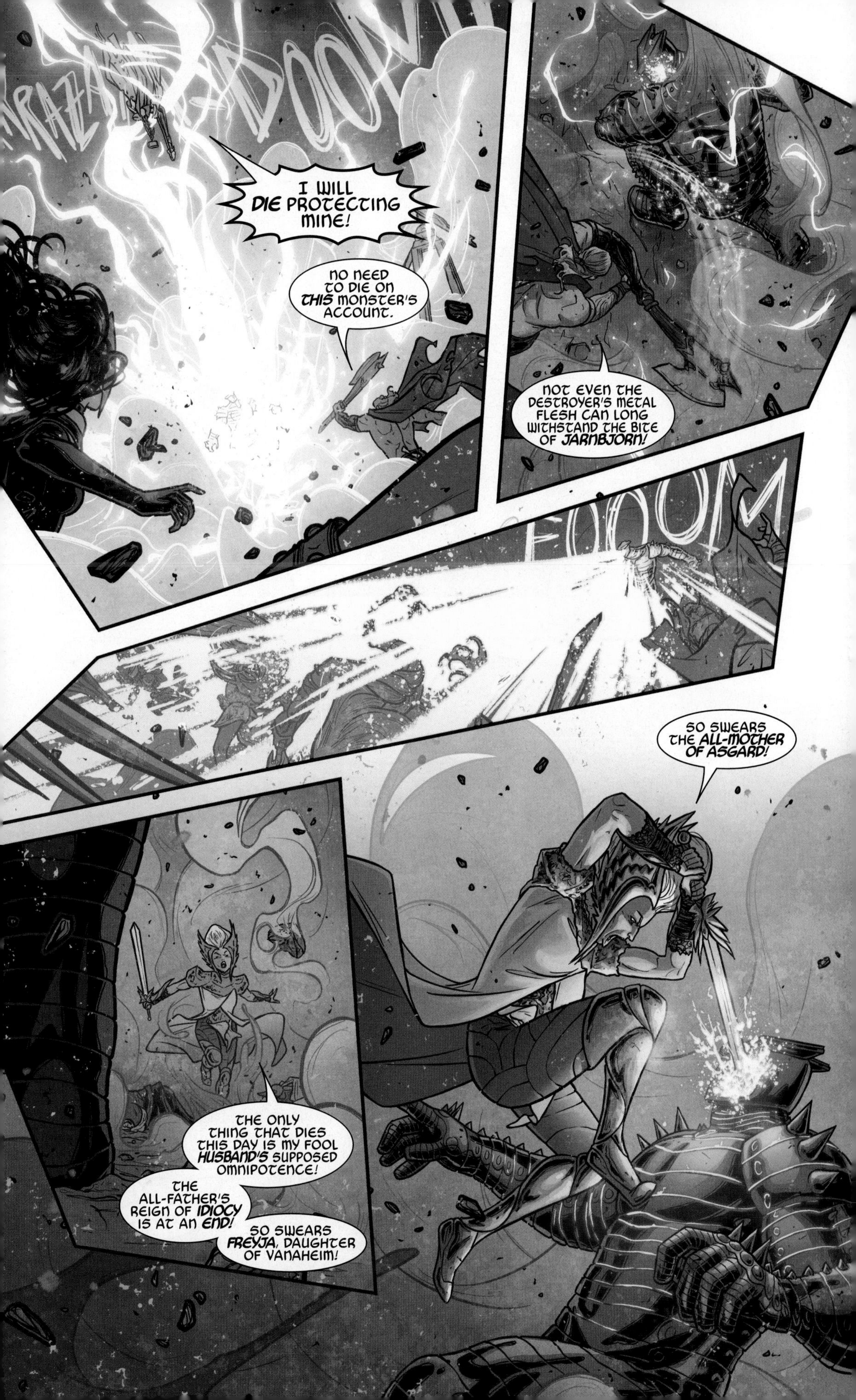

KRAZA-DOOM
I WILL DIE PROTECTING MINE!
NO NEED TO DIE ON THIS MONSTER'S ACCOUNT.
NOT EVEN THE DESTROYER'S METAL FLESH CAN LONG WITHSTAND THE BITE OF JARNBJORN!
FOOOM
SO SWEARS THE ALL-MOTHER OF ASGARD!
THE ONLY THING THAT DIES THIS DAY IS MY FOOL HUSBAND'S SUPPOSED OMNIPOTENCE!
THE ALL-FATHER'S REIGN OF IDIOCY IS AT AN END!
SO SWEARS FREYJA, DAUGHTER OF VANAHEIM!

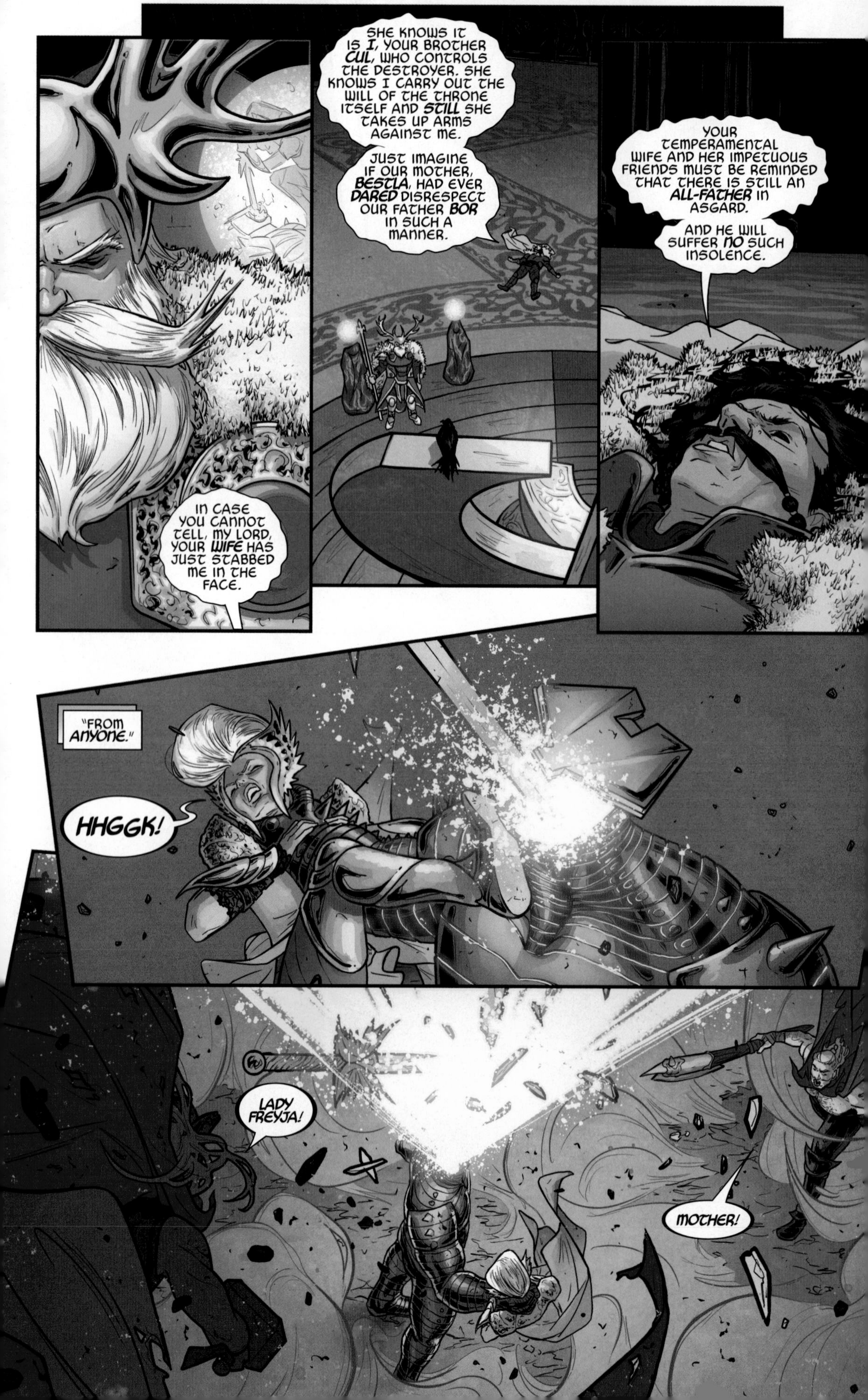

In case you cannot tell, my lord, your wife has just stabbed me in the face.
She knows it is I, your brother Cul, who controls the Destroyer. She knows I carry out the will of the throne itself and still she takes up arms against me.
Just imagine if our mother, Bestla, had ever dared disrespect our father Bor in such a manner.
Your temperamental wife and her impetuous friends must be reminded that there is still an All-Father in Asgard.
And he will suffer no such insolence.
"From anyone."
HHGGK!
Lady Freyja!
Mother!

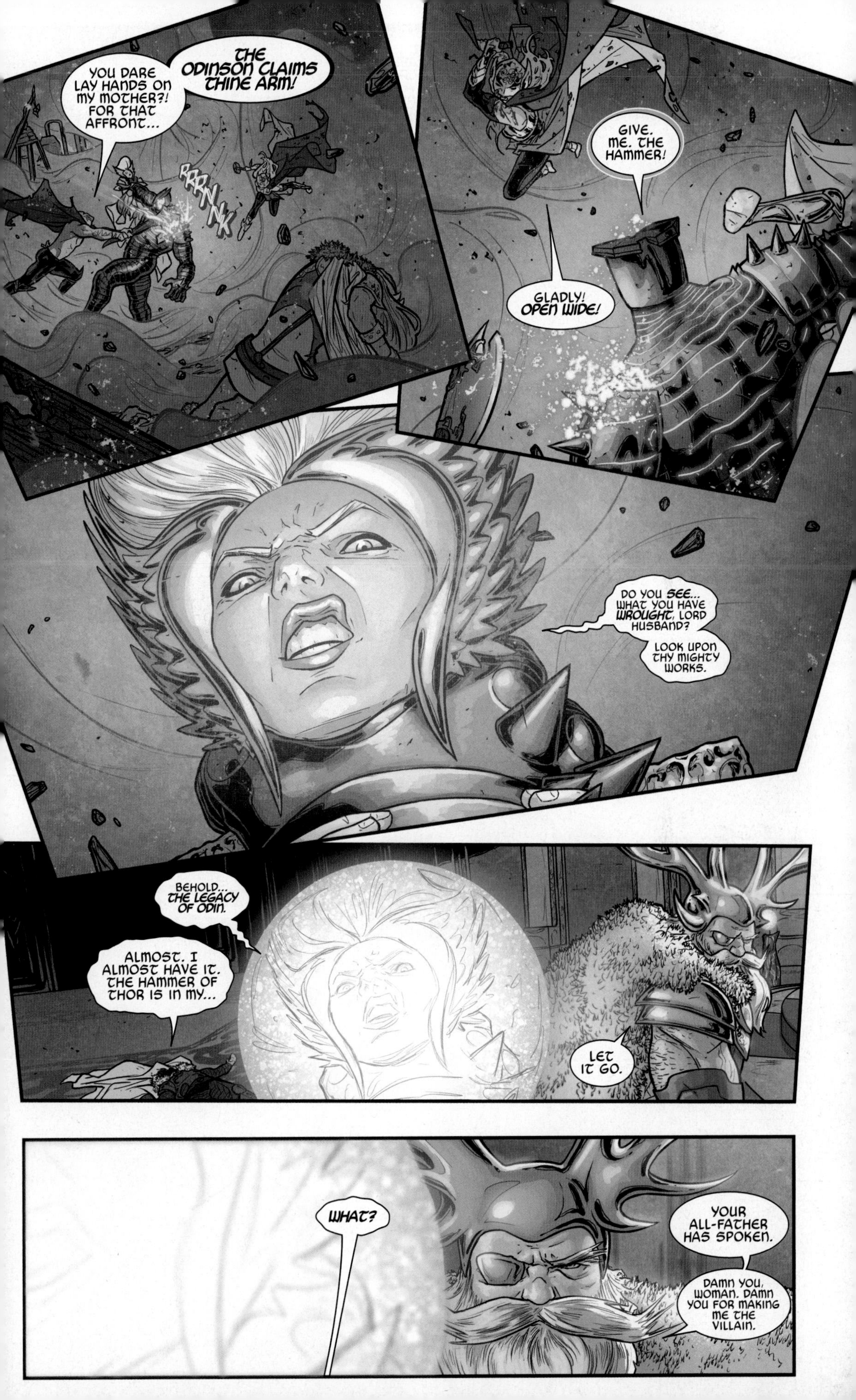
YOU DARE LAY HANDS ON MY MOTHER?! FOR THAT AFFRONT...
THE ODINSON CLAIMS THINE ARM!
RRRNNK
GIVE. ME. THE HAMMER!
GLADLY! OPEN WIDE!
DO YOU SEE... WHAT YOU HAVE WROUGHT, LORD HUSBAND?
LOOK UPON THY MIGHTY WORKS.
BEHOLD... THE LEGACY OF ODIN.
ALMOST. I ALMOST HAVE IT. THE HAMMER OF THOR IS IN MY...
LET IT GO.
WHAT?
YOUR ALL-FATHER HAS SPOKEN.
DAMN YOU, WOMAN. DAMN YOU FOR MAKING ME THE VILLAIN.

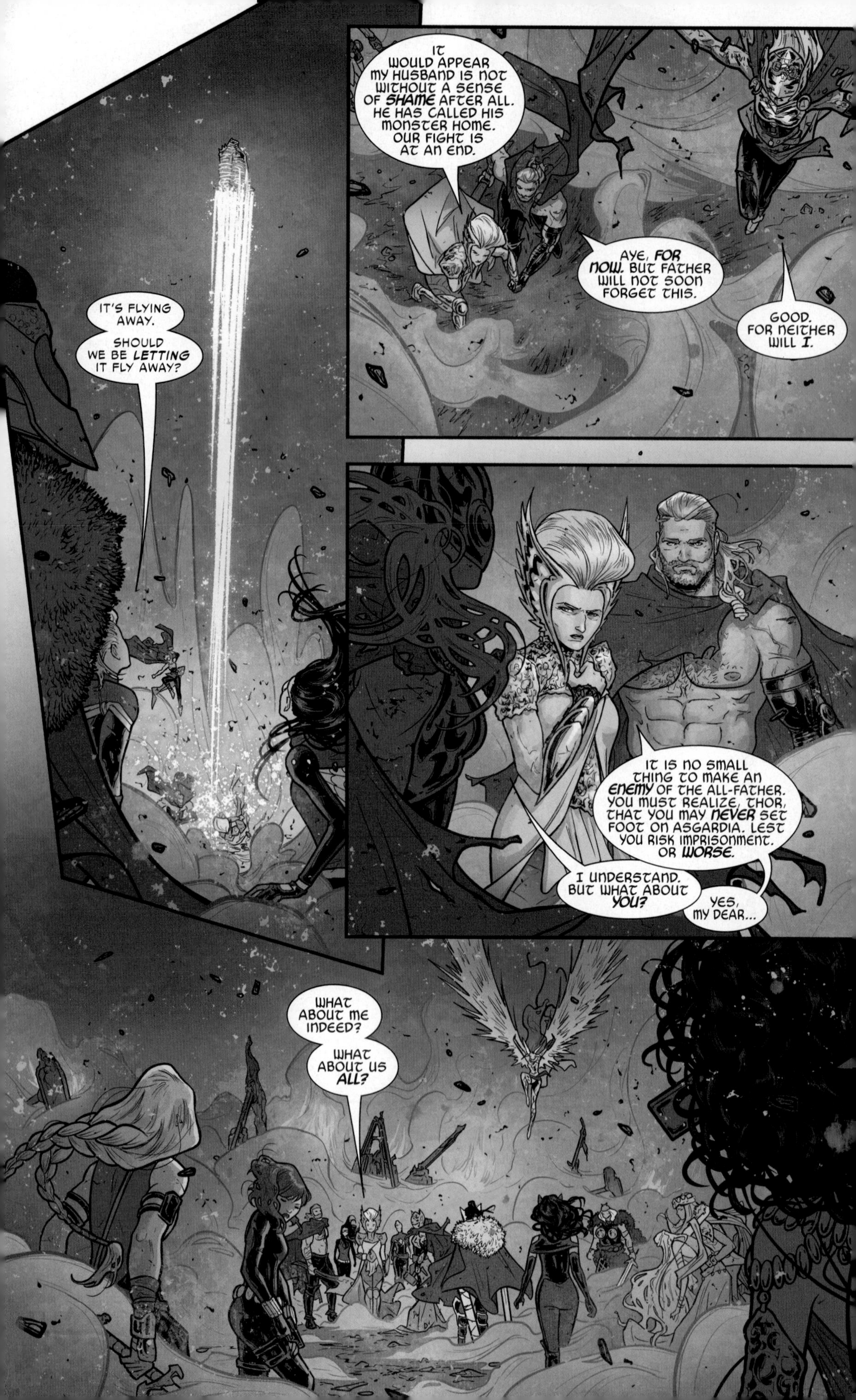

IT WOULD APPEAR MY HUSBAND IS NOT WITHOUT A SENSE OF SHAME AFTER ALL. HE HAS CALLED HIS MONSTER HOME. OUR FIGHT IS AT AN END.
AYE, FOR NOW. BUT FATHER WILL NOT SOON FORGET THIS.
GOOD. FOR NEITHER WILL I.
IT'S FLYING AWAY.
SHOULD WE BE LETTING IT FLY AWAY?
IT IS NO SMALL THING TO MAKE AN ENEMY OF THE ALL-FATHER. YOU MUST REALIZE, THOR, THAT YOU MAY NEVER SET FOOT ON ASGARDIA. LEST YOU RISK IMPRISONMENT. OR WORSE.
I UNDERSTAND. BUT WHAT ABOUT YOU?
YES, MY DEAR...
WHAT ABOUT ME INDEED?
WHAT ABOUT US ALL?

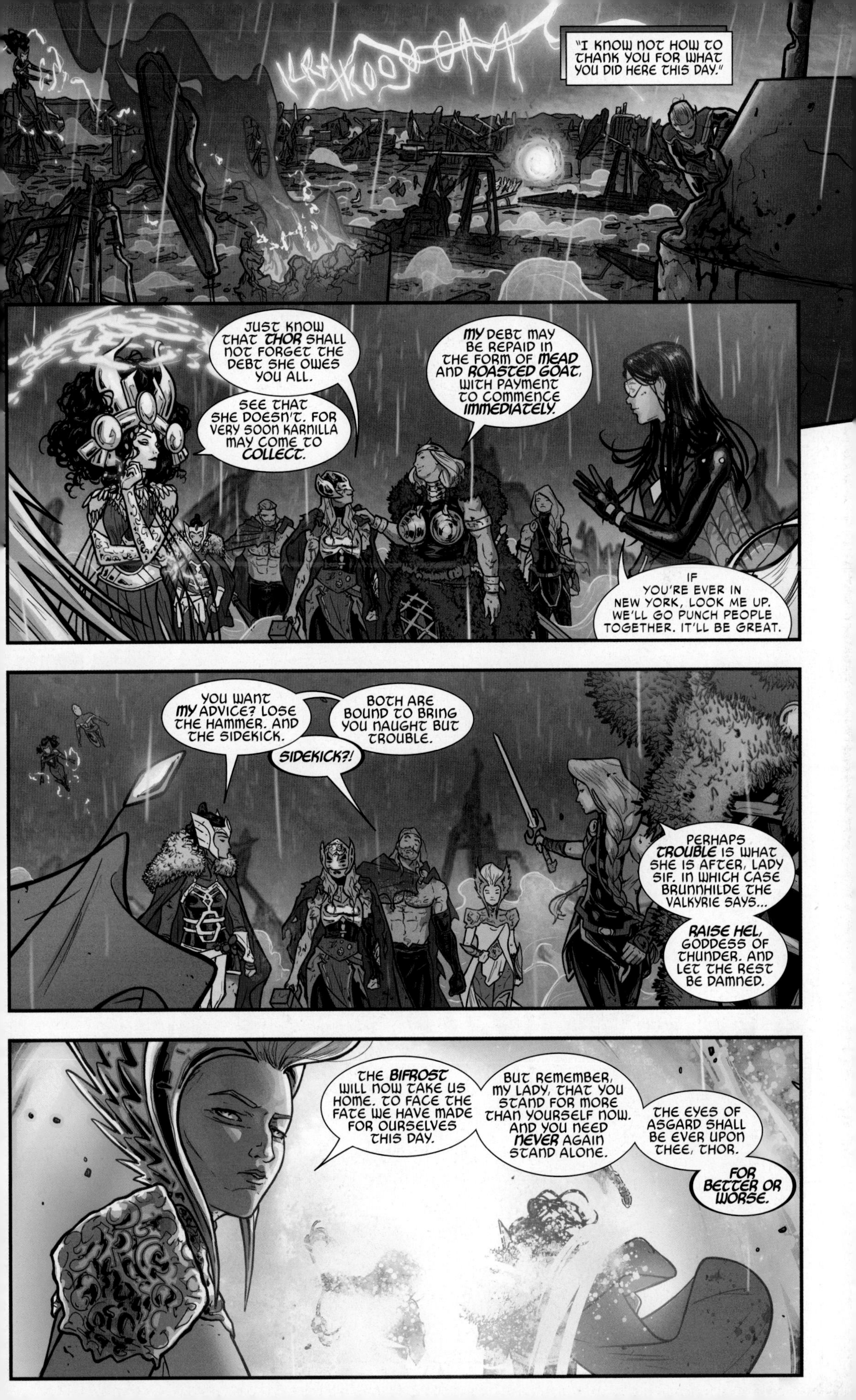
KRRAKOOOOOM
"I KNOW NOT HOW TO THANK YOU FOR WHAT YOU DID HERE THIS DAY."
JUST KNOW THAT THOR SHALL NOT FORGET THE DEBT SHE OWES YOU ALL.
SEE THAT SHE DOESN'T. FOR VERY SOON KARNILLA MAY COME TO COLLECT.
MY DEBT MAY BE REPAID IN THE FORM OF MEAD AND ROASTED GOAT, WITH PAYMENT TO COMMENCE IMMEDIATELY.
IF YOU'RE EVER IN NEW YORK, LOOK ME UP. WE'LL GO PUNCH PEOPLE TOGETHER. IT'LL BE GREAT.
YOU WANT MY ADVICE? LOSE THE HAMMER. AND THE SIDEKICK.
BOTH ARE BOUND TO BRING YOU NAUGHT BUT TROUBLE.
SIDEKICK?!
PERHAPS TROUBLE IS WHAT SHE IS AFTER, LADY SIF. IN WHICH CASE BRUNNHILDE THE VALKYRIE SAYS...
RAISE HEL, GODDESS OF THUNDER. AND LET THE REST BE DAMNED.
THE BIFROST WILL NOW TAKE US HOME. TO FACE THE FATE WE HAVE MADE FOR OURSELVES THIS DAY.
BUT REMEMBER, MY LADY, THAT YOU STAND FOR MORE THAN YOURSELF NOW. AND YOU NEED NEVER AGAIN STAND ALONE.
THE EYES OF ASGARD SHALL BE EVER UPON THEE, THOR.
FOR BETTER OR WORSE.

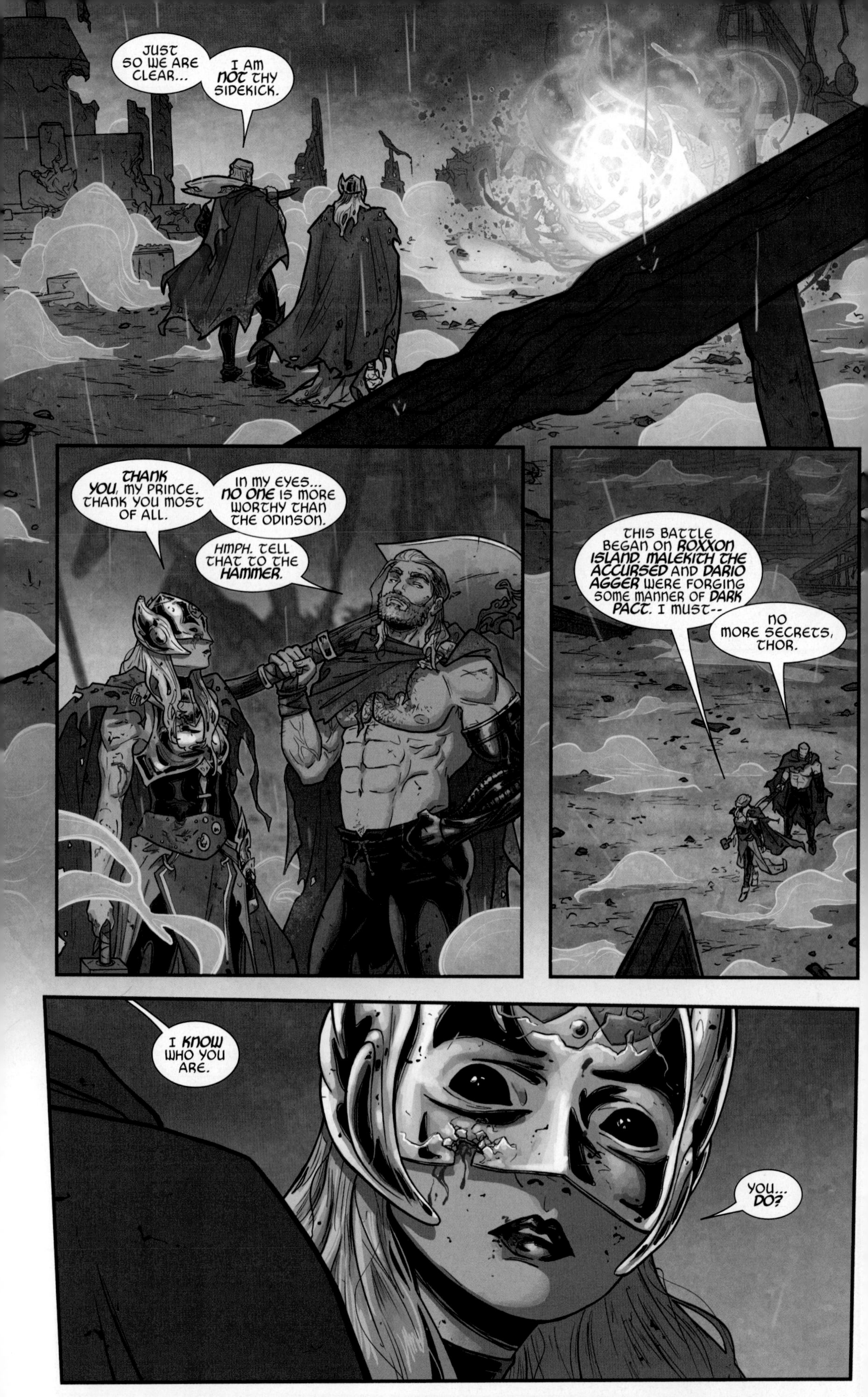
JUST SO WE ARE CLEAR...
I AM NOT THY SIDEKICK.
THANK YOU, MY PRINCE. THANK YOU MOST OF ALL.
IN MY EYES... NO ONE IS MORE WORTHY THAN THE ODINSON.
HMPH. TELL THAT TO THE HAMMER.
THIS BATTLE BEGAN ON ROXXON ISLAND. MALEKITH THE ACCURSED AND DARIO AGGER WERE FORGING SOME MANNER OF DARK PACT. I MUST--
NO MORE SECRETS, THOR.
I KNOW WHO YOU ARE.
YOU... DO?

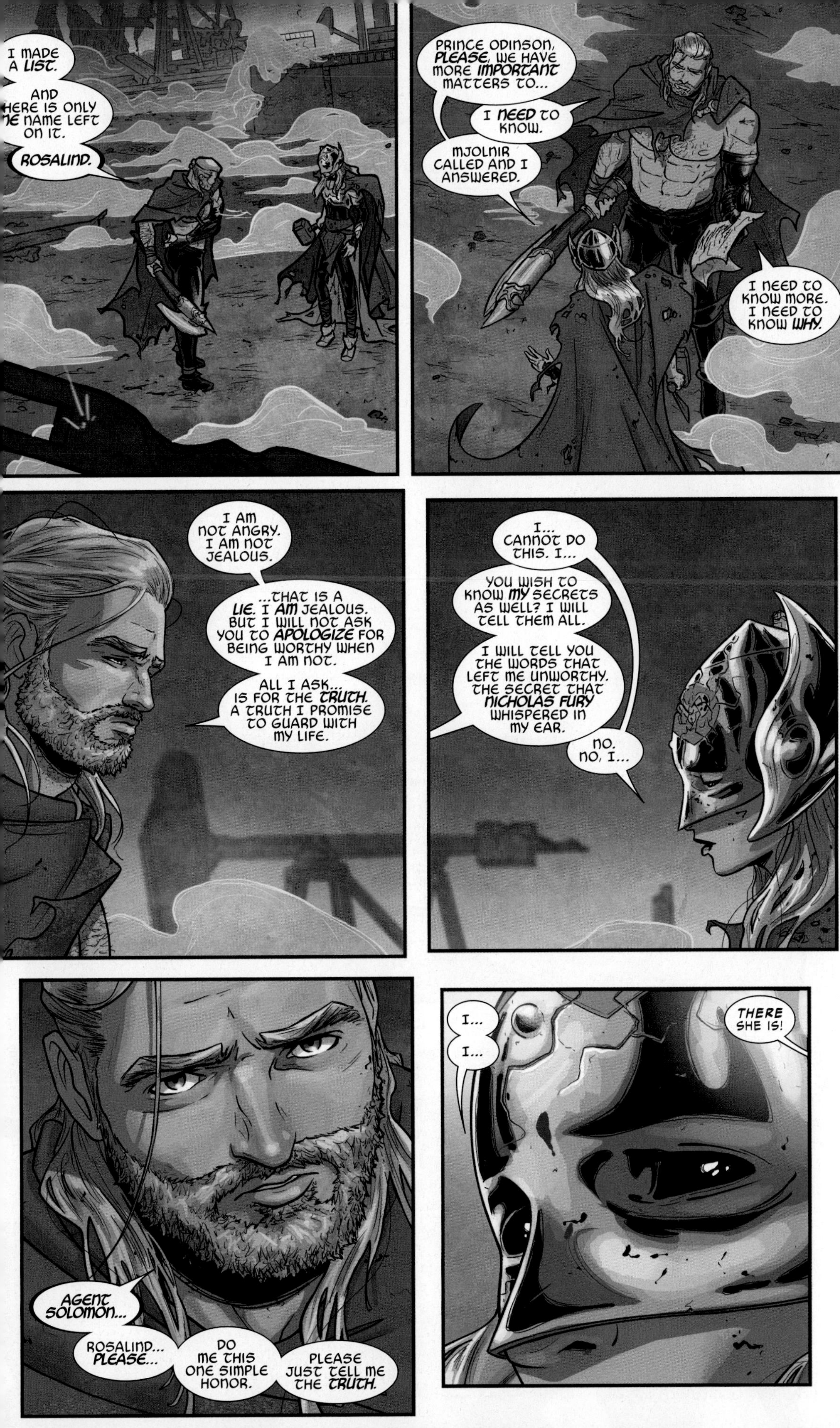

I MADE A LIST.
AND HERE IS ONLY NE NAME LEFT ON IT.
ROSALIND.
PRINCE ODINSON, PLEASE, WE HAVE MORE IMPORTANT MATTERS TO...
I NEED TO KNOW.
MJOLNIR CALLED AND I ANSWERED.
I NEED TO KNOW MORE. I NEED TO KNOW WHY.
I AM NOT ANGRY. I AM NOT JEALOUS.
...THAT IS A LIE. I AM JEALOUS. BUT I WILL NOT ASK YOU TO APOLOGIZE FOR BEING WORTHY WHEN I AM NOT.
ALL I ASK... IS FOR THE TRUTH. A TRUTH I PROMISE TO GUARD WITH MY LIFE.
I... CANNOT DO THIS. I...
YOU WISH TO KNOW MY SECRETS AS WELL? I WILL TELL THEM ALL.
I WILL TELL YOU THE WORDS THAT LEFT ME UNWORTHY. THE SECRET THAT NICHOLAS FURY WHISPERED IN MY EAR.
NO. NO, I...
AGENT SOLOMON...
ROSALIND... PLEASE...
DO ME THIS ONE SIMPLE HONOR.
PLEASE JUST TELL ME THE TRUTH.
I...
I...
THERE SHE IS!

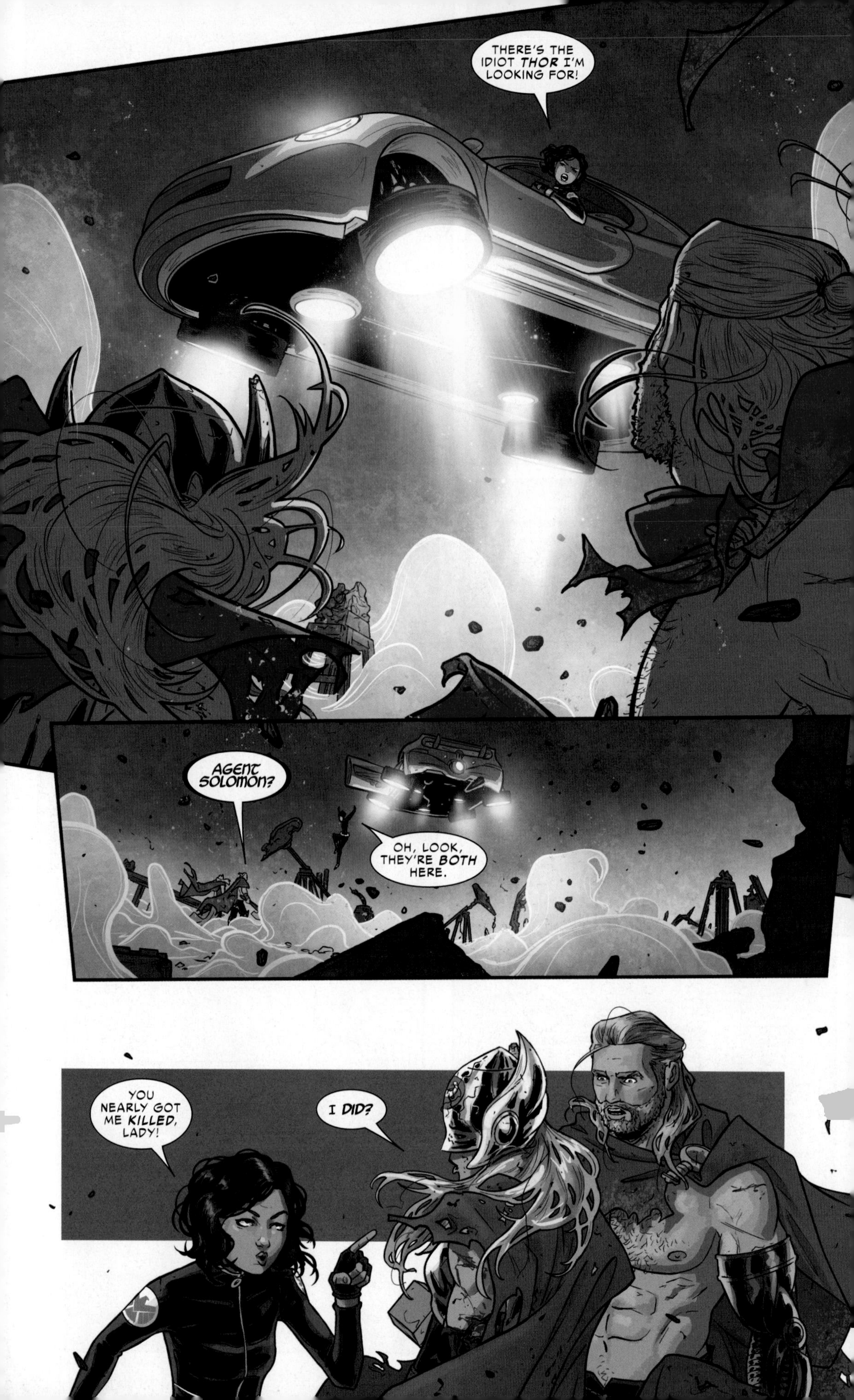
THERE'S THE IDIOT THOR I'M LOOKING FOR!
AGENT SOLOMON?
OH, LOOK, THEY'RE BOTH HERE.
YOU NEARLY GOT ME KILLED, LADY!
I DID?

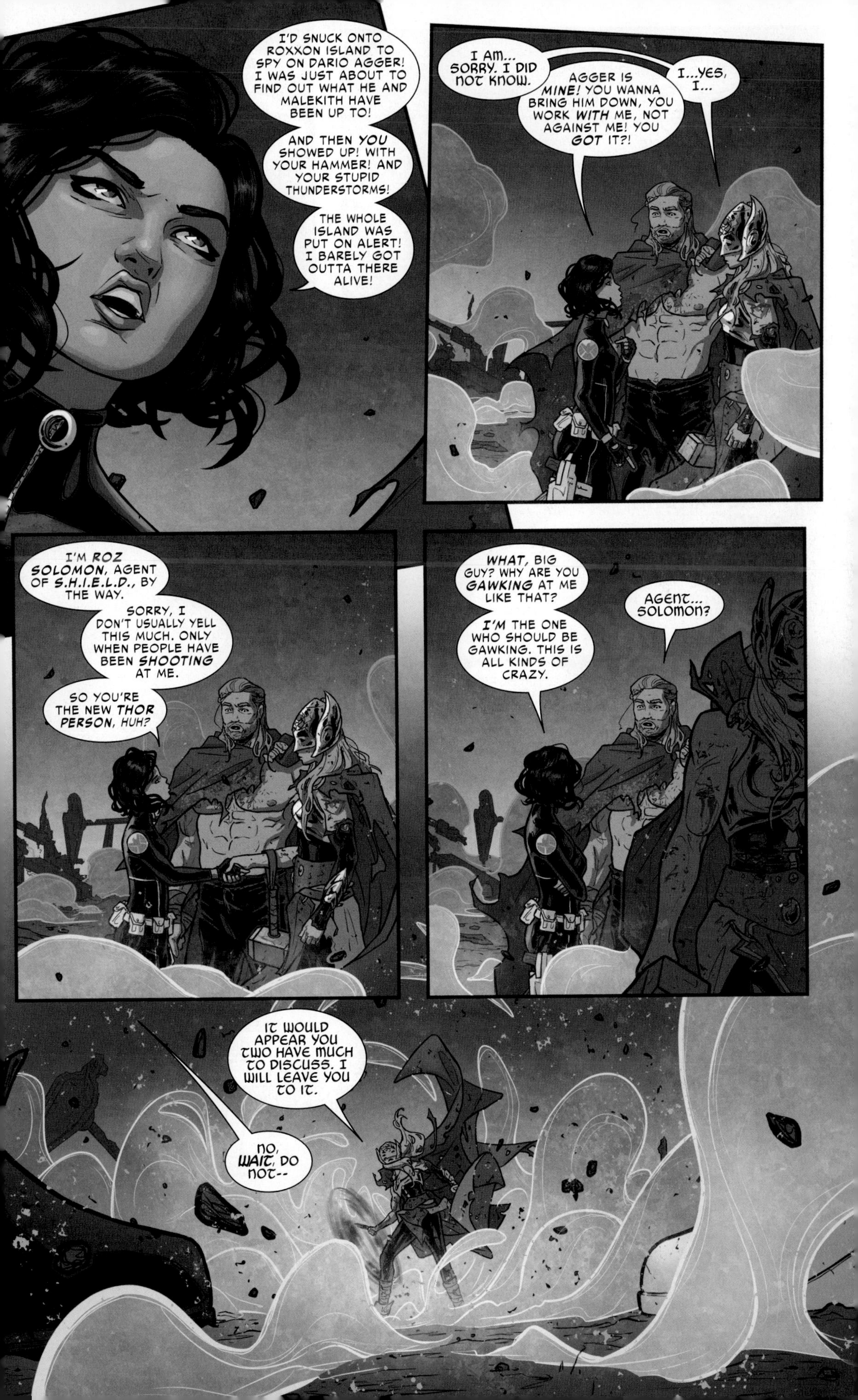
I'D SNUCK ONTO ROXXON ISLAND TO SPY ON DARIO AGGER! I WAS JUST ABOUT TO FIND OUT WHAT HE AND MALEKITH HAVE BEEN UP TO!
AND THEN YOU SHOWED UP! WITH YOUR HAMMER! AND YOUR STUPID THUNDERSTORMS!
THE WHOLE ISLAND WAS PUT ON ALERT! I BARELY GOT OUTTA THERE ALIVE!
I AM... SORRY. I DID NOT KNOW.
AGGER IS MINE! YOU WANNA BRING HIM DOWN, YOU WORK WITH ME, NOT AGAINST ME! YOU GOT IT?!
I...YES, I...
I'M ROZ SOLOMON, AGENT OF S.H.I.E.L.D., BY THE WAY.
SORRY, I DON'T USUALLY YELL THIS MUCH. ONLY WHEN PEOPLE HAVE BEEN SHOOTING AT ME.
SO YOU'RE THE NEW THOR PERSON, HUH?
WHAT, BIG GUY? WHY ARE YOU GAWKING AT ME LIKE THAT?
I'M THE ONE WHO SHOULD BE GAWKING. THIS IS ALL KINDS OF CRAZY.
AGENT... SOLOMON?
IT WOULD APPEAR YOU TWO HAVE MUCH TO DISCUSS. I WILL LEAVE YOU TO IT.
NO, WAIT, DO NOT--

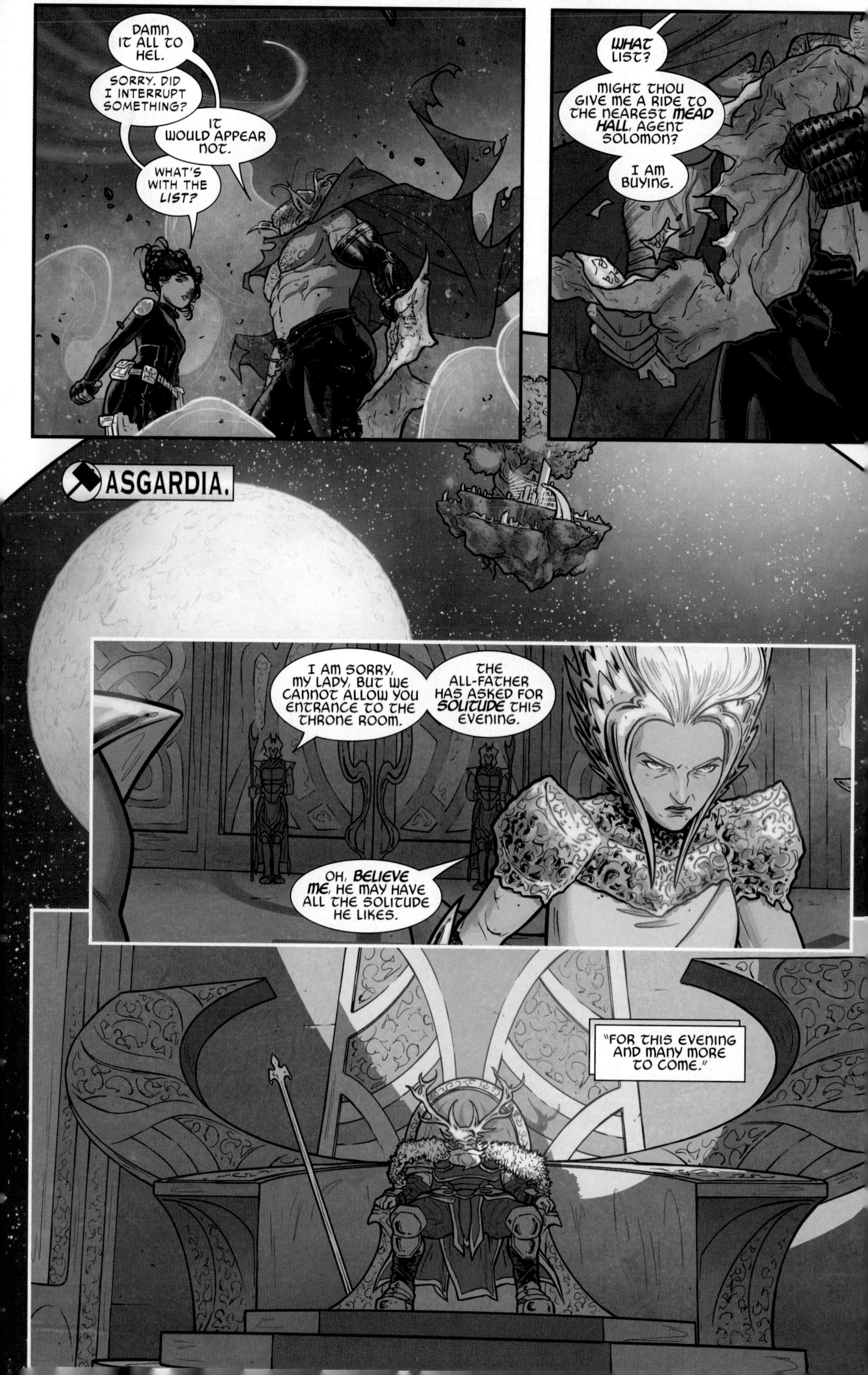
DAMN IT ALL TO HEL.
SORRY. DID I INTERRUPT SOMETHING?
IT WOULD APPEAR NOT.
WHAT'S WITH THE LIST?
WHAT LIST?
MIGHT THOU GIVE ME A RIDE TO THE NEAREST MEAD HALL, AGENT SOLOMON?
I AM BUYING.
ASGARDIA.
I AM SORRY, MY LADY, BUT WE CANNOT ALLOW YOU ENTRANCE TO THE THRONE ROOM.
THE ALL-FATHER HAS ASKED FOR SOLITUDE THIS EVENING.
OH, BELIEVE ME, HE MAY HAVE ALL THE SOLITUDE HE LIKES.
"FOR THIS EVENING AND MANY MORE TO COME."

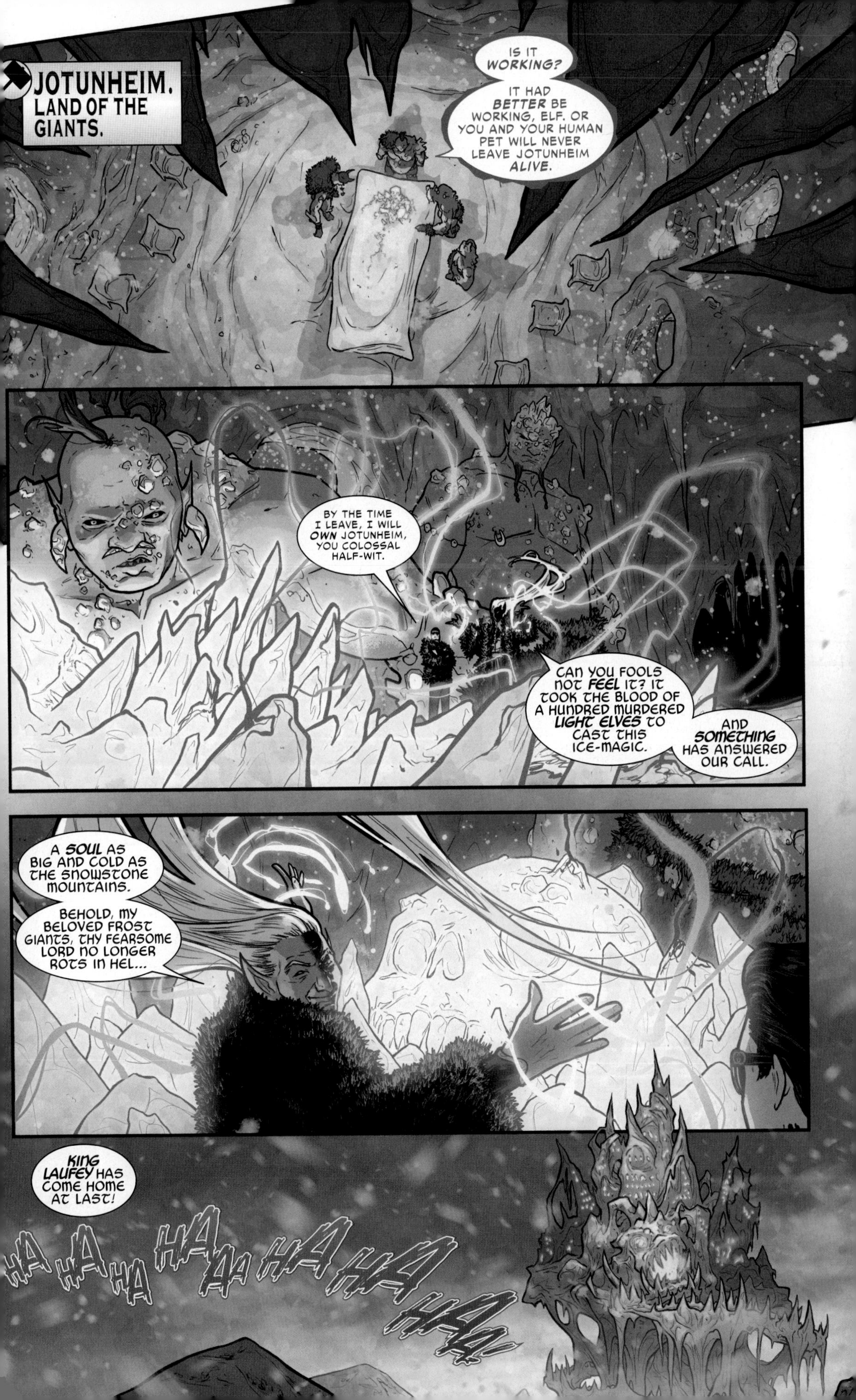
JOTUNHEIM. LAND OF THE GIANTS.
IS IT WORKING?
IT HAD BETTER BE WORKING, ELF. OR YOU AND YOUR HUMAN PET WILL NEVER LEAVE JOTUNHEIM ALIVE.
BY THE TIME I LEAVE, I WILL OWN JOTUNHEIM, YOU COLOSSAL HALF-WIT.
CAN YOU FOOLS NOT FEEL IT? IT TOOK THE BLOOD OF A HUNDRED MURDERED LIGHT ELVES TO CAST THIS ICE-MAGIC.
AND SOMETHING HAS ANSWERED OUR CALL.
A SOUL AS BIG AND COLD AS THE SNOWSTONE MOUNTAINS.
BEHOLD, MY BELOVED FROST GIANTS, THY FEARSOME LORD NO LONGER ROTS IN HEL...
KING LAUFEY HAS COME HOME AT LAST!
HA HA HA HA HA HA HA HA HA HA HA

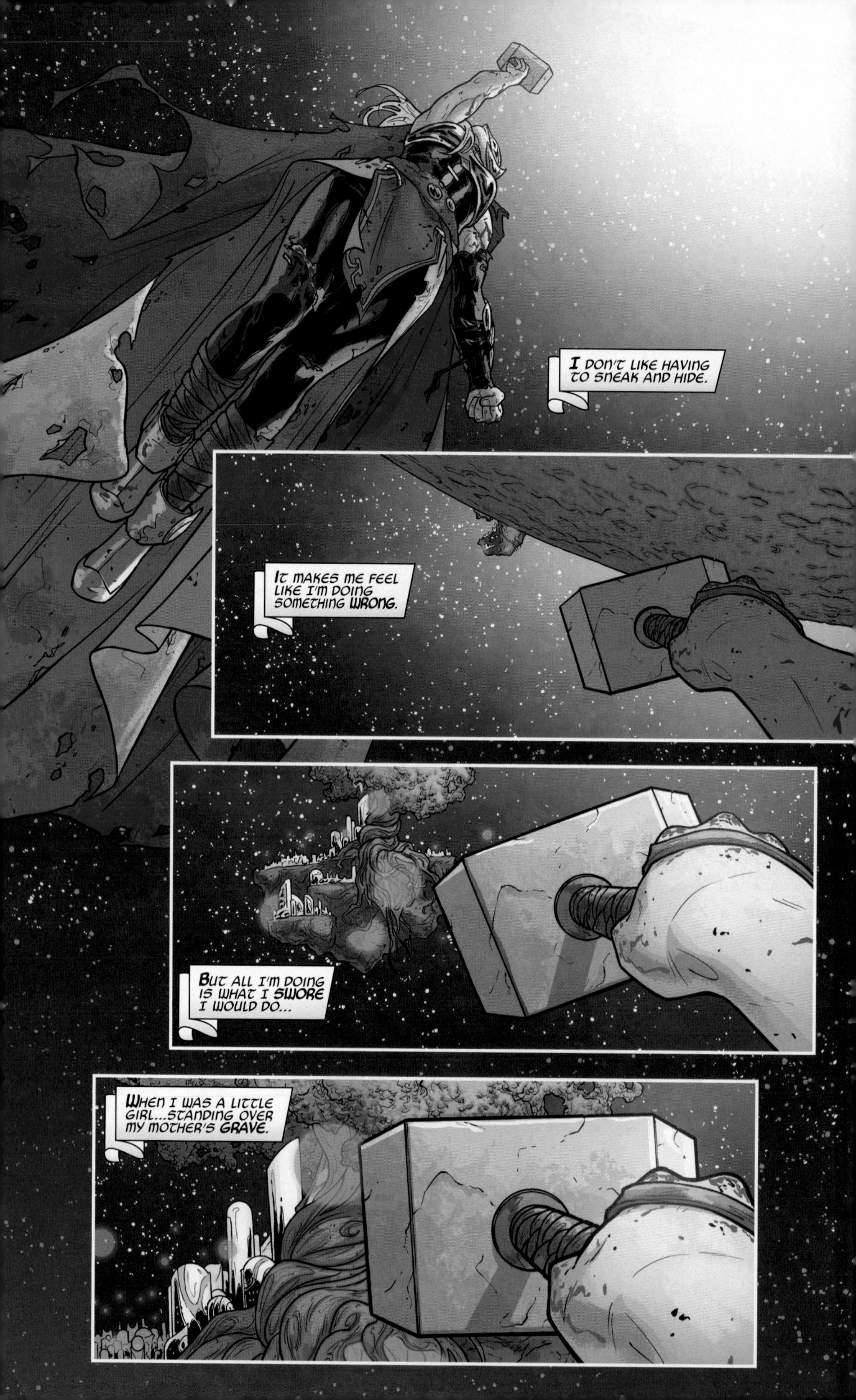

I DON'T LIKE HAVING TO SNEAK AND HIDE.
IT MAKES ME FEEL LIKE I'M DOING SOMETHING WRONG.
BUT ALL I'M DOING IS WHAT I SWORE I WOULD DO...
WHEN I WAS A LITTLE GIRL...STANDING OVER MY MOTHER'S GRAVE.

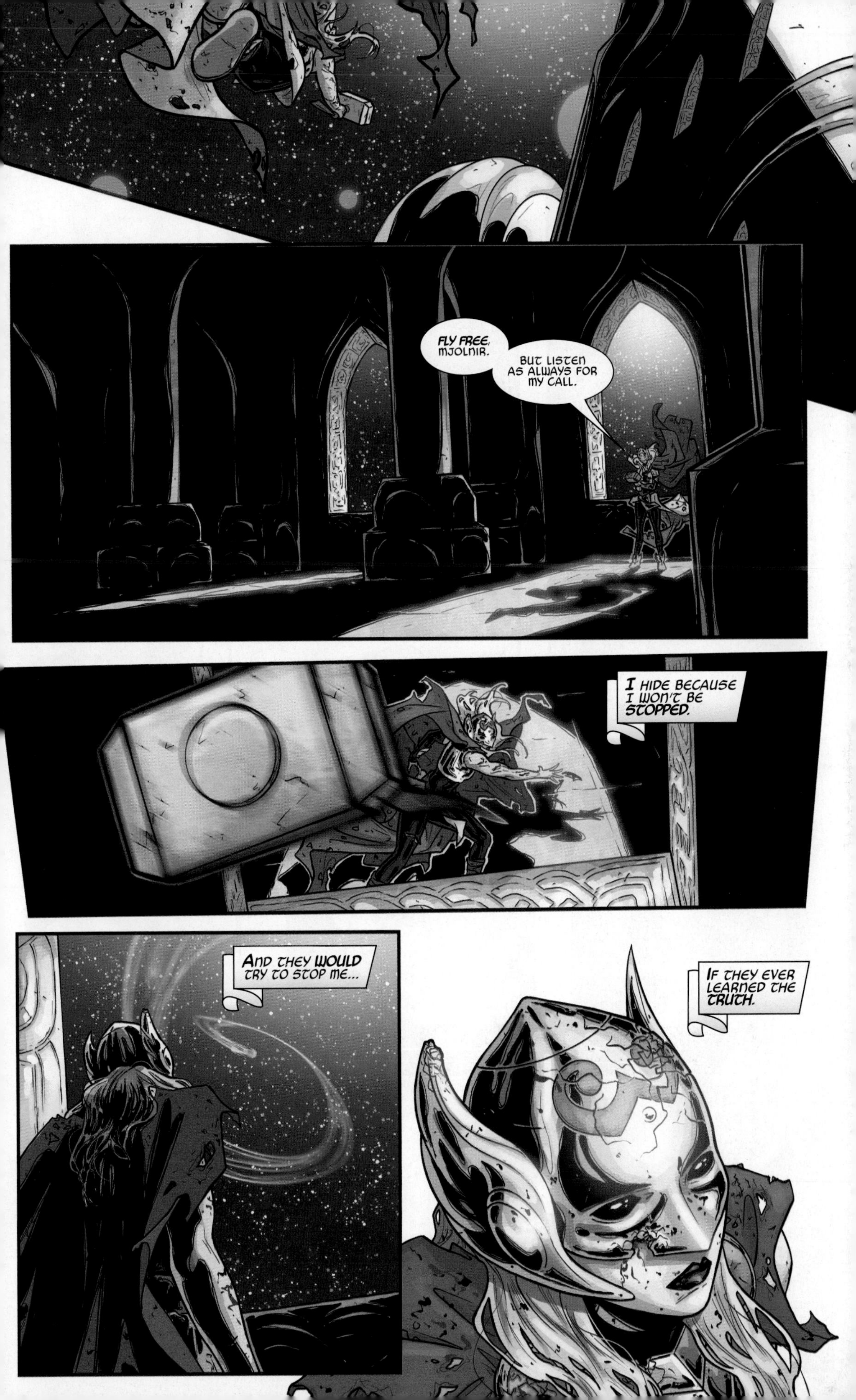
FLY FREE, MJOLNIR.
BUT LISTEN AS ALWAYS FOR MY CALL.
I HIDE BECAUSE I WON'T BE STOPPED.
AND THEY WOULD TRY TO STOP ME...
IF THEY EVER LEARNED THE TRUTH.

THE WORLD NEEDS A THOR. THAT'S ALL THAT REALLY MATTERS.

WE NEED A GOD WHO UNDERSTANDS WHAT IT MEANS TO BE HUMBLED. TO BE MORTAL.

A GOD WHO KNOWS HOW PRECIOUS LIFE IS. HOW DELICATE.

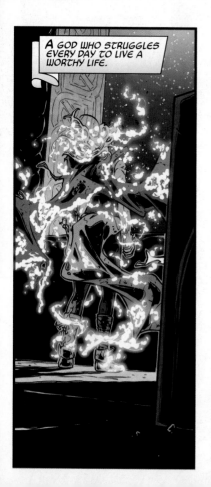

A GOD WHO STRUGGLES EVERY DAY TO LIVE A WORTHY LIFE.

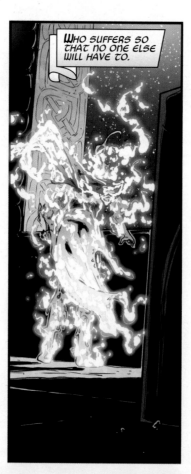

WHO SUFFERS SO THAT NO ONE ELSE WILL HAVE TO.

A GOD WHO LOVES THE EARTH ENOUGH TO DIE FOR IT.

UGGHH

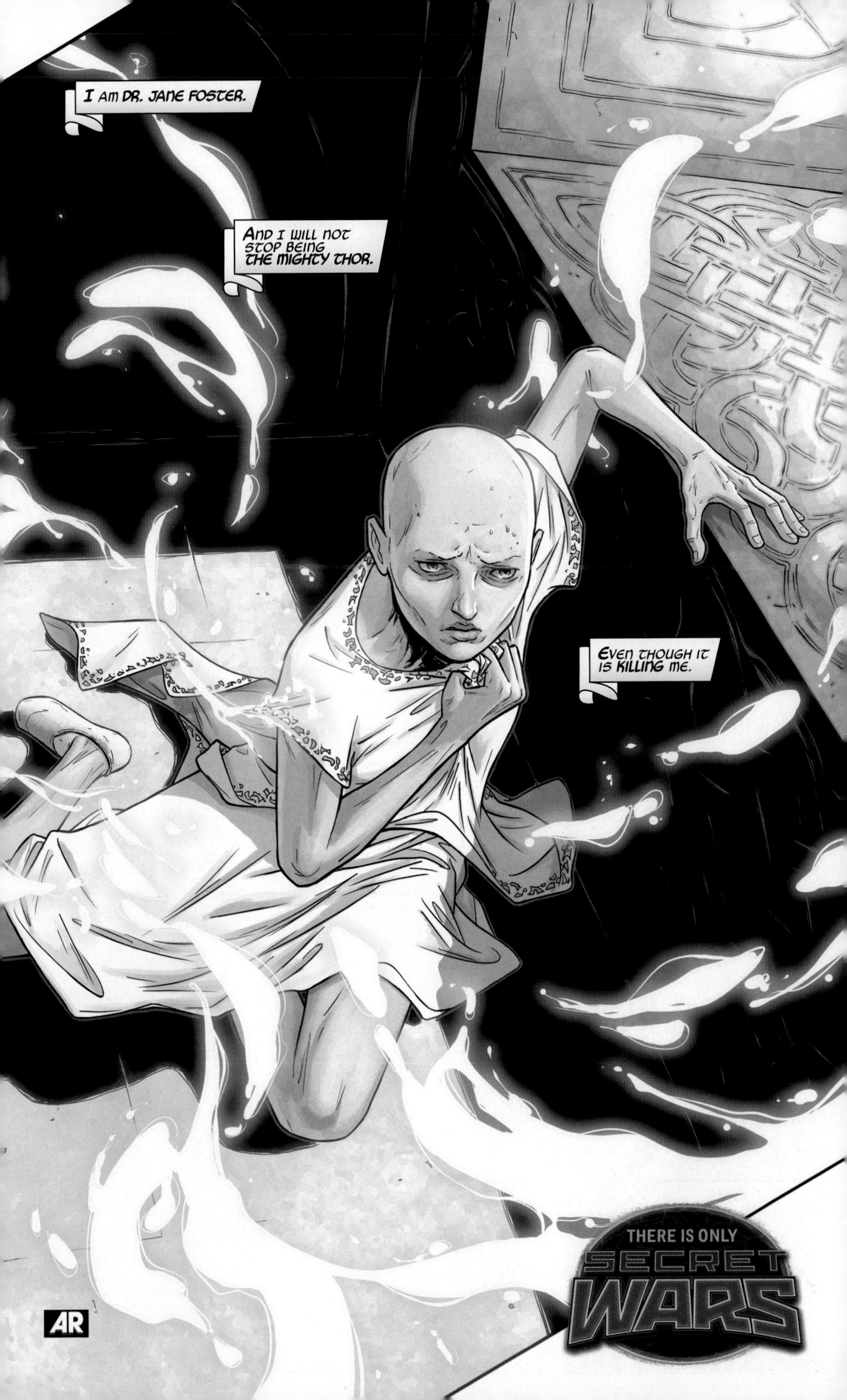
I AM DR. JANE FOSTER.
AND I WILL NOT STOP BEING THE MIGHTY THOR.
EVEN THOUGH IT IS KILLING ME.
THERE IS ONLY SECRET WARS
AR

ANNUAL 1

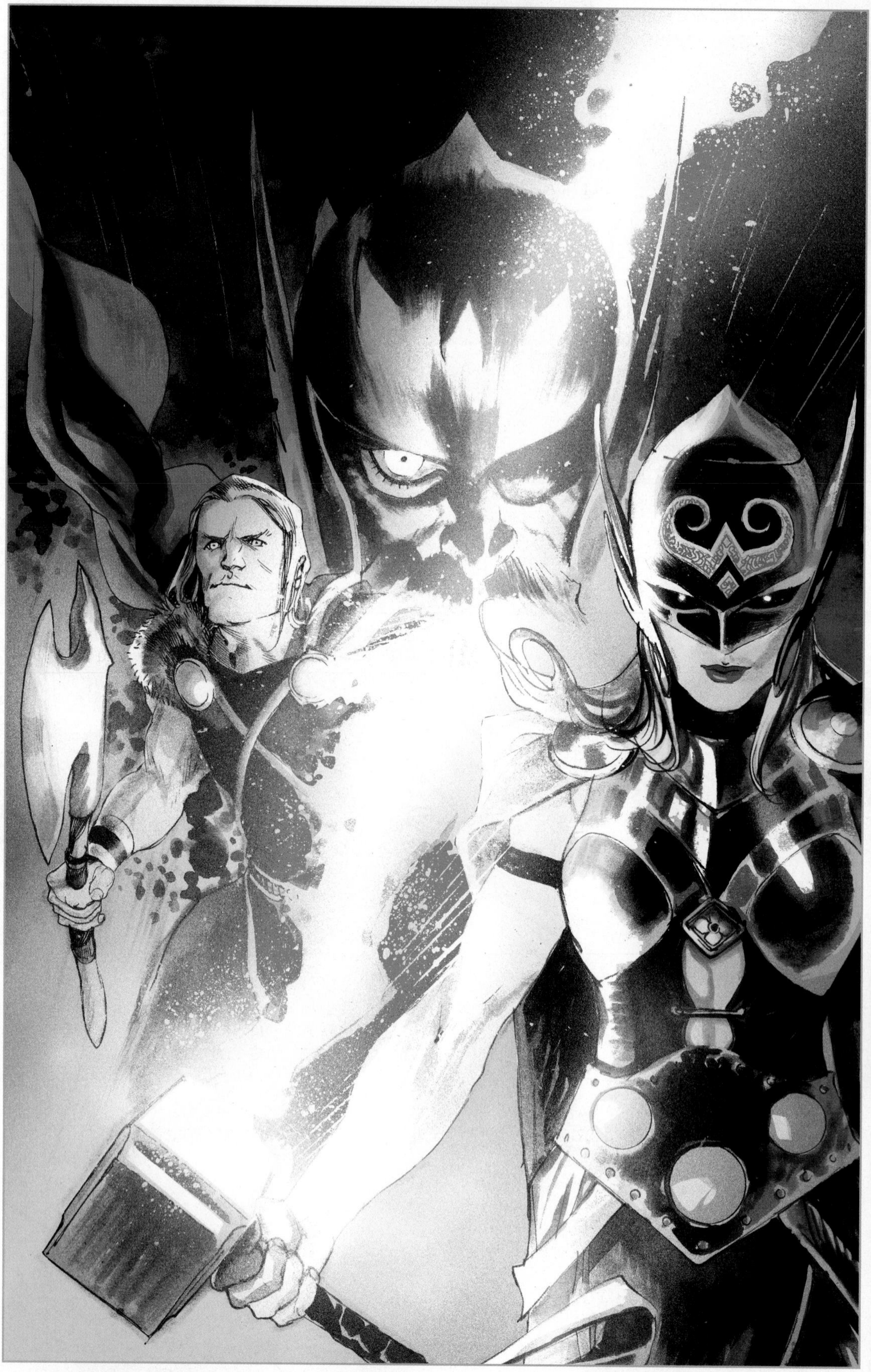

KING THOR, THOR & YOUNG THOR

TALES OF THUNDER

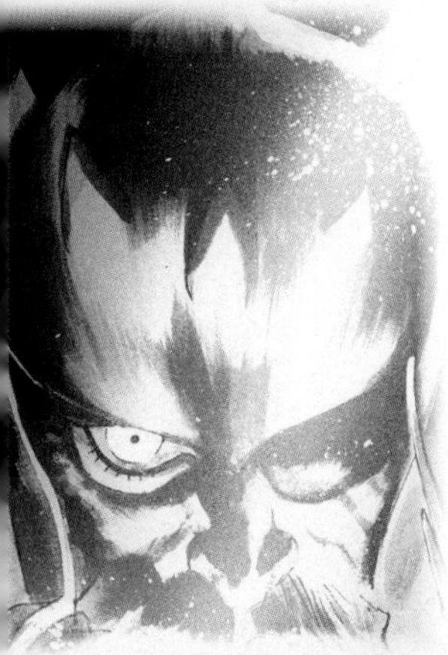

KING THOR

The God of Thunder of the far future. He rules Asgard and has three granddaughters—Frigg, Ellisiv, and Atli—known as the Girls of Thunder. Together, they recently helped bring life back to Earth after it had been dead and barren for quite some time.

JASON AARON writer
TIMOTHY TRUMAN artist
FRANK MARTIN colorist
JOE SABINO letterer
JON MOISAN assistant editor
WIL MOSS editor

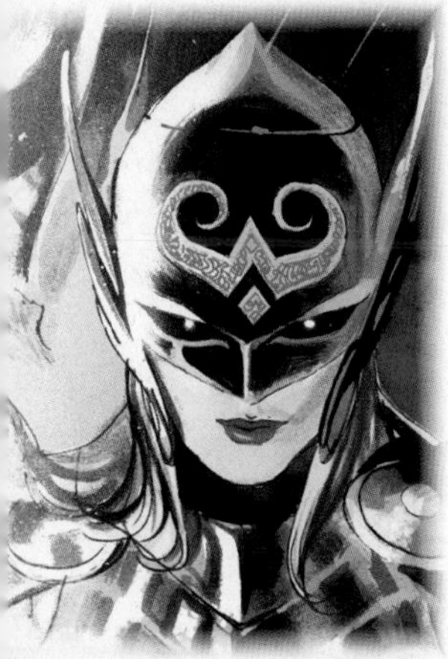

THOR

The Goddess of Thunder of the present. Recently, after Thor found himself suddenly unworthy to lift Mjolnir, a mysterious woman was able to lift the enchanted hammer, becoming the new Thor! Her true identity remains a secret to all.

NOELLE STEVENSON writer
MARGUERITE SAUVAGE artist
JOE SABINO letterer
JON MOISAN assistant editor
WIL MOSS editor

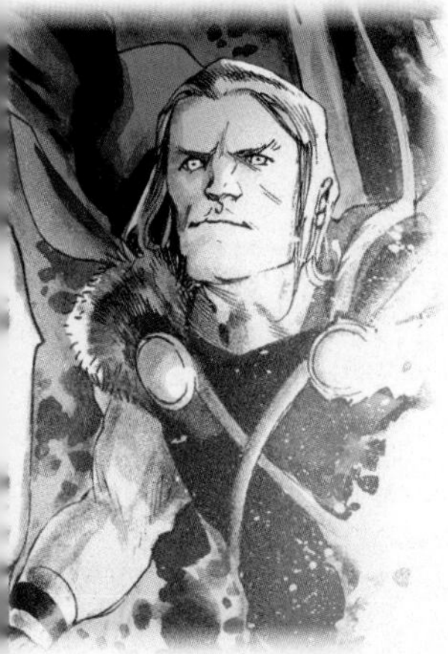

YOUNG THOR

The God of Thunder of the distant past. This Thor is not yet worthy to wield Mjolnir. He is worshipped by Vikings and beloved by his fellow Asgardians, but is best known for his mead-fueled escapades.

CM PUNK writer
ROB GUILLORY artist
JOE SABINO letterer
JON MOISAN editor
WIL MOSS consulting editor

RAFAEL ALBUQUERQUE cover artist
ROB GUILLORY; MARGUERITE SAUVAGE variant cover artists

AXEL ALONSO editor in chief
JOE QUESADA chief creative officer
DAN BUCKLEY publisher
ALAN FINE executive producer

THOR created by STAN LEE, LARRY LIEBER & JACK KIRBY

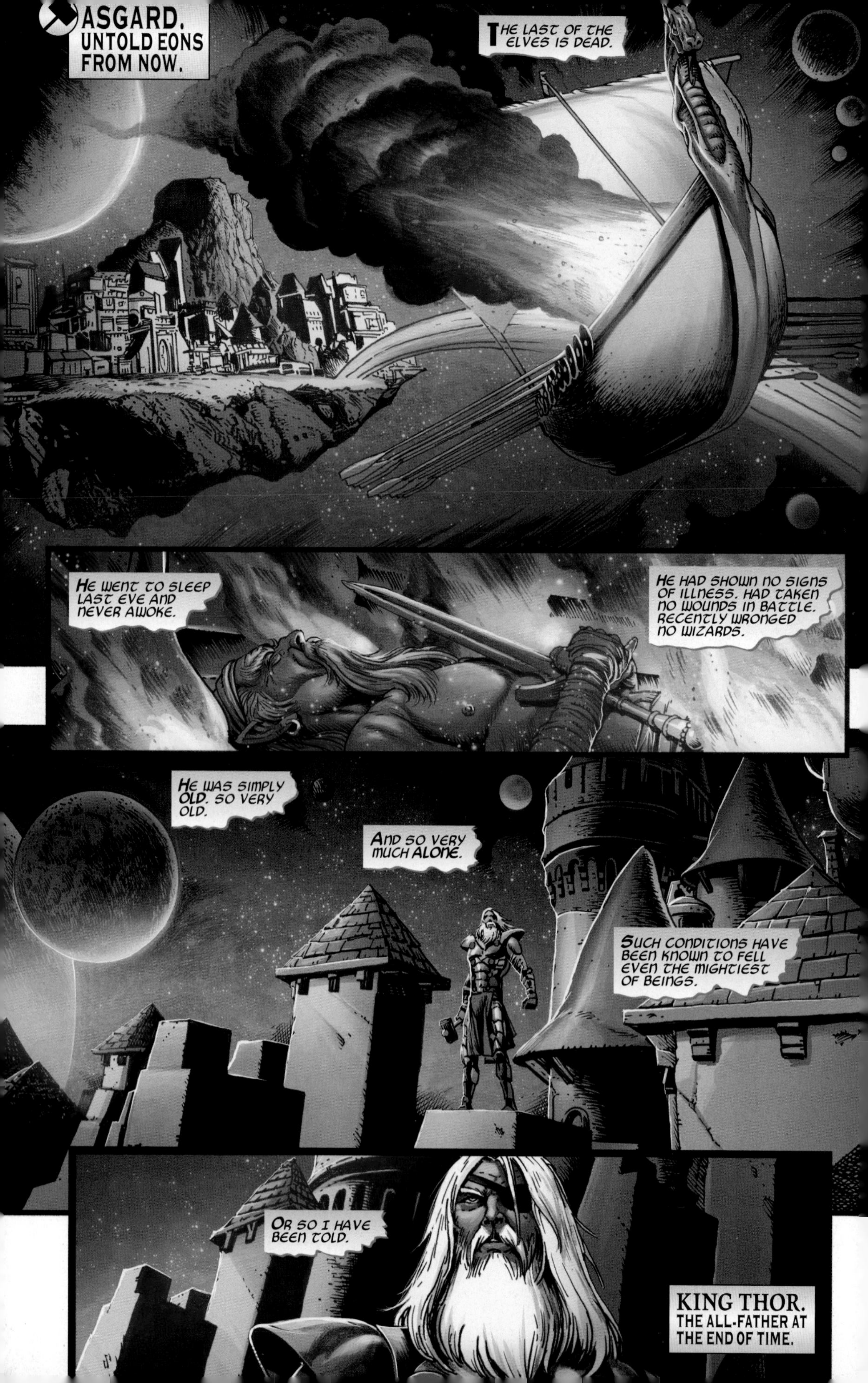
ASGARD. UNTOLD EONS FROM NOW.
THE LAST OF THE ELVES IS DEAD.
HE WENT TO SLEEP LAST EVE AND NEVER AWOKE.
HE HAD SHOWN NO SIGNS OF ILLNESS. HAD TAKEN NO WOUNDS IN BATTLE. RECENTLY WRONGED NO WIZARDS.
HE WAS SIMPLY OLD. SO VERY OLD.
AND SO VERY MUCH ALONE.
SUCH CONDITIONS HAVE BEEN KNOWN TO FELL EVEN THE MIGHTIEST OF BEINGS.
OR SO I HAVE BEEN TOLD.
KING THOR. THE ALL-FATHER AT THE END OF TIME.

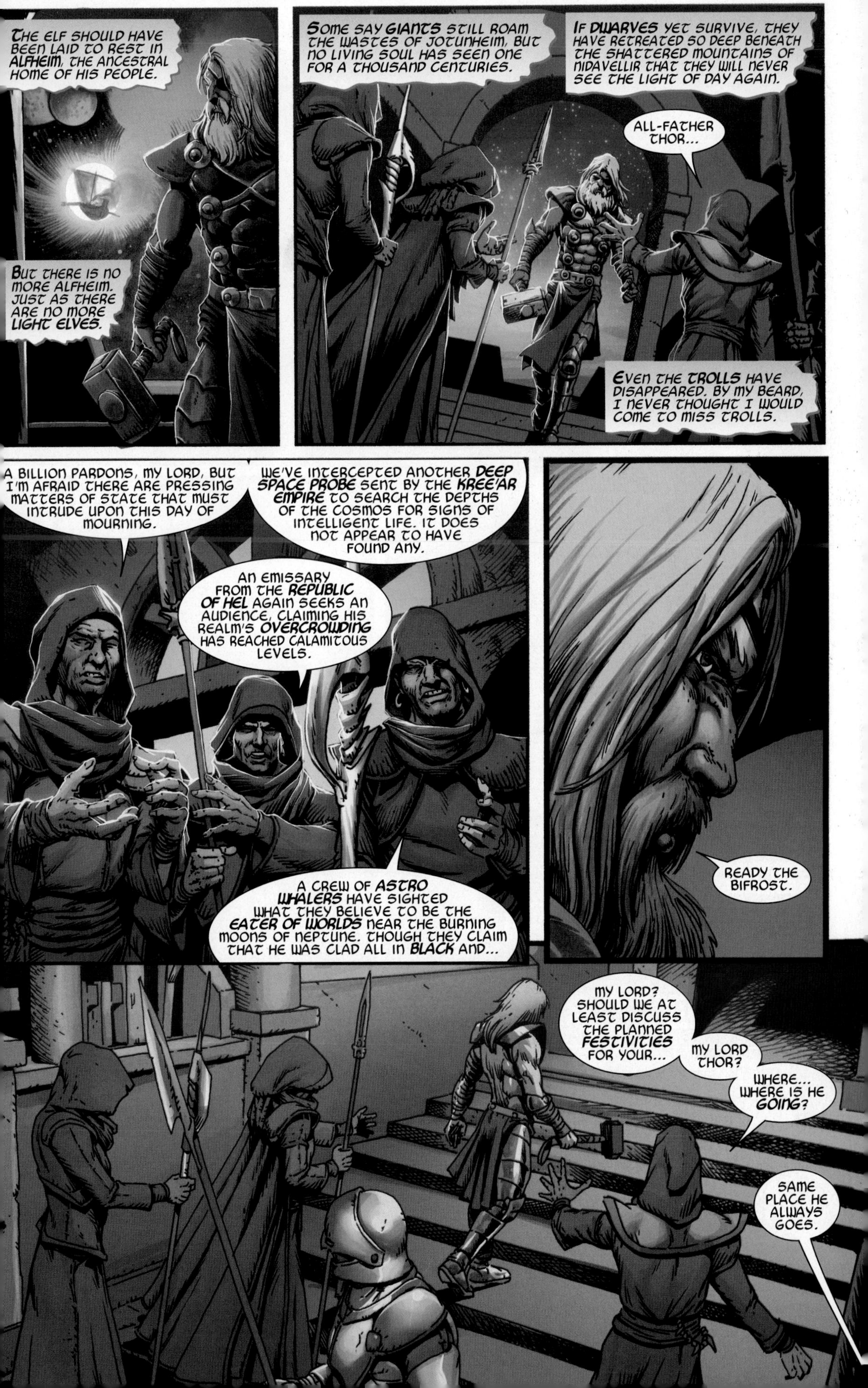
THE ELF SHOULD HAVE BEEN LAID TO REST IN ALFHEIM, THE ANCESTRAL HOME OF HIS PEOPLE.
BUT THERE IS NO MORE ALFHEIM. JUST AS THERE ARE NO MORE LIGHT ELVES.
SOME SAY GIANTS STILL ROAM THE WASTES OF JOTUNHEIM, BUT NO LIVING SOUL HAS SEEN ONE FOR A THOUSAND CENTURIES.
IF DWARVES YET SURVIVE, THEY HAVE RETREATED SO DEEP BENEATH THE SHATTERED MOUNTAINS OF NIDAVELLIR THAT THEY WILL NEVER SEE THE LIGHT OF DAY AGAIN.
ALL-FATHER THOR...
EVEN THE TROLLS HAVE DISAPPEARED. BY MY BEARD, I NEVER THOUGHT I WOULD COME TO MISS TROLLS.
A BILLION PARDONS, MY LORD, BUT I'M AFRAID THERE ARE PRESSING MATTERS OF STATE THAT MUST INTRUDE UPON THIS DAY OF MOURNING.
WE'VE INTERCEPTED ANOTHER DEEP SPACE PROBE SENT BY THE KREE'AR EMPIRE TO SEARCH THE DEPTHS OF THE COSMOS FOR SIGNS OF INTELLIGENT LIFE. IT DOES NOT APPEAR TO HAVE FOUND ANY.
AN EMISSARY FROM THE REPUBLIC OF HEL AGAIN SEEKS AN AUDIENCE, CLAIMING HIS REALM'S OVERCROWDING HAS REACHED CALAMITOUS LEVELS.
A CREW OF ASTRO WHALERS HAVE SIGHTED WHAT THEY BELIEVE TO BE THE EATER OF WORLDS NEAR THE BURNING MOONS OF NEPTUNE. THOUGH THEY CLAIM THAT HE WAS CLAD ALL IN BLACK AND...
READY THE BIFROST.
MY LORD? SHOULD WE AT LEAST DISCUSS THE PLANNED FESTIVITIES FOR YOUR...
MY LORD THOR?
WHERE... WHERE IS HE GOING?
SAME PLACE HE ALWAYS GOES.

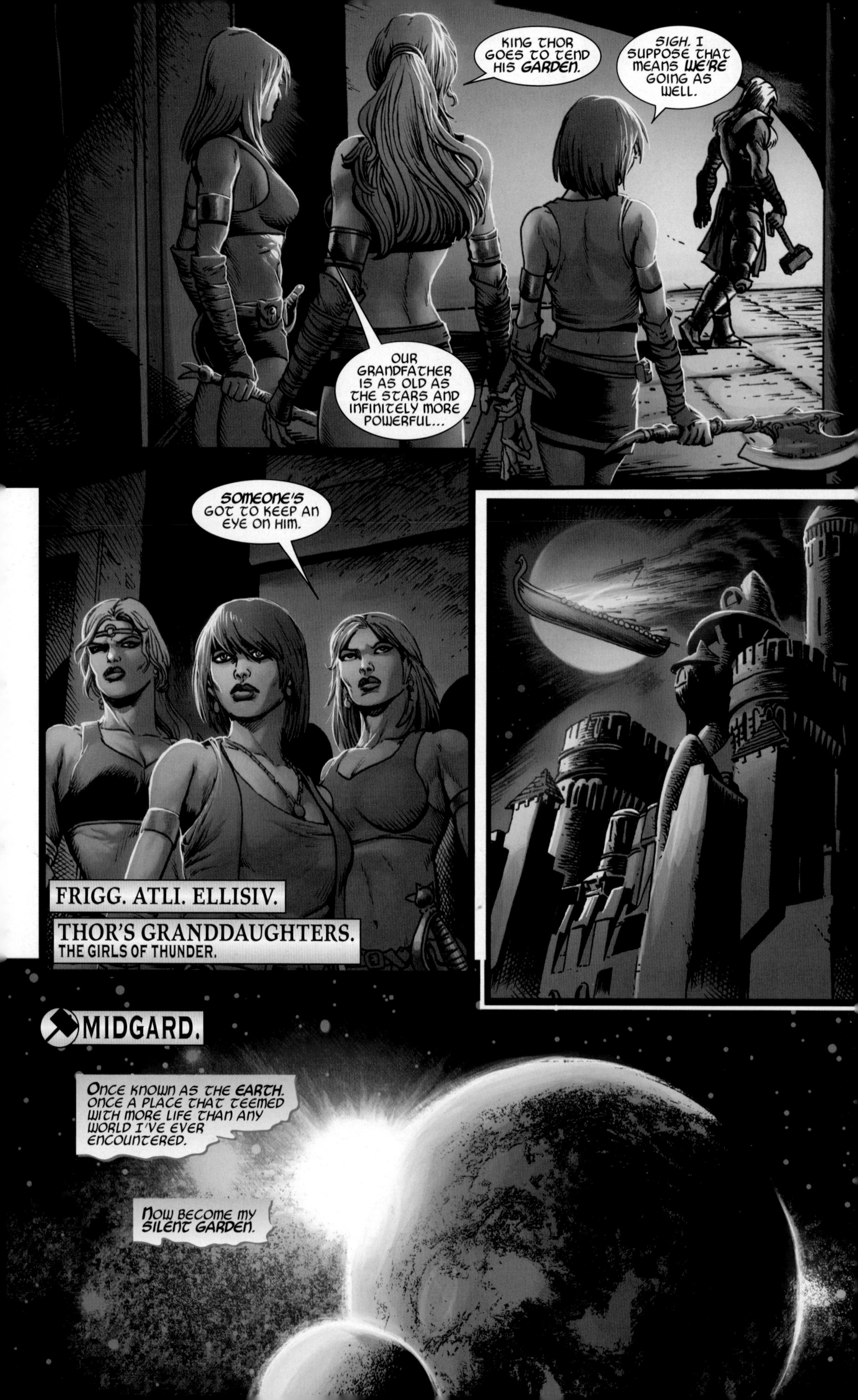
KING THOR GOES TO TEND HIS GARDEN.
SIGH. I SUPPOSE THAT MEANS WE'RE GOING AS WELL.
OUR GRANDFATHER IS AS OLD AS THE STARS AND INFINITELY MORE POWERFUL...
SOMEONE'S GOT TO KEEP AN EYE ON HIM.
FRIGG. ATLI. ELLISIV.
THOR'S GRANDDAUGHTERS.
THE GIRLS OF THUNDER.
MIDGARD.
ONCE KNOWN AS THE EARTH. ONCE A PLACE THAT TEEMED WITH MORE LIFE THAN ANY WORLD I'VE EVER ENCOUNTERED.
NOW BECOME MY SILENT GARDEN.

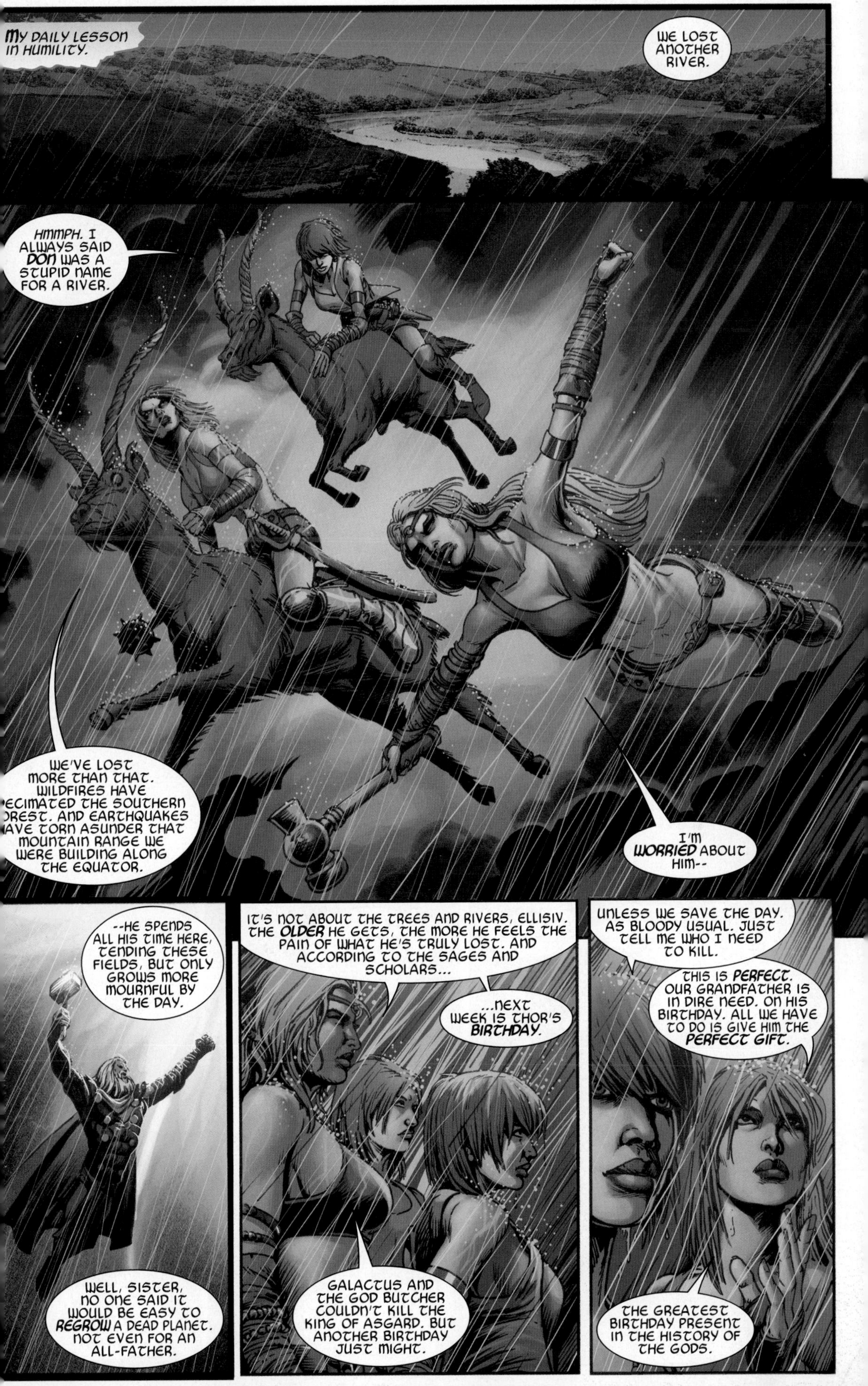

MY DAILY LESSON IN HUMILITY.
WE LOST ANOTHER RIVER.
HMMPH. I ALWAYS SAID DON WAS A STUPID NAME FOR A RIVER.
WE'VE LOST MORE THAN THAT. WILDFIRES HAVE ECIMATED THE SOUTHERN OREST. AND EARTHQUAKES AVE TORN ASUNDER THAT MOUNTAIN RANGE WE WERE BUILDING ALONG THE EQUATOR.
I'M WORRIED ABOUT HIM--
--HE SPENDS ALL HIS TIME HERE, TENDING THESE FIELDS, BUT ONLY GROWS MORE MOURNFUL BY THE DAY.
WELL, SISTER, NO ONE SAID IT WOULD BE EASY TO REGROW A DEAD PLANET. NOT EVEN FOR AN ALL-FATHER.
IT'S NOT ABOUT THE TREES AND RIVERS, ELLISIV. THE OLDER HE GETS, THE MORE HE FEELS THE PAIN OF WHAT HE'S TRULY LOST. AND ACCORDING TO THE SAGES AND SCHOLARS...
...NEXT WEEK IS THOR'S BIRTHDAY.
GALACTUS AND THE GOD BUTCHER COULDN'T KILL THE KING OF ASGARD. BUT ANOTHER BIRTHDAY JUST MIGHT.
UNLESS WE SAVE THE DAY. AS BLOODY USUAL. JUST TELL ME WHO I NEED TO KILL.
THIS IS PERFECT. OUR GRANDFATHER IS IN DIRE NEED. ON HIS BIRTHDAY. ALL WE HAVE TO DO IS GIVE HIM THE PERFECT GIFT.
THE GREATEST BIRTHDAY PRESENT IN THE HISTORY OF THE GODS.

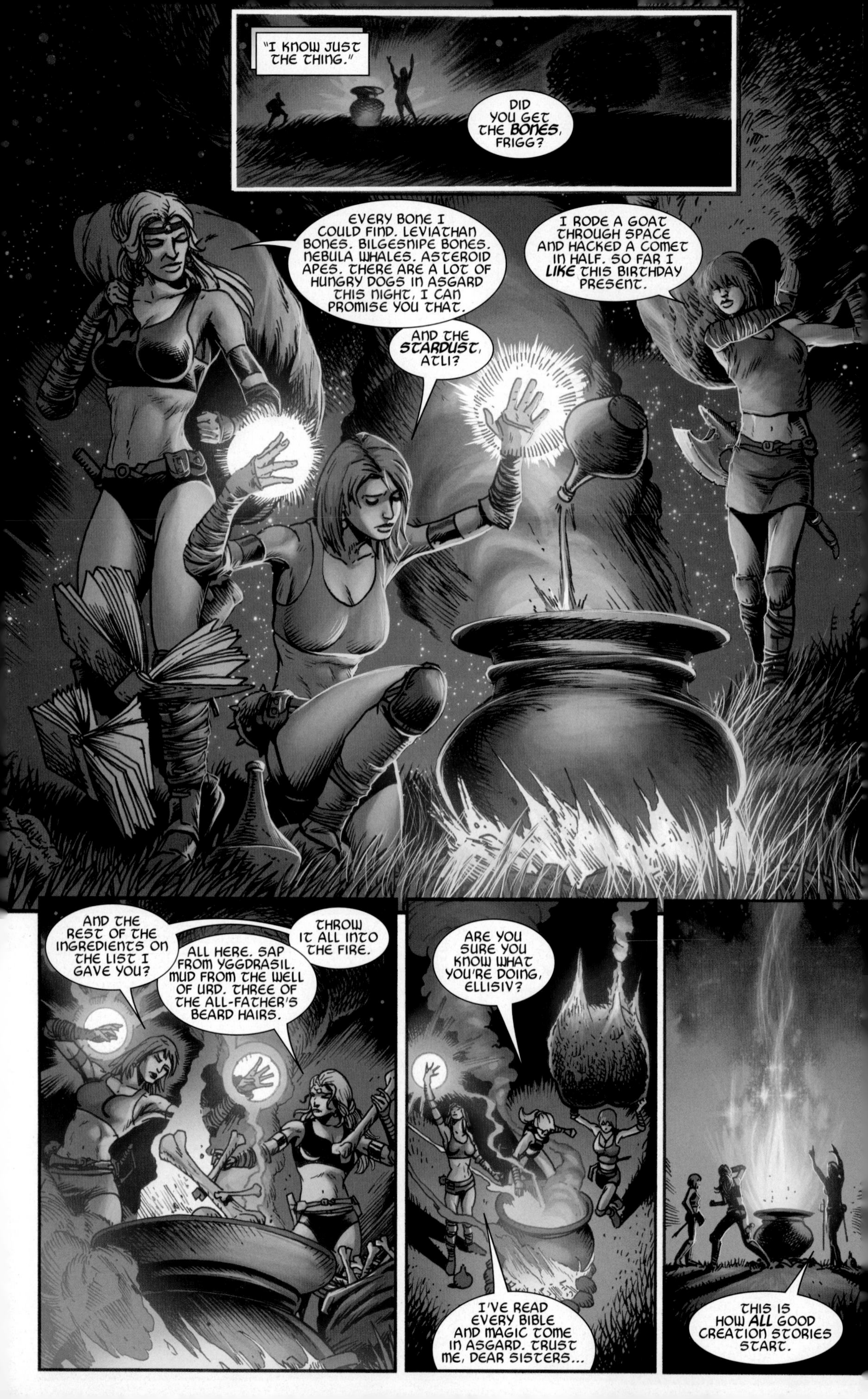
"I KNOW JUST THE THING."
DID YOU GET THE BONES, FRIGG?
EVERY BONE I COULD FIND. LEVIATHAN BONES. BILGESNIPE BONES. NEBULA WHALES. ASTEROID APES. THERE ARE A LOT OF HUNGRY DOGS IN ASGARD THIS NIGHT, I CAN PROMISE YOU THAT.
I RODE A GOAT THROUGH SPACE AND HACKED A COMET IN HALF. SO FAR I LIKE THIS BIRTHDAY PRESENT.
AND THE STARDUST, ATLI?
AND THE REST OF THE INGREDIENTS ON THE LIST I GAVE YOU?
ALL HERE. SAP FROM YGGDRASIL. MUD FROM THE WELL OF URD. THREE OF THE ALL-FATHER'S BEARD HAIRS.
THROW IT ALL INTO THE FIRE.
ARE YOU SURE YOU KNOW WHAT YOU'RE DOING, ELLISIV?
I'VE READ EVERY BIBLE AND MAGIC TOME IN ASGARD. TRUST ME, DEAR SISTERS...
THIS IS HOW ALL GOOD CREATION STORIES START.

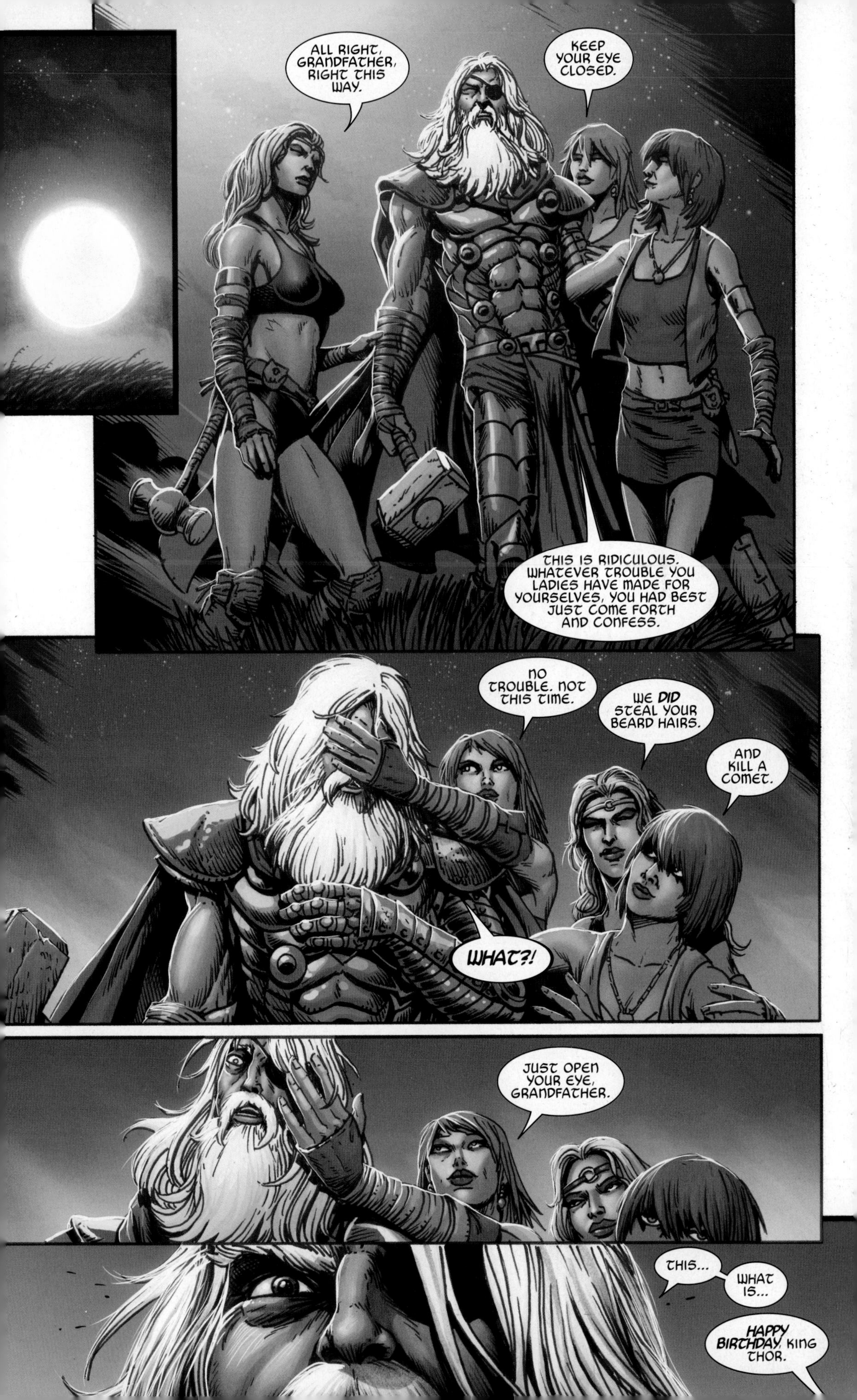
ALL RIGHT, GRANDFATHER, RIGHT THIS WAY.
KEEP YOUR EYE CLOSED.
THIS IS RIDICULOUS. WHATEVER TROUBLE YOU LADIES HAVE MADE FOR YOURSELVES, YOU HAD BEST JUST COME FORTH AND CONFESS.
NO TROUBLE. NOT THIS TIME.
WE DID STEAL YOUR BEARD HAIRS.
AND KILL A COMET.
WHAT?!
JUST OPEN YOUR EYE, GRANDFATHER.
THIS...
WHAT IS...
HAPPY BIRTHDAY, KING THOR.

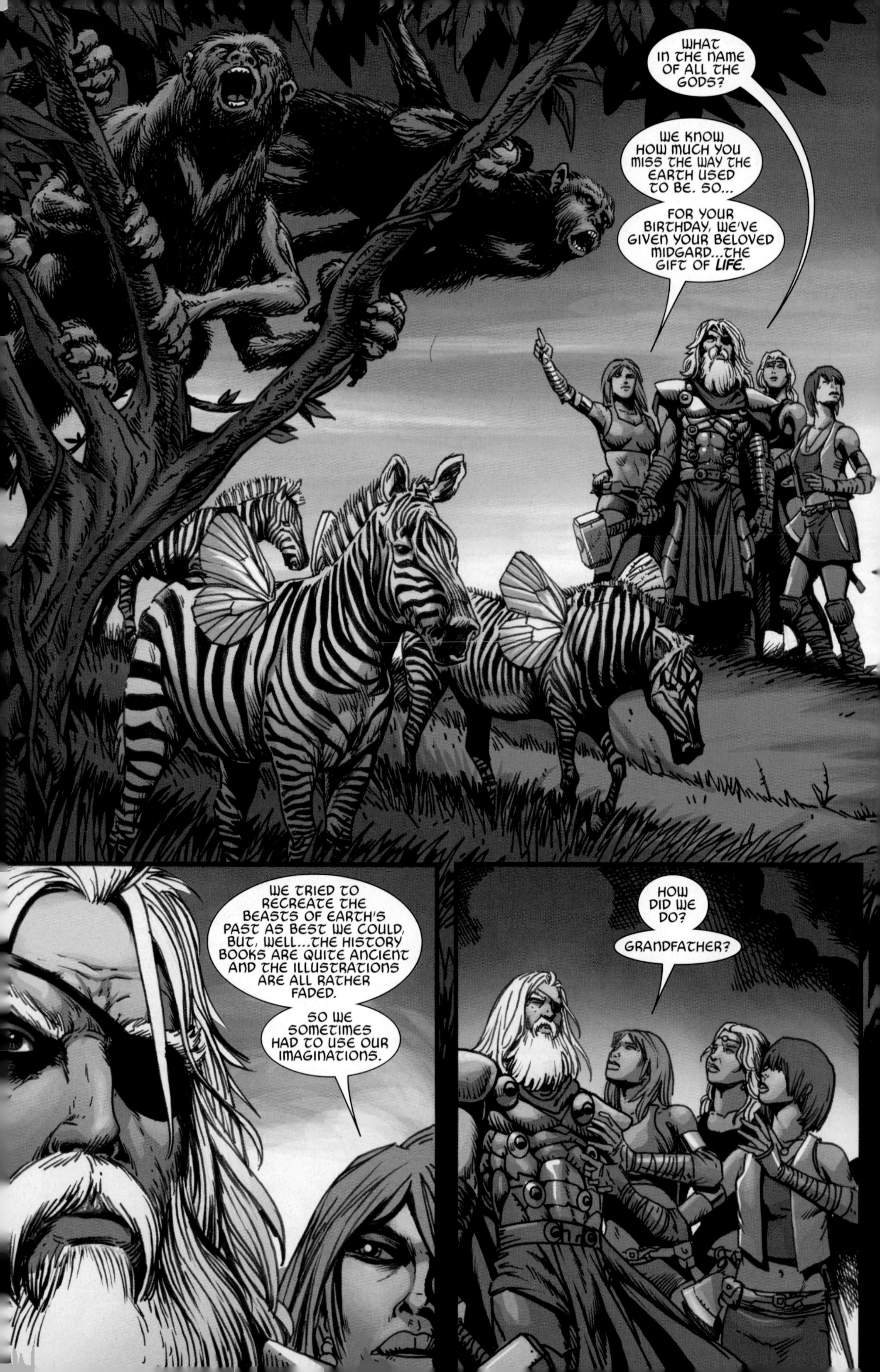
WHAT IN THE NAME OF ALL THE GODS?
WE KNOW HOW MUCH YOU MISS THE WAY THE EARTH USED TO BE. SO...
FOR YOUR BIRTHDAY, WE'VE GIVEN YOUR BELOVED MIDGARD...THE GIFT OF *LIFE*.
WE TRIED TO RECREATE THE BEASTS OF EARTH'S PAST AS BEST WE COULD, BUT, WELL...THE HISTORY BOOKS ARE QUITE ANCIENT AND THE ILLUSTRATIONS ARE ALL RATHER FADED.
SO WE SOMETIMES HAD TO USE OUR IMAGINATIONS.
HOW DID WE DO?
GRANDFATHER?

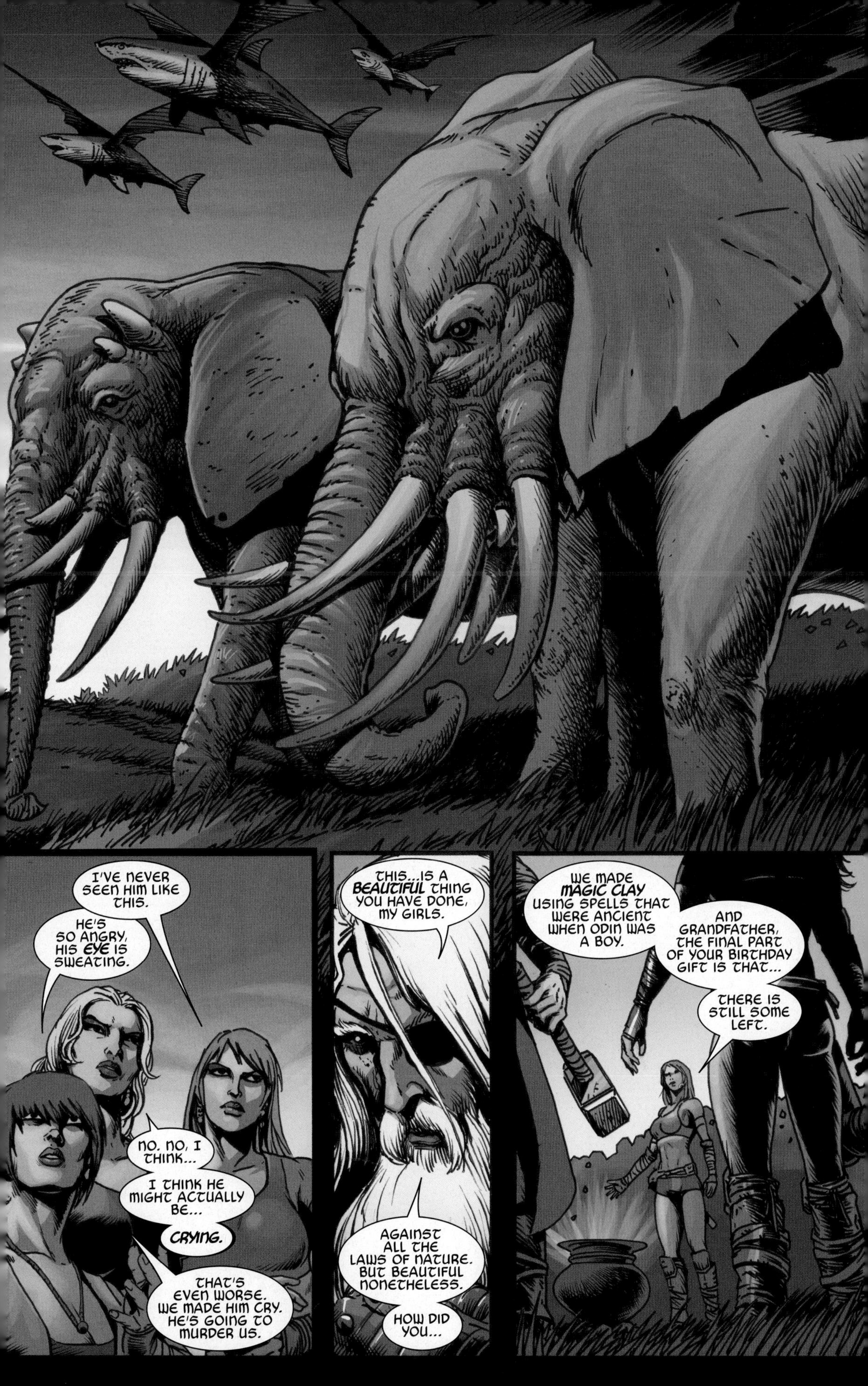
I'VE NEVER SEEN HIM LIKE THIS.
HE'S SO ANGRY, HIS *EYE* IS SWEATING.
NO. NO, I THINK...
I THINK HE MIGHT ACTUALLY BE...
CRYING.
THAT'S EVEN WORSE. WE MADE HIM CRY. HE'S GOING TO MURDER US.
THIS...IS A *BEAUTIFUL* THING YOU HAVE DONE, MY GIRLS.
AGAINST ALL THE LAWS OF NATURE. BUT BEAUTIFUL NONETHELESS.
HOW DID YOU...
WE MADE *MAGIC CLAY* USING SPELLS THAT WERE ANCIENT WHEN ODIN WAS A BOY.
AND GRANDFATHER, THE FINAL PART OF YOUR BIRTHDAY GIFT IS THAT...
THERE IS STILL SOME LEFT.

KRAKAKOOOM!!

A GREAT FEAST WAS PREPARED IN ASGARD TO MARK THE ANNIVERSARY OF MY BIRTH.

IT WAS A MONUMENTALLY LAVISH AFFAIR.

OR SO THEY TELL ME.

I WAS UNABLE TO ATTEND.

WHAT SORT OF ANIMAL IS HE MAKING? IT DOESN'T EVEN HAVE WINGS.

I THOUGHT HE MIGHT MAKE A DRAGON OR MAYBE SOME WHALES, BUT THIS...THIS IS...

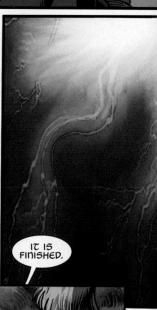

IT IS FINISHED.

AND SO IT BEGINS.

GRANDFATHER...

IS THAT WHAT I THINK IT IS?

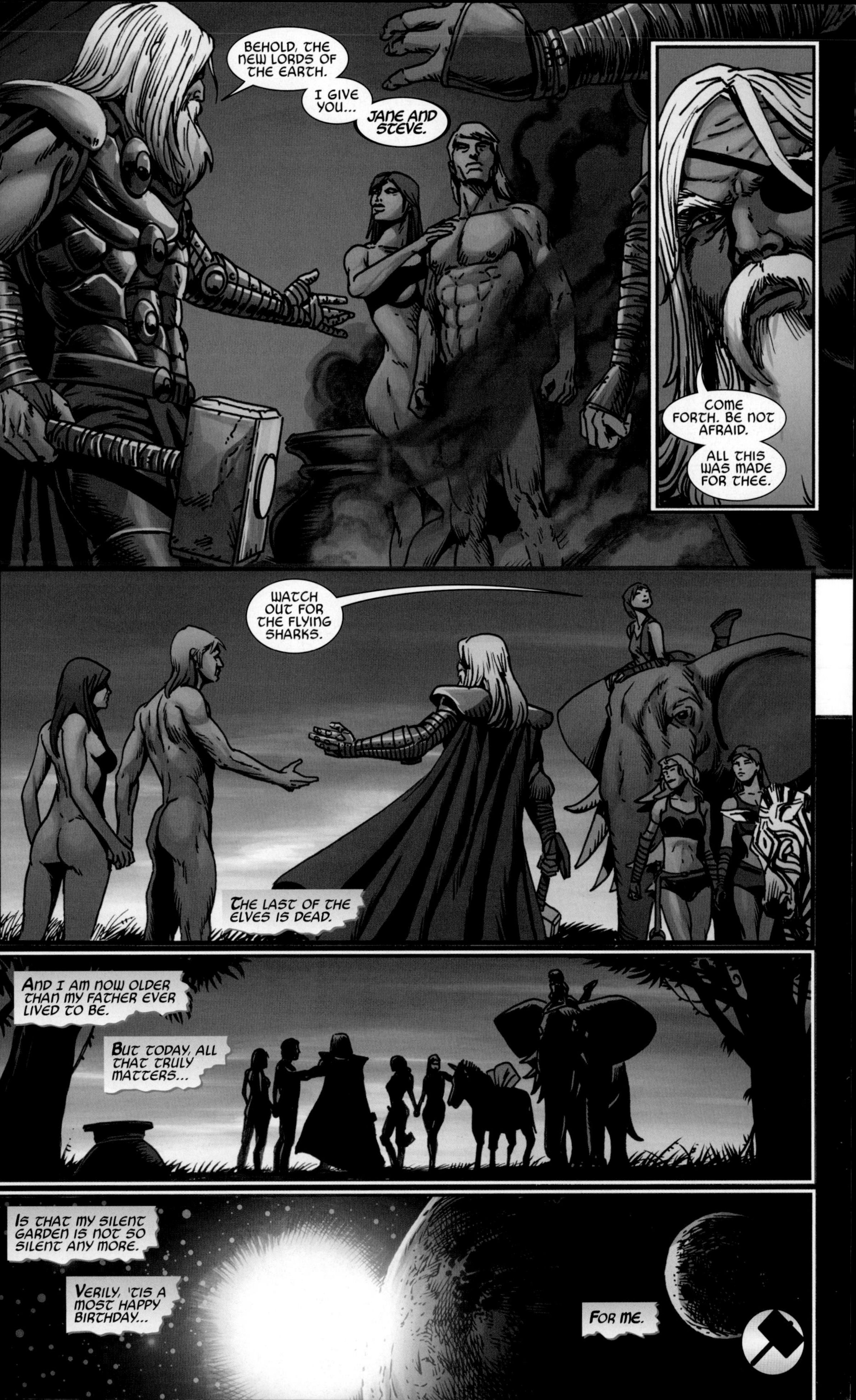
BEHOLD, THE NEW LORDS OF THE EARTH.
I GIVE YOU...
JANE AND STEVE.
COME FORTH. BE NOT AFRAID.
ALL THIS WAS MADE FOR THEE.
WATCH OUT FOR THE FLYING SHARKS.
THE LAST OF THE ELVES IS DEAD.
AND I AM NOW OLDER THAN MY FATHER EVER LIVED TO BE.
BUT TODAY, ALL THAT TRULY MATTERS...
IS THAT MY SILENT GARDEN IS NOT SO SILENT ANY MORE.
VERILY, 'TIS A MOST HAPPY BIRTHDAY...
FOR ME.

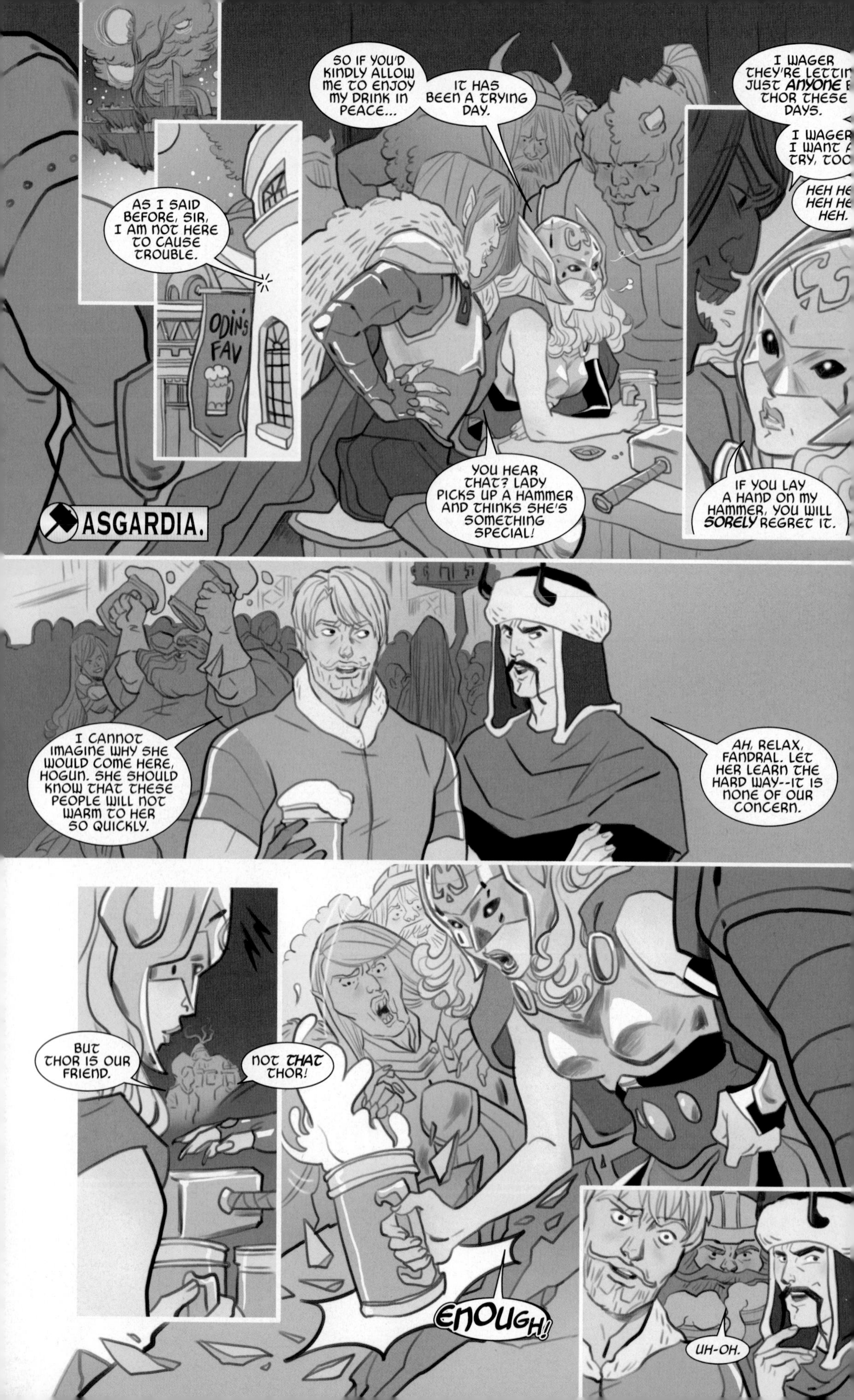
ASGARDIA.
AS I SAID BEFORE, SIR, I AM NOT HERE TO CAUSE TROUBLE.
ODIN'S FAV
SO IF YOU'D KINDLY ALLOW ME TO ENJOY MY DRINK IN PEACE...
IT HAS BEEN A TRYING DAY.
YOU HEAR THAT? LADY PICKS UP A HAMMER AND THINKS SHE'S SOMETHING SPECIAL!
I WAGER THEY'RE LETTIN JUST ANYONE B THOR THESE DAYS.
I WAGER I WANT A TRY, TOO
HEH HE HEH HE HEH.
IF YOU LAY A HAND ON MY HAMMER, YOU WILL SORELY REGRET IT.
I CANNOT IMAGINE WHY SHE WOULD COME HERE, HOGUN. SHE SHOULD KNOW THAT THESE PEOPLE WILL NOT WARM TO HER SO QUICKLY.
AH, RELAX, FANDRAL. LET HER LEARN THE HARD WAY--IT IS NONE OF OUR CONCERN.
BUT THOR IS OUR FRIEND.
NOT THAT THOR!
ENOUGH!
UH-OH.

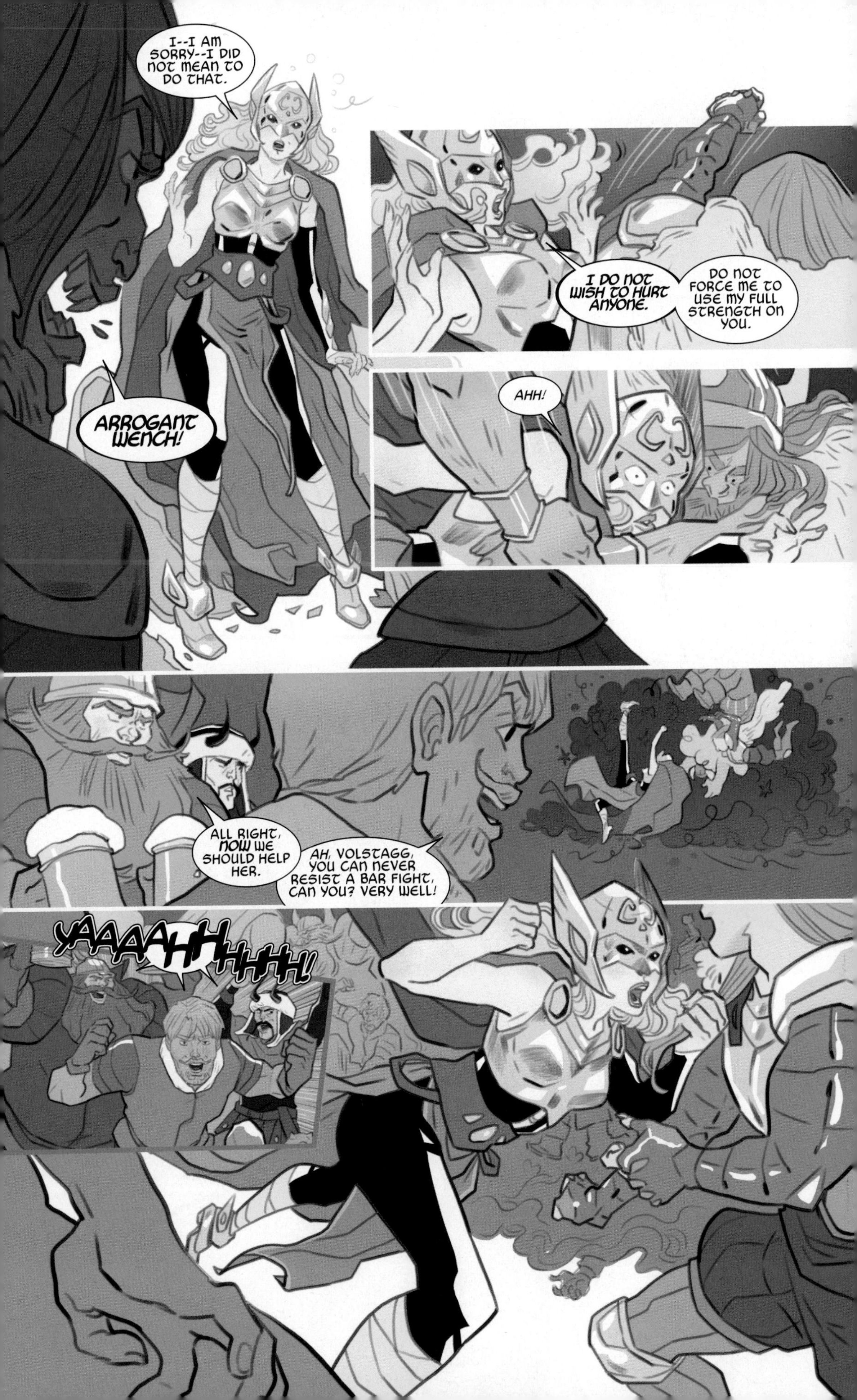
I--I AM SORRY--I DID NOT MEAN TO DO THAT.
ARROGANT WENCH!
I DO NOT WISH TO HURT ANYONE.
DO NOT FORCE ME TO USE MY FULL STRENGTH ON YOU.
AHH!
ALL RIGHT, NOW WE SHOULD HELP HER.
AH, VOLSTAGG, YOU CAN NEVER RESIST A BAR FIGHT, CAN YOU? VERY WELL!
YAAAAHHHHHH!

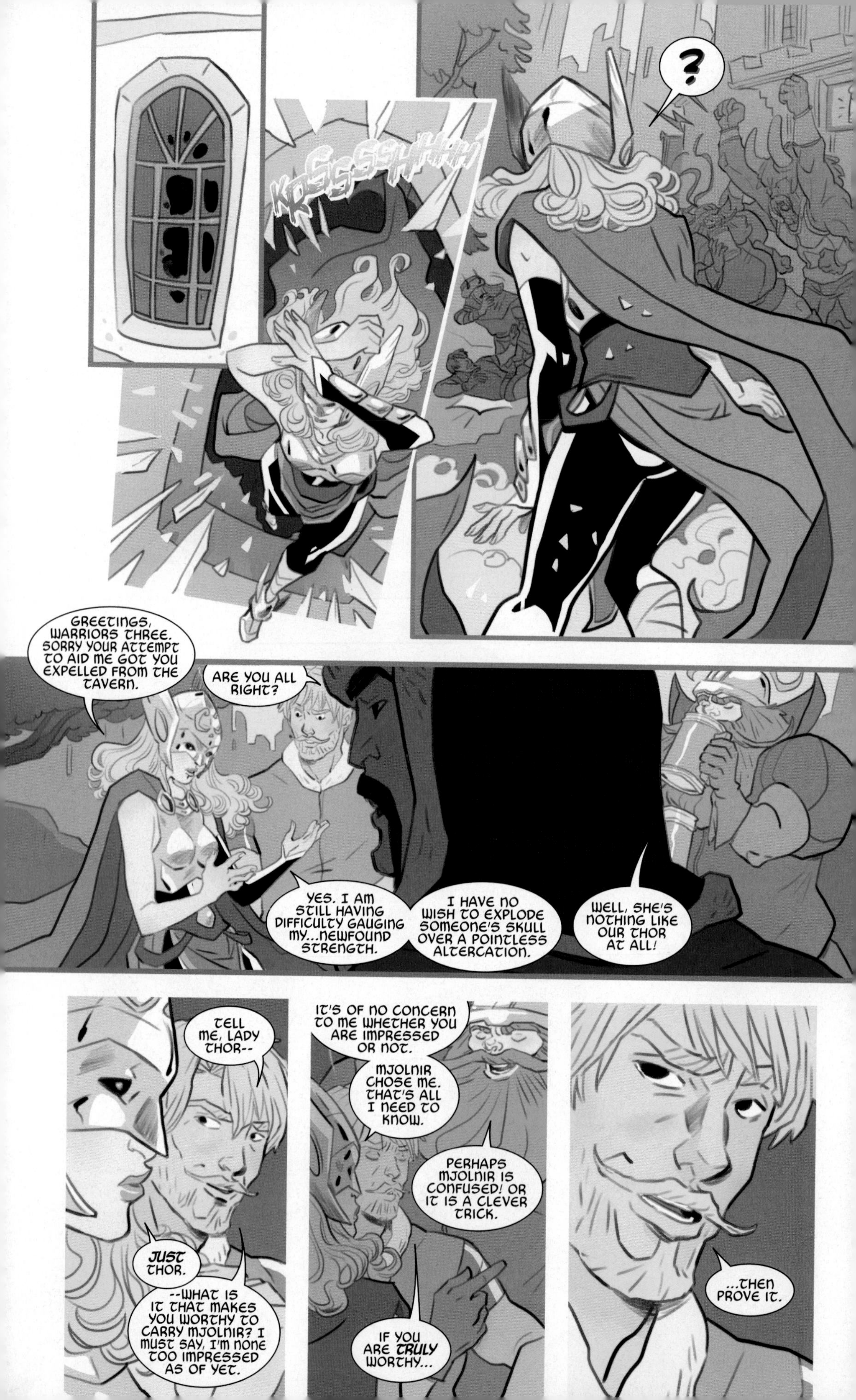
KRSSSSHHHH
?
GREETINGS, WARRIORS THREE. SORRY YOUR ATTEMPT TO AID ME GOT YOU EXPELLED FROM THE TAVERN.
ARE YOU ALL RIGHT?
YES. I AM STILL HAVING DIFFICULTY GAUGING MY...NEWFOUND STRENGTH.
I HAVE NO WISH TO EXPLODE SOMEONE'S SKULL OVER A POINTLESS ALTERCATION.
WELL, SHE'S NOTHING LIKE OUR THOR AT ALL!
TELL ME, LADY THOR--
JUST THOR.
--WHAT IS IT THAT MAKES YOU WORTHY TO CARRY MJOLNIR? I MUST SAY, I'M NONE TOO IMPRESSED AS OF YET.
IT'S OF NO CONCERN TO ME WHETHER YOU ARE IMPRESSED OR NOT.
MJOLNIR CHOSE ME. THAT'S ALL I NEED TO KNOW.
PERHAPS MJOLNIR IS CONFUSED! OR IT IS A CLEVER TRICK.
IF YOU ARE TRULY WORTHY...
...THEN PROVE IT.

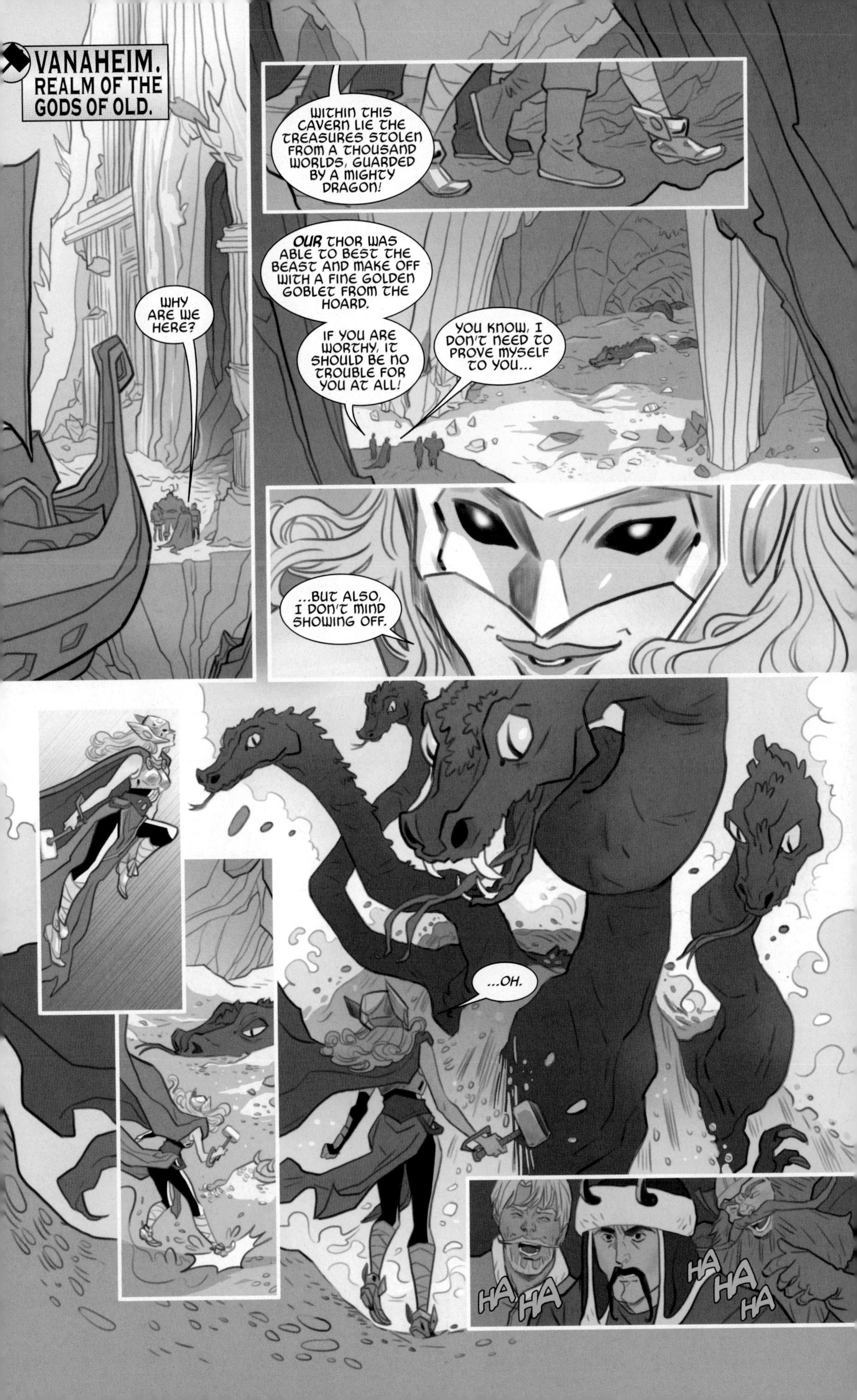
VANAHEIM. REALM OF THE GODS OF OLD.
WHY ARE WE HERE?
WITHIN THIS CAVERN LIE THE TREASURES STOLEN FROM A THOUSAND WORLDS, GUARDED BY A MIGHTY DRAGON!
OUR THOR WAS ABLE TO BEST THE BEAST AND MAKE OFF WITH A FINE GOLDEN GOBLET FROM THE HOARD.
IF YOU ARE WORTHY, IT SHOULD BE NO TROUBLE FOR YOU AT ALL!
YOU KNOW, I DON'T NEED TO PROVE MYSELF TO YOU...
...BUT ALSO, I DON'T MIND SHOWING OFF.
...OH.
HA HA
HA HA HA

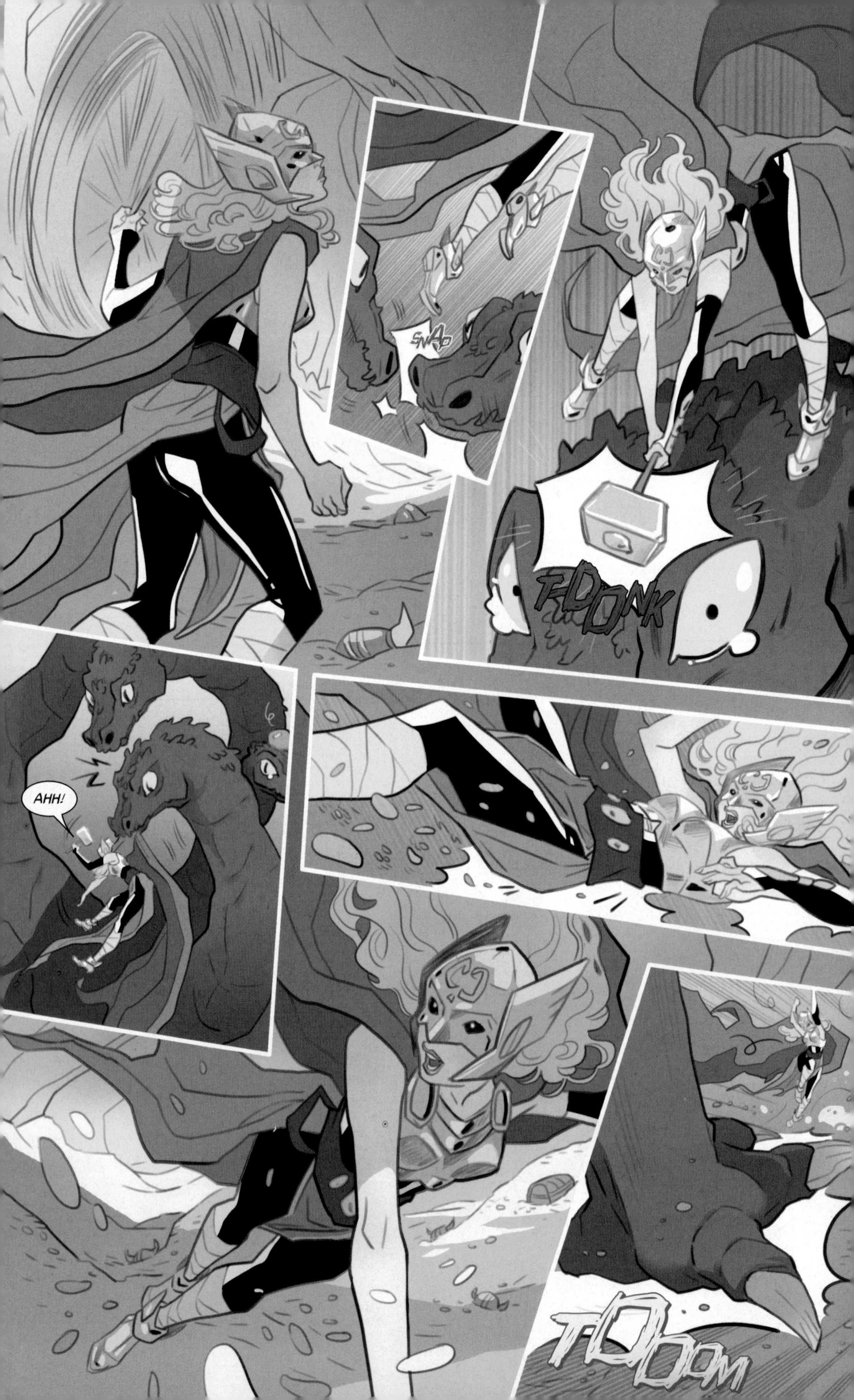
SNAP
TDOONK
AHH!
TOOOOM

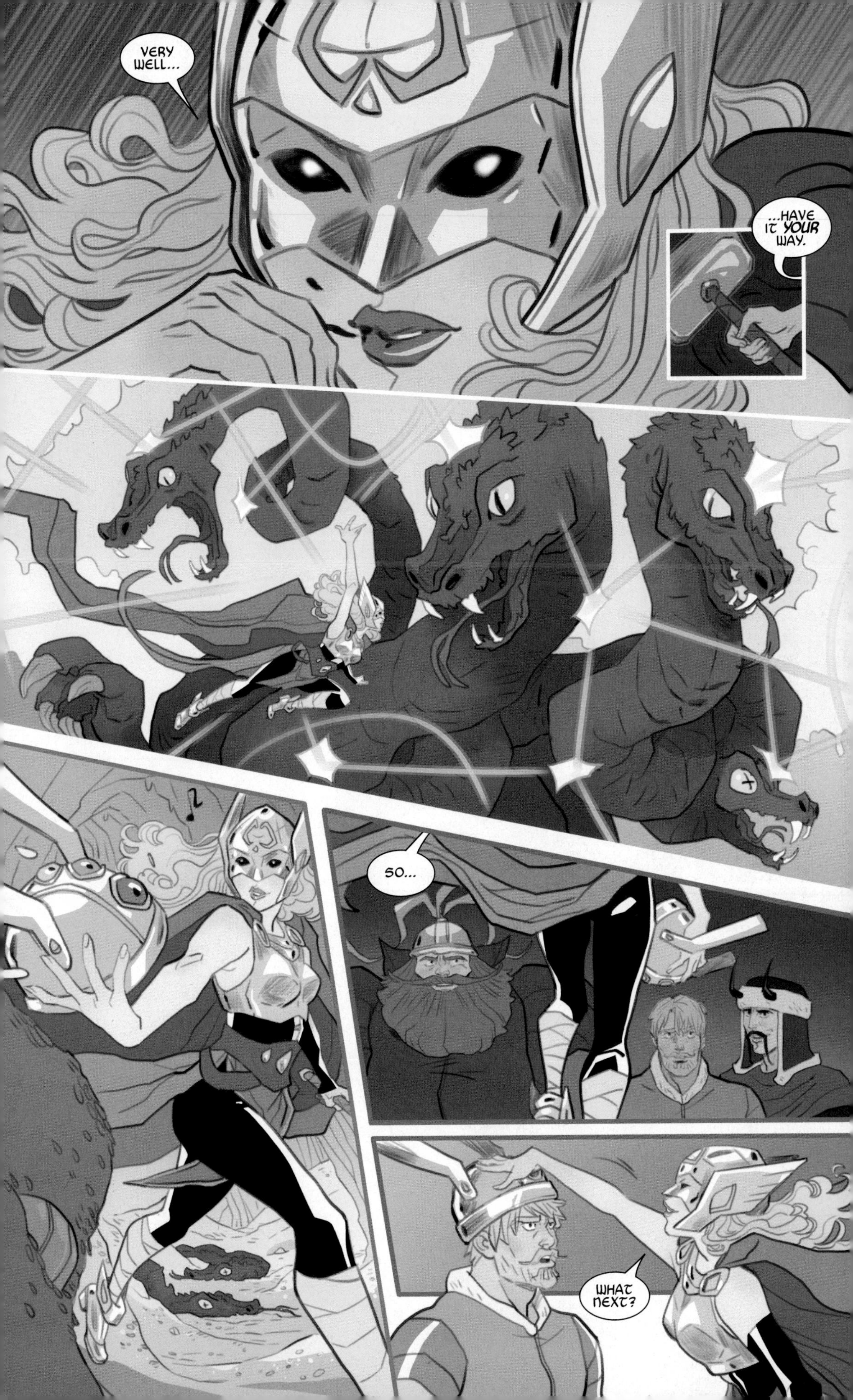
VERY WELL...
...HAVE IT YOUR WAY.
SO...
WHAT NEXT?

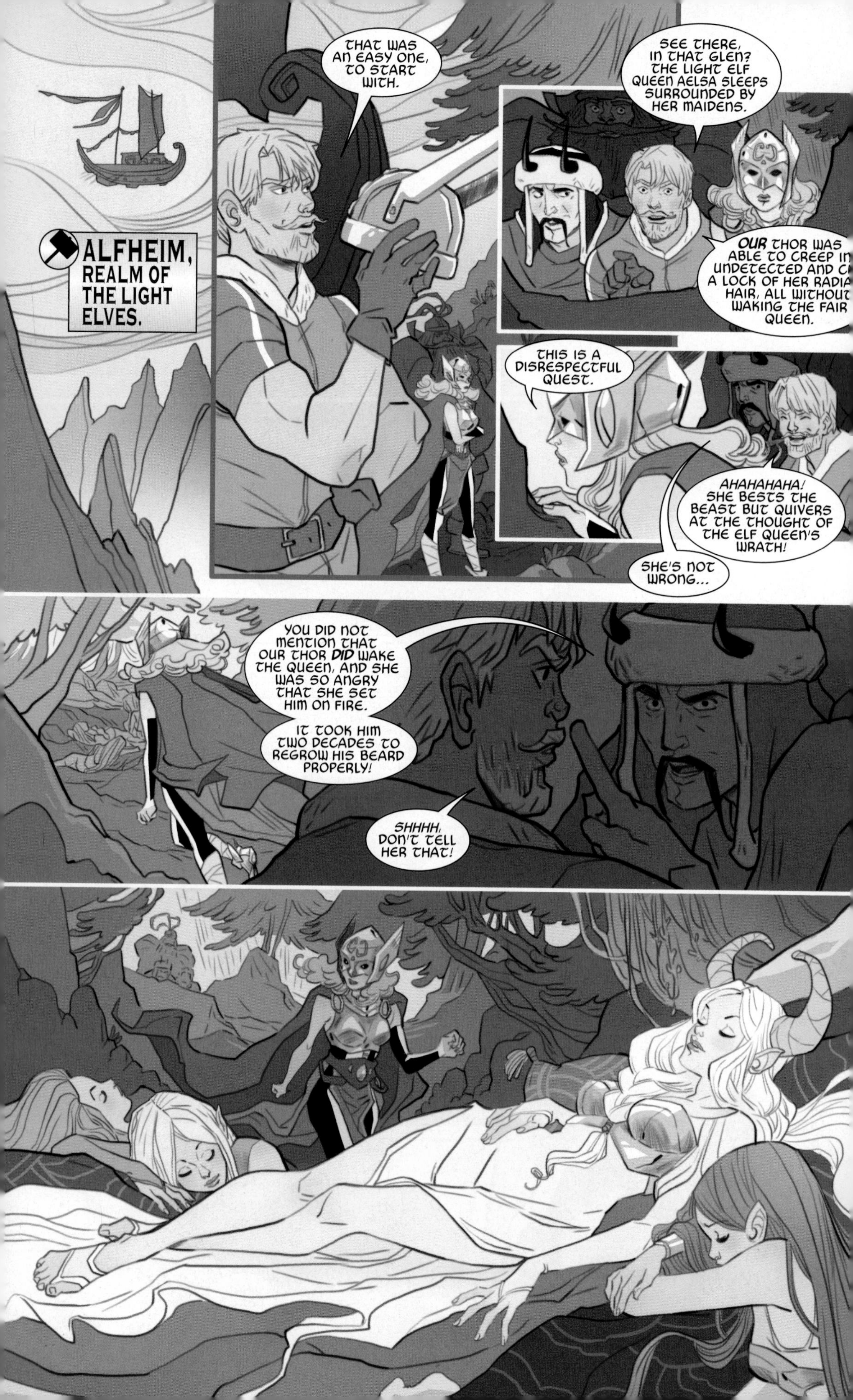

ALFHEIM, REALM OF THE LIGHT ELVES.
THAT WAS AN EASY ONE, TO START WITH.
SEE THERE, IN THAT GLEN? THE LIGHT ELF QUEEN AELSA SLEEPS SURROUNDED BY HER MAIDENS.
OUR THOR WAS ABLE TO CREEP IN UNDETECTED AND C A LOCK OF HER RADIA HAIR, ALL WITHOUT WAKING THE FAIR QUEEN.
THIS IS A DISRESPECTFUL QUEST.
AHAHAHAHA! SHE BESTS THE BEAST BUT QUIVERS AT THE THOUGHT OF THE ELF QUEEN'S WRATH!
SHE'S NOT WRONG...
YOU DID NOT MENTION THAT OUR THOR DID WAKE THE QUEEN, AND SHE WAS SO ANGRY THAT SHE SET HIM ON FIRE.
IT TOOK HIM TWO DECADES TO REGROW HIS BEARD PROPERLY!
SHHHH, DON'T TELL HER THAT!

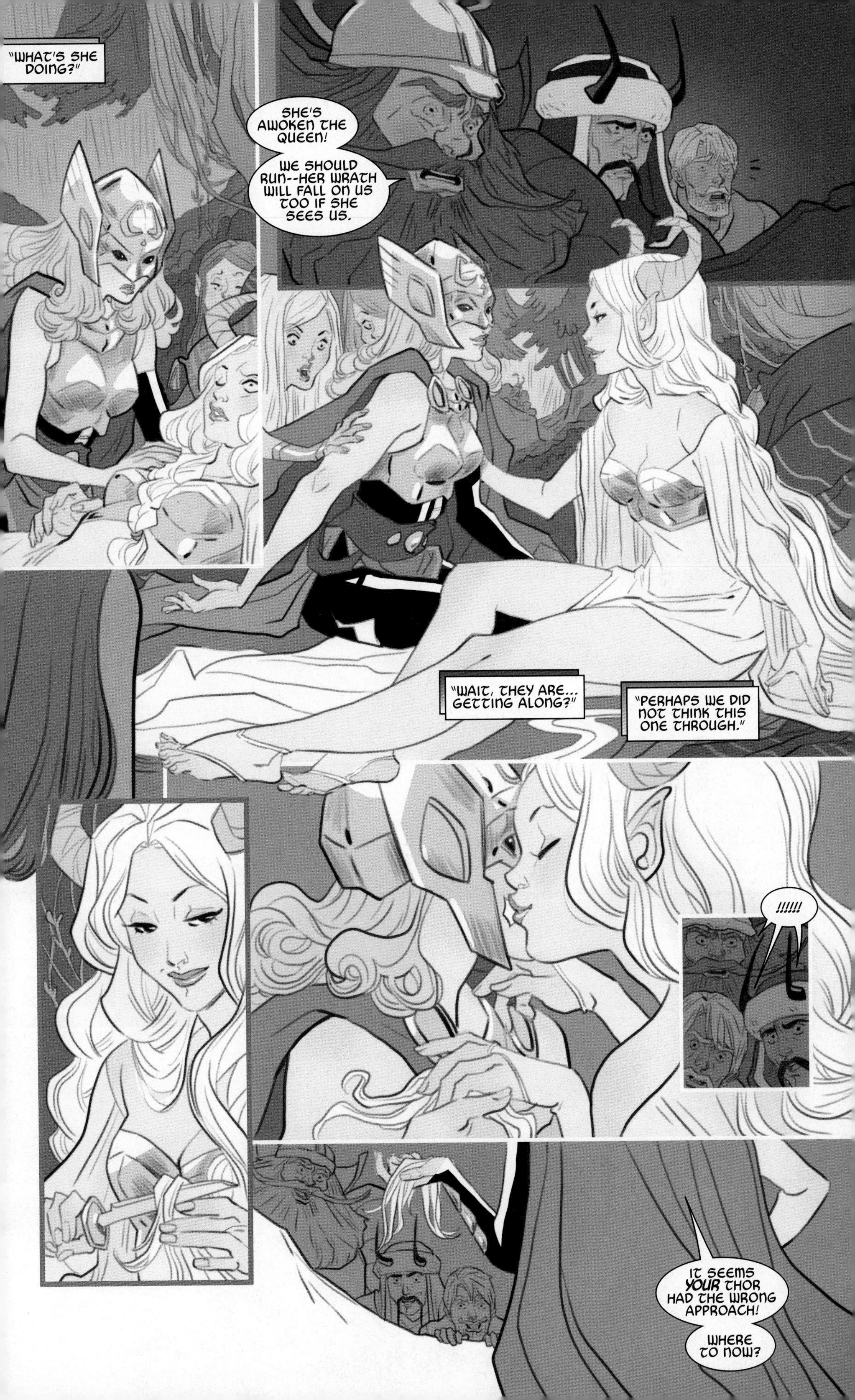
"WHAT'S SHE DOING?"
SHE'S AWOKEN THE QUEEN!
WE SHOULD RUN--HER WRATH WILL FALL ON US TOO IF SHE SEES US.
"WAIT, THEY ARE... GETTING ALONG?"
"PERHAPS WE DID NOT THINK THIS ONE THROUGH."
!!!!!!
IT SEEMS *YOUR* THOR HAD THE WRONG APPROACH!
WHERE TO NOW?

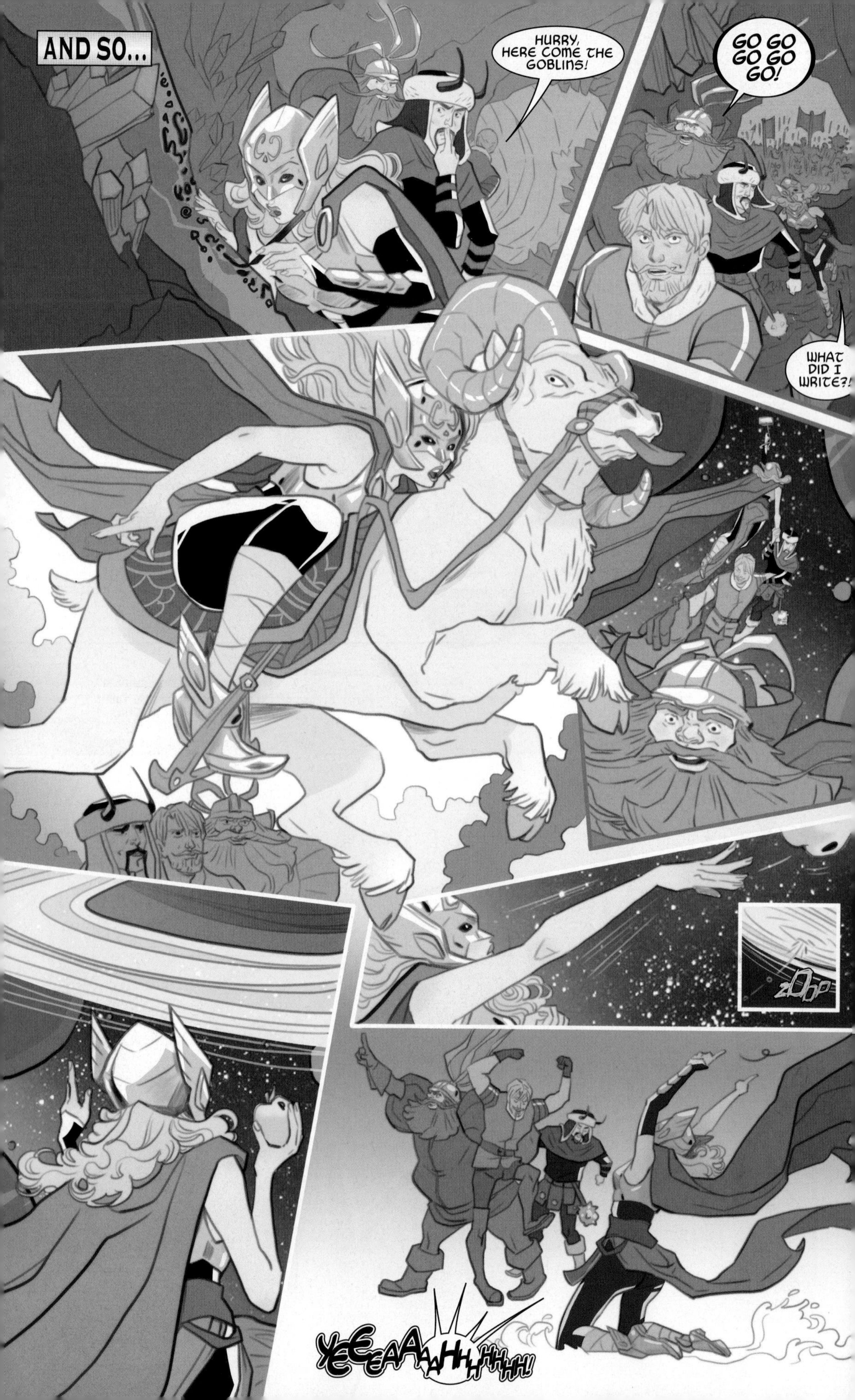
AND SO...
HURRY, HERE COME THE GOBLINS!
GO GO GO GO GO!
WHAT DID I WRITE?!
ZOOP
YEEEAAAAAHHHHHHH!

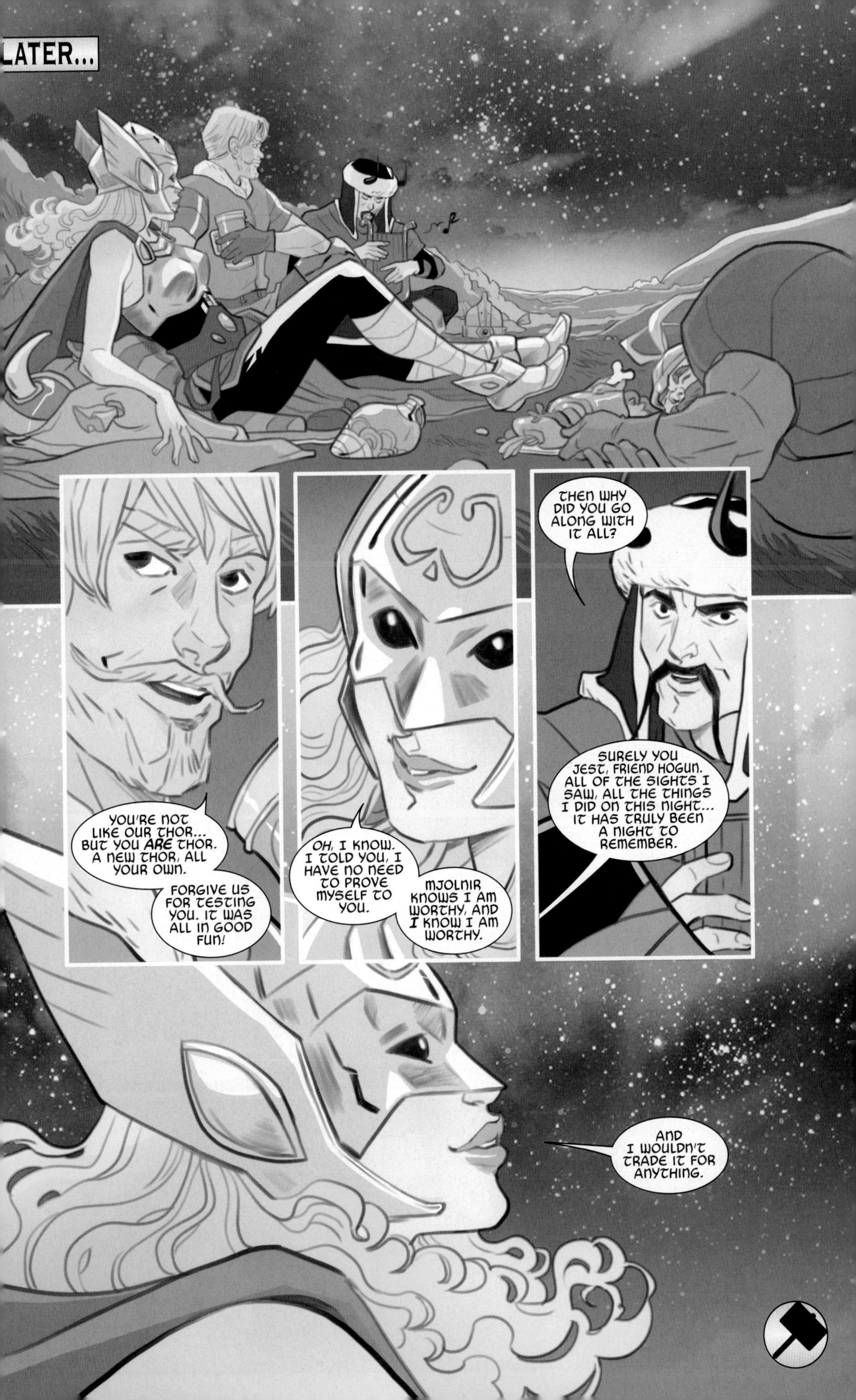
LATER...
YOU'RE NOT LIKE OUR THOR... BUT YOU ARE THOR. A NEW THOR, ALL YOUR OWN.
FORGIVE US FOR TESTING YOU. IT WAS ALL IN GOOD FUN!
OH, I KNOW. I TOLD YOU, I HAVE NO NEED TO PROVE MYSELF TO YOU.
MJOLNIR KNOWS I AM WORTHY, AND I KNOW I AM WORTHY.
THEN WHY DID YOU GO ALONG WITH IT ALL?
SURELY YOU JEST, FRIEND HOGUN. ALL OF THE SIGHTS I SAW, ALL THE THINGS I DID ON THIS NIGHT... IT HAS TRULY BEEN A NIGHT TO REMEMBER.
AND I WOULDN'T TRADE IT FOR ANYTHING.

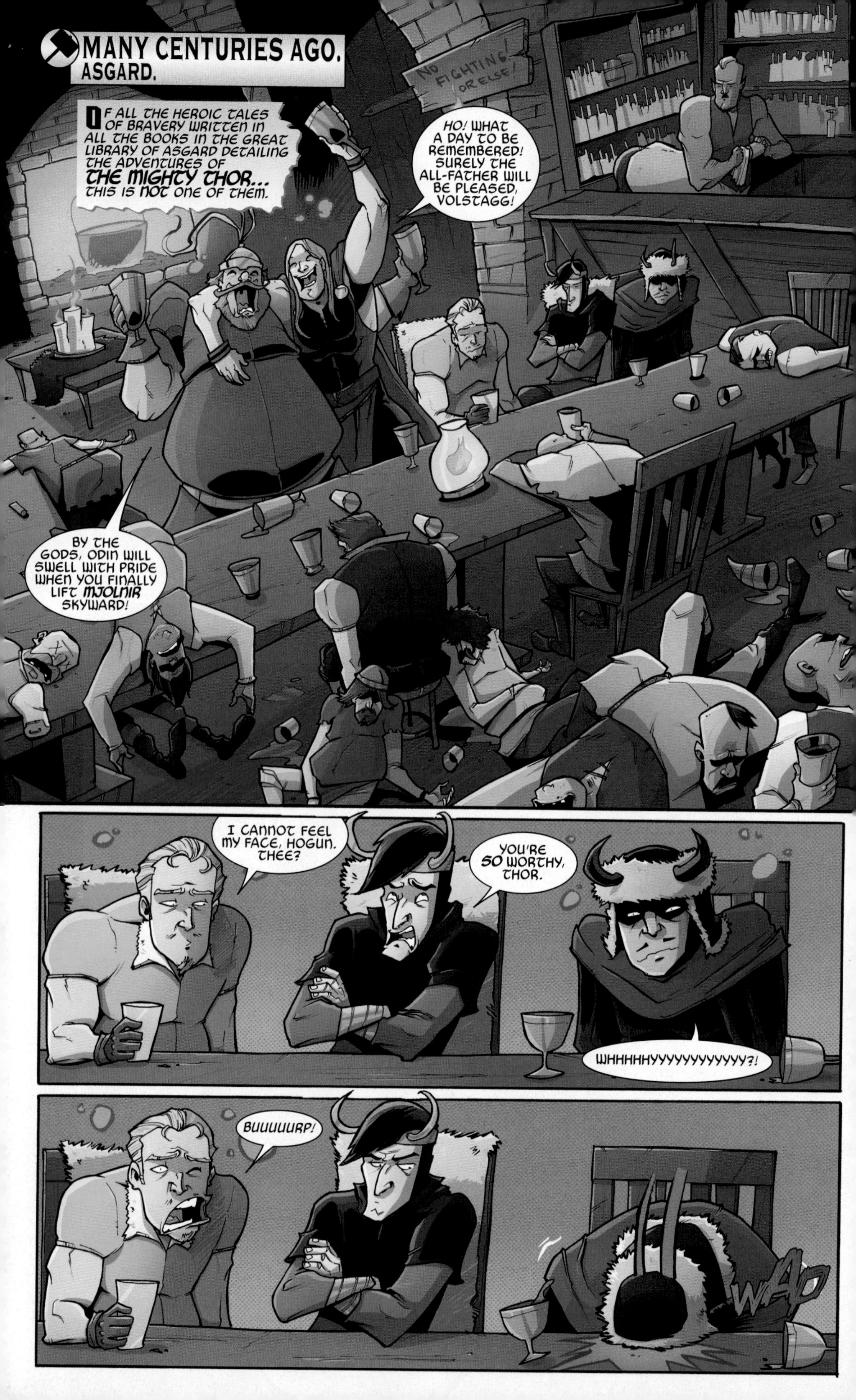
MANY CENTURIES AGO.
ASGARD.
NO FIGHTING! OR ELSE!
OF ALL THE HEROIC TALES OF BRAVERY WRITTEN IN ALL THE BOOKS IN THE GREAT LIBRARY OF ASGARD DETAILING THE ADVENTURES OF THE MIGHTY THOR... THIS IS NOT ONE OF THEM.
HO! WHAT A DAY TO BE REMEMBERED! SURELY THE ALL-FATHER WILL BE PLEASED, VOLSTAGG!
BY THE GODS, ODIN WILL SWELL WITH PRIDE WHEN YOU FINALLY LIFT MJOLNIR SKYWARD!
I CANNOT FEEL MY FACE, HOGUN. THEE?
YOU'RE SO WORTHY, THOR.
WHHHHHYYYYYYYYYYYY?!
BUUUUURP!
WAP

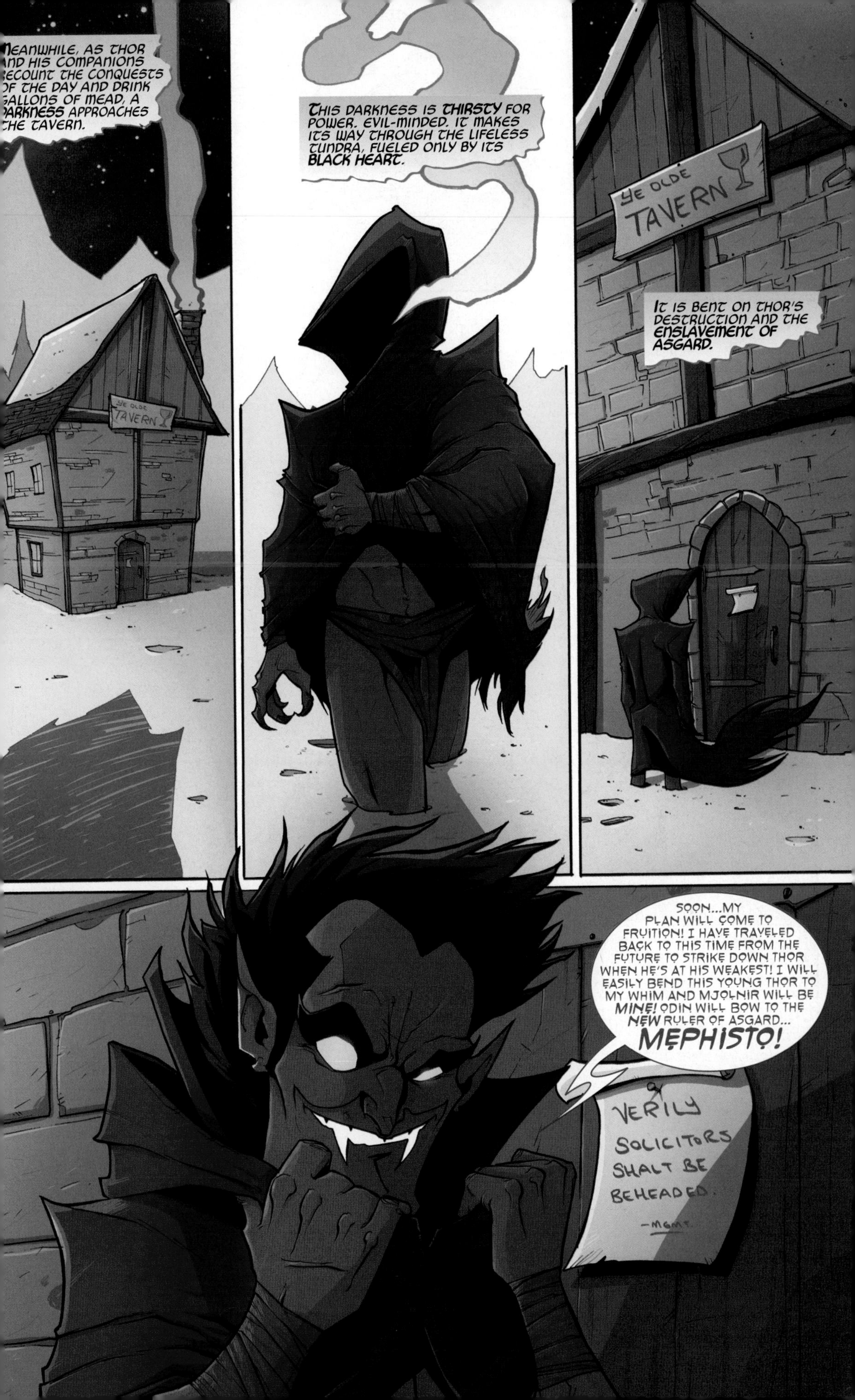
MEANWHILE, AS THOR AND HIS COMPANIONS RECOUNT THE CONQUESTS OF THE DAY AND DRINK GALLONS OF MEAD, A DARKNESS APPROACHES THE TAVERN.
YE OLDE TAVERN
THIS DARKNESS IS THIRSTY FOR POWER. EVIL-MINDED, IT MAKES ITS WAY THROUGH THE LIFELESS TUNDRA, FUELED ONLY BY ITS BLACK HEART.
YE OLDE TAVERN
IT IS BENT ON THOR'S DESTRUCTION AND THE ENSLAVEMENT OF ASGARD.
SOON...MY PLAN WILL COME TO FRUITION! I HAVE TRAVELED BACK TO THIS TIME FROM THE FUTURE TO STRIKE DOWN THOR WHEN HE'S AT HIS WEAKEST! I WILL EASILY BEND THIS YOUNG THOR TO MY WHIM AND MJOLNIR WILL BE MINE! ODIN WILL BOW TO THE NEW RULER OF ASGARD... MEPHISTO!
VERILY SOLICITORS SHALT BE BEHEADED.
-MGMT.

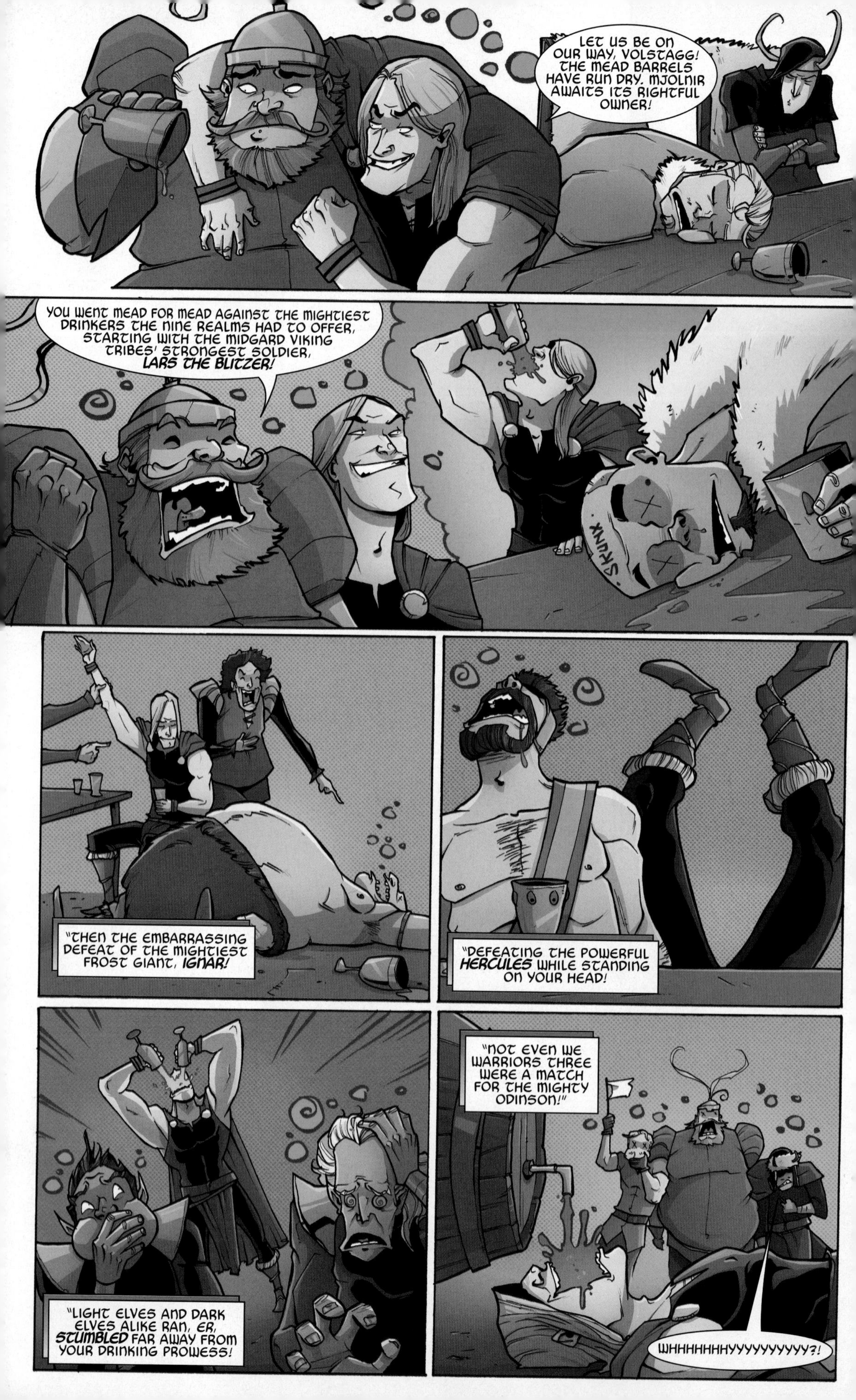
LET US BE ON OUR WAY, VOLSTAGG! THE MEAD BARRELS HAVE RUN DRY. MJOLNIR AWAITS ITS RIGHTFUL OWNER!
YOU WENT MEAD FOR MEAD AGAINST THE MIGHTIEST DRINKERS THE NINE REALMS HAD TO OFFER, STARTING WITH THE MIDGARD VIKING TRIBES' STRONGEST SOLDIER, LARS THE BLITZER!
SKUNK
"THEN THE EMBARRASSING DEFEAT OF THE MIGHTIEST FROST GIANT, IGNAR!
"DEFEATING THE POWERFUL HERCULES WHILE STANDING ON YOUR HEAD!
"LIGHT ELVES AND DARK ELVES ALIKE RAN, ER, STUMBLED FAR AWAY FROM YOUR DRINKING PROWESS!
"NOT EVEN WE WARRIORS THREE WERE A MATCH FOR THE MIGHTY ODINSON!"
WHHHHHHHYYYYYYYYYY?!

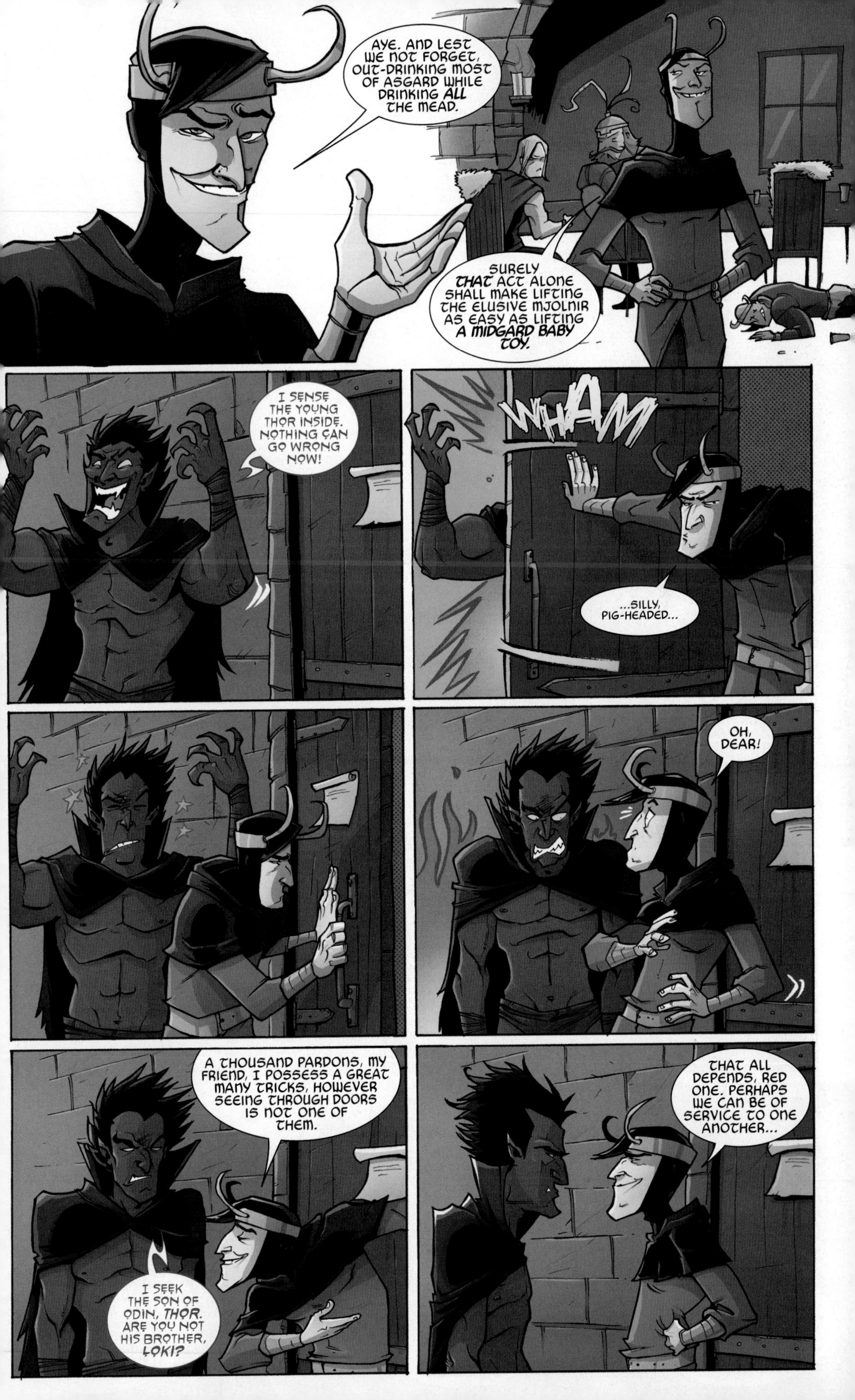
AYE. AND LEST WE NOT FORGET, OUT-DRINKING MOST OF ASGARD WHILE DRINKING ALL THE MEAD.
SURELY THAT ACT ALONE SHALL MAKE LIFTING THE ELUSIVE MJOLNIR AS EASY AS LIFTING A MIDGARD BABY TOY.
I SENSE THE YOUNG THOR INSIDE. NOTHING CAN GO WRONG NOW!
WHAM
...SILLY, PIG-HEADED...
OH, DEAR!
I SEEK THE SON OF ODIN, THOR. ARE YOU NOT HIS BROTHER, LOKI?
A THOUSAND PARDONS, MY FRIEND, I POSSESS A GREAT MANY TRICKS, HOWEVER SEEING THROUGH DOORS IS NOT ONE OF THEM.
THAT ALL DEPENDS, RED ONE. PERHAPS WE CAN BE OF SERVICE TO ONE ANOTHER...

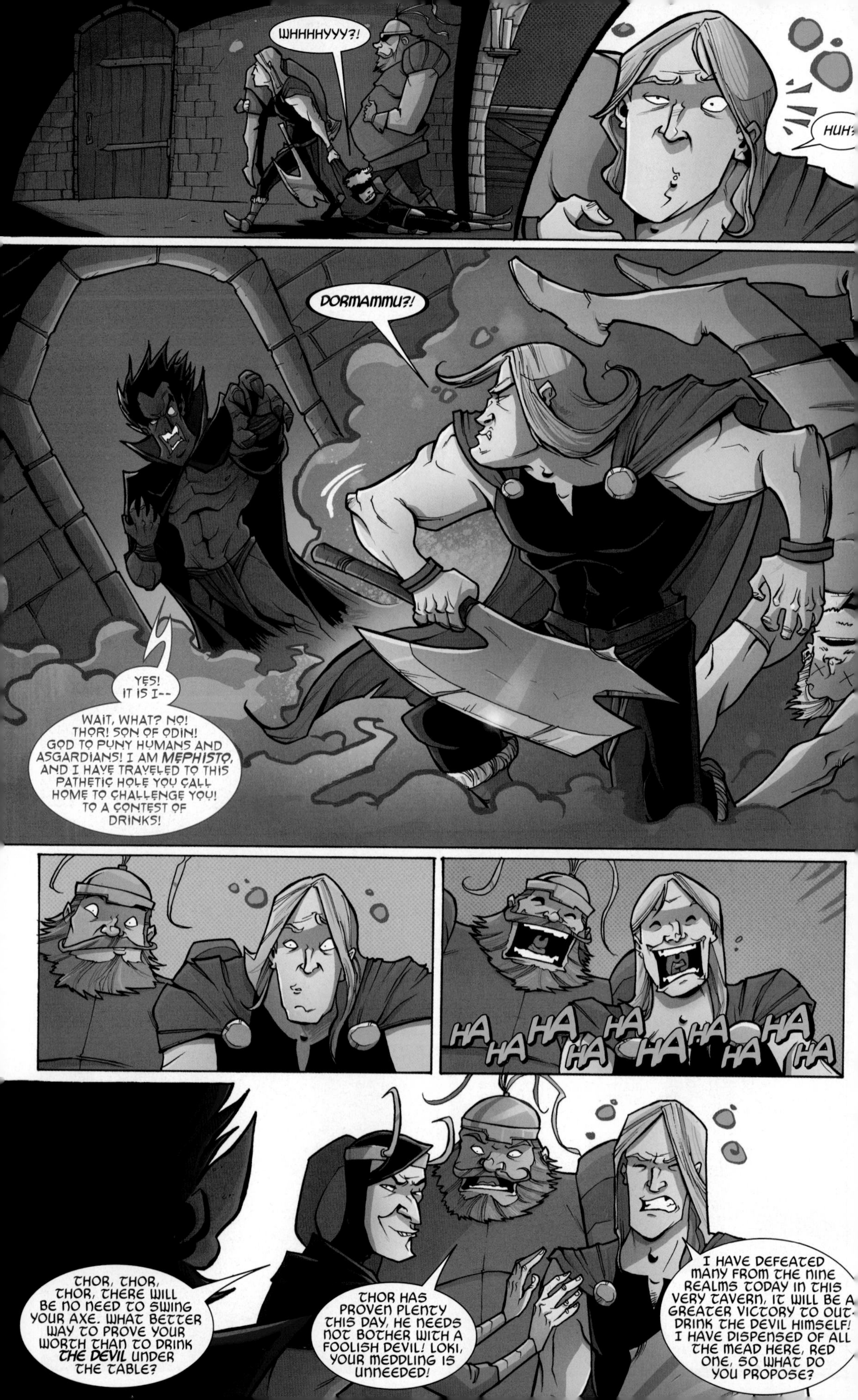
WHHHHYYY?!
HUH?
DORMAMMU?!
YES! IT IS I--
WAIT, WHAT? NO! THOR! SON OF ODIN! GOD TO PUNY HUMANS AND ASGARDIANS! I AM MEPHISTO, AND I HAVE TRAVELED TO THIS PATHETIC HOLE YOU CALL HOME TO CHALLENGE YOU! TO A CONTEST OF DRINKS!
HA HA HA HA HA HA HA HA HA HA HA
THOR, THOR, THOR, THERE WILL BE NO NEED TO SWING YOUR AXE. WHAT BETTER WAY TO PROVE YOUR WORTH THAN TO DRINK THE DEVIL UNDER THE TABLE?
THOR HAS PROVEN PLENTY THIS DAY, HE NEEDS NOT BOTHER WITH A FOOLISH DEVIL! LOKI, YOUR MEDDLING IS UNNEEDED!
I HAVE DEFEATED MANY FROM THE NINE REALMS TODAY IN THIS VERY TAVERN, IT WILL BE A GREATER VICTORY TO OUT-DRINK THE DEVIL HIMSELF! I HAVE DISPENSED OF ALL THE MEAD HERE, RED ONE, SO WHAT DO YOU PROPOSE?

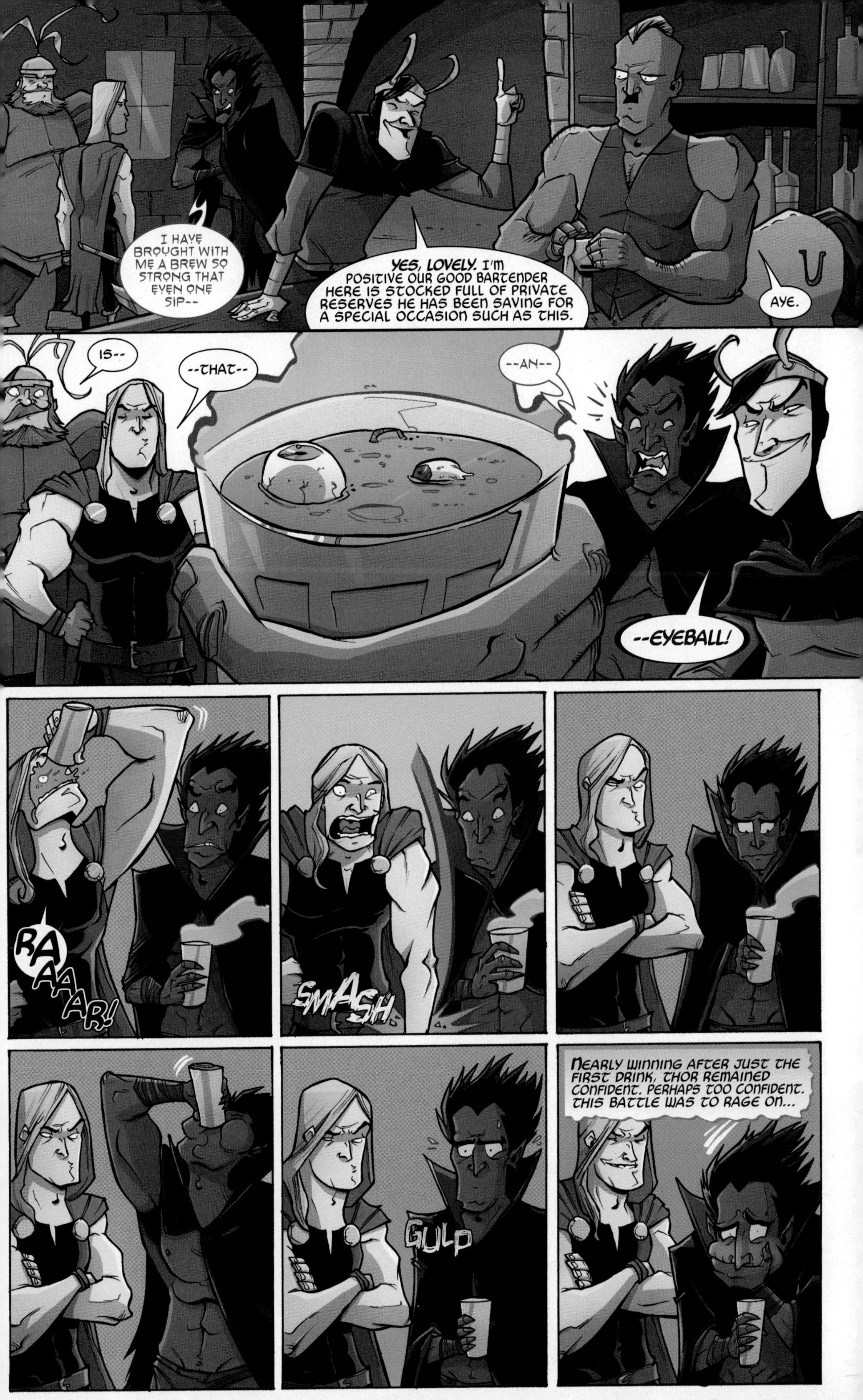
I HAVE BROUGHT WITH ME A BREW SO STRONG THAT EVEN ONE SIP--
YES, LOVELY. I'M POSITIVE OUR GOOD BARTENDER HERE IS STOCKED FULL OF PRIVATE RESERVES HE HAS BEEN SAVING FOR A SPECIAL OCCASION SUCH AS THIS.
AYE.
IS--
--THAT--
--AN--
--EYEBALL!
RAAAAR!
SMASH
NEARLY WINNING AFTER JUST THE FIRST DRINK, THOR REMAINED CONFIDENT. PERHAPS TOO CONFIDENT. THIS BATTLE WAS TO RAGE ON...
GULP

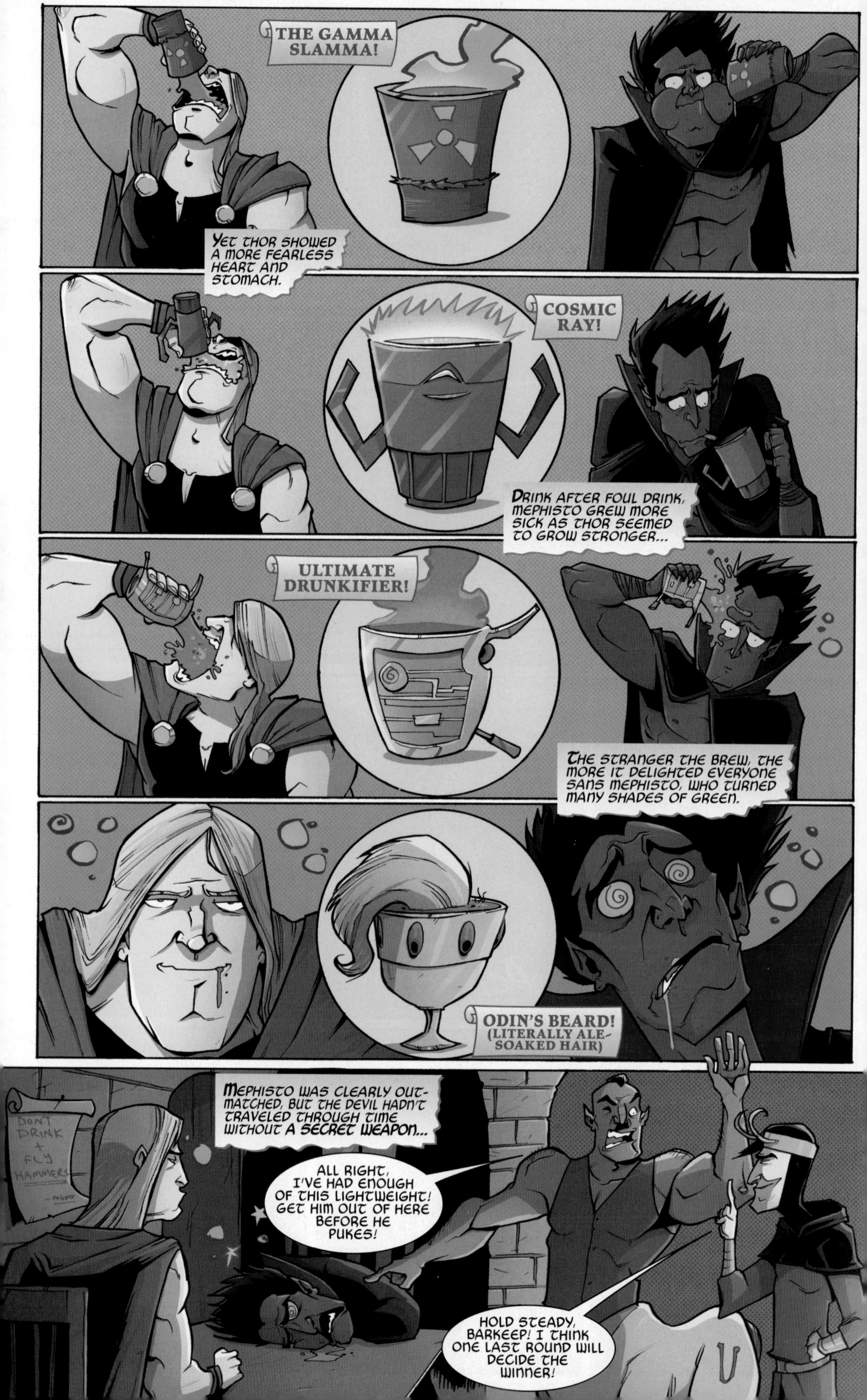
THE GAMMA SLAMMA!
YET THOR SHOWED A MORE FEARLESS HEART AND STOMACH.
COSMIC RAY!
DRINK AFTER FOUL DRINK, MEPHISTO GREW MORE SICK AS THOR SEEMED TO GROW STRONGER...
ULTIMATE DRUNKIFIER!
THE STRANGER THE BREW, THE MORE IT DELIGHTED EVERYONE SANS MEPHISTO, WHO TURNED MANY SHADES OF GREEN.
ODIN'S BEARD! (LITERALLY ALE-SOAKED HAIR)
MEPHISTO WAS CLEARLY OUT-MATCHED, BUT THE DEVIL HADN'T TRAVELED THROUGH TIME WITHOUT A SECRET WEAPON...
DONT DRINK + FLY HAMMERS
ALL RIGHT, I'VE HAD ENOUGH OF THIS LIGHTWEIGHT! GET HIM OUT OF HERE BEFORE HE PUKES!
HOLD STEADY, BARKEEP! I THINK ONE LAST ROUND WILL DECIDE THE WINNER!

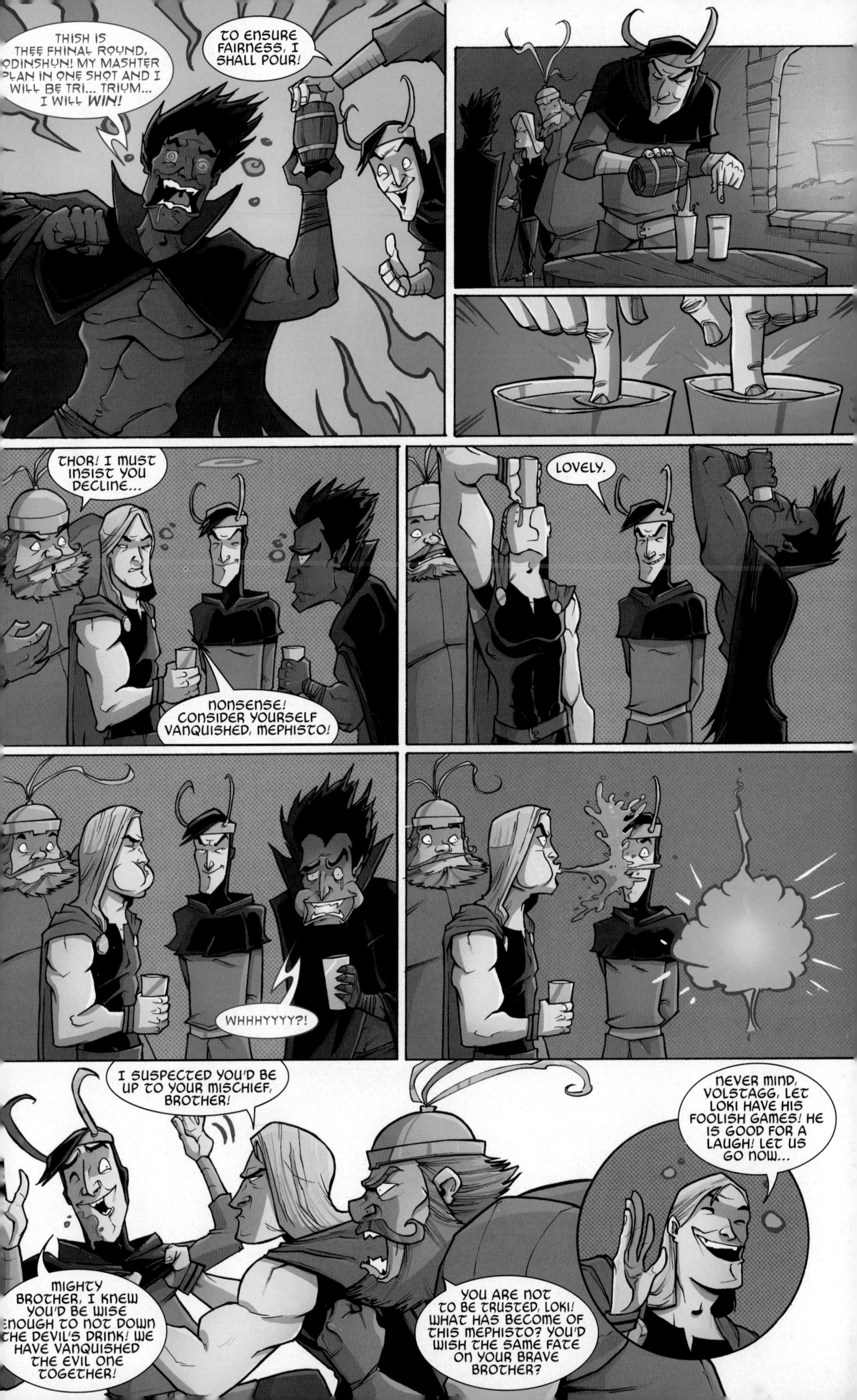
THISH IS THEE FHINAL ROUND, ODINSHUN! MY MASHTER PLAN IN ONE SHOT AND I WILL BE TRI... TRIUM... I WILL WIN!
TO ENSURE FAIRNESS, I SHALL POUR!
THOR! I MUST INSIST YOU DECLINE...
NONSENSE! CONSIDER YOURSELF VANQUISHED, MEPHISTO!
LOVELY.
WHHHYYYY?!
I SUSPECTED YOU'D BE UP TO YOUR MISCHIEF, BROTHER!
MIGHTY BROTHER, I KNEW YOU'D BE WISE ENOUGH TO NOT DOWN THE DEVIL'S DRINK! WE HAVE VANQUISHED THE EVIL ONE TOGETHER!
YOU ARE NOT TO BE TRUSTED, LOKI! WHAT HAS BECOME OF THIS MEPHISTO? YOU'D WISH THE SAME FATE ON YOUR BRAVE BROTHER?
NEVER MIND, VOLSTAGG, LET LOKI HAVE HIS FOOLISH GAMES! HE IS GOOD FOR A LAUGH! LET US GO NOW...

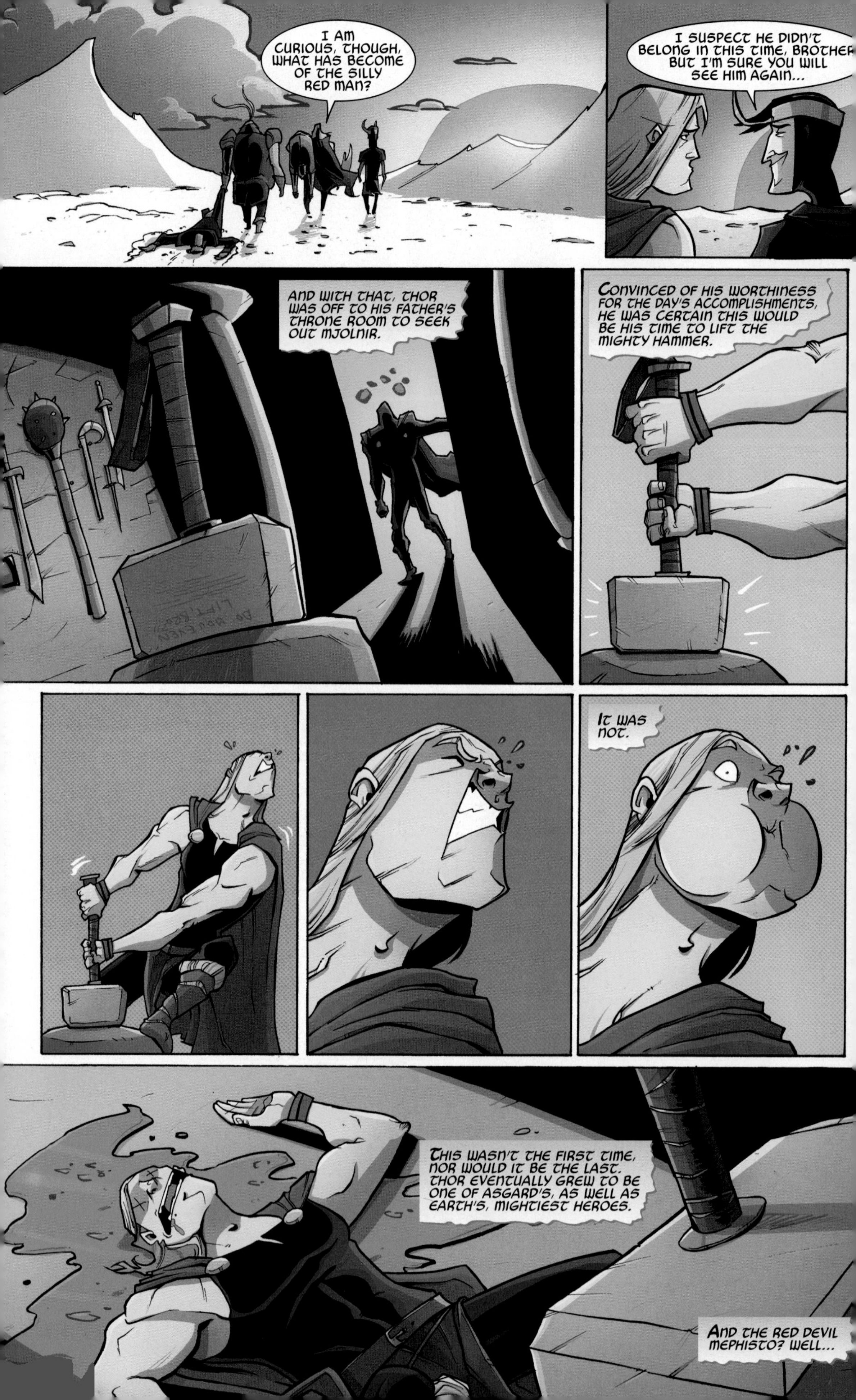

I AM CURIOUS, THOUGH, WHAT HAS BECOME OF THE SILLY RED MAN?
I SUSPECT HE DIDN'T BELONG IN THIS TIME, BROTHER BUT I'M SURE YOU WILL SEE HIM AGAIN...
AND WITH THAT, THOR WAS OFF TO HIS FATHER'S THRONE ROOM TO SEEK OUT MJOLNIR.
CONVINCED OF HIS WORTHINESS FOR THE DAY'S ACCOMPLISHMENTS, HE WAS CERTAIN THIS WOULD BE HIS TIME TO LIFT THE MIGHTY HAMMER.
IT WAS NOT.
THIS WASN'T THE FIRST TIME, NOR WOULD IT BE THE LAST. THOR EVENTUALLY GREW TO BE ONE OF ASGARD'S, AS WELL AS EARTH'S, MIGHTIEST HEROES.
AND THE RED DEVIL MEPHISTO? WELL...

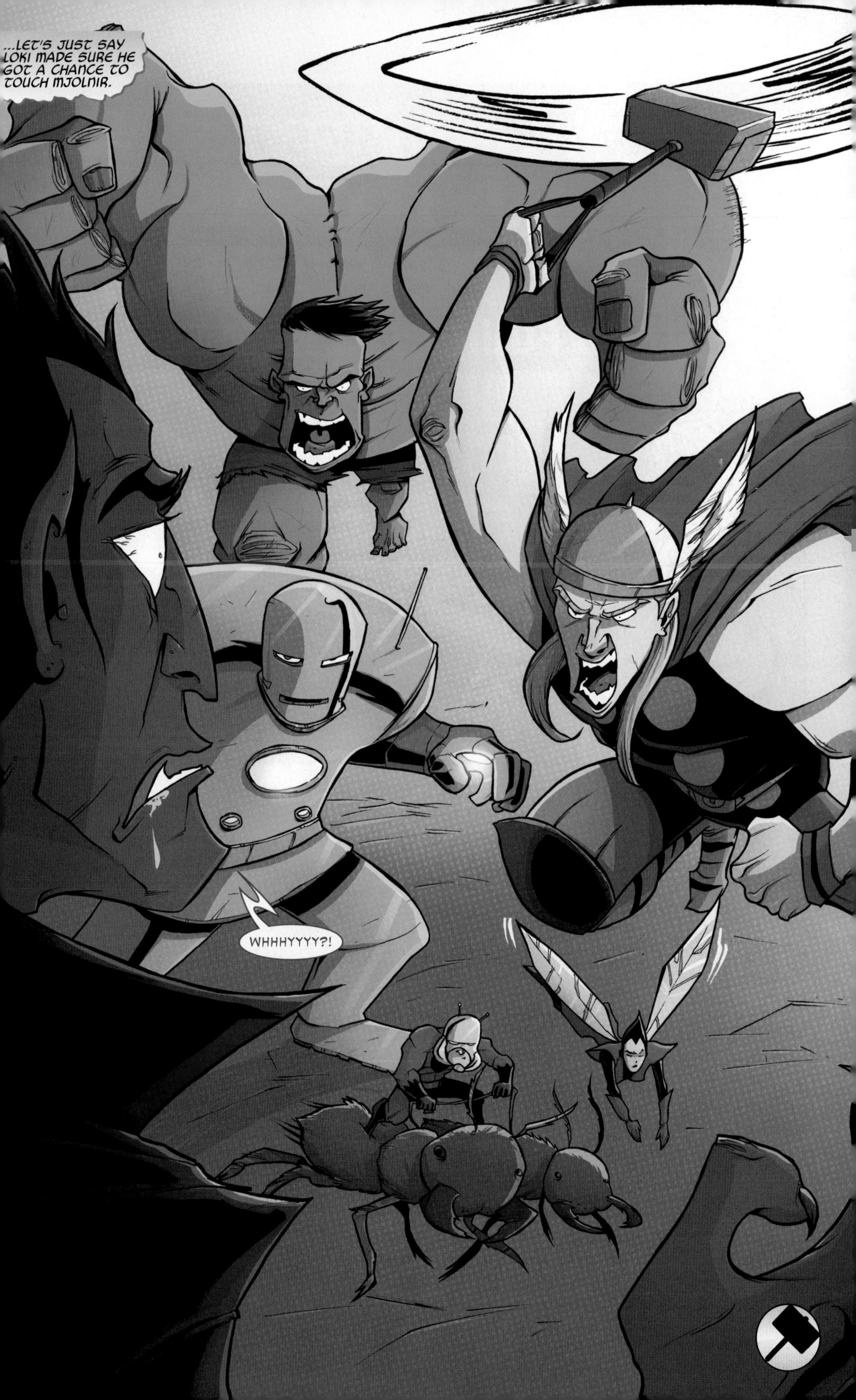
...LET'S JUST SAY LOKI MADE SURE HE GOT A CHANCE TO TOUCH MJOLNIR.
WHHHYYYY?!

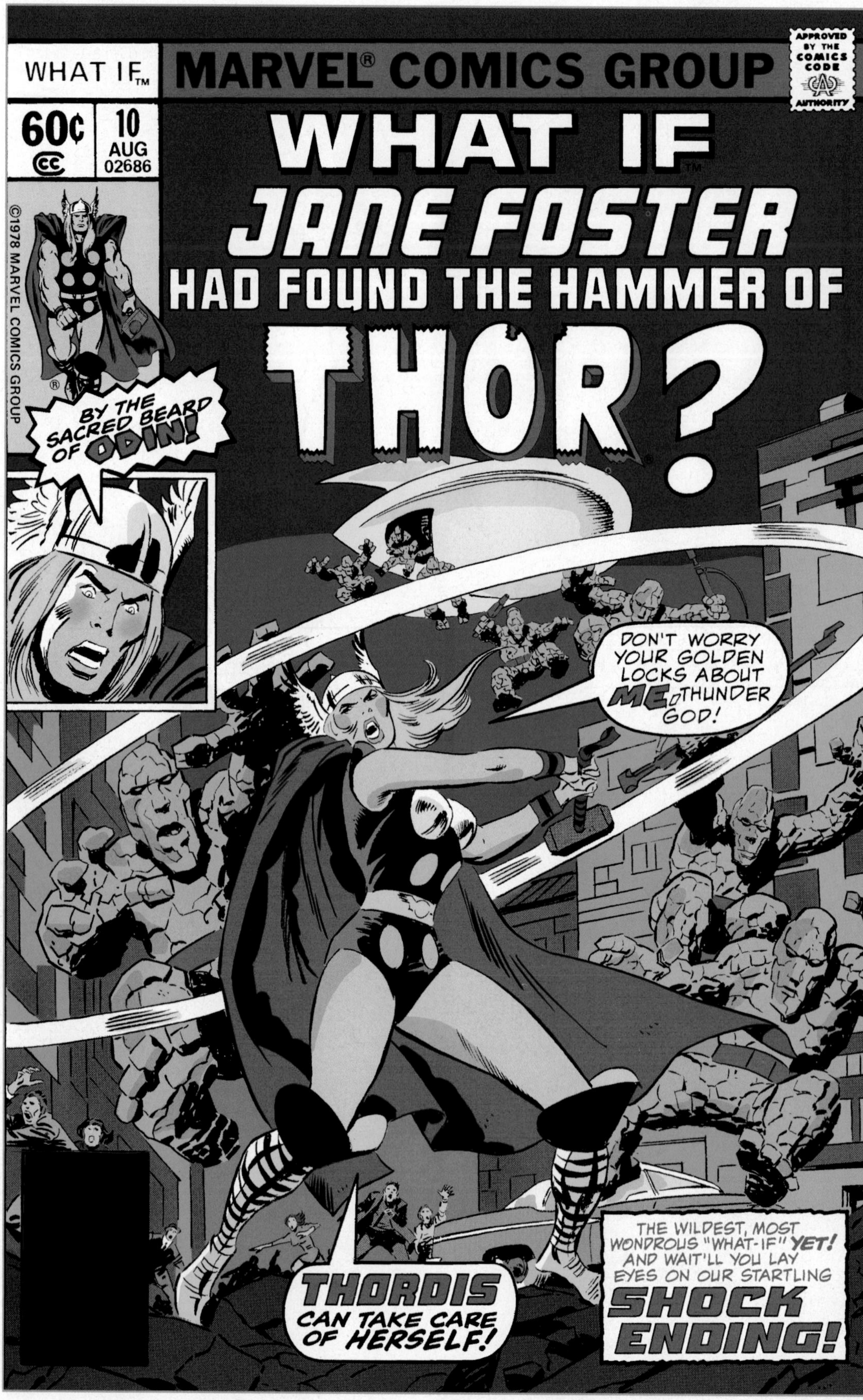
WHAT IF™
MARVEL® COMICS GROUP
APPROVED BY THE COMICS CODE AUTHORITY
60¢
10 AUG 02686
WHAT IF™
JANE FOSTER
HAD FOUND THE HAMMER OF
THOR?
©1978 MARVEL COMICS GROUP
BY THE SACRED BEARD OF ODIN!
DON'T WORRY YOUR GOLDEN LOCKS ABOUT ME, THUNDER GOD!
THORDIS CAN TAKE CARE OF HERSELF!
THE WILDEST, MOST WONDROUS "WHAT-IF" YET! AND WAIT'LL YOU LAY EYES ON OUR STARTLING SHOCK ENDING!

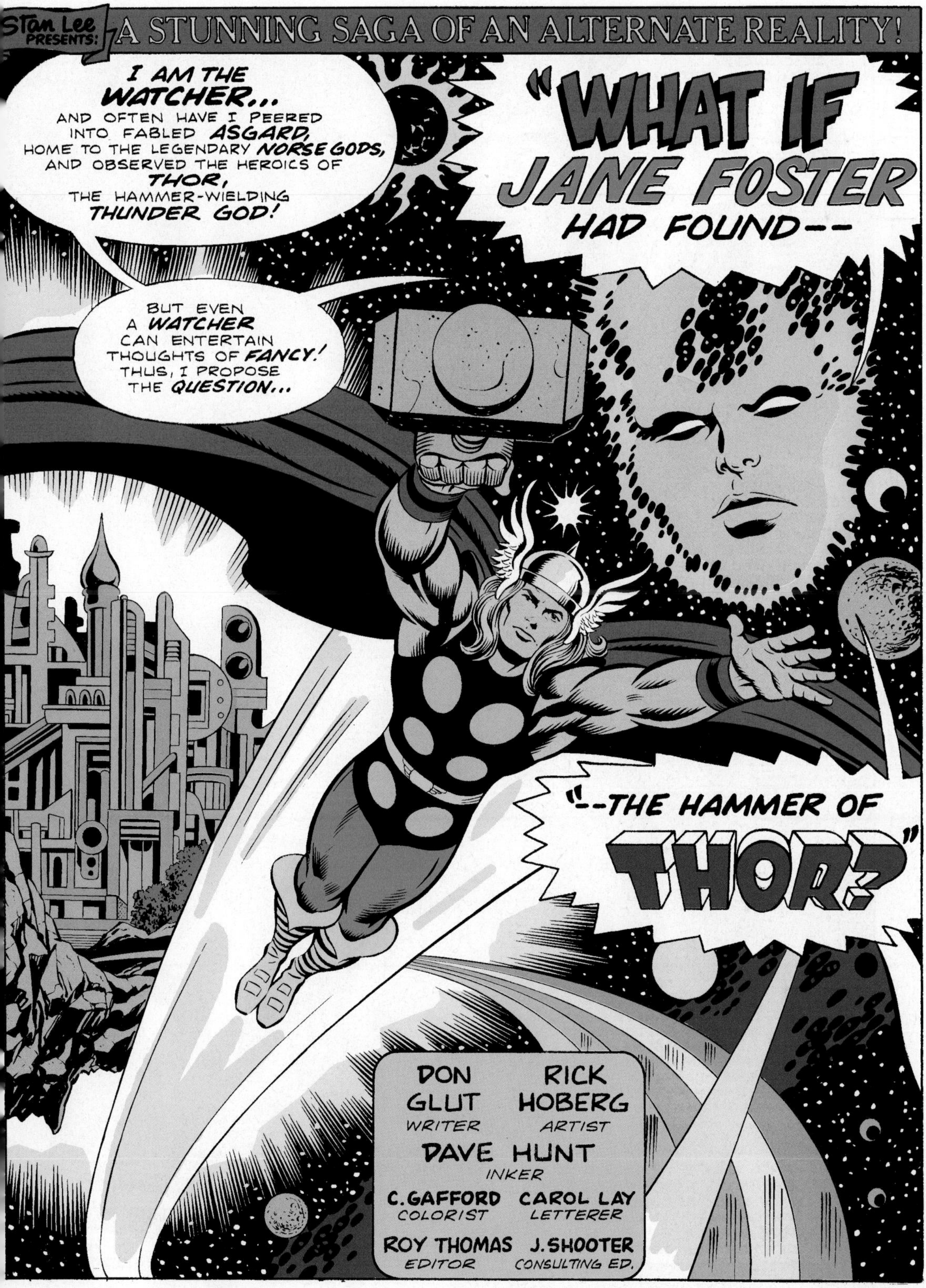

Stan Lee PRESENTS: A STUNNING SAGA OF AN ALTERNATE REALITY!
I AM THE WATCHER... AND OFTEN HAVE I PEERED INTO FABLED ASGARD, HOME TO THE LEGENDARY NORSE GODS, AND OBSERVED THE HEROICS OF THOR, THE HAMMER-WIELDING THUNDER GOD!
BUT EVEN A WATCHER CAN ENTERTAIN THOUGHTS OF FANCY! THUS, I PROPOSE THE QUESTION...
"WHAT IF JANE FOSTER HAD FOUND--
"--THE HAMMER OF THOR?"
DON GLUT WRITER
RICK HOBERG ARTIST
DAVE HUNT INKER
C. GAFFORD COLORIST
CAROL LAY LETTERER
ROY THOMAS EDITOR
J. SHOOTER CONSULTING ED.

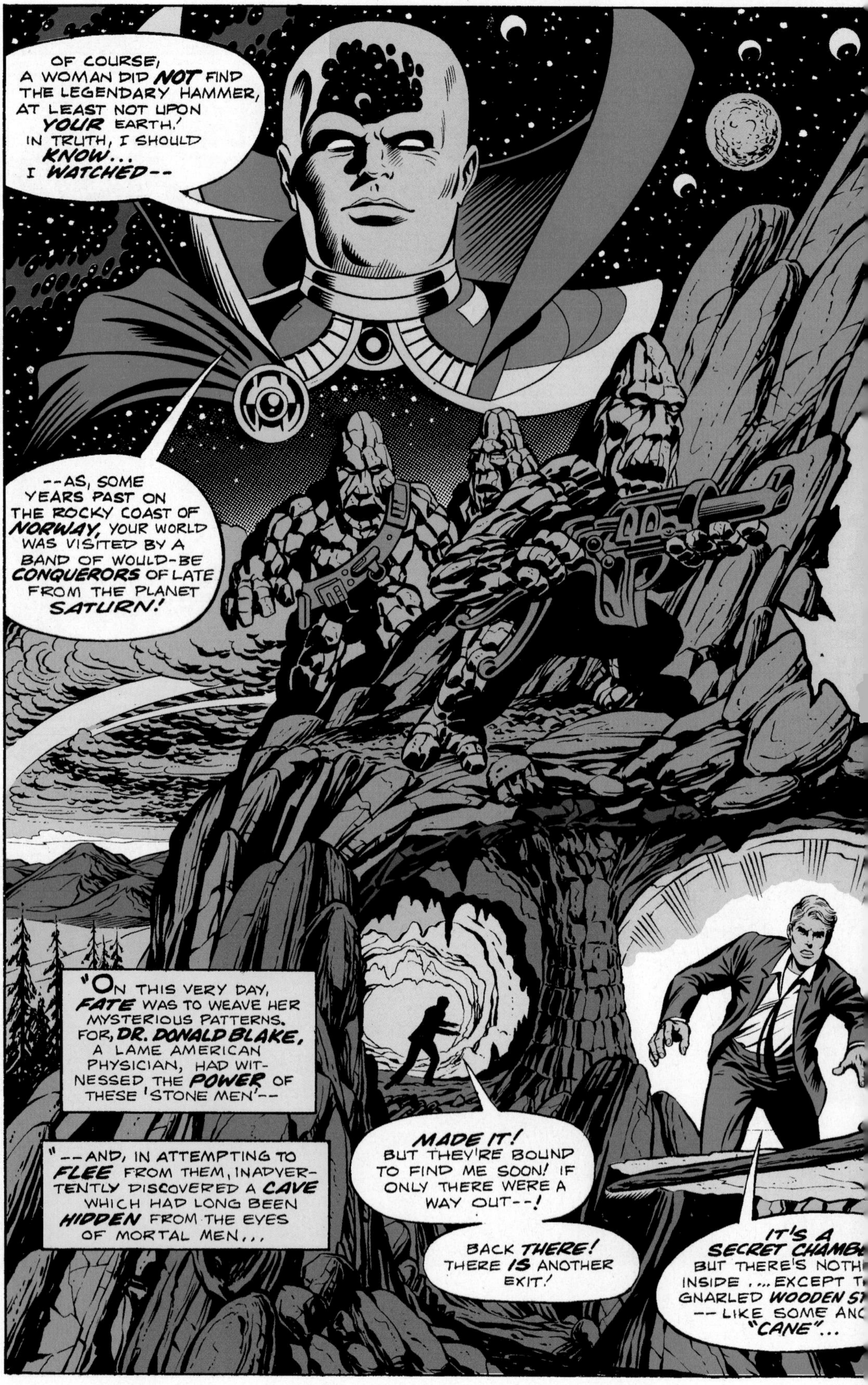
OF COURSE, A WOMAN DID NOT FIND THE LEGENDARY HAMMER, AT LEAST NOT UPON YOUR EARTH! IN TRUTH, I SHOULD KNOW... I WATCHED--
--AS, SOME YEARS PAST ON THE ROCKY COAST OF NORWAY, YOUR WORLD WAS VISITED BY A BAND OF WOULD-BE CONQUERORS OF LATE FROM THE PLANET SATURN!
"ON THIS VERY DAY, FATE WAS TO WEAVE HER MYSTERIOUS PATTERNS. FOR, DR. DONALD BLAKE, A LAME AMERICAN PHYSICIAN, HAD WITNESSED THE POWER OF THESE 'STONE MEN'--
"--AND, IN ATTEMPTING TO FLEE FROM THEM, INADVERTENTLY DISCOVERED A CAVE WHICH HAD LONG BEEN HIDDEN FROM THE EYES OF MORTAL MEN...
MADE IT! BUT THEY'RE BOUND TO FIND ME SOON! IF ONLY THERE WERE A WAY OUT--!
BACK THERE! THERE IS ANOTHER EXIT!

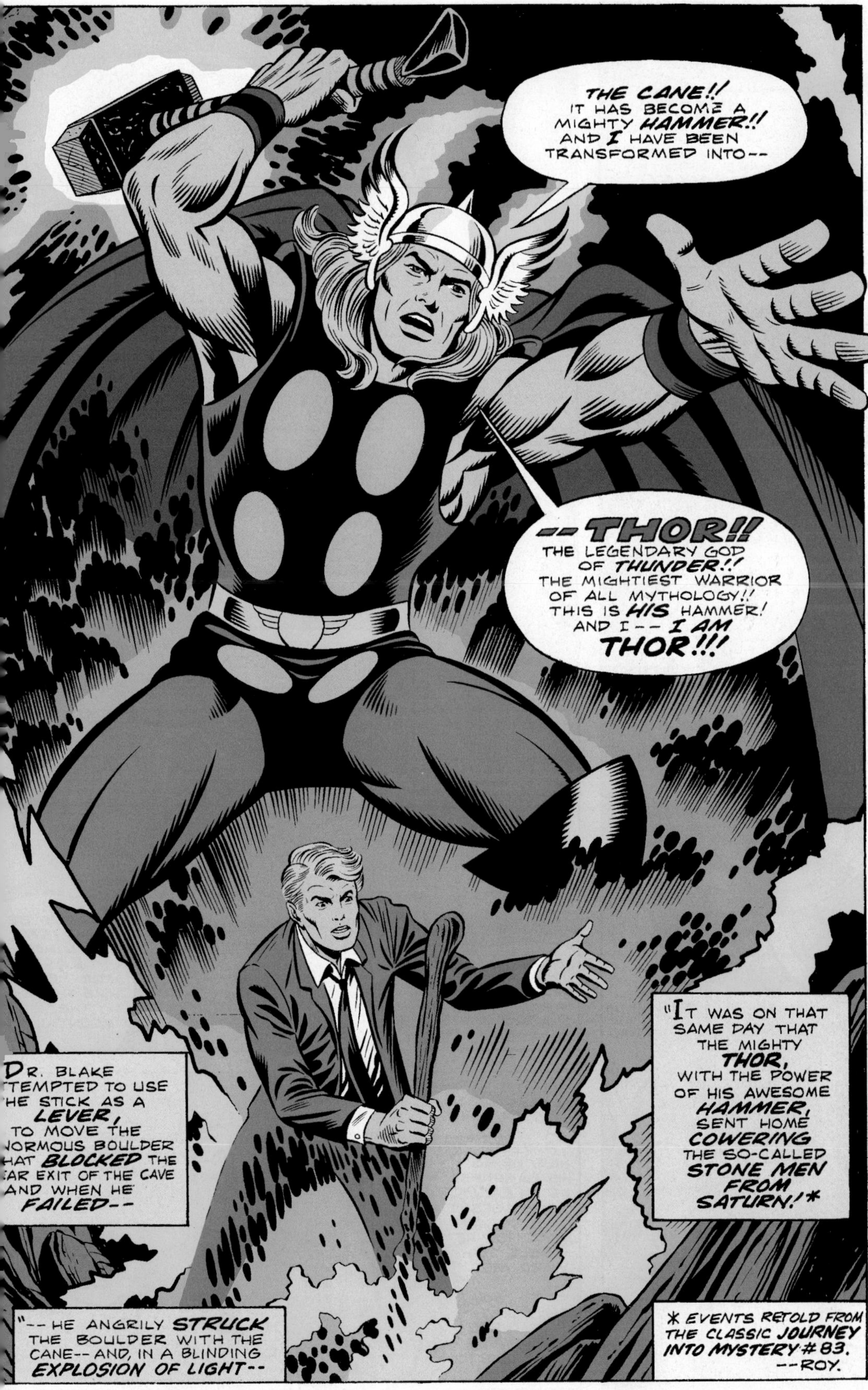
THE CANE!! IT HAS BECOME A MIGHTY HAMMER!! AND I HAVE BEEN TRANSFORMED INTO--
--THOR!! THE LEGENDARY GOD OF THUNDER!! THE MIGHTIEST WARRIOR OF ALL MYTHOLOGY!! THIS IS HIS HAMMER! AND I -- I AM THOR!!!
DR. BLAKE TEMPTED TO USE HE STICK AS A LEVER, TO MOVE THE NORMOUS BOULDER HAT BLOCKED THE EAR EXIT OF THE CAVE AND WHEN HE FAILED--
"-- HE ANGRILY STRUCK THE BOULDER WITH THE CANE-- AND, IN A BLINDING EXPLOSION OF LIGHT--
"IT WAS ON THAT SAME DAY THAT THE MIGHTY THOR, WITH THE POWER OF HIS AWESOME HAMMER, SENT HOME COWERING THE SO-CALLED STONE MEN FROM SATURN!*
* EVENTS RETOLD FROM THE CLASSIC JOURNEY INTO MYSTERY #83. --ROY.

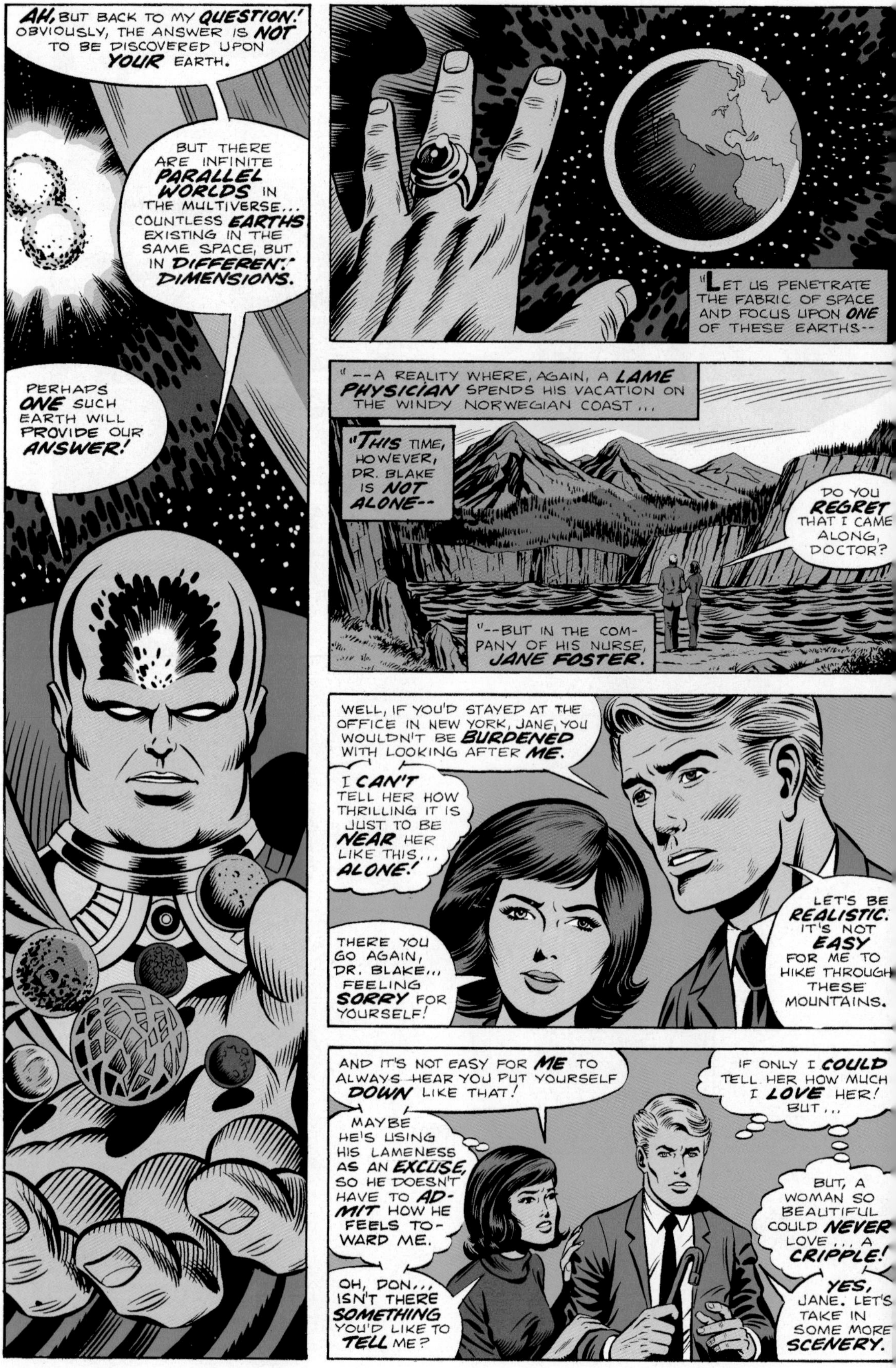
AH, BUT BACK TO MY QUESTION! OBVIOUSLY, THE ANSWER IS NOT TO BE DISCOVERED UPON YOUR EARTH.
BUT THERE ARE INFINITE PARALLEL WORLDS IN THE MULTIVERSE... COUNTLESS EARTHS EXISTING IN THE SAME SPACE, BUT IN DIFFERENT DIMENSIONS.
PERHAPS ONE SUCH EARTH WILL PROVIDE OUR ANSWER!
"LET US PENETRATE THE FABRIC OF SPACE AND FOCUS UPON ONE OF THESE EARTHS--
"--A REALITY WHERE, AGAIN, A LAME PHYSICIAN SPENDS HIS VACATION ON THE WINDY NORWEGIAN COAST...
"THIS TIME, HOWEVER, DR. BLAKE IS NOT ALONE--
"--BUT IN THE COMPANY OF HIS NURSE, JANE FOSTER.
DO YOU REGRET THAT I CAME ALONG, DOCTOR?
WELL, IF YOU'D STAYED AT THE OFFICE IN NEW YORK, JANE, YOU WOULDN'T BE BURDENED WITH LOOKING AFTER ME.
I CAN'T TELL HER HOW THRILLING IT IS JUST TO BE NEAR HER LIKE THIS... ALONE!
THERE YOU GO AGAIN, DR. BLAKE... FEELING SORRY FOR YOURSELF!
LET'S BE REALISTIC. IT'S NOT EASY FOR ME TO HIKE THROUGH THESE MOUNTAINS.
AND IT'S NOT EASY FOR ME TO ALWAYS HEAR YOU PUT YOURSELF DOWN LIKE THAT!
MAYBE HE'S USING HIS LAMENESS AS AN EXCUSE, SO HE DOESN'T HAVE TO ADMIT HOW HE FEELS TOWARD ME.
OH, DON... ISN'T THERE SOMETHING YOU'D LIKE TO TELL ME?
IF ONLY I COULD TELL HER HOW MUCH I LOVE HER! BUT...
BUT, A WOMAN SO BEAUTIFUL COULD NEVER LOVE... A CRIPPLE!
YES, JANE. LET'S TAKE IN SOME MORE SCENERY.

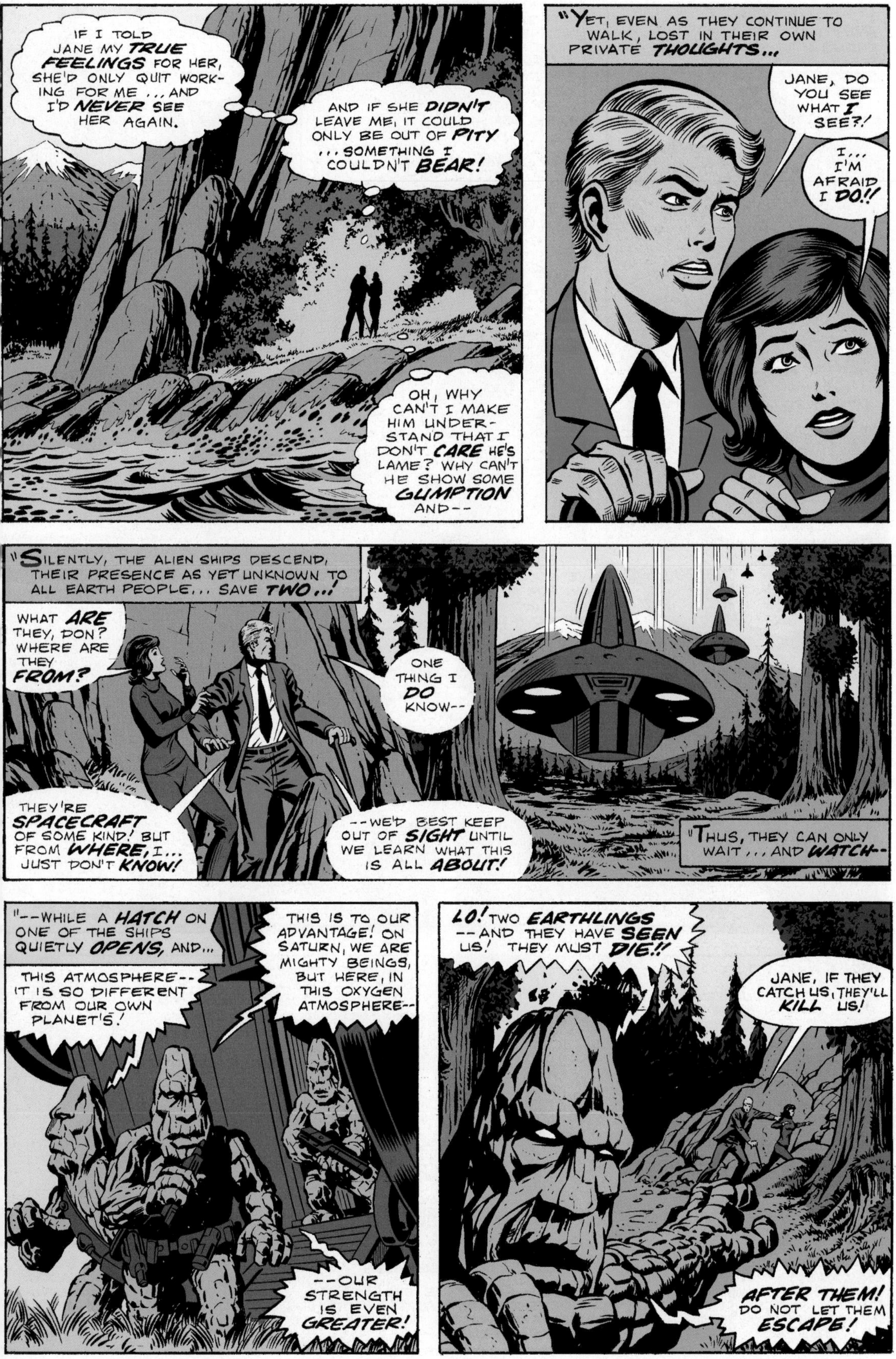
IF I TOLD JANE MY TRUE FEELINGS FOR HER, SHE'D ONLY QUIT WORKING FOR ME ..., AND I'D NEVER SEE HER AGAIN.
AND IF SHE DIDN'T LEAVE ME, IT COULD ONLY BE OUT OF PITY ... SOMETHING I COULDN'T BEAR!
OH, WHY CAN'T I MAKE HIM UNDERSTAND THAT I DON'T CARE HE'S LAME? WHY CAN'T HE SHOW SOME GUMPTION AND--
"YET, EVEN AS THEY CONTINUE TO WALK, LOST IN THEIR OWN PRIVATE THOUGHTS...
JANE, DO YOU SEE WHAT I SEE?!
I... I'M AFRAID I DO!!
"SILENTLY, THE ALIEN SHIPS DESCEND, THEIR PRESENCE AS YET UNKNOWN TO ALL EARTH PEOPLE... SAVE TWO...!
WHAT ARE THEY, DON? WHERE ARE THEY FROM?
ONE THING I DO KNOW--
THEY'RE SPACECRAFT OF SOME KIND! BUT FROM WHERE, I... JUST DON'T KNOW!
--WE'D BEST KEEP OUT OF SIGHT UNTIL WE LEARN WHAT THIS IS ALL ABOUT!
"THUS, THEY CAN ONLY WAIT ... AND WATCH--
"--WHILE A HATCH ON ONE OF THE SHIPS QUIETLY OPENS, AND...
THIS ATMOSPHERE-- IT IS SO DIFFERENT FROM OUR OWN PLANET'S!
THIS IS TO OUR ADVANTAGE! ON SATURN, WE ARE MIGHTY BEINGS, BUT HERE, IN THIS OXYGEN ATMOSPHERE--
--OUR STRENGTH IS EVEN GREATER!
LO! TWO EARTHLINGS --AND THEY HAVE SEEN US! THEY MUST DIE!!
JANE, IF THEY CATCH US, THEY'LL KILL US!
AFTER THEM! DO NOT LET THEM ESCAPE!

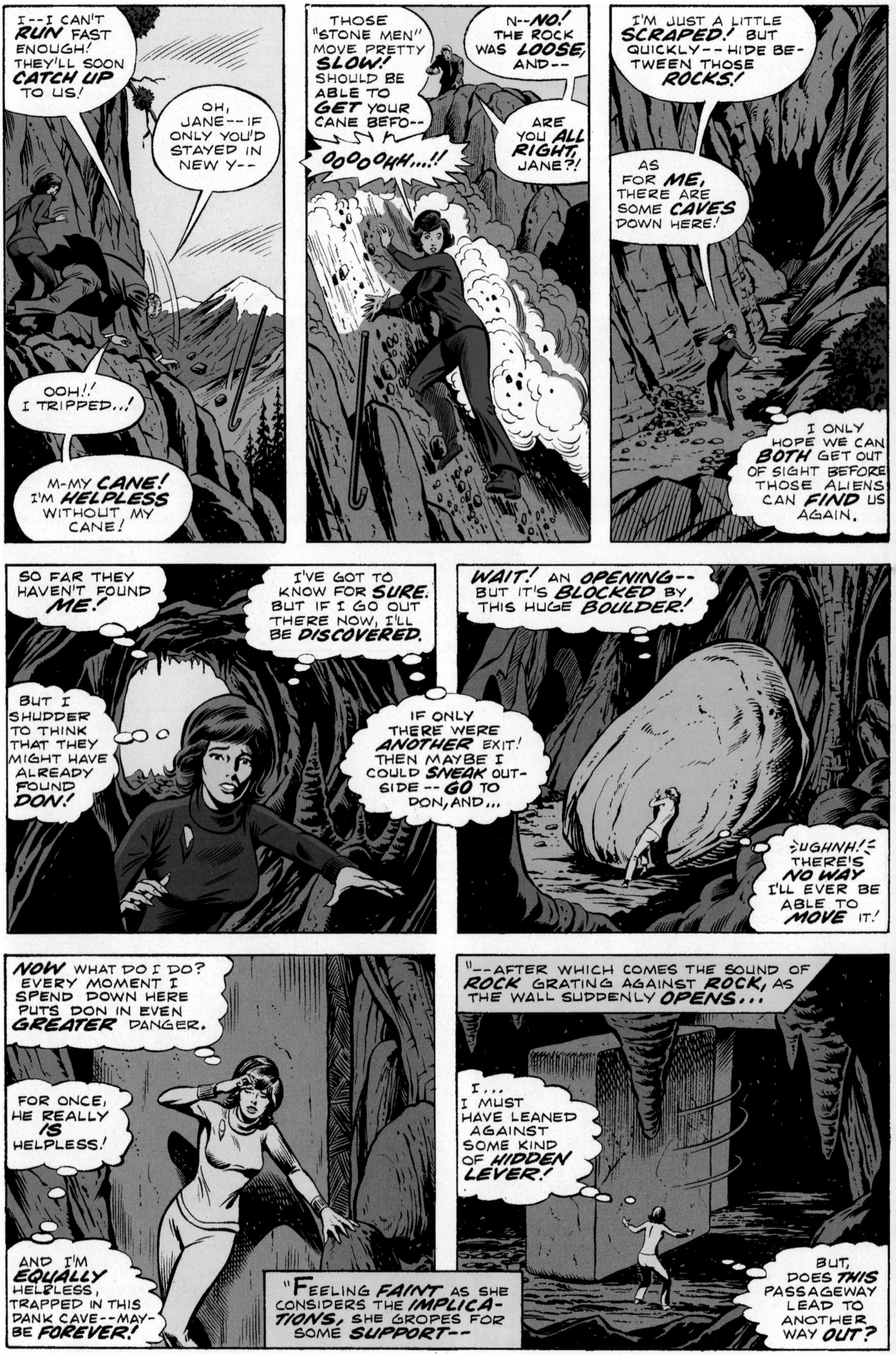

I--I CAN'T RUN FAST ENOUGH! THEY'LL SOON CATCH UP TO US!
OH, JANE--IF ONLY YOU'D STAYED IN NEW Y--
OOH!! I TRIPPED..!
M-MY CANE! I'M HELPLESS WITHOUT MY CANE!
THOSE "STONE MEN" MOVE PRETTY SLOW! SHOULD BE ABLE TO GET YOUR CANE BEFO--
OOOOOHH...!!
N--NO! THE ROCK WAS LOOSE, AND--
ARE YOU ALL RIGHT, JANE?!
I'M JUST A LITTLE SCRAPED! BUT QUICKLY--HIDE BETWEEN THOSE ROCKS!
AS FOR ME, THERE ARE SOME CAVES DOWN HERE!
I ONLY HOPE WE CAN BOTH GET OUT OF SIGHT BEFORE THOSE ALIENS CAN FIND US AGAIN.
SO FAR THEY HAVEN'T FOUND ME!
I'VE GOT TO KNOW FOR SURE. BUT IF I GO OUT THERE NOW, I'LL BE DISCOVERED.
BUT I SHUDDER TO THINK THAT THEY MIGHT HAVE ALREADY FOUND DON!
IF ONLY THERE WERE ANOTHER EXIT! THEN MAYBE I COULD SNEAK OUTSIDE--GO TO DON, AND...
WAIT! AN OPENING--BUT IT'S BLOCKED BY THIS HUGE BOULDER!
UGHNH! THERE'S NO WAY I'LL EVER BE ABLE TO MOVE IT!
NOW WHAT DO I DO? EVERY MOMENT I SPEND DOWN HERE PUTS DON IN EVEN GREATER DANGER.
FOR ONCE, HE REALLY IS HELPLESS!
AND I'M EQUALLY HELPLESS, TRAPPED IN THIS DANK CAVE--MAYBE FOREVER!
"FEELING FAINT AS SHE CONSIDERS THE IMPLICATIONS, SHE GROPES FOR SOME SUPPORT--
"--AFTER WHICH COMES THE SOUND OF ROCK GRATING AGAINST ROCK, AS THE WALL SUDDENLY OPENS...
I... I MUST HAVE LEANED AGAINST SOME KIND OF HIDDEN LEVER!
BUT, DOES THIS PASSAGEWAY LEAD TO ANOTHER WAY OUT?

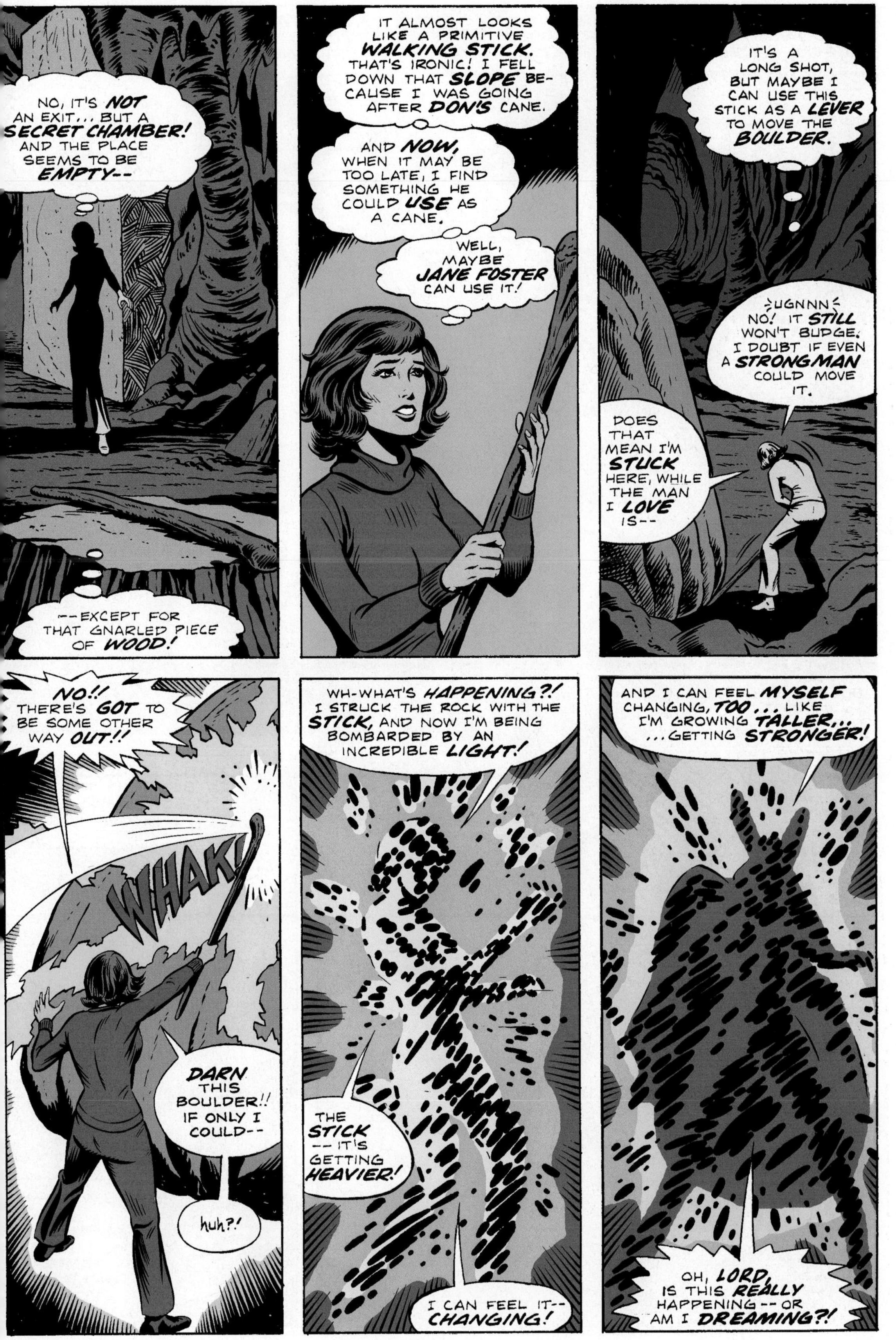
NO, IT'S NOT AN EXIT... BUT A SECRET CHAMBER! AND THE PLACE SEEMS TO BE EMPTY--
--EXCEPT FOR THAT GNARLED PIECE OF WOOD!
IT ALMOST LOOKS LIKE A PRIMITIVE WALKING STICK. THAT'S IRONIC! I FELL DOWN THAT SLOPE BE-CAUSE I WAS GOING AFTER DON'S CANE.
AND NOW, WHEN IT MAY BE TOO LATE, I FIND SOMETHING HE COULD USE AS A CANE.
WELL, MAYBE JANE FOSTER CAN USE IT!
IT'S A LONG SHOT, BUT MAYBE I CAN USE THIS STICK AS A LEVER TO MOVE THE BOULDER.
UGNNN NO! IT STILL WON'T BUDGE. I DOUBT IF EVEN A STRONGMAN COULD MOVE IT.
DOES THAT MEAN I'M STUCK HERE, WHILE THE MAN I LOVE IS--
NO!! THERE'S GOT TO BE SOME OTHER WAY OUT!!
WHAK!
DARN THIS BOULDER!! IF ONLY I COULD--
huh?!
WH-WHAT'S HAPPENING?! I STRUCK THE ROCK WITH THE STICK, AND NOW I'M BEING BOMBARDED BY AN INCREDIBLE LIGHT!
THE STICK -- IT'S GETTING HEAVIER!
I CAN FEEL IT-- CHANGING!
AND I CAN FEEL MYSELF CHANGING, TOO... LIKE I'M GROWING TALLER... ...GETTING STRONGER!
OH, LORD, IS THIS REALLY HAPPENING -- OR AM I DREAMING?!

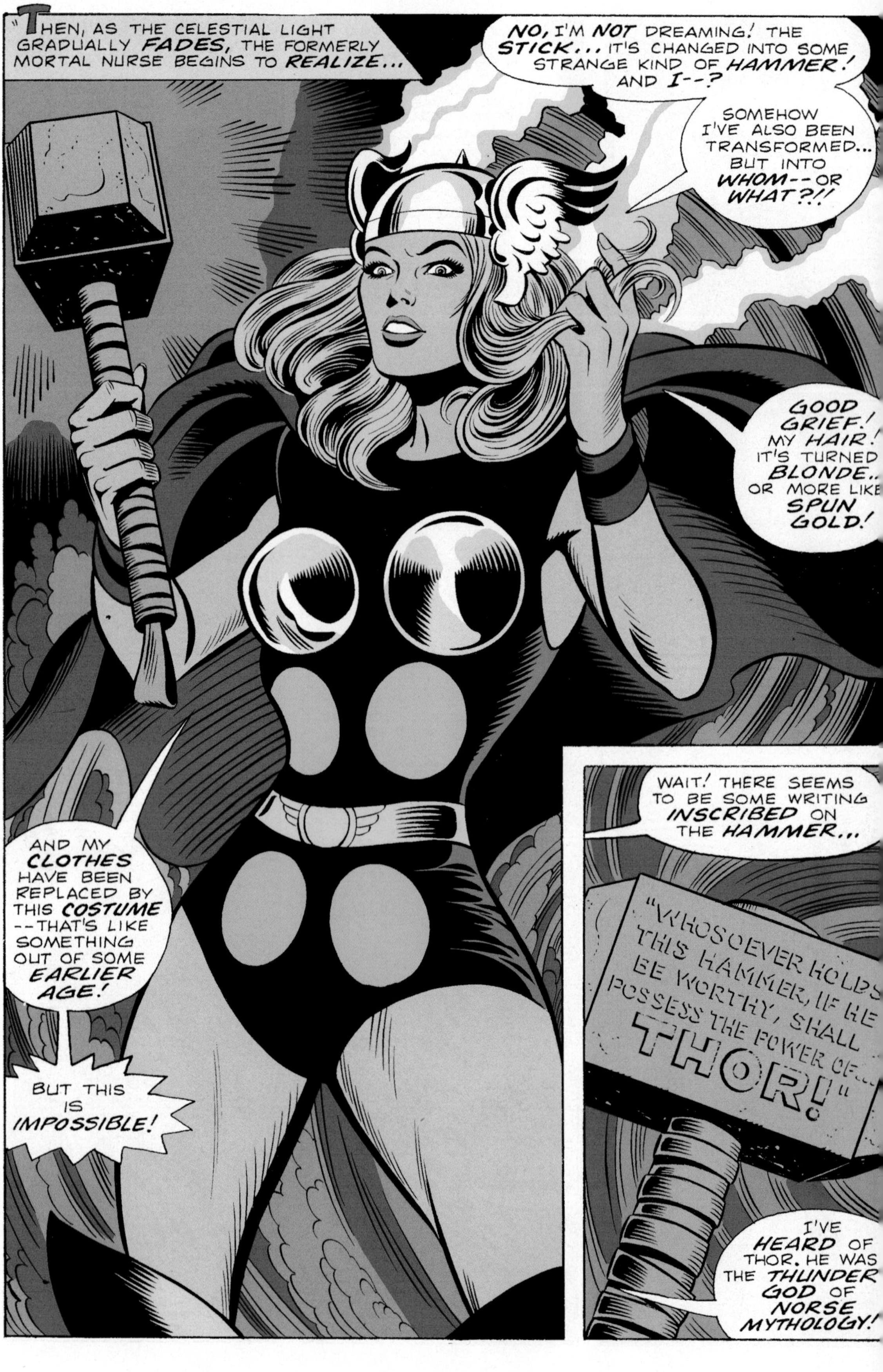
"THEN, AS THE CELESTIAL LIGHT GRADUALLY FADES, THE FORMERLY MORTAL NURSE BEGINS TO REALIZE...
NO, I'M NOT DREAMING! THE STICK... IT'S CHANGED INTO SOME STRANGE KIND OF HAMMER! AND I--?
SOMEHOW I'VE ALSO BEEN TRANSFORMED... BUT INTO WHOM--OR WHAT?!!
GOOD GRIEF! MY HAIR! IT'S TURNED BLONDE.. OR MORE LIKE SPUN GOLD!
AND MY CLOTHES HAVE BEEN REPLACED BY THIS COSTUME --THAT'S LIKE SOMETHING OUT OF SOME EARLIER AGE!
BUT THIS IS IMPOSSIBLE!
WAIT! THERE SEEMS TO BE SOME WRITING INSCRIBED ON THE HAMMER...
"WHOSOEVER HOLDS THIS HAMMER, IF HE BE WORTHY, SHALL POSSESS THE POWER OF... THOR!"
I'VE HEARD OF THOR. HE WAS THE THUNDER GOD OF NORSE MYTHOLOGY!

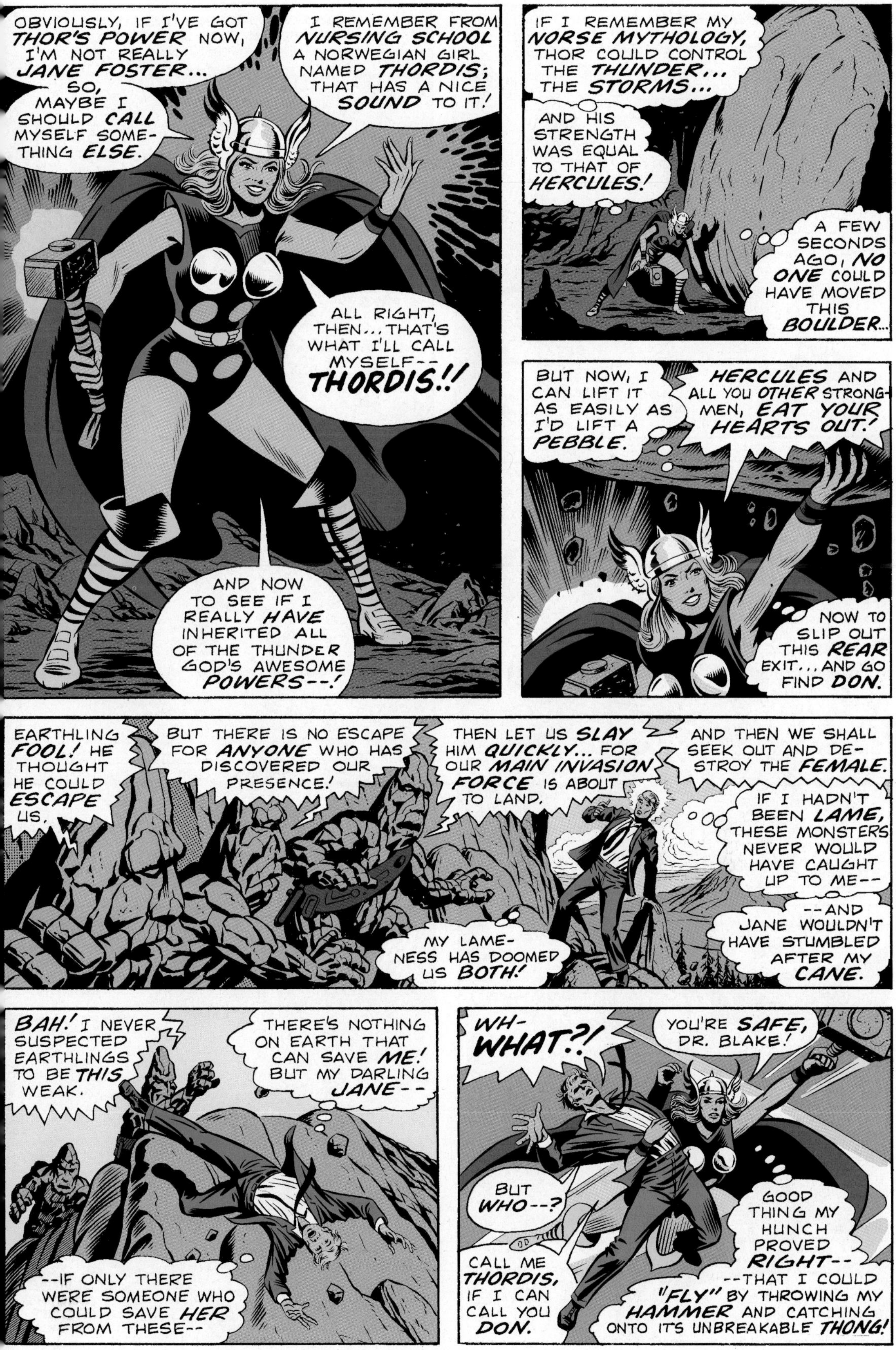
OBVIOUSLY, IF I'VE GOT THOR'S POWER NOW, I'M NOT REALLY JANE FOSTER... SO, MAYBE I SHOULD CALL MYSELF SOMETHING ELSE.
I REMEMBER FROM NURSING SCHOOL A NORWEGIAN GIRL NAMED THORDIS; THAT HAS A NICE SOUND TO IT!
ALL RIGHT, THEN... THAT'S WHAT I'LL CALL MYSELF-- THORDIS!!
AND NOW TO SEE IF I REALLY HAVE INHERITED ALL OF THE THUNDER GOD'S AWESOME POWERS--!
IF I REMEMBER MY NORSE MYTHOLOGY, THOR COULD CONTROL THE THUNDER... THE STORMS...
AND HIS STRENGTH WAS EQUAL TO THAT OF HERCULES!
A FEW SECONDS AGO, NO ONE COULD HAVE MOVED THIS BOULDER...
BUT NOW, I CAN LIFT IT AS EASILY AS I'D LIFT A PEBBLE.
HERCULES AND ALL YOU OTHER STRONG-MEN, EAT YOUR HEARTS OUT!
NOW TO SLIP OUT THIS REAR EXIT... AND GO FIND DON.
EARTHLING FOOL! HE THOUGHT HE COULD ESCAPE US.
BUT THERE IS NO ESCAPE FOR ANYONE WHO HAS DISCOVERED OUR PRESENCE!
THEN LET US SLAY HIM QUICKLY... FOR OUR MAIN INVASION FORCE IS ABOUT TO LAND.
AND THEN WE SHALL SEEK OUT AND DESTROY THE FEMALE.
IF I HADN'T BEEN LAME, THESE MONSTERS NEVER WOULD HAVE CAUGHT UP TO ME--
--AND JANE WOULDN'T HAVE STUMBLED AFTER MY CANE.
MY LAMENESS HAS DOOMED US BOTH!
BAH! I NEVER SUSPECTED EARTHLINGS TO BE THIS WEAK.
THERE'S NOTHING ON EARTH THAT CAN SAVE ME! BUT MY DARLING JANE--
--IF ONLY THERE WERE SOMEONE WHO COULD SAVE HER FROM THESE--
WH-WHAT?!
YOU'RE SAFE, DR. BLAKE!
BUT WHO--?
CALL ME THORDIS, IF I CAN CALL YOU DON.
GOOD THING MY HUNCH PROVED RIGHT--
--THAT I COULD "FLY" BY THROWING MY HAMMER AND CATCHING ONTO IT'S UNBREAKABLE THONG!

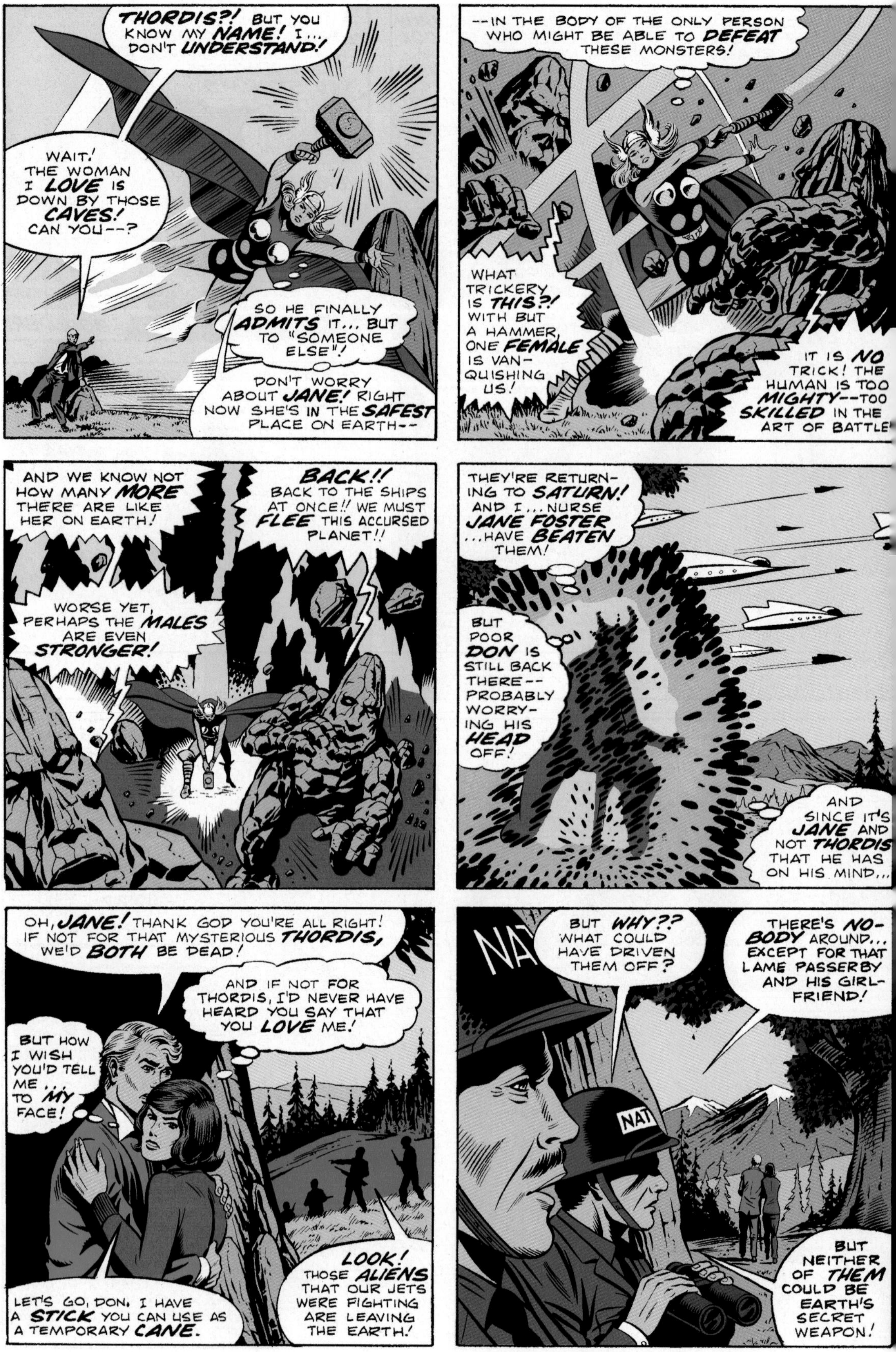
THORDIS?! BUT YOU KNOW MY NAME! I... DON'T UNDERSTAND!
WAIT! THE WOMAN I LOVE IS DOWN BY THOSE CAVES! CAN YOU--?
SO HE FINALLY ADMITS IT... BUT TO "SOMEONE ELSE"!
DON'T WORRY ABOUT JANE! RIGHT NOW SHE'S IN THE SAFEST PLACE ON EARTH--
--IN THE BODY OF THE ONLY PERSON WHO MIGHT BE ABLE TO DEFEAT THESE MONSTERS!
WHAT TRICKERY IS THIS?! WITH BUT A HAMMER, ONE FEMALE IS VANQUISHING US!
IT IS NO TRICK! THE HUMAN IS TOO MIGHTY--TOO SKILLED IN THE ART OF BATTLE!
AND WE KNOW NOT HOW MANY MORE THERE ARE LIKE HER ON EARTH!
BACK!! BACK TO THE SHIPS AT ONCE!! WE MUST FLEE THIS ACCURSED PLANET!!
WORSE YET, PERHAPS THE MALES ARE EVEN STRONGER!
THEY'RE RETURNING TO SATURN! AND I... NURSE JANE FOSTER ...HAVE BEATEN THEM!
BUT POOR DON IS STILL BACK THERE--PROBABLY WORRYING HIS HEAD OFF!
AND SINCE IT'S JANE AND NOT THORDIS THAT HE HAS ON HIS MIND...
OH, JANE! THANK GOD YOU'RE ALL RIGHT! IF NOT FOR THAT MYSTERIOUS THORDIS, WE'D BOTH BE DEAD!
AND IF NOT FOR THORDIS, I'D NEVER HAVE HEARD YOU SAY THAT YOU LOVE ME!
BUT HOW I WISH YOU'D TELL ME... TO MY FACE!
LET'S GO, DON. I HAVE A STICK YOU CAN USE AS A TEMPORARY CANE.
LOOK! THOSE ALIENS THAT OUR JETS WERE FIGHTING ARE LEAVING THE EARTH!
BUT WHY?? WHAT COULD HAVE DRIVEN THEM OFF?
THERE'S NOBODY AROUND... EXCEPT FOR THAT LAME PASSERBY AND HIS GIRLFRIEND!
BUT NEITHER OF THEM COULD BE EARTH'S SECRET WEAPON!

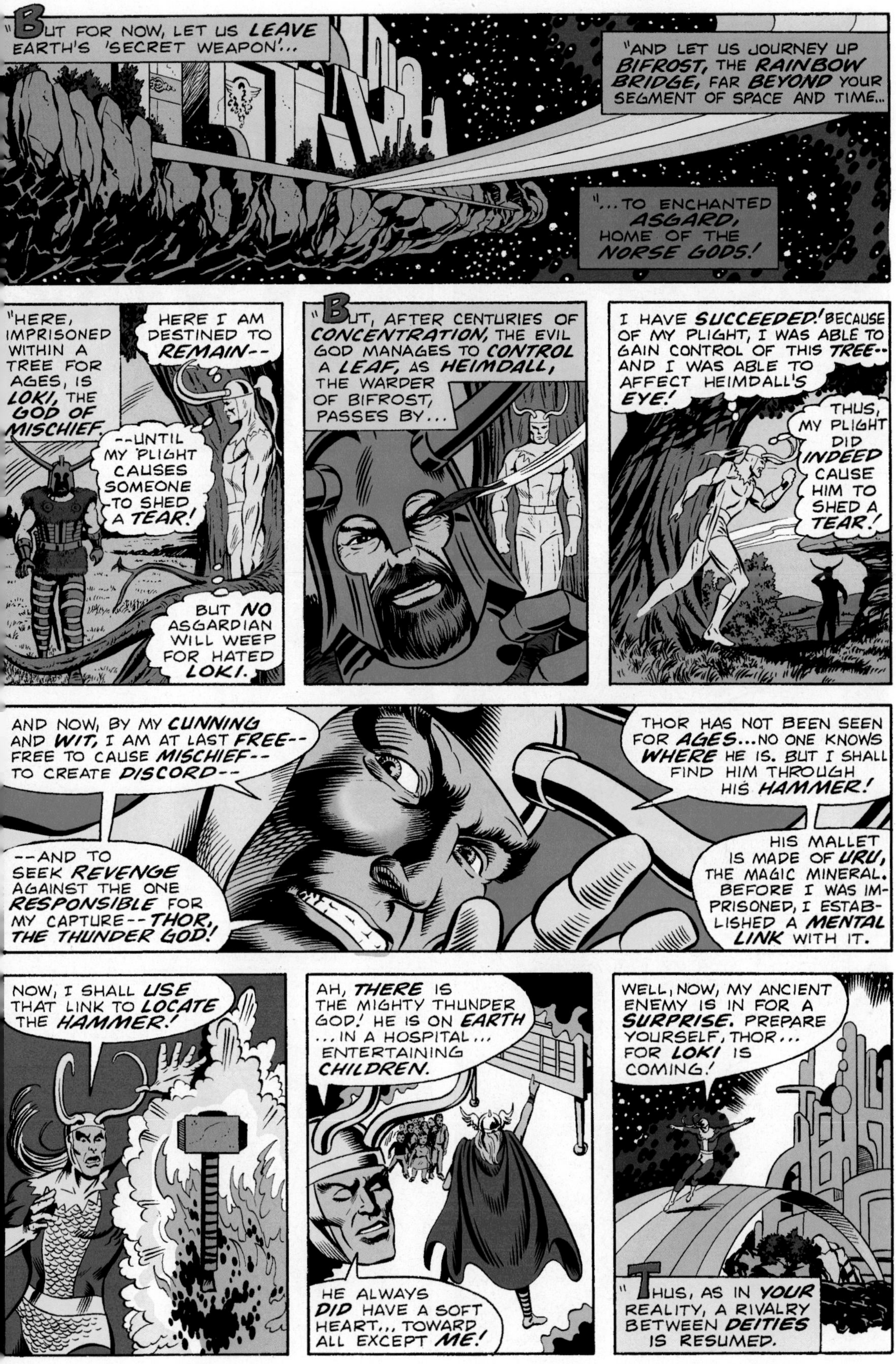
"BUT FOR NOW, LET US LEAVE EARTH'S 'SECRET WEAPON'...
"AND LET US JOURNEY UP BIFROST, THE RAINBOW BRIDGE, FAR BEYOND YOUR SEGMENT OF SPACE AND TIME...
"...TO ENCHANTED ASGARD, HOME OF THE NORSE GODS!
"HERE, IMPRISONED WITHIN A TREE FOR AGES, IS LOKI, THE GOD OF MISCHIEF.
HERE I AM DESTINED TO REMAIN--
--UNTIL MY PLIGHT CAUSES SOMEONE TO SHED A TEAR!
BUT NO ASGARDIAN WILL WEEP FOR HATED LOKI.
"BUT, AFTER CENTURIES OF CONCENTRATION, THE EVIL GOD MANAGES TO CONTROL A LEAF, AS HEIMDALL, THE WARDER OF BIFROST, PASSES BY...
I HAVE SUCCEEDED! BECAUSE OF MY PLIGHT, I WAS ABLE TO GAIN CONTROL OF THIS TREE-- AND I WAS ABLE TO AFFECT HEIMDALL'S EYE!
THUS, MY PLIGHT DID INDEED CAUSE HIM TO SHED A TEAR!
AND NOW, BY MY CUNNING AND WIT, I AM AT LAST FREE-- FREE TO CAUSE MISCHIEF-- TO CREATE DISCORD--
--AND TO SEEK REVENGE AGAINST THE ONE RESPONSIBLE FOR MY CAPTURE--THOR, THE THUNDER GOD!
THOR HAS NOT BEEN SEEN FOR AGES...NO ONE KNOWS WHERE HE IS. BUT I SHALL FIND HIM THROUGH HIS HAMMER!
HIS MALLET IS MADE OF URU, THE MAGIC MINERAL. BEFORE I WAS IMPRISONED, I ESTABLISHED A MENTAL LINK WITH IT.
NOW, I SHALL USE THAT LINK TO LOCATE THE HAMMER!
AH, THERE IS THE MIGHTY THUNDER GOD! HE IS ON EARTH ...IN A HOSPITAL... ENTERTAINING CHILDREN.
HE ALWAYS DID HAVE A SOFT HEART... TOWARD ALL EXCEPT ME!
WELL, NOW, MY ANCIENT ENEMY IS IN FOR A SURPRISE. PREPARE YOURSELF, THOR... FOR LOKI IS COMING!
"THUS, AS IN YOUR REALITY, A RIVALRY BETWEEN DEITIES IS RESUMED.

"MUCH HAS *CHANGED* UPON MIDGARD, THE NORSE GODS' NAME FOR YOUR *EARTH*, SINCE LOKI'S LAST VISIT...

"YET, NOT EVEN THE *GOD OF MISCHIEF* SUSPECTS THE MOST *SIGNIFICANT* CHANGE OF ALL...

YOU KNOW, JANE, THERE'S *FEWER* OF US *MD'S* MAKING HOUSE-CALLS EVERY DA--

OH, *LORD*, DON --*LOOK!*

HOLY CRIPES! WILL YA LOOKIT *THAT?!*

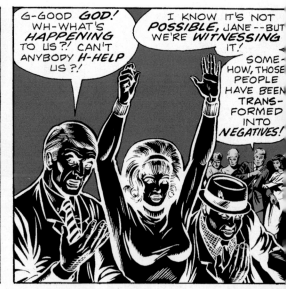

G-GOOD *GOD!* WH-WHAT'S *HAPPENING* TO US?! CAN'T ANYBODY H-HELP US?!

I KNOW IT'S NOT *POSSIBLE*, JANE--BUT WE'RE *WITNESSING* IT!

SOME-HOW, THOSE PEOPLE HAVE BEEN TRANS-FORMED INTO *NEGATIVES!*

I FEEL SO *HELPLESS!* AS A DOCTOR, I SHOULD *DO* SOMETHING. BUT WHAT'S HAPPENING GOES *BEYOND* MEDICAL SCIENCE!

DON'S *RIGHT!* NO FORCE THAT *SCIENCE* CAN EXPLAIN DID *THAT!*

IF I DIDN'T *KNOW* BETTER, I'D THINK THIS WAS SOME-THING *SUPERNATUR-AL*, BUT... JANE?

DON WAS TOO CONCERNED WITH THOSE *PEOPLE* TO NOTICE ME SLIPPING INTO THIS *ALLEY.*

NOW I CAN TAKE OUT THIS *HAIRBRUSH* --SHAPED FROM A PIECE OF *NORWEGIAN WOOD.*

BUT I'M *NOT* GOING TO BRUSH MY *HAIR!*

JUST ONE *TAP* AGAINST THE PAVEMENT WITH MY INNOCENT-LOOKING BRUSH, AND I BECOME--

KR AK!

THORDIS, GODDESS OF THUNDER!

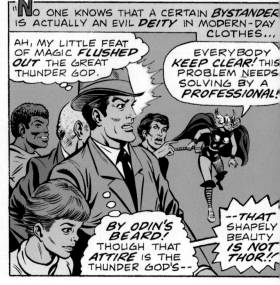

"NO ONE KNOWS THAT A CERTAIN *BYSTANDER* IS ACTUALLY AN EVIL *DEITY* IN MODERN-DAY CLOTHES...

AH, MY LITTLE FEAT OF MAGIC *FLUSHED OUT* THE GREAT THUNDER GOD.

EVERYBODY *KEEP CLEAR!* THIS PROBLEM *NEEDS* SOLVING BY A *PROFESSIONAL!*

BY ODIN'S *BEARD!* THOUGH THAT *ATTIRE* IS THE THUNDER GOD'S--

--THAT SHAPELY BEAUTY *IS NOT THOR.!!*

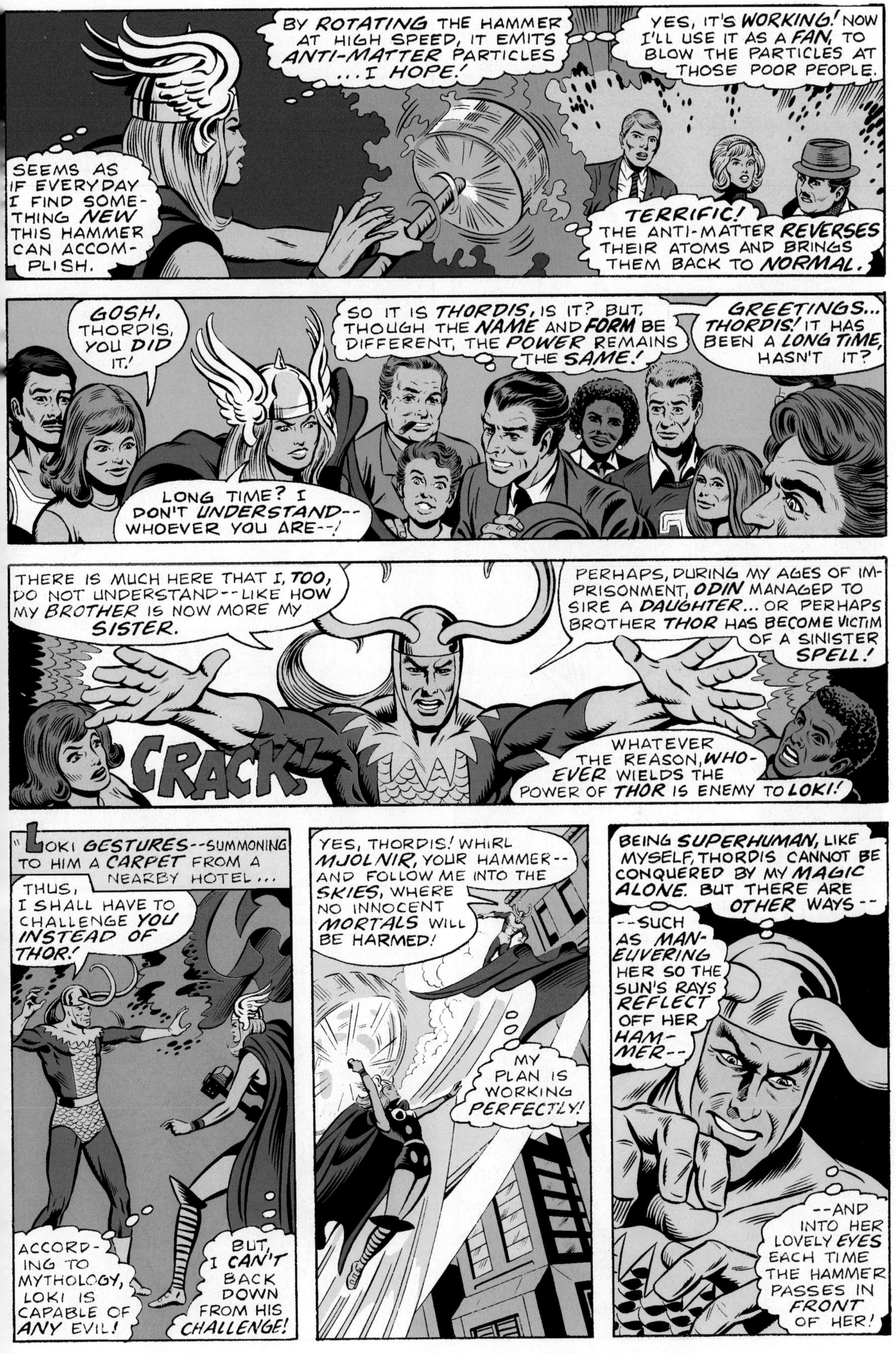
BY ROTATING THE HAMMER AT HIGH SPEED, IT EMITS ANTI-MATTER PARTICLES ...I HOPE!
SEEMS AS IF EVERYDAY I FIND SOMETHING NEW THIS HAMMER CAN ACCOMPLISH.
YES, IT'S WORKING! NOW I'LL USE IT AS A FAN, TO BLOW THE PARTICLES AT THOSE POOR PEOPLE.
TERRIFIC! THE ANTI-MATTER REVERSES THEIR ATOMS AND BRINGS THEM BACK TO NORMAL.
GOSH, THORDIS, YOU DID IT!
LONG TIME? I DON'T UNDERSTAND-- WHOEVER YOU ARE--!
SO IT IS THORDIS, IS IT? BUT, THOUGH THE NAME AND FORM BE DIFFERENT, THE POWER REMAINS THE SAME!
GREETINGS... THORDIS! IT HAS BEEN A LONG TIME, HASN'T IT?
THERE IS MUCH HERE THAT I, TOO, DO NOT UNDERSTAND--LIKE HOW MY BROTHER IS NOW MORE MY SISTER.
PERHAPS, DURING MY AGES OF IMPRISONMENT, ODIN MANAGED TO SIRE A DAUGHTER... OR PERHAPS BROTHER THOR HAS BECOME VICTIM OF A SINISTER SPELL!
CRACK!
WHATEVER THE REASON, WHOEVER WIELDS THE POWER OF THOR IS ENEMY TO LOKI!
LOKI GESTURES--SUMMONING TO HIM A CARPET FROM A NEARBY HOTEL...
THUS, I SHALL HAVE TO CHALLENGE YOU INSTEAD OF THOR!
ACCORDING TO MYTHOLOGY, LOKI IS CAPABLE OF ANY EVIL!
BUT, I CAN'T BACK DOWN FROM HIS CHALLENGE!
YES, THORDIS! WHIRL MJOLNIR, YOUR HAMMER-- AND FOLLOW ME INTO THE SKIES, WHERE NO INNOCENT MORTALS WILL BE HARMED!
MY PLAN IS WORKING PERFECTLY!
BEING SUPERHUMAN, LIKE MYSELF, THORDIS CANNOT BE CONQUERED BY MY MAGIC ALONE. BUT THERE ARE OTHER WAYS--
--SUCH AS MANEUVERING HER SO THE SUN'S RAYS REFLECT OFF HER HAMMER--
--AND INTO HER LOVELY EYES EACH TIME THE HAMMER PASSES IN FRONT OF HER!

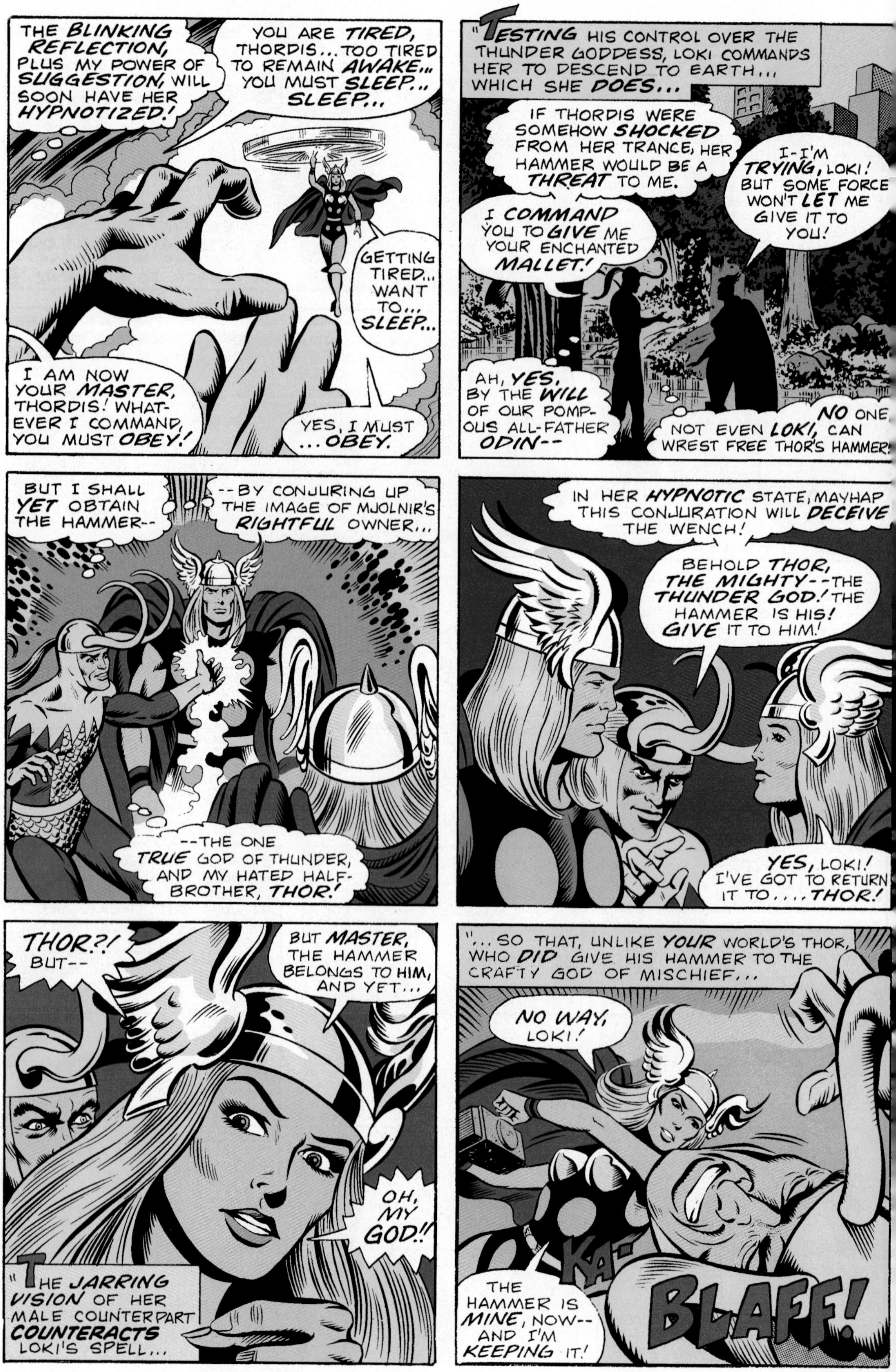
THE BLINKING REFLECTION, PLUS MY POWER OF SUGGESTION, WILL SOON HAVE HER HYPNOTIZED!
YOU ARE TIRED, THORDIS... TOO TIRED TO REMAIN AWAKE... YOU MUST SLEEP... SLEEP...
GETTING TIRED... WANT TO... SLEEP...
I AM NOW YOUR MASTER, THORDIS! WHATEVER I COMMAND, YOU MUST OBEY!
YES, I MUST ...OBEY.
"TESTING HIS CONTROL OVER THE THUNDER GODDESS, LOKI COMMANDS HER TO DESCEND TO EARTH... WHICH SHE DOES...
IF THORDIS WERE SOMEHOW SHOCKED FROM HER TRANCE, HER HAMMER WOULD BE A THREAT TO ME.
I COMMAND YOU TO GIVE ME YOUR ENCHANTED MALLET!
I-I'M TRYING, LOKI! BUT SOME FORCE WON'T LET ME GIVE IT TO YOU!
AH, YES. BY THE WILL OF OUR POMPOUS ALL-FATHER ODIN--
NO ONE, NOT EVEN LOKI, CAN WREST FREE THOR'S HAMMER!
BUT I SHALL YET OBTAIN THE HAMMER--
--BY CONJURING UP THE IMAGE OF MJOLNIR'S RIGHTFUL OWNER...
--THE ONE TRUE GOD OF THUNDER, AND MY HATED HALF-BROTHER, THOR!
IN HER HYPNOTIC STATE, MAYHAP THIS CONJURATION WILL DECEIVE THE WENCH!
BEHOLD THOR, THE MIGHTY--THE THUNDER GOD! THE HAMMER IS HIS! GIVE IT TO HIM!
YES, LOKI! I'VE GOT TO RETURN IT TO.... THOR!
THOR?! BUT--
BUT MASTER, THE HAMMER BELONGS TO HIM, AND YET...
OH, MY GOD!!
"THE JARRING VISION OF HER MALE COUNTERPART COUNTERACTS LOKI'S SPELL...
"...SO THAT, UNLIKE YOUR WORLD'S THOR, WHO DID GIVE HIS HAMMER TO THE CRAFTY GOD OF MISCHIEF...
NO WAY, LOKI!
KA-BLAFF!
THE HAMMER IS MINE, NOW-- AND I'M KEEPING IT!

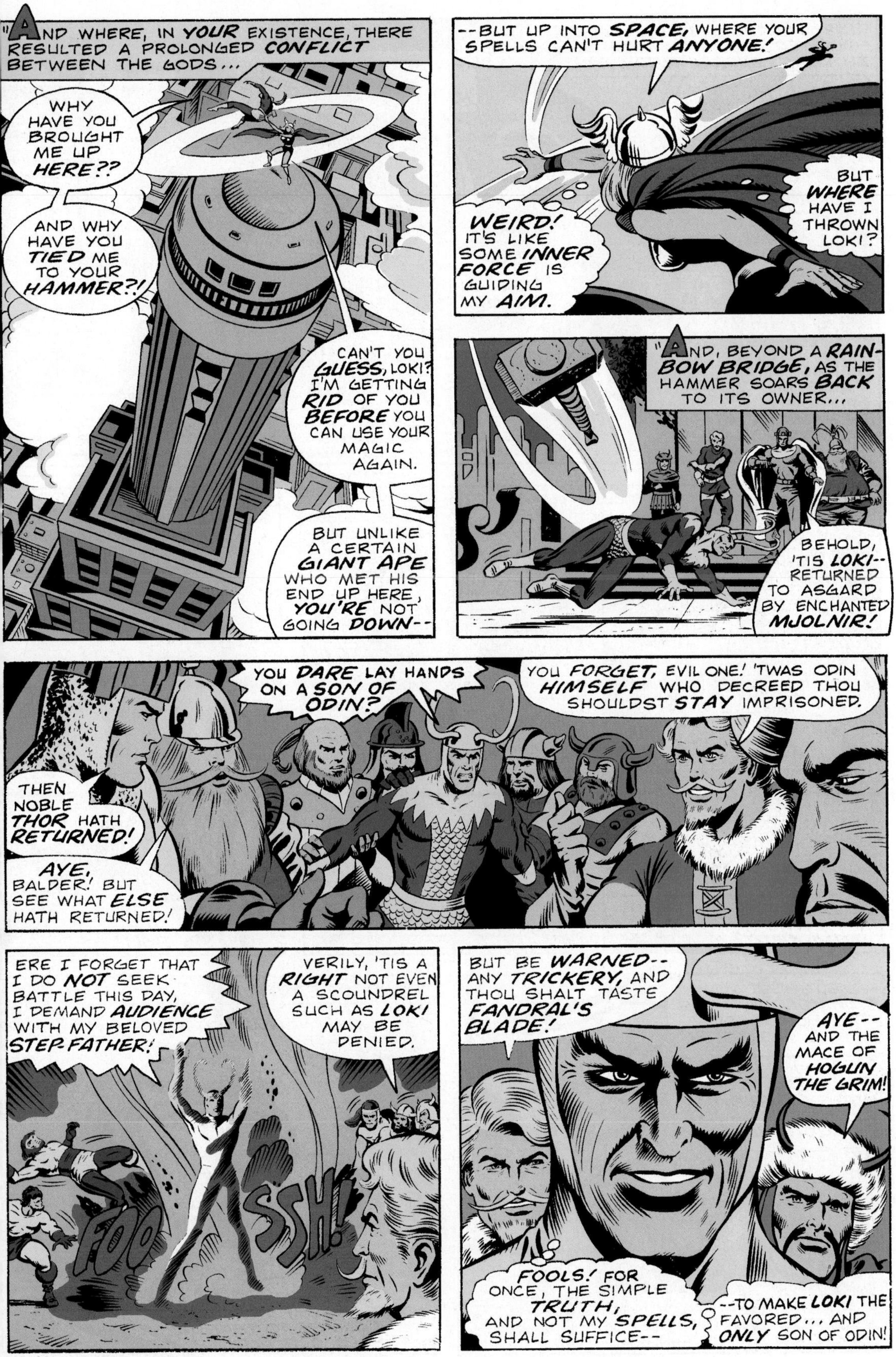
"AND WHERE, IN YOUR EXISTENCE, THERE RESULTED A PROLONGED CONFLICT BETWEEN THE GODS...
WHY HAVE YOU BROUGHT ME UP HERE??
AND WHY HAVE YOU TIED ME TO YOUR HAMMER?!
CAN'T YOU GUESS, LOKI? I'M GETTING RID OF YOU BEFORE YOU CAN USE YOUR MAGIC AGAIN.
BUT UNLIKE A CERTAIN GIANT APE WHO MET HIS END UP HERE, YOU'RE NOT GOING DOWN--
--BUT UP INTO SPACE, WHERE YOUR SPELLS CAN'T HURT ANYONE!
WEIRD! IT'S LIKE SOME INNER FORCE IS GUIDING MY AIM.
BUT WHERE HAVE I THROWN LOKI?
"AND, BEYOND A RAINBOW BRIDGE, AS THE HAMMER SOARS BACK TO ITS OWNER...
BEHOLD, 'TIS LOKI-- RETURNED TO ASGARD BY ENCHANTED MJOLNIR!
THEN NOBLE THOR HATH RETURNED!
AYE, BALDER! BUT SEE WHAT ELSE HATH RETURNED!
YOU DARE LAY HANDS ON A SON OF ODIN?
YOU FORGET, EVIL ONE! 'TWAS ODIN HIMSELF WHO DECREED THOU SHOULDST STAY IMPRISONED.
ERE I FORGET THAT I DO NOT SEEK BATTLE THIS DAY, I DEMAND AUDIENCE WITH MY BELOVED STEP-FATHER!
VERILY, 'TIS A RIGHT NOT EVEN A SCOUNDREL SUCH AS LOKI MAY BE DENIED.
FOOSSH!
BUT BE WARNED-- ANY TRICKERY, AND THOU SHALT TASTE FANDRAL'S BLADE!
AYE-- AND THE MACE OF HOGUN THE GRIM!
FOOLS! FOR ONCE, THE SIMPLE TRUTH, AND NOT MY SPELLS, SHALL SUFFICE--
--TO MAKE LOKI THE FAVORED... AND ONLY SON OF ODIN!

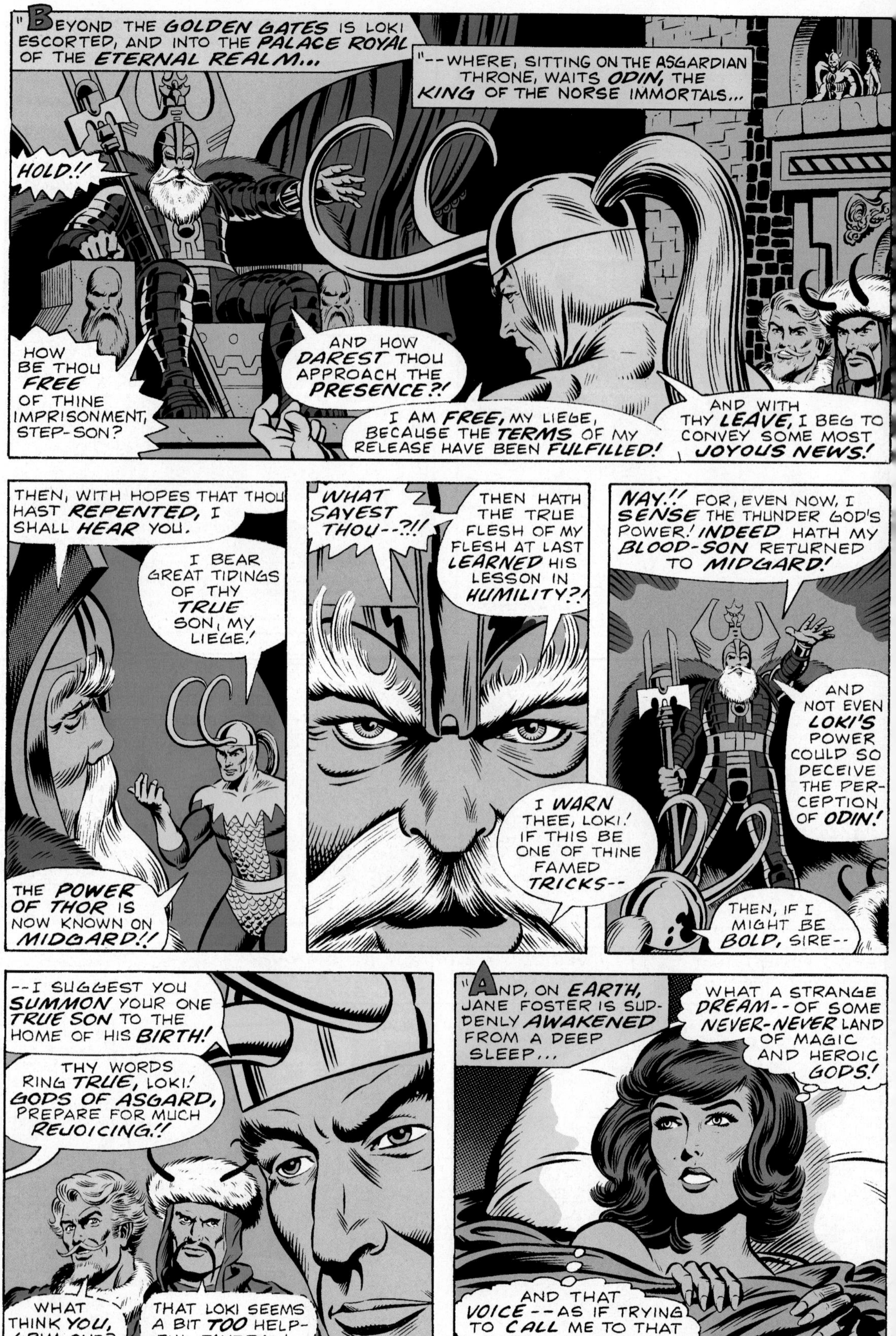
"BEYOND THE GOLDEN GATES IS LOKI ESCORTED, AND INTO THE PALACE ROYAL OF THE ETERNAL REALM...
"--WHERE, SITTING ON THE ASGARDIAN THRONE, WAITS ODIN, THE KING OF THE NORSE IMMORTALS...
HOLD!!
HOW BE THOU FREE OF THINE IMPRISONMENT, STEP-SON?
AND HOW DAREST THOU APPROACH THE PRESENCE?!
I AM FREE, MY LIEGE, BECAUSE THE TERMS OF MY RELEASE HAVE BEEN FULFILLED!
AND WITH THY LEAVE, I BEG TO CONVEY SOME MOST JOYOUS NEWS!
THEN, WITH HOPES THAT THOU HAST REPENTED, I SHALL HEAR YOU.
I BEAR GREAT TIDINGS OF THY TRUE SON, MY LIEGE!
THE POWER OF THOR IS NOW KNOWN ON MIDGARD!!
WHAT SAYEST THOU--?!!
THEN HATH THE TRUE FLESH OF MY FLESH AT LAST LEARNED HIS LESSON IN HUMILITY?!
I WARN THEE, LOKI! IF THIS BE ONE OF THINE FAMED TRICKS--
NAY!! FOR, EVEN NOW, I SENSE THE THUNDER GOD'S POWER! INDEED HATH MY BLOOD-SON RETURNED TO MIDGARD!
AND NOT EVEN LOKI'S POWER COULD SO DECEIVE THE PERCEPTION OF ODIN!
THEN, IF I MIGHT BE BOLD, SIRE--
--I SUGGEST YOU SUMMON YOUR ONE TRUE SON TO THE HOME OF HIS BIRTH!
THY WORDS RING TRUE, LOKI! GODS OF ASGARD, PREPARE FOR MUCH REJOICING!!
WHAT THINK YOU, GRIM ONE?
THAT LOKI SEEMS A BIT TOO HELPFUL, FANDRAL!
"AND, ON EARTH, JANE FOSTER IS SUDDENLY AWAKENED FROM A DEEP SLEEP...
WHAT A STRANGE DREAM--OF SOME NEVER-NEVER LAND OF MAGIC AND HEROIC GODS!
AND THAT VOICE--AS IF TRYING TO CALL ME TO THAT FABULOUS PLACE!

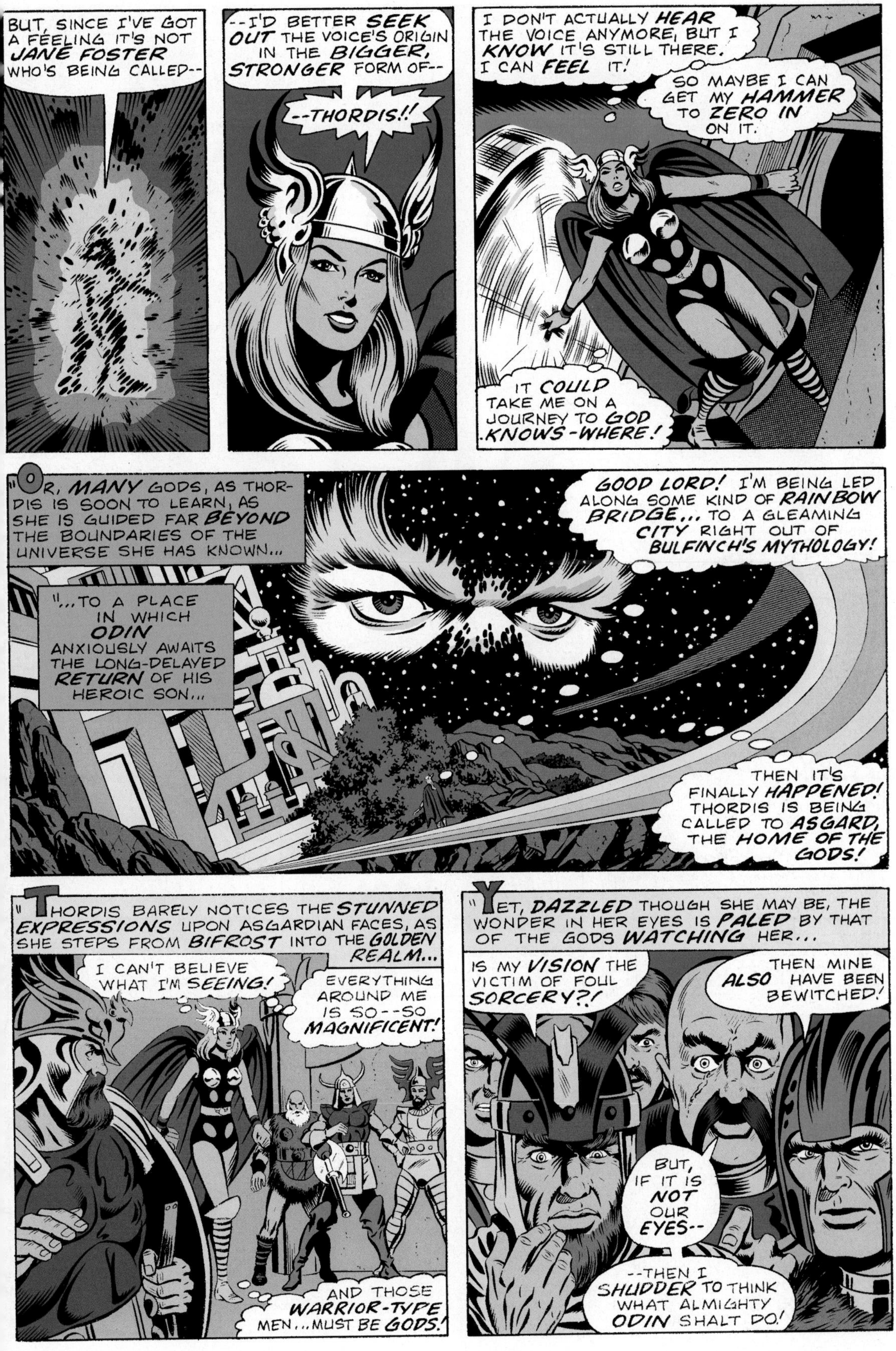

BUT, SINCE I'VE GOT A FEELING IT'S NOT JANE FOSTER WHO'S BEING CALLED--
--I'D BETTER SEEK OUT THE VOICE'S ORIGIN IN THE BIGGER, STRONGER FORM OF--
--THORDIS!!
I DON'T ACTUALLY HEAR THE VOICE ANYMORE, BUT I KNOW IT'S STILL THERE. I CAN FEEL IT!
SO MAYBE I CAN GET MY HAMMER TO ZERO IN ON IT.
IT COULD TAKE ME ON A JOURNEY TO GOD KNOWS-WHERE!
"OR, MANY GODS, AS THORDIS IS SOON TO LEARN, AS SHE IS GUIDED FAR BEYOND THE BOUNDARIES OF THE UNIVERSE SHE HAS KNOWN...
GOOD LORD! I'M BEING LED ALONG SOME KIND OF RAINBOW BRIDGE... TO A GLEAMING CITY RIGHT OUT OF BULFINCH'S MYTHOLOGY!
"...TO A PLACE IN WHICH ODIN ANXIOUSLY AWAITS THE LONG-DELAYED RETURN OF HIS HEROIC SON...
THEN IT'S FINALLY HAPPENED! THORDIS IS BEING CALLED TO ASGARD, THE HOME OF THE GODS!
"THORDIS BARELY NOTICES THE STUNNED EXPRESSIONS UPON ASGARDIAN FACES, AS SHE STEPS FROM BIFROST INTO THE GOLDEN REALM...
I CAN'T BELIEVE WHAT I'M SEEING!
EVERYTHING AROUND ME IS SO--SO MAGNIFICENT!
AND THOSE WARRIOR-TYPE MEN... MUST BE GODS!
"YET, DAZZLED THOUGH SHE MAY BE, THE WONDER IN HER EYES IS PALED BY THAT OF THE GODS WATCHING HER...
IS MY VISION THE VICTIM OF FOUL SORCERY?!
THEN MINE ALSO HAVE BEEN BEWITCHED!
BUT, IF IT IS NOT OUR EYES--
--THEN I SHUDDER TO THINK WHAT ALMIGHTY ODIN SHALT DO!

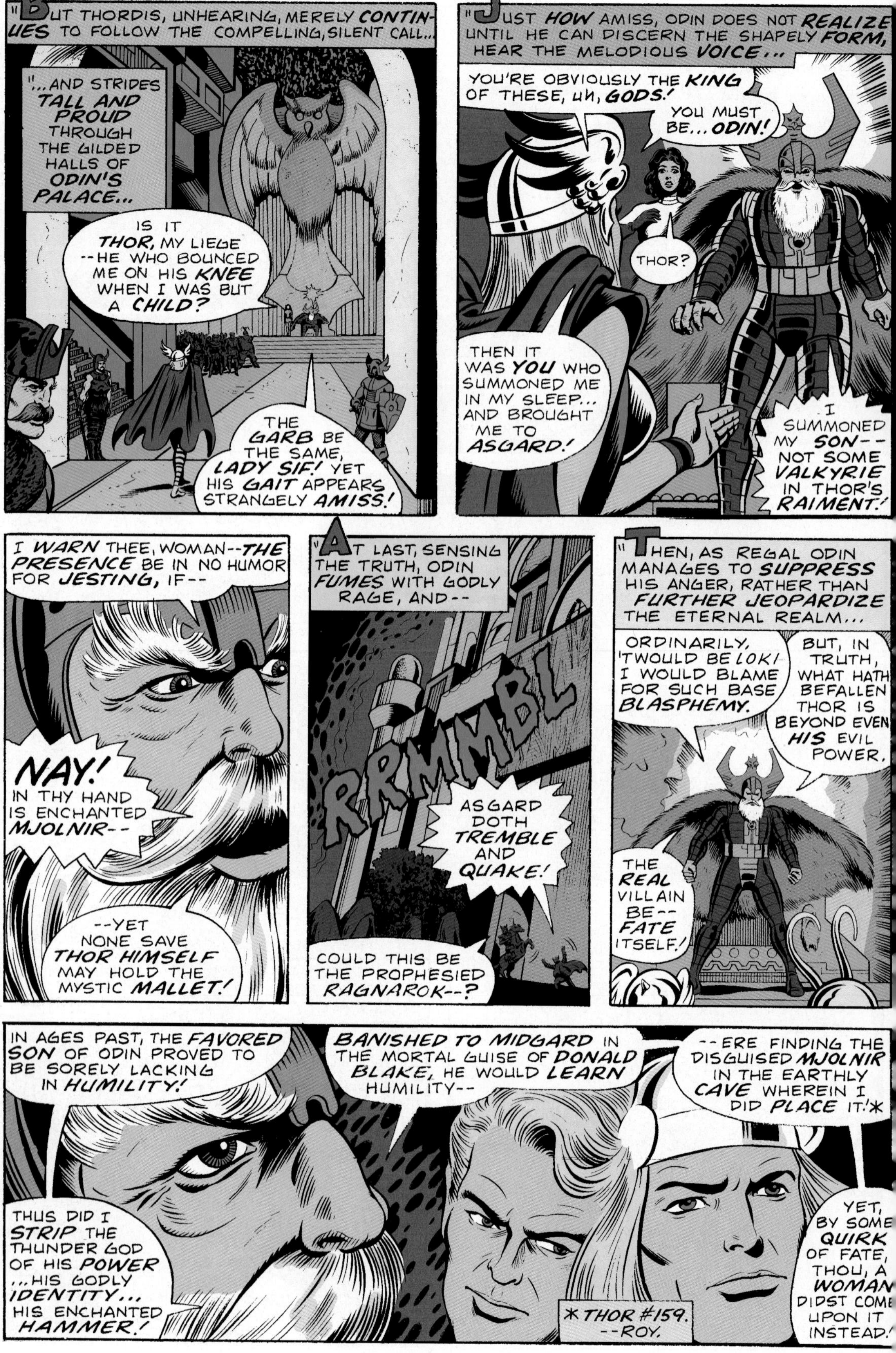
"BUT THORDIS, UNHEARING, MERELY CONTINUES TO FOLLOW THE COMPELLING, SILENT CALL...
"...AND STRIDES TALL AND PROUD THROUGH THE GILDED HALLS OF ODIN'S PALACE...
IS IT THOR, MY LIEGE --HE WHO BOUNCED ME ON HIS KNEE WHEN I WAS BUT A CHILD?
THE GARB BE THE SAME, LADY SIF! YET HIS GAIT APPEARS STRANGELY AMISS!
"JUST HOW AMISS, ODIN DOES NOT REALIZE UNTIL HE CAN DISCERN THE SHAPELY FORM, HEAR THE MELODIOUS VOICE...
YOU'RE OBVIOUSLY THE KING OF THESE, UH, GODS!
YOU MUST BE... ODIN!
THOR?
THEN IT WAS YOU WHO SUMMONED ME IN MY SLEEP... AND BROUGHT ME TO ASGARD!
I SUMMONED MY SON--NOT SOME VALKYRIE IN THOR'S RAIMENT!
I WARN THEE, WOMAN--THE PRESENCE BE IN NO HUMOR FOR JESTING, IF--
NAY! IN THY HAND IS ENCHANTED MJOLNIR--
--YET NONE SAVE THOR HIMSELF MAY HOLD THE MYSTIC MALLET!
"AT LAST, SENSING THE TRUTH, ODIN FUMES WITH GODLY RAGE, AND--
RRMMMBL
ASGARD DOTH TREMBLE AND QUAKE!
COULD THIS BE THE PROPHESIED RAGNAROK--?
"THEN, AS REGAL ODIN MANAGES TO SUPPRESS HIS ANGER, RATHER THAN FURTHER JEOPARDIZE THE ETERNAL REALM...
ORDINARILY, 'TWOULD BE LOKI I WOULD BLAME FOR SUCH BASE BLASPHEMY.
BUT, IN TRUTH, WHAT HATH BEFALLEN THOR IS BEYOND EVEN HIS EVIL POWER.
THE REAL VILLAIN BE--FATE ITSELF!
IN AGES PAST, THE FAVORED SON OF ODIN PROVED TO BE SORELY LACKING IN HUMILITY!
BANISHED TO MIDGARD IN THE MORTAL GUISE OF DONALD BLAKE, HE WOULD LEARN HUMILITY--
--ERE FINDING THE DISGUISED MJOLNIR IN THE EARTHLY CAVE WHEREIN I DID PLACE IT!*
THUS DID I STRIP THE THUNDER GOD OF HIS POWER ...HIS GODLY IDENTITY... HIS ENCHANTED HAMMER!
*THOR #159. --ROY.
YET, BY SOME QUIRK OF FATE, THOU, A WOMAN DIDST COME UPON IT INSTEAD!

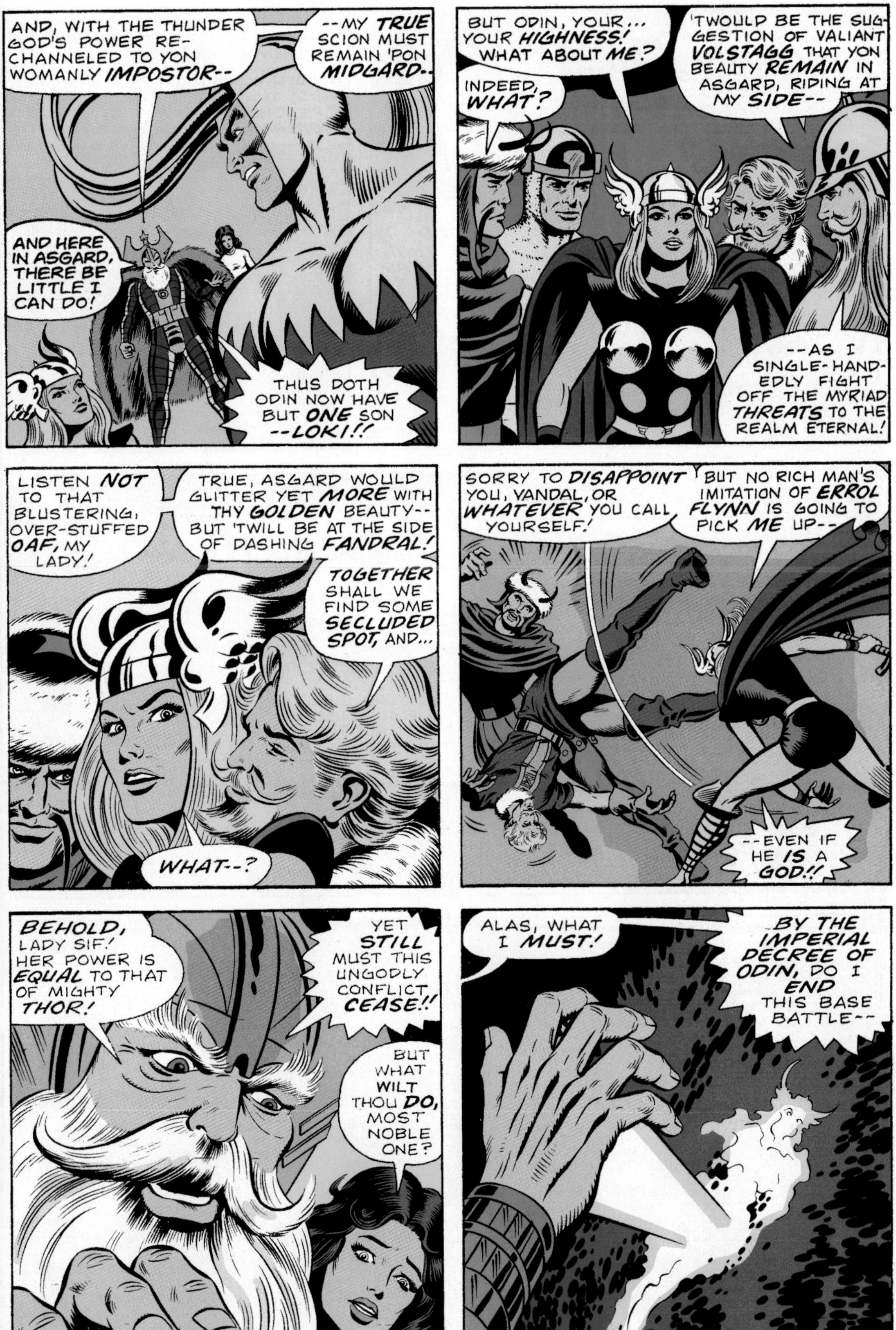
AND, WITH THE THUNDER GOD'S POWER RE-CHANNELED TO YON WOMANLY IMPOSTOR--
--MY TRUE SCION MUST REMAIN 'PON MIDGARD--
AND HERE IN ASGARD, THERE BE LITTLE I CAN DO!
THUS DOTH ODIN NOW HAVE BUT ONE SON --LOKI!!
BUT ODIN, YOUR... YOUR HIGHNESS! WHAT ABOUT ME?
INDEED, WHAT?
'TWOULD BE THE SUGGESTION OF VALIANT VOLSTAGG THAT YON BEAUTY REMAIN IN ASGARD, RIDING AT MY SIDE--
--AS I SINGLE-HANDEDLY FIGHT OFF THE MYRIAD THREATS TO THE REALM ETERNAL!
LISTEN NOT TO THAT BLUSTERING, OVER-STUFFED OAF, MY LADY!
TRUE, ASGARD WOULD GLITTER YET MORE WITH THY GOLDEN BEAUTY-- BUT 'TWILL BE AT THE SIDE OF DASHING FANDRAL!
TOGETHER SHALL WE FIND SOME SECLUDED SPOT, AND...
WHAT--?
SORRY TO DISAPPOINT YOU, VANDAL, OR WHATEVER YOU CALL YOURSELF!
BUT NO RICH MAN'S IMITATION OF ERROL FLYNN IS GOING TO PICK ME UP--
--EVEN IF HE IS A GOD!!
BEHOLD, LADY SIF! HER POWER IS EQUAL TO THAT OF MIGHTY THOR!
YET STILL MUST THIS UNGODLY CONFLICT CEASE!!
BUT WHAT WILT THOU DO, MOST NOBLE ONE?
ALAS, WHAT I MUST!
BY THE IMPERIAL DECREE OF ODIN, DO I END THIS BASE BATTLE--

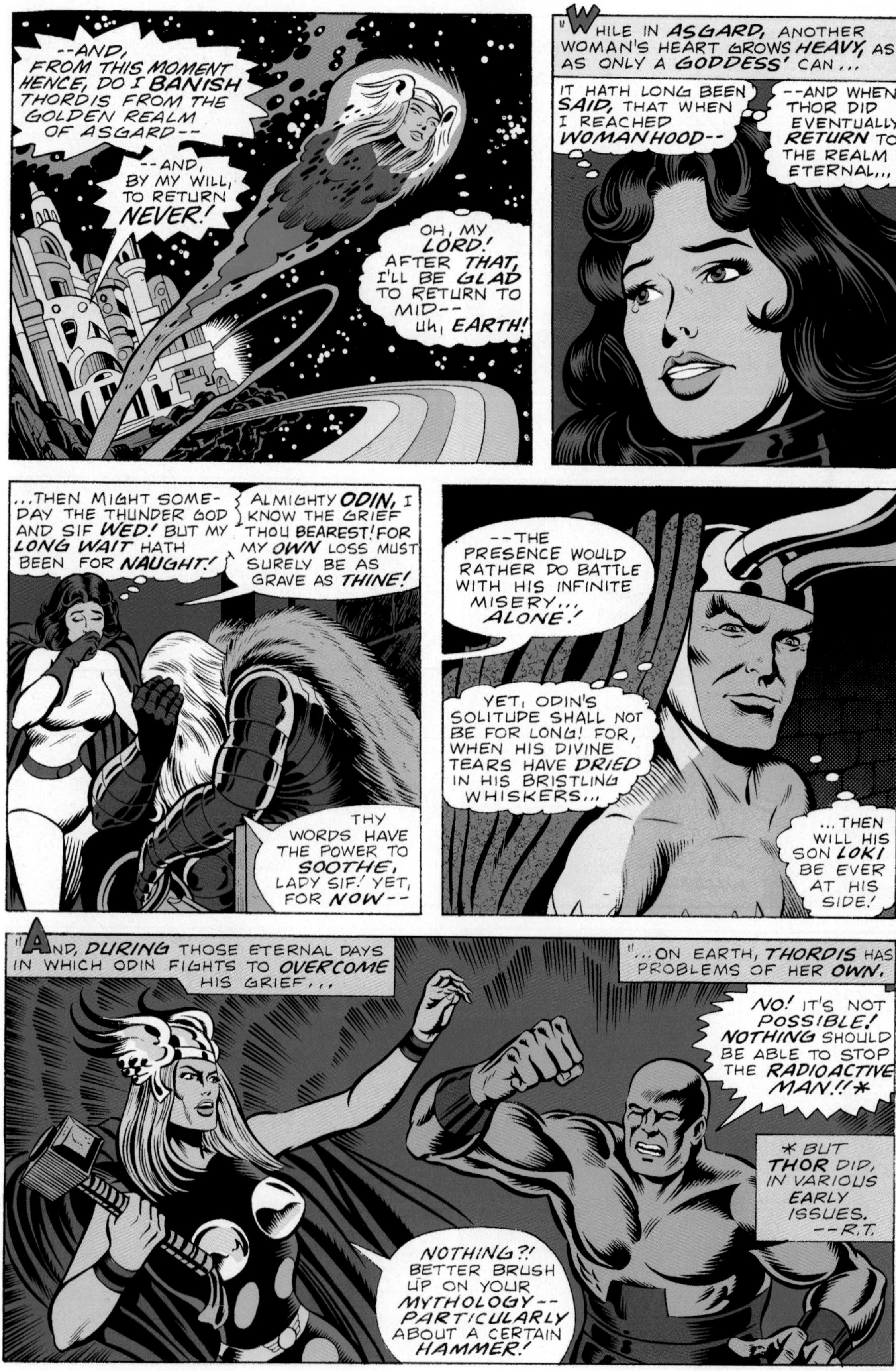
--AND, FROM THIS MOMENT HENCE, DO I BANISH THORDIS FROM THE GOLDEN REALM OF ASGARD--
--AND, BY MY WILL, TO RETURN NEVER!
OH, MY LORD! AFTER THAT, I'LL BE GLAD TO RETURN TO MID-- uh, EARTH!
"WHILE IN ASGARD, ANOTHER WOMAN'S HEART GROWS HEAVY, AS AS ONLY A GODDESS' CAN...
IT HATH LONG BEEN SAID, THAT WHEN I REACHED WOMANHOOD--
--AND WHEN THOR DID EVENTUALLY RETURN TO THE REALM ETERNAL...
...THEN MIGHT SOME-DAY THE THUNDER GOD AND SIF WED! BUT MY LONG WAIT HATH BEEN FOR NAUGHT!
ALMIGHTY ODIN, I KNOW THE GRIEF THOU BEAREST! FOR MY OWN LOSS MUST SURELY BE AS GRAVE AS THINE!
THY WORDS HAVE THE POWER TO SOOTHE, LADY SIF! YET, FOR NOW--
--THE PRESENCE WOULD RATHER DO BATTLE WITH HIS INFINITE MISERY... ALONE!
YET, ODIN'S SOLITUDE SHALL NOT BE FOR LONG! FOR, WHEN HIS DIVINE TEARS HAVE DRIED IN HIS BRISTLING WHISKERS...
...THEN WILL HIS SON LOKI BE EVER AT HIS SIDE!
"AND, DURING THOSE ETERNAL DAYS IN WHICH ODIN FIGHTS TO OVERCOME HIS GRIEF...
"...ON EARTH, THORDIS HAS PROBLEMS OF HER OWN.
NO! IT'S NOT POSSIBLE! NOTHING SHOULD BE ABLE TO STOP THE RADIOACTIVE MAN!!*
*BUT THOR DID, IN VARIOUS EARLY ISSUES. --R.T.
NOTHING?! BETTER BRUSH UP ON YOUR MYTHOLOGY--PARTICULARLY ABOUT A CERTAIN HAMMER!

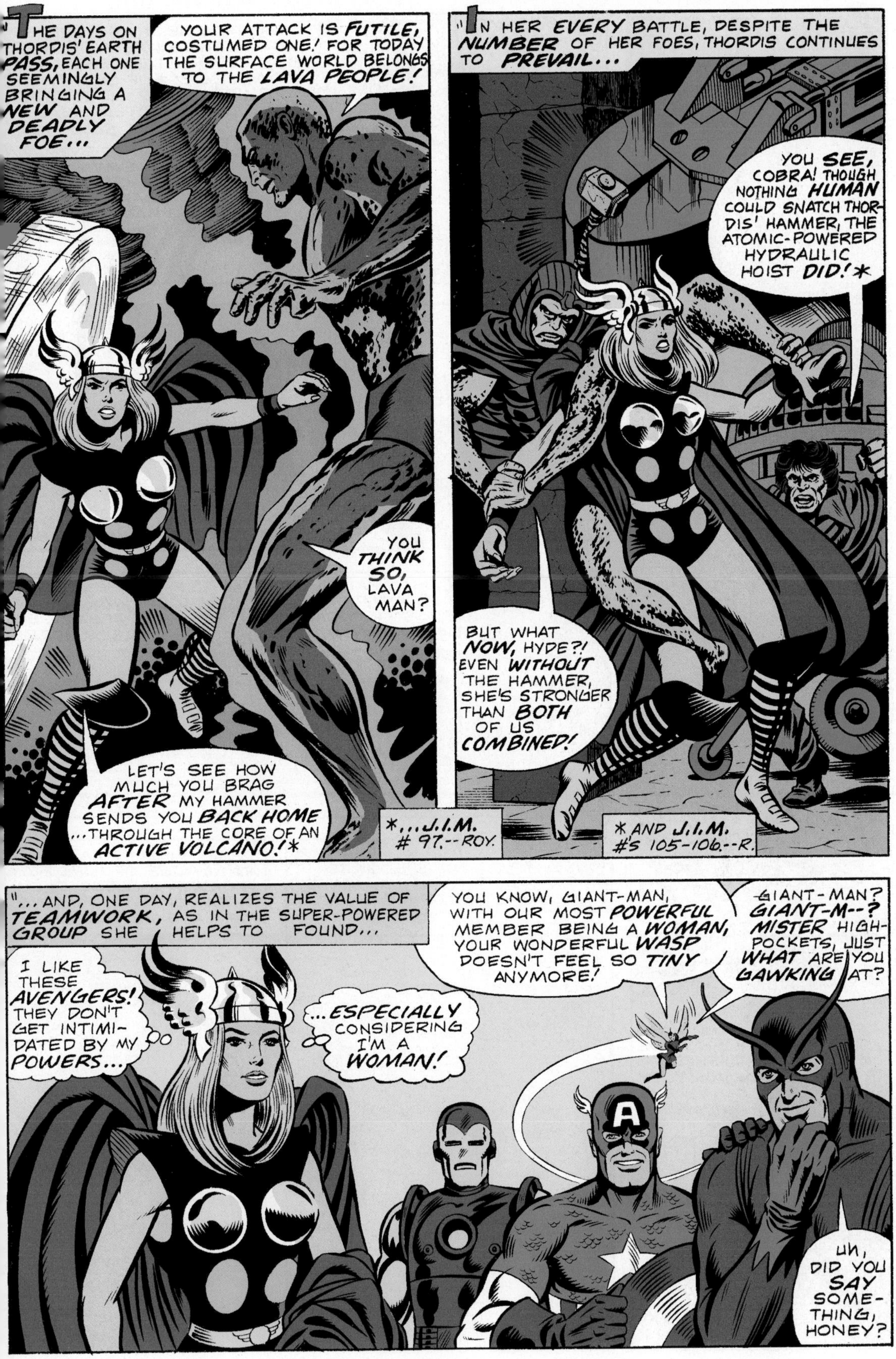

THE DAYS ON THORDIS' EARTH PASS, EACH ONE SEEMINGLY BRINGING A NEW AND DEADLY FOE...
YOUR ATTACK IS FUTILE, COSTUMED ONE! FOR TODAY THE SURFACE WORLD BELONGS TO THE LAVA PEOPLE!
YOU THINK SO, LAVA MAN?
LET'S SEE HOW MUCH YOU BRAG AFTER MY HAMMER SENDS YOU BACK HOME ...THROUGH THE CORE OF AN ACTIVE VOLCANO!*
*...J.I.M. # 97.--ROY.
IN HER EVERY BATTLE, DESPITE THE NUMBER OF HER FOES, THORDIS CONTINUES TO PREVAIL...
YOU SEE, COBRA! THOUGH NOTHING HUMAN COULD SNATCH THORDIS' HAMMER, THE ATOMIC-POWERED HYDRAULIC HOIST DID!*
BUT WHAT NOW, HYDE?! EVEN WITHOUT THE HAMMER, SHE'S STRONGER THAN BOTH OF US COMBINED!
* AND J.I.M. #'S 105-106.--R.
"...AND, ONE DAY, REALIZES THE VALUE OF TEAMWORK, AS IN THE SUPER-POWERED GROUP SHE HELPS TO FOUND...
I LIKE THESE AVENGERS! THEY DON'T GET INTIMIDATED BY MY POWERS...
...ESPECIALLY CONSIDERING I'M A WOMAN!
YOU KNOW, GIANT-MAN, WITH OUR MOST POWERFUL MEMBER BEING A WOMAN, YOUR WONDERFUL WASP DOESN'T FEEL SO TINY ANYMORE!
GIANT-MAN? GIANT-M--? MISTER HIGH-POCKETS, JUST WHAT ARE YOU GAWKING AT?
UH, DID YOU SAY SOMETHING, HONEY?

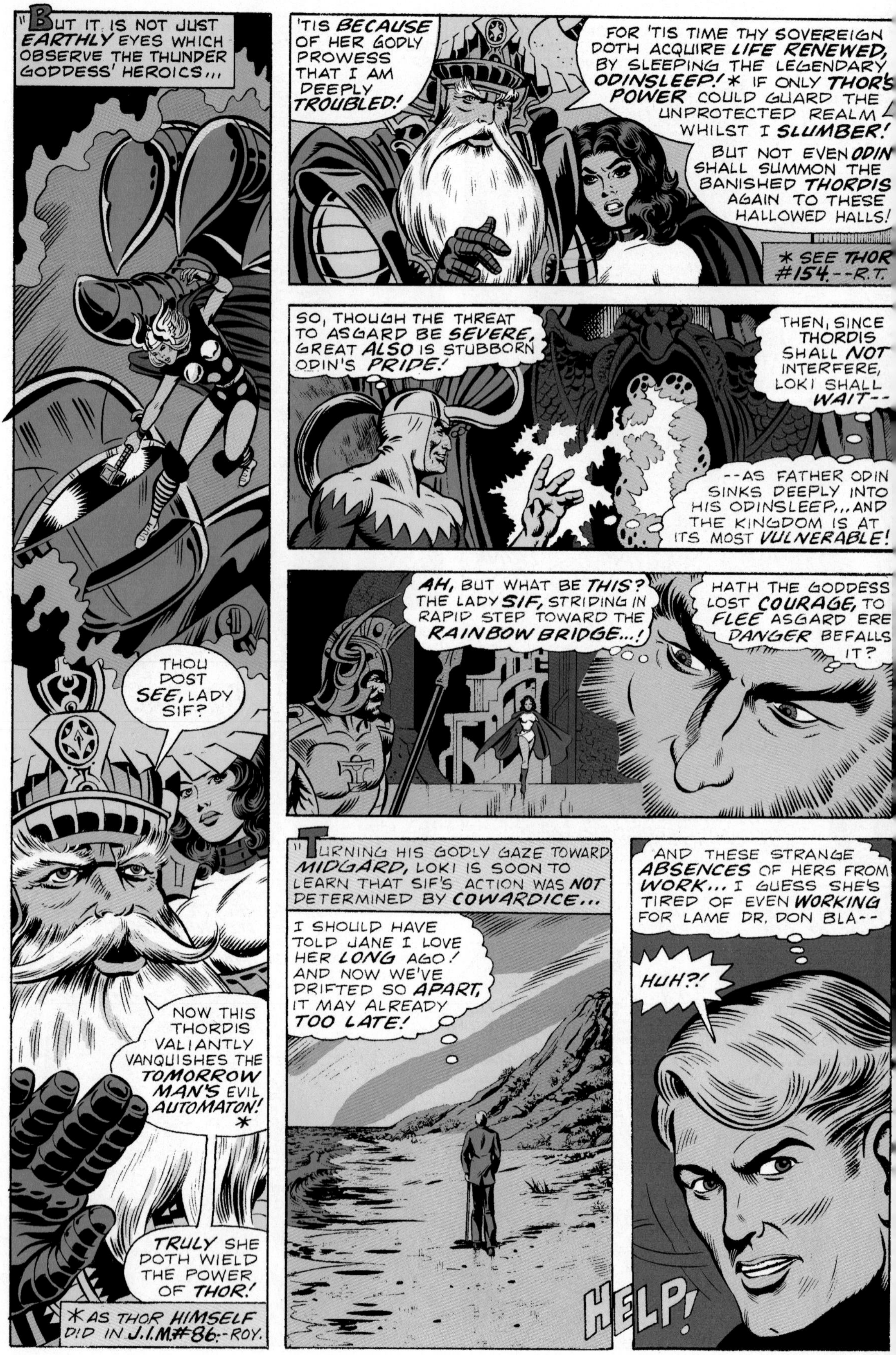
"BUT IT IS NOT JUST EARTHLY EYES WHICH OBSERVE THE THUNDER GODDESS' HEROICS...
THOU DOST SEE, LADY SIF?
NOW THIS THORDIS VALIANTLY VANQUISHES THE TOMORROW MAN'S EVIL AUTOMATON! *
TRULY SHE DOTH WIELD THE POWER OF THOR!
* AS THOR HIMSELF DID IN J.I.M.#86.-ROY.
'TIS BECAUSE OF HER GODLY PROWESS THAT I AM DEEPLY TROUBLED!
FOR 'TIS TIME THY SOVEREIGN DOTH ACQUIRE LIFE RENEWED, BY SLEEPING THE LEGENDARY ODINSLEEP! * IF ONLY THOR'S POWER COULD GUARD THE UNPROTECTED REALM WHILST I SLUMBER!
BUT NOT EVEN ODIN SHALL SUMMON THE BANISHED THORDIS AGAIN TO THESE HALLOWED HALLS!
* SEE THOR #154.--R.T.
SO, THOUGH THE THREAT TO ASGARD BE SEVERE, GREAT ALSO IS STUBBORN ODIN'S PRIDE!
THEN, SINCE THORDIS SHALL NOT INTERFERE, LOKI SHALL WAIT--
--AS FATHER ODIN SINKS DEEPLY INTO HIS ODINSLEEP... AND THE KINGDOM IS AT ITS MOST VULNERABLE!
AH, BUT WHAT BE THIS? THE LADY SIF, STRIDING IN RAPID STEP TOWARD THE RAINBOW BRIDGE...!
HATH THE GODDESS LOST COURAGE, TO FLEE ASGARD ERE DANGER BEFALLS IT?
"TURNING HIS GODLY GAZE TOWARD MIDGARD, LOKI IS SOON TO LEARN THAT SIF'S ACTION WAS NOT DETERMINED BY COWARDICE...
I SHOULD HAVE TOLD JANE I LOVE HER LONG AGO! AND NOW WE'VE DRIFTED SO APART, IT MAY ALREADY TOO LATE!
AND THESE STRANGE ABSENCES OF HERS FROM WORK... I GUESS SHE'S TIRED OF EVEN WORKING FOR LAME DR. DON BLA--
HUH?!
HELP!

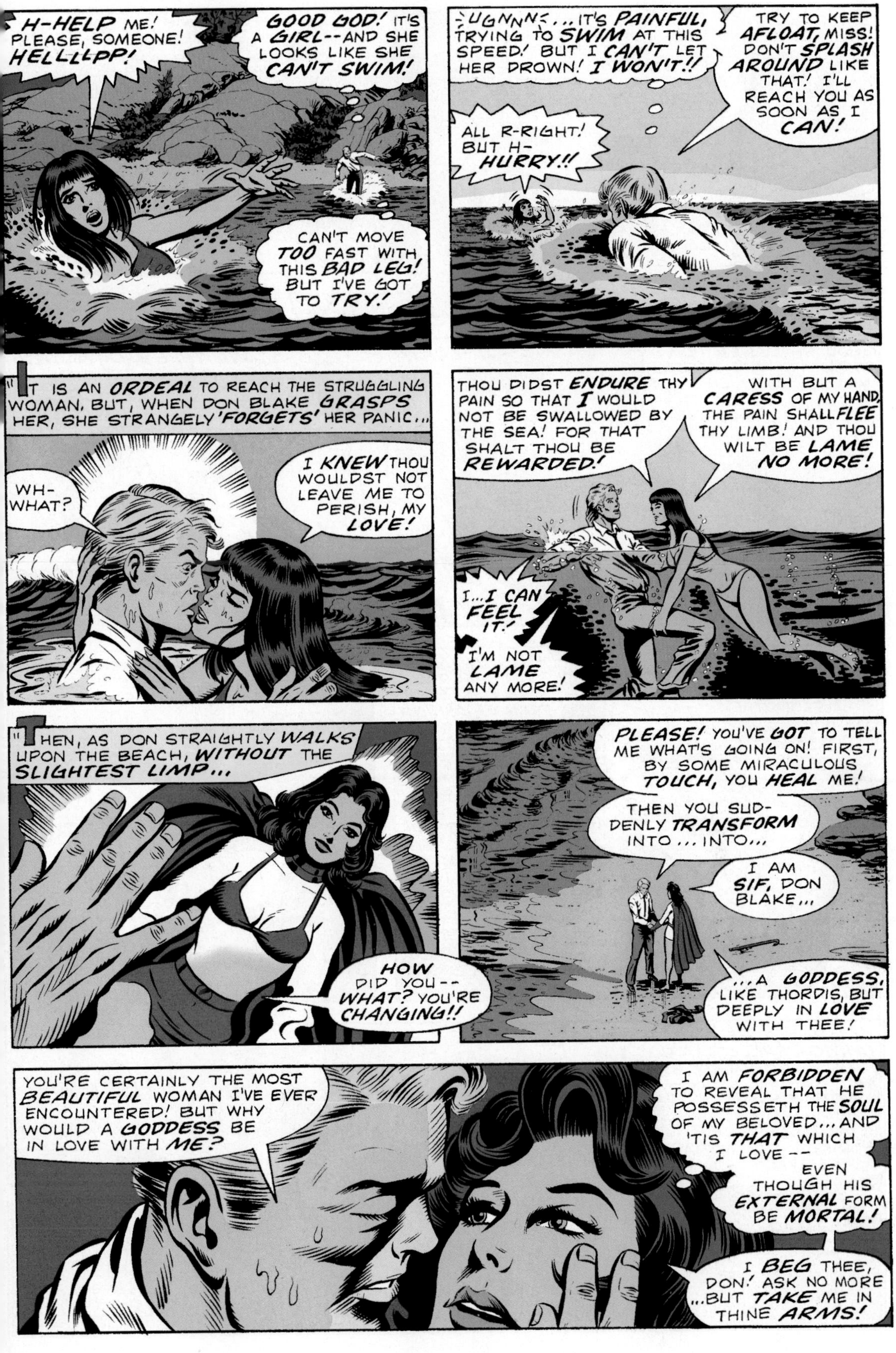

H-HELP ME! PLEASE, SOMEONE! HELLLLPP!
GOOD GOD! IT'S A GIRL--AND SHE LOOKS LIKE SHE CAN'T SWIM!
CAN'T MOVE TOO FAST WITH THIS BAD LEG! BUT I'VE GOT TO TRY!
UGNNN... IT'S PAINFUL, TRYING TO SWIM AT THIS SPEED! BUT I CAN'T LET HER DROWN! I WON'T!!
TRY TO KEEP AFLOAT, MISS! DON'T SPLASH AROUND LIKE THAT! I'LL REACH YOU AS SOON AS I CAN!
ALL R-RIGHT! BUT H-HURRY!!
IT IS AN ORDEAL TO REACH THE STRUGGLING WOMAN, BUT, WHEN DON BLAKE GRASPS HER, SHE STRANGELY 'FORGETS' HER PANIC...
WH-WHAT?
I KNEW THOU WOULDST NOT LEAVE ME TO PERISH, MY LOVE!
THOU DIDST ENDURE THY PAIN SO THAT I WOULD NOT BE SWALLOWED BY THE SEA! FOR THAT SHALT THOU BE REWARDED!
WITH BUT A CARESS OF MY HAND, THE PAIN SHALL FLEE THY LIMB! AND THOU WILT BE LAME NO MORE!
I... I CAN FEEL IT!
I'M NOT LAME ANY MORE!
THEN, AS DON STRAIGHTLY WALKS UPON THE BEACH, WITHOUT THE SLIGHTEST LIMP...
HOW DID YOU-- WHAT? YOU'RE CHANGING!!
PLEASE! YOU'VE GOT TO TELL ME WHAT'S GOING ON! FIRST, BY SOME MIRACULOUS TOUCH, YOU HEAL ME!
THEN YOU SUDDENLY TRANSFORM INTO... INTO...
I AM SIF, DON BLAKE...
...A GODDESS, LIKE THORDIS, BUT DEEPLY IN LOVE WITH THEE!
YOU'RE CERTAINLY THE MOST BEAUTIFUL WOMAN I'VE EVER ENCOUNTERED! BUT WHY WOULD A GODDESS BE IN LOVE WITH ME?
I AM FORBIDDEN TO REVEAL THAT HE POSSESSETH THE SOUL OF MY BELOVED... AND 'TIS THAT WHICH I LOVE -- EVEN THOUGH HIS EXTERNAL FORM BE MORTAL!
I BEG THEE, DON! ASK NO MORE ...BUT TAKE ME IN THINE ARMS!

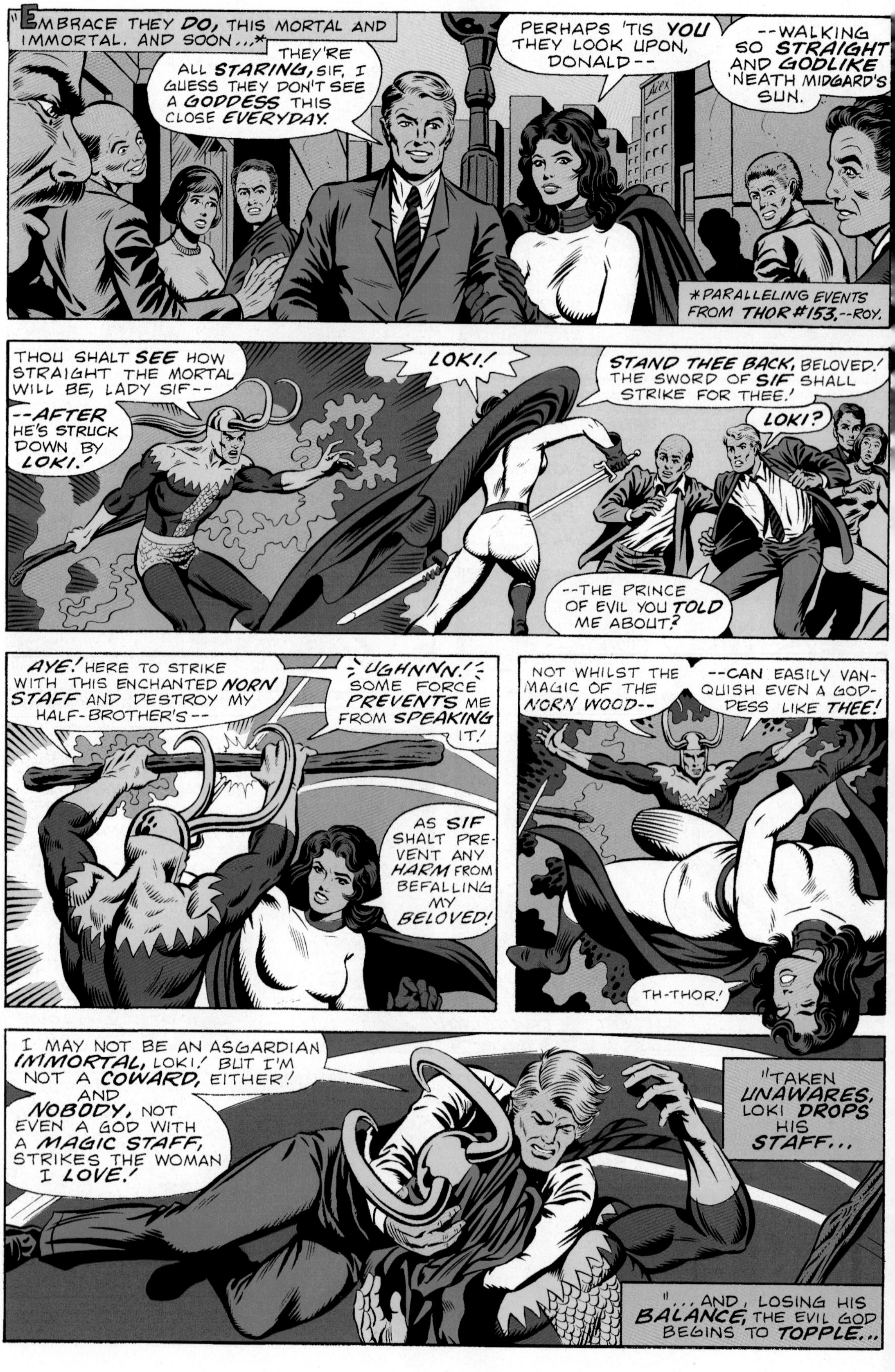
"EMBRACE THEY DO, THIS MORTAL AND IMMORTAL. AND SOON...*
THEY'RE ALL STARING, SIF. I GUESS THEY DON'T SEE A GODDESS THIS CLOSE EVERYDAY.
PERHAPS 'TIS YOU THEY LOOK UPON, DONALD--
--WALKING SO STRAIGHT AND GODLIKE 'NEATH MIDGARD'S SUN.
*PARALLELING EVENTS FROM THOR #153.--ROY.
THOU SHALT SEE HOW STRAIGHT THE MORTAL WILL BE, LADY SIF--
--AFTER HE'S STRUCK DOWN BY LOKI!
LOKI!
STAND THEE BACK, BELOVED! THE SWORD OF SIF SHALL STRIKE FOR THEE!
LOKI?
--THE PRINCE OF EVIL YOU TOLD ME ABOUT?
AYE! HERE TO STRIKE WITH THIS ENCHANTED NORN STAFF AND DESTROY MY HALF-BROTHER'S--
UGHNNN! SOME FORCE PREVENTS ME FROM SPEAKING IT!
AS SIF SHALT PREVENT ANY HARM FROM BEFALLING MY BELOVED!
NOT WHILST THE MAGIC OF THE NORN WOOD--
--CAN EASILY VANQUISH EVEN A GODDESS LIKE THEE!
TH-THOR!
I MAY NOT BE AN ASGARDIAN IMMORTAL, LOKI! BUT I'M NOT A COWARD, EITHER!
AND NOBODY, NOT EVEN A GOD WITH A MAGIC STAFF, STRIKES THE WOMAN I LOVE!
"TAKEN UNAWARES, LOKI DROPS HIS STAFF...
"...AND, LOSING HIS BALANCE, THE EVIL GOD BEGINS TO TOPPLE...

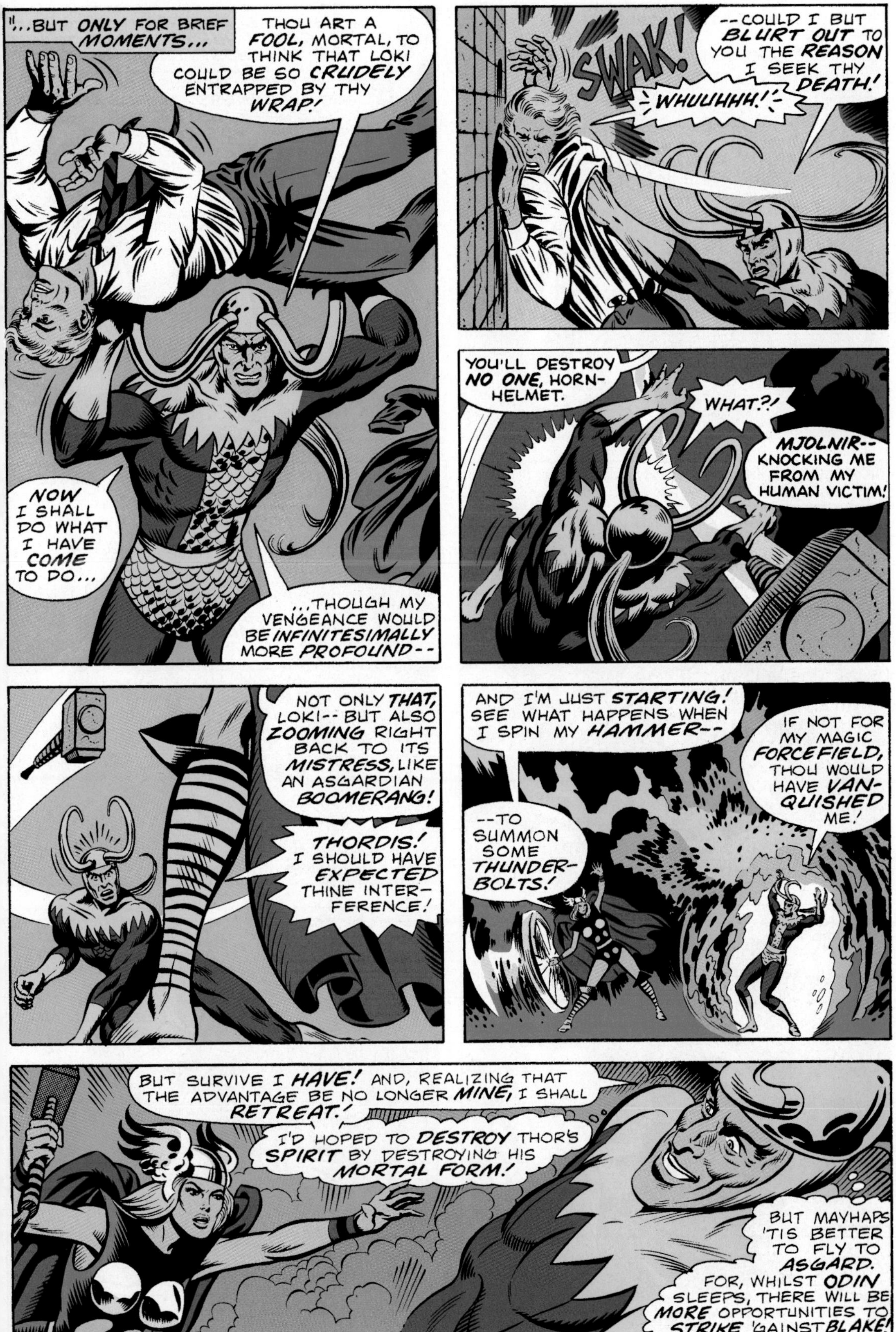

"...BUT ONLY FOR BRIEF MOMENTS...
THOU ART A FOOL, MORTAL, TO THINK THAT LOKI COULD BE SO CRUDELY ENTRAPPED BY THY WRAP!
NOW I SHALL DO WHAT I HAVE COME TO DO...
...THOUGH MY VENGEANCE WOULD BE INFINITESIMALLY MORE PROFOUND--
SWAK!
--COULD I BUT BLURT OUT TO YOU THE REASON I SEEK THY DEATH!
WHUUHHH!
YOU'LL DESTROY NO ONE, HORN-HELMET.
WHAT?!
MJOLNIR--KNOCKING ME FROM MY HUMAN VICTIM!
NOT ONLY THAT, LOKI--BUT ALSO ZOOMING RIGHT BACK TO ITS MISTRESS, LIKE AN ASGARDIAN BOOMERANG!
THORDIS! I SHOULD HAVE EXPECTED THINE INTER-FERENCE!
AND I'M JUST STARTING! SEE WHAT HAPPENS WHEN I SPIN MY HAMMER--
--TO SUMMON SOME THUNDER-BOLTS!
IF NOT FOR MY MAGIC FORCEFIELD, THOU WOULD HAVE VAN-QUISHED ME!
BUT SURVIVE I HAVE! AND, REALIZING THAT THE ADVANTAGE BE NO LONGER MINE, I SHALL RETREAT!
I'D HOPED TO DESTROY THOR'S SPIRIT BY DESTROYING HIS MORTAL FORM!
BUT MAYHAPS 'TIS BETTER TO FLY TO ASGARD. FOR, WHILST ODIN SLEEPS, THERE WILL BE MORE OPPORTUNITIES TO STRIKE 'GAINST BLAKE!

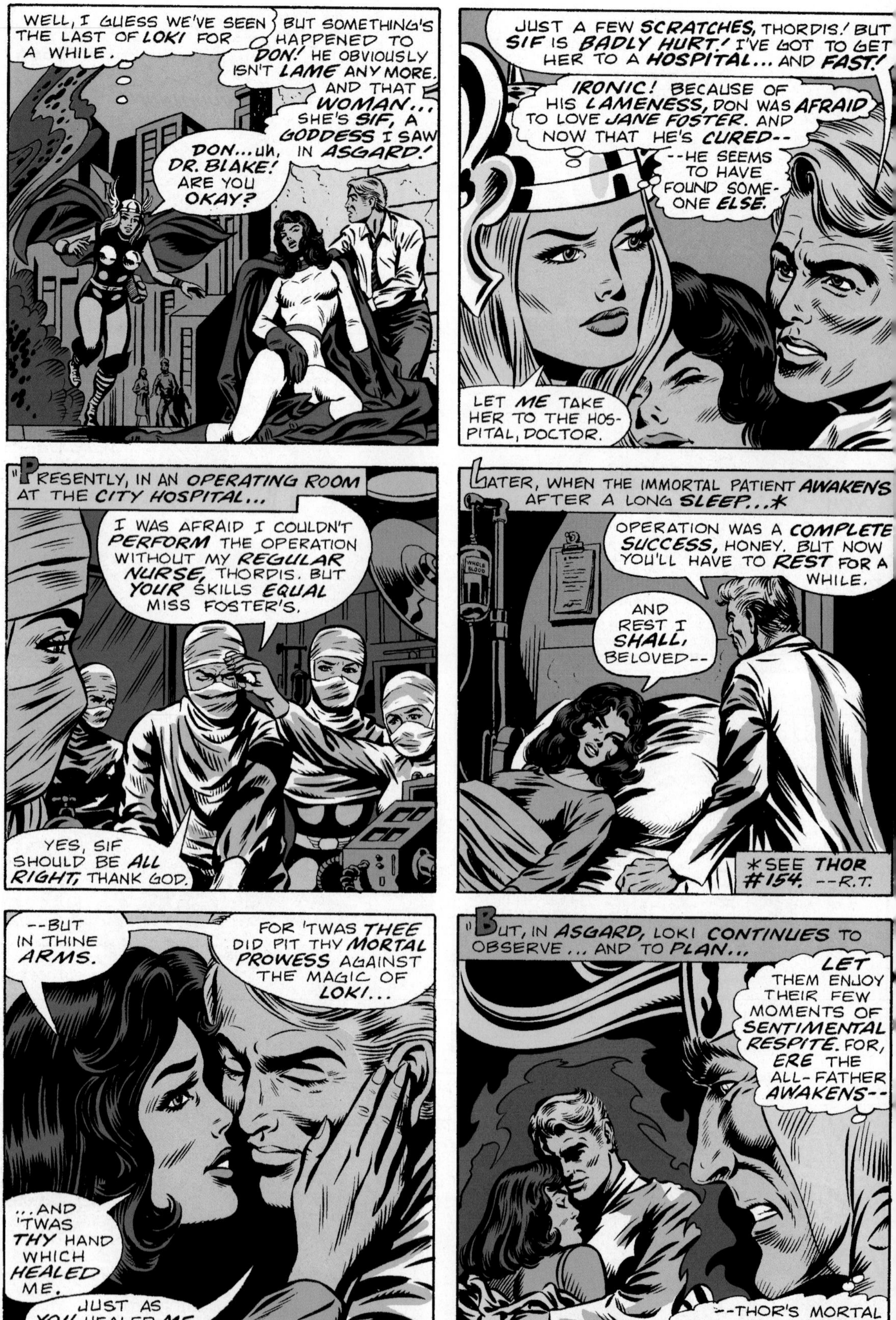
WELL, I GUESS WE'VE SEEN THE LAST OF LOKI FOR A WHILE.
BUT SOMETHING'S HAPPENED TO DON! HE OBVIOUSLY ISN'T LAME ANY MORE. AND THAT WOMAN... SHE'S SIF, A GODDESS I SAW IN ASGARD!
DON... uh, DR. BLAKE! ARE YOU OKAY?
JUST A FEW SCRATCHES, THORDIS! BUT SIF IS BADLY HURT! I'VE GOT TO GET HER TO A HOSPITAL... AND FAST!
IRONIC! BECAUSE OF HIS LAMENESS, DON WAS AFRAID TO LOVE JANE FOSTER. AND NOW THAT HE'S CURED--
--HE SEEMS TO HAVE FOUND SOMEONE ELSE.
LET ME TAKE HER TO THE HOSPITAL, DOCTOR.
PRESENTLY, IN AN OPERATING ROOM AT THE CITY HOSPITAL...
I WAS AFRAID I COULDN'T PERFORM THE OPERATION WITHOUT MY REGULAR NURSE, THORDIS. BUT YOUR SKILLS EQUAL MISS FOSTER'S.
YES, SIF SHOULD BE ALL RIGHT, THANK GOD.
LATER, WHEN THE IMMORTAL PATIENT AWAKENS AFTER A LONG SLEEP...*
OPERATION WAS A COMPLETE SUCCESS, HONEY. BUT NOW YOU'LL HAVE TO REST FOR A WHILE.
AND REST I SHALL, BELOVED--
*SEE THOR #154. --R.T.
--BUT IN THINE ARMS.
FOR 'TWAS THEE DID PIT THY MORTAL PROWESS AGAINST THE MAGIC OF LOKI...
...AND 'TWAS THY HAND WHICH HEALED ME.
JUST AS YOU HEALED ME REMEMBER?
BUT, IN ASGARD, LOKI CONTINUES TO OBSERVE... AND TO PLAN...
LET THEM ENJOY THEIR FEW MOMENTS OF SENTIMENTAL RESPITE. FOR, ERE THE ALL-FATHER AWAKENS--
--THOR'S MORTAL SHELL SHALL PERISH, NEVER TO RISE AGAIN!

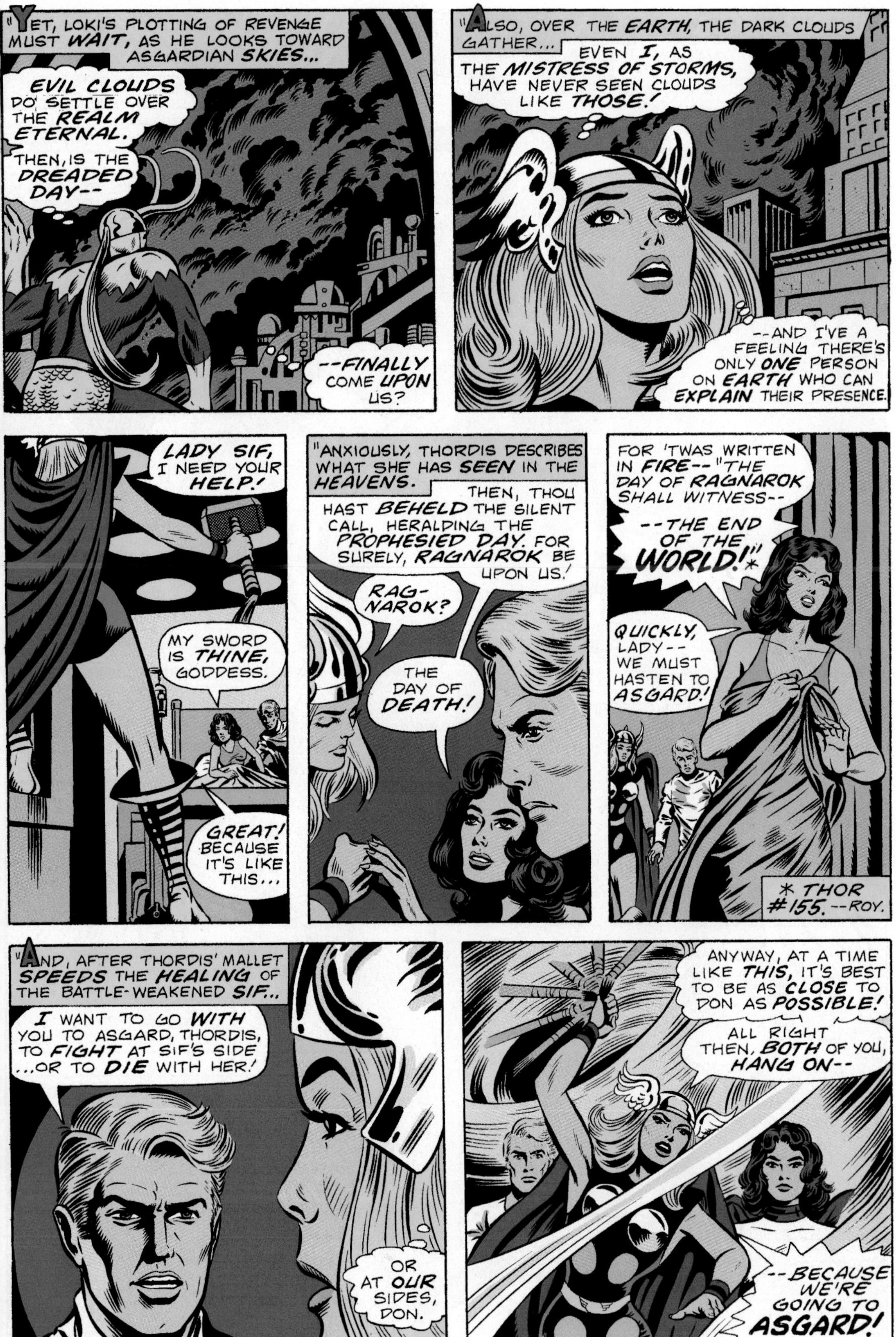
"YET, LOKI'S PLOTTING OF REVENGE MUST WAIT, AS HE LOOKS TOWARD ASGARDIAN SKIES...
EVIL CLOUDS DO SETTLE OVER THE REALM ETERNAL.
THEN, IS THE DREADED DAY--
--FINALLY COME UPON US?
"ALSO, OVER THE EARTH, THE DARK CLOUDS GATHER...
EVEN I, AS THE MISTRESS OF STORMS, HAVE NEVER SEEN CLOUDS LIKE THOSE!
--AND I'VE A FEELING THERE'S ONLY ONE PERSON ON EARTH WHO CAN EXPLAIN THEIR PRESENCE.
LADY SIF, I NEED YOUR HELP!
MY SWORD IS THINE, GODDESS.
GREAT! BECAUSE IT'S LIKE THIS...
"ANXIOUSLY, THORDIS DESCRIBES WHAT SHE HAS SEEN IN THE HEAVENS.
THEN, THOU HAST BEHELD THE SILENT CALL, HERALDING THE PROPHESIED DAY. FOR SURELY, RAGNAROK BE UPON US!
RAG-NAROK?
THE DAY OF DEATH!
FOR 'TWAS WRITTEN IN FIRE-- "THE DAY OF RAGNAROK SHALL WITNESS--
--THE END OF THE WORLD!"*
QUICKLY, LADY-- WE MUST HASTEN TO ASGARD!
* THOR #155. --ROY.
"AND, AFTER THORDIS' MALLET SPEEDS THE HEALING OF THE BATTLE-WEAKENED SIF...
I WANT TO GO WITH YOU TO ASGARD, THORDIS, TO FIGHT AT SIF'S SIDE ...OR TO DIE WITH HER!
OR AT OUR SIDES, DON.
ANYWAY, AT A TIME LIKE THIS, IT'S BEST TO BE AS CLOSE TO DON AS POSSIBLE!
ALL RIGHT THEN. BOTH OF YOU, HANG ON--
--BECAUSE WE'RE GOING TO ASGARD!

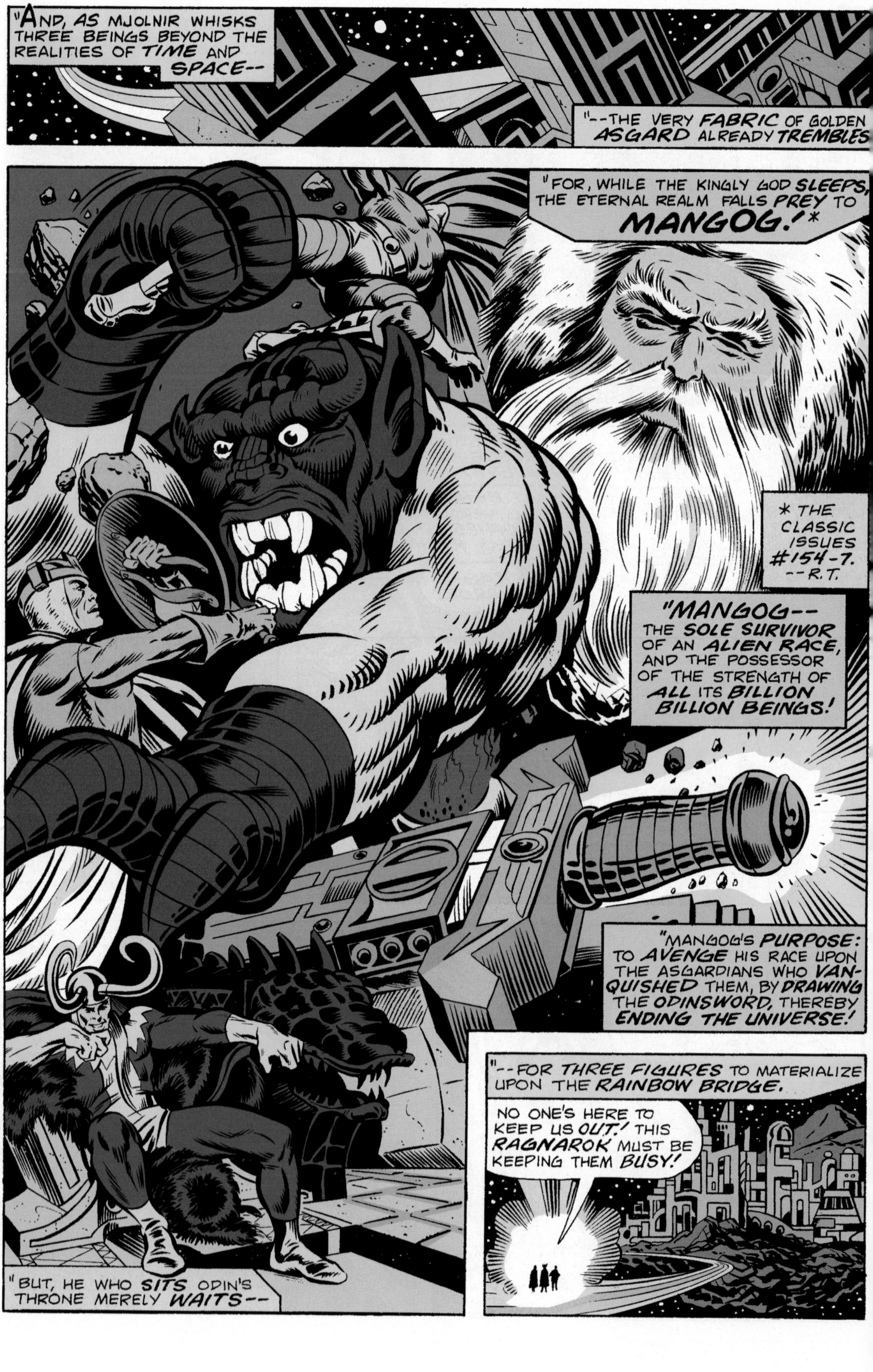
"AND, AS MJOLNIR WHISKS THREE BEINGS BEYOND THE REALITIES OF TIME AND SPACE--
"--THE VERY FABRIC OF GOLDEN ASGARD ALREADY TREMBLES
"FOR, WHILE THE KINGLY GOD SLEEPS, THE ETERNAL REALM FALLS PREY TO MANGOG!"*
* THE CLASSIC ISSUES #154-7. --R.T.
"MANGOG-- THE SOLE SURVIVOR OF AN ALIEN RACE, AND THE POSSESSOR OF THE STRENGTH OF ALL ITS BILLION BILLION BEINGS!
"MANGOG'S PURPOSE: TO AVENGE HIS RACE UPON THE ASGARDIANS WHO VANQUISHED THEM, BY DRAWING THE ODINSWORD, THEREBY ENDING THE UNIVERSE!
"BUT, HE WHO SITS ODIN'S THRONE MERELY WAITS--
"--FOR THREE FIGURES TO MATERIALIZE UPON THE RAINBOW BRIDGE.
NO ONE'S HERE TO KEEP US OUT! THIS RAGNAROK MUST BE KEEPING THEM BUSY!

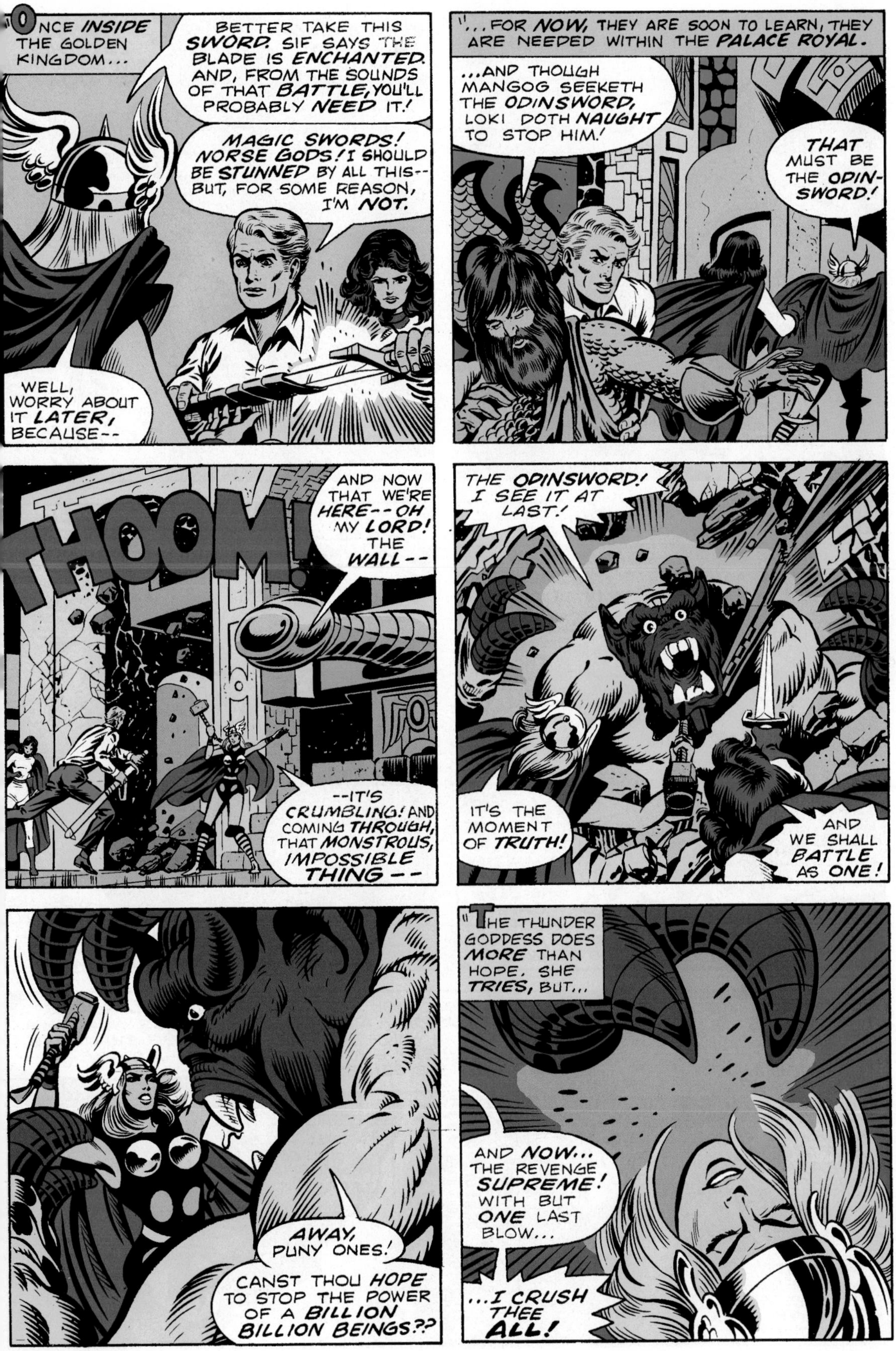
ONCE INSIDE THE GOLDEN KINGDOM...
BETTER TAKE THIS SWORD. SIF SAYS THE BLADE IS ENCHANTED. AND, FROM THE SOUNDS OF THAT BATTLE, YOU'LL PROBABLY NEED IT!
MAGIC SWORDS! NORSE GODS! I SHOULD BE STUNNED BY ALL THIS-- BUT, FOR SOME REASON, I'M NOT.
WELL, WORRY ABOUT IT LATER, BECAUSE--
"...FOR NOW, THEY ARE SOON TO LEARN, THEY ARE NEEDED WITHIN THE PALACE ROYAL.
...AND THOUGH MANGOG SEEKETH THE ODINSWORD, LOKI DOTH NAUGHT TO STOP HIM!
THAT MUST BE THE ODINSWORD!
THOOM!
AND NOW THAT WE'RE HERE--OH MY LORD! THE WALL--
--IT'S CRUMBLING! AND COMING THROUGH, THAT MONSTROUS, IMPOSSIBLE THING--
THE ODINSWORD! I SEE IT AT LAST!
IT'S THE MOMENT OF TRUTH!
AND WE SHALL BATTLE AS ONE!
AWAY, PUNY ONES!
CANST THOU HOPE TO STOP THE POWER OF A BILLION BILLION BEINGS??
"THE THUNDER GODDESS DOES MORE THAN HOPE. SHE TRIES, BUT...
AND NOW... THE REVENGE SUPREME! WITH BUT ONE LAST BLOW...
...I CRUSH THEE ALL!

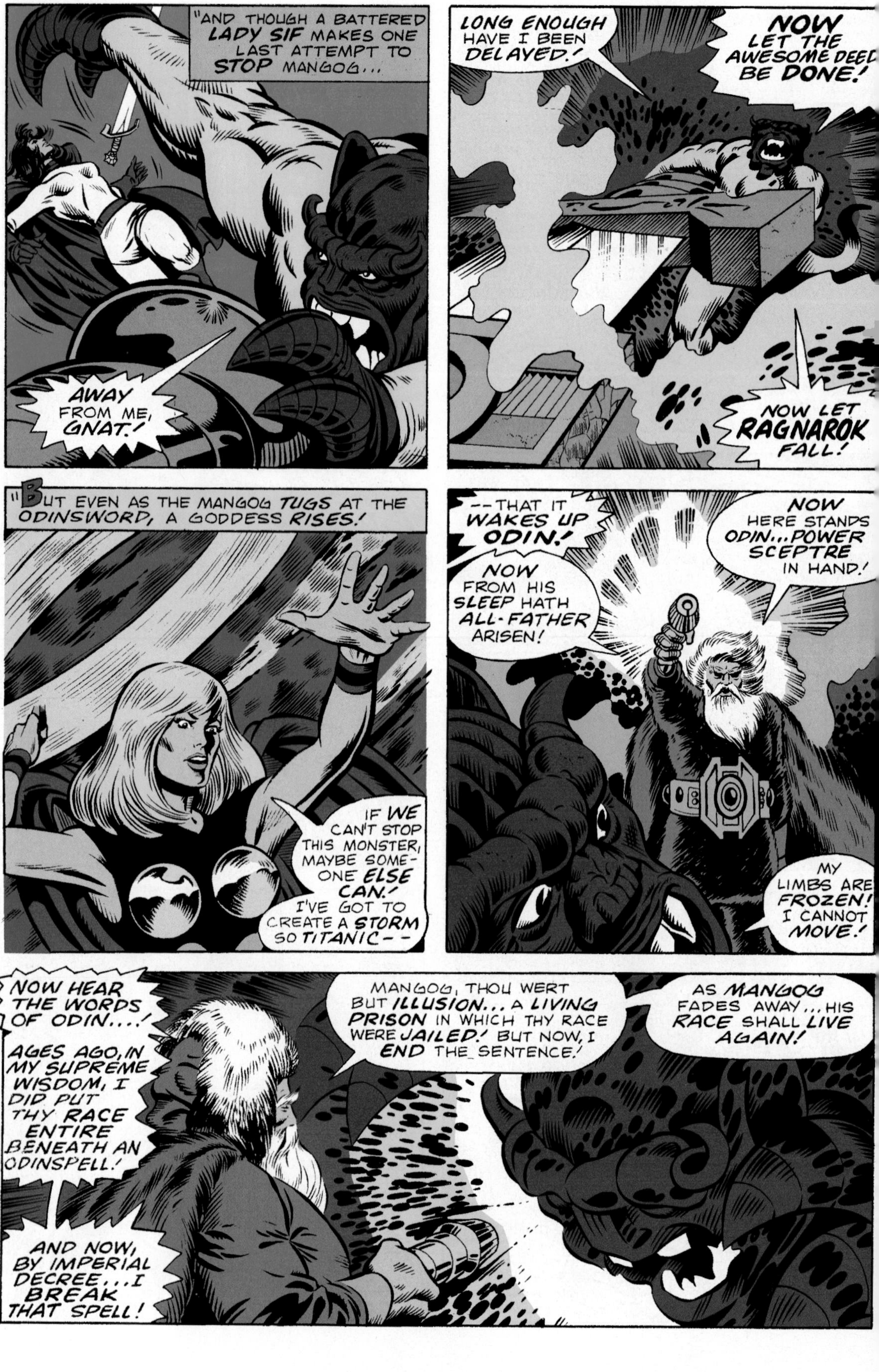

"AND THOUGH A BATTERED LADY SIF MAKES ONE LAST ATTEMPT TO STOP MANGOG...
AWAY FROM ME, GNAT!
LONG ENOUGH HAVE I BEEN DELAYED!
NOW LET THE AWESOME DEED BE DONE!
NOW LET RAGNAROK FALL!
"BUT EVEN AS THE MANGOG TUGS AT THE ODINSWORD, A GODDESS RISES!
IF WE CAN'T STOP THIS MONSTER, MAYBE SOME-ONE ELSE CAN! I'VE GOT TO CREATE A STORM SO TITANIC--
--THAT IT WAKES UP ODIN!
NOW FROM HIS SLEEP HATH ALL-FATHER ARISEN!
NOW HERE STANDS ODIN...POWER SCEPTRE IN HAND!
MY LIMBS ARE FROZEN! I CANNOT MOVE!
NOW HEAR THE WORDS OF ODIN...!
AGES AGO, IN MY SUPREME WISDOM, I DID PUT THY RACE ENTIRE BENEATH AN ODINSPELL!
AND NOW, BY IMPERIAL DECREE...I BREAK THAT SPELL!
MANGOG, THOU WERT BUT ILLUSION... A LIVING PRISON IN WHICH THY RACE WERE JAILED! BUT NOW, I END THE SENTENCE!
AS MANGOG FADES AWAY...HIS RACE SHALL LIVE AGAIN!

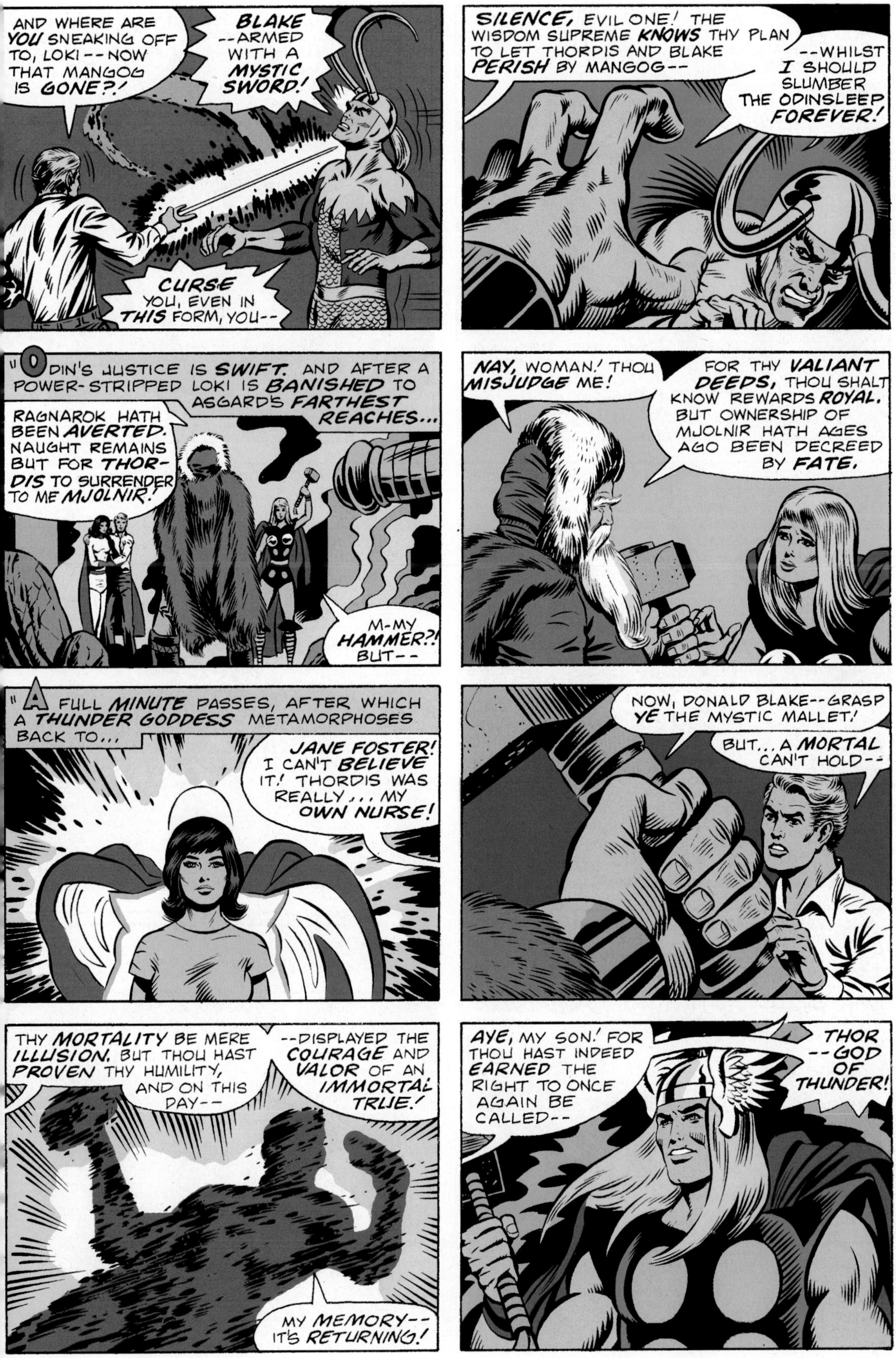
AND WHERE ARE YOU SNEAKING OFF TO, LOKI--NOW THAT MANGOG IS GONE?!
BLAKE --ARMED WITH A MYSTIC SWORD!
CURSE YOU, EVEN IN THIS FORM, YOU--
SILENCE, EVIL ONE! THE WISDOM SUPREME KNOWS THY PLAN TO LET THORDIS AND BLAKE PERISH BY MANGOG--
--WHILST I SHOULD SLUMBER THE ODINSLEEP FOREVER!
"ODIN'S JUSTICE IS SWIFT. AND AFTER A POWER-STRIPPED LOKI IS BANISHED TO ASGARD'S FARTHEST REACHES...
RAGNAROK HATH BEEN AVERTED. NAUGHT REMAINS BUT FOR THORDIS TO SURRENDER TO ME MJOLNIR!
M-MY HAMMER?! BUT--
NAY, WOMAN! THOU MISJUDGE ME!
FOR THY VALIANT DEEDS, THOU SHALT KNOW REWARDS ROYAL. BUT OWNERSHIP OF MJOLNIR HATH AGES AGO BEEN DECREED BY FATE.
"A FULL MINUTE PASSES, AFTER WHICH A THUNDER GODDESS METAMORPHOSES BACK TO...
JANE FOSTER! I CAN'T BELIEVE IT! THORDIS WAS REALLY... MY OWN NURSE!
NOW, DONALD BLAKE--GRASP YE THE MYSTIC MALLET!
BUT... A MORTAL CAN'T HOLD--
THY MORTALITY BE MERE ILLUSION. BUT THOU HAST PROVEN THY HUMILITY, AND ON THIS DAY--
--DISPLAYED THE COURAGE AND VALOR OF AN IMMORTAL TRUE!
MY MEMORY-- IT'S RETURNING!
AYE, MY SON! FOR THOU HAST INDEED EARNED THE RIGHT TO ONCE AGAIN BE CALLED--
THOR --GOD OF THUNDER!

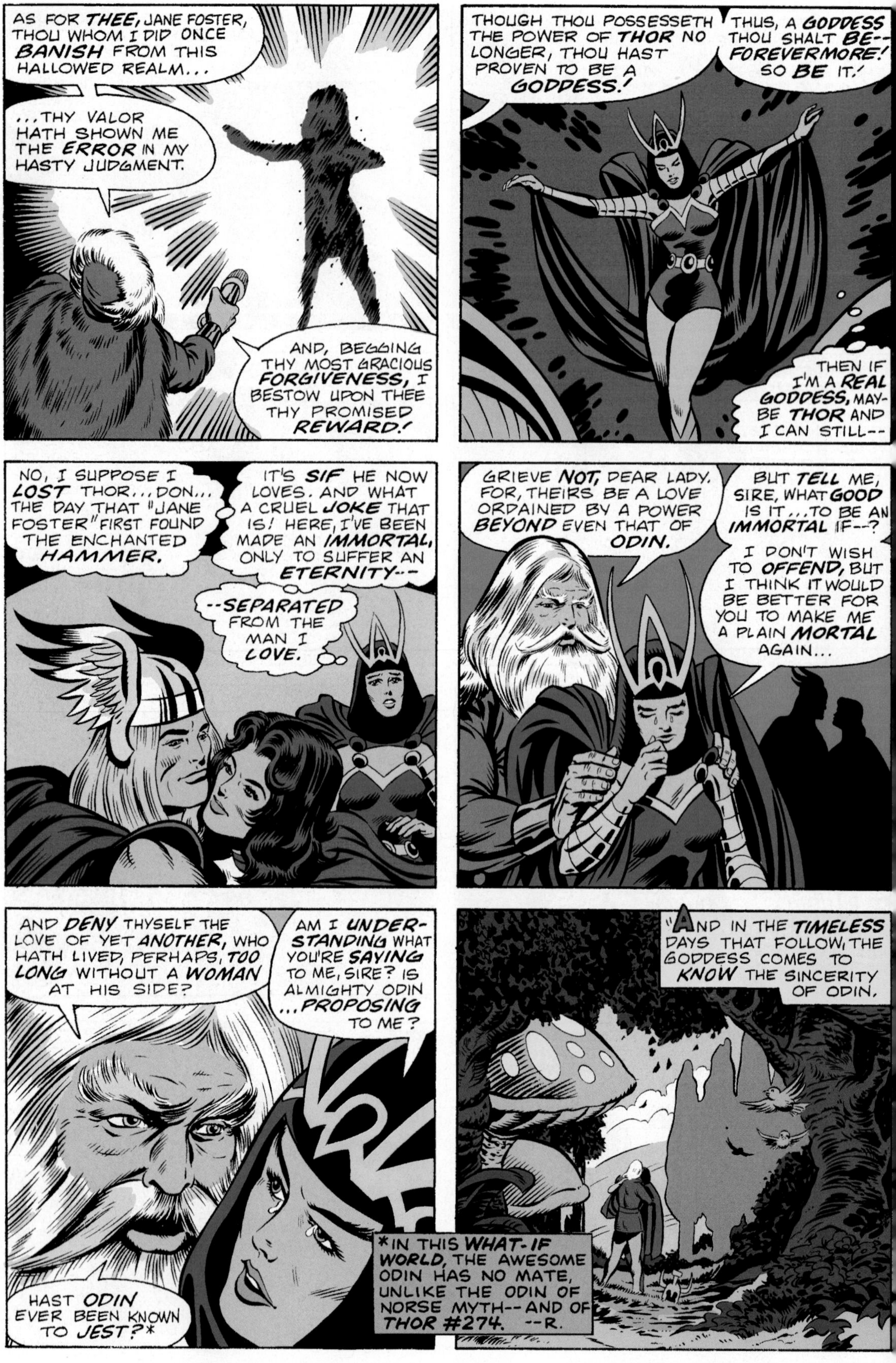
AS FOR THEE, JANE FOSTER, THOU WHOM I DID ONCE BANISH FROM THIS HALLOWED REALM...
...THY VALOR HATH SHOWN ME THE ERROR IN MY HASTY JUDGMENT.
AND, BEGGING THY MOST GRACIOUS FORGIVENESS, I BESTOW UPON THEE THY PROMISED REWARD!
THOUGH THOU POSSESSETH THE POWER OF THOR NO LONGER, THOU HAST PROVEN TO BE A GODDESS!
THUS, A GODDESS THOU SHALT BE-- FOREVERMORE! SO BE IT!
THEN IF I'M A REAL GODDESS, MAYBE THOR AND I CAN STILL--
NO, I SUPPOSE I LOST THOR...DON... THE DAY THAT "JANE FOSTER" FIRST FOUND THE ENCHANTED HAMMER.
IT'S SIF HE NOW LOVES. AND WHAT A CRUEL JOKE THAT IS! HERE, I'VE BEEN MADE AN IMMORTAL, ONLY TO SUFFER AN ETERNITY--
--SEPARATED FROM THE MAN I LOVE.
GRIEVE NOT, DEAR LADY. FOR, THEIRS BE A LOVE ORDAINED BY A POWER BEYOND EVEN THAT OF ODIN.
BUT TELL ME, SIRE, WHAT GOOD IS IT...TO BE AN IMMORTAL IF--?
I DON'T WISH TO OFFEND, BUT I THINK IT WOULD BE BETTER FOR YOU TO MAKE ME A PLAIN MORTAL AGAIN...
AND DENY THYSELF THE LOVE OF YET ANOTHER, WHO HATH LIVED, PERHAPS, TOO LONG WITHOUT A WOMAN AT HIS SIDE?
AM I UNDERSTANDING WHAT YOU'RE SAYING TO ME, SIRE? IS ALMIGHTY ODIN ...PROPOSING TO ME?
HAST ODIN EVER BEEN KNOWN TO JEST?*
*IN THIS WHAT-IF WORLD, THE AWESOME ODIN HAS NO MATE, UNLIKE THE ODIN OF NORSE MYTH--AND OF THOR #274. --R.
"AND IN THE TIMELESS DAYS THAT FOLLOW, THE GODDESS COMES TO KNOW THE SINCERITY OF ODIN.

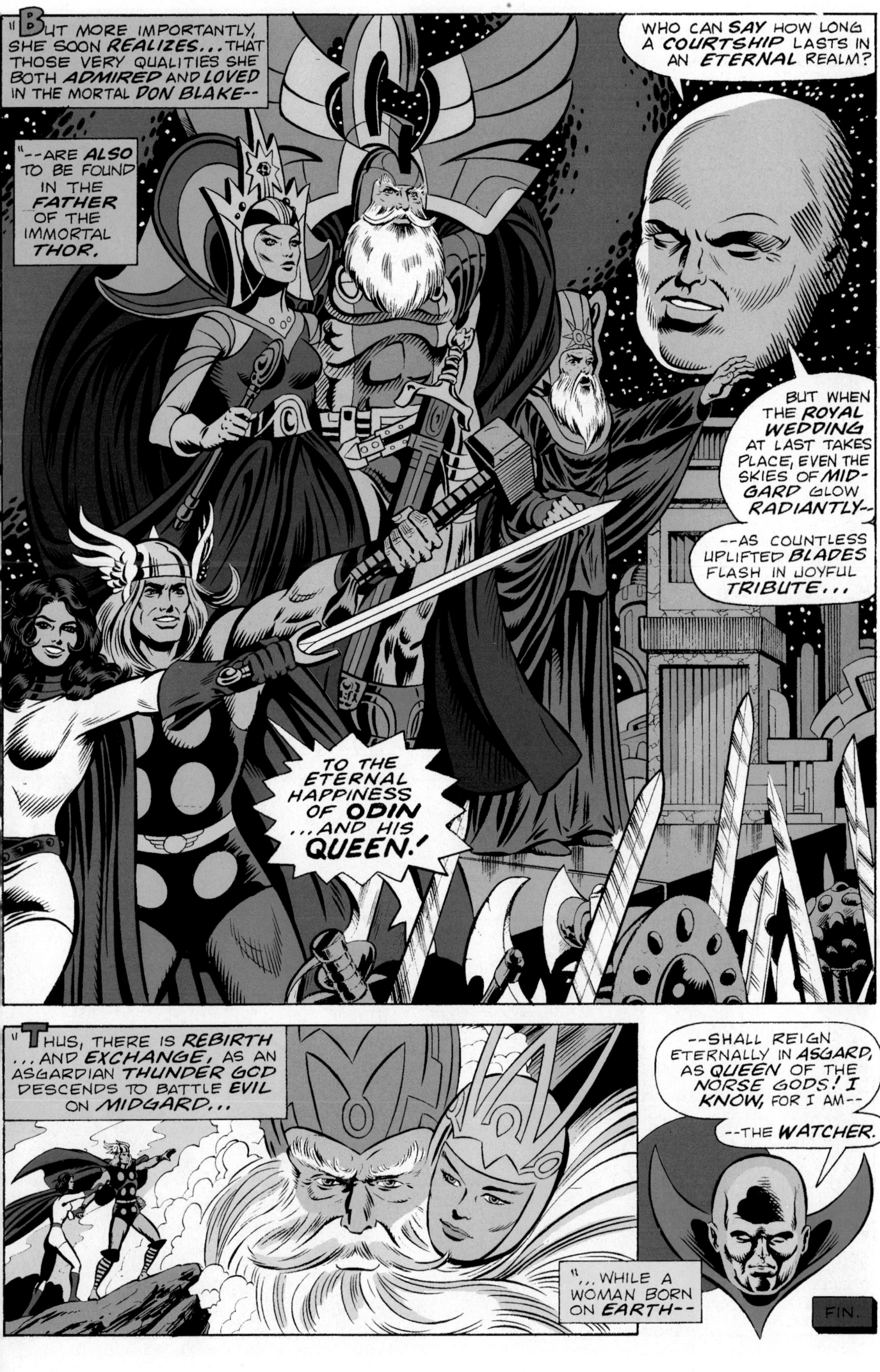
"But more importantly, she soon realizes... that those very qualities she both admired and loved in the mortal Don Blake--
"--are also to be found in the father of the immortal Thor.
Who can say how long a courtship lasts in an eternal realm?
But when the royal wedding at last takes place, even the skies of Midgard glow radiantly--
--as countless uplifted blades flash in joyful tribute...
To the eternal happiness of Odin ...and his queen!
"Thus, there is rebirth ...and exchange, as an Asgardian thunder god descends to battle evil on Midgard...
"...while a woman born on Earth--
--shall reign eternally in Asgard, as queen of the Norse gods! I know, for I am--
--the Watcher.
Fin.

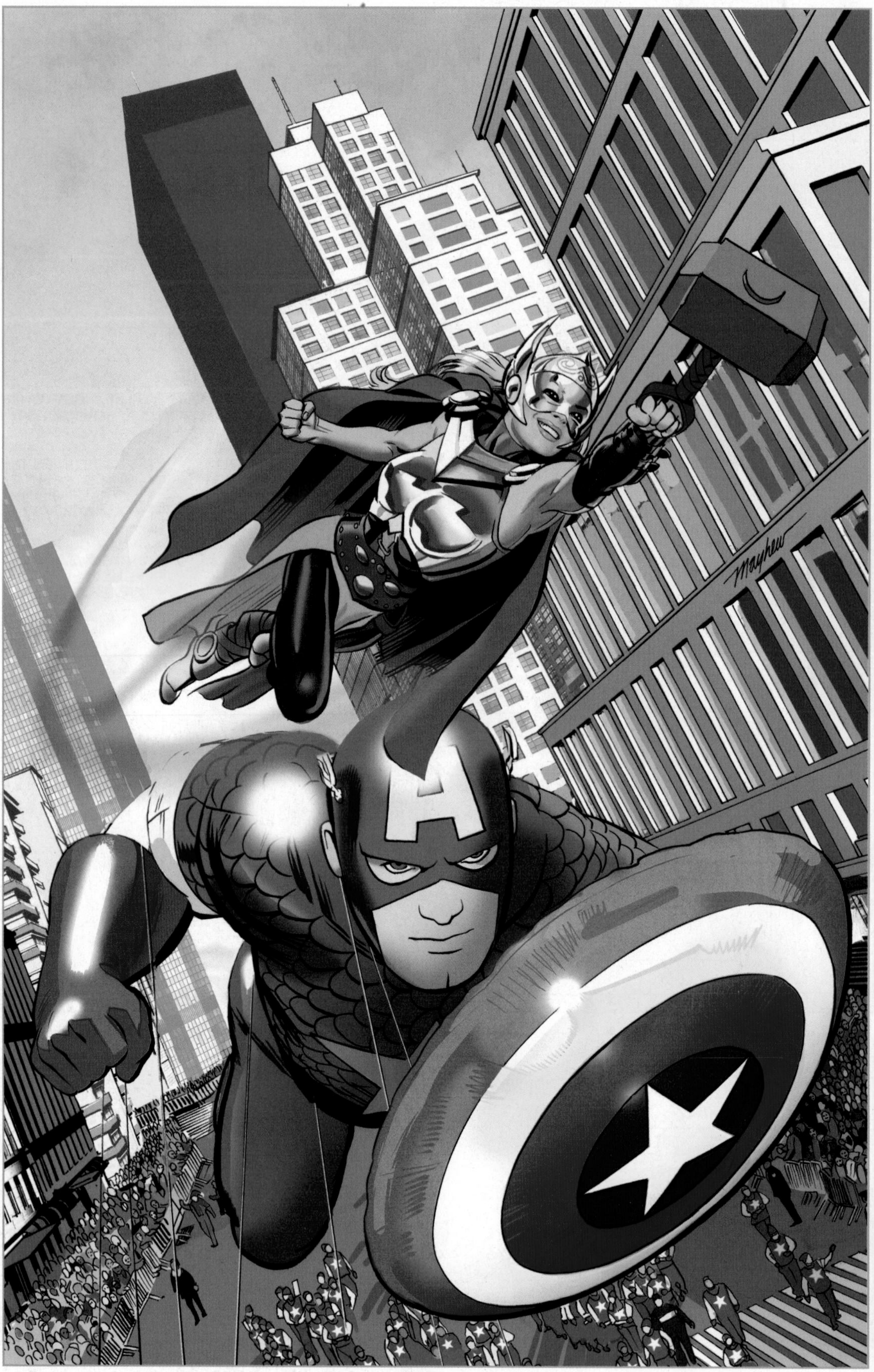
Mayhew

THOR # 8 NYC VARIANT
BY **MIKE MAYHEW**

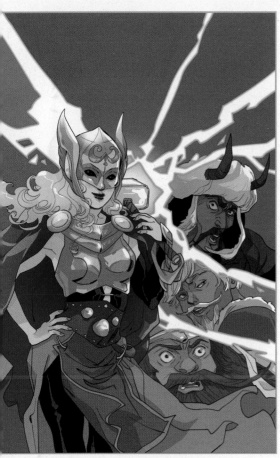

THOR ANNUAL # 1 VARIANT
BY **MARGUERITE SAUVAGE**

1
VARIANT EDITION
ANNUAL
MARVEL
THOR
MIGHTY MARVEL MIND CONTROL MATCH-UP!!!
WHO IS LOKI'S MYSTERY WRESTLER??!!
EDITOR'S NOTE: THIS DOES NOT HAPPEN IN THIS ISSUE.

THOR ANNUAL # 1 VARIANT
BY **ROB GUILLORY**

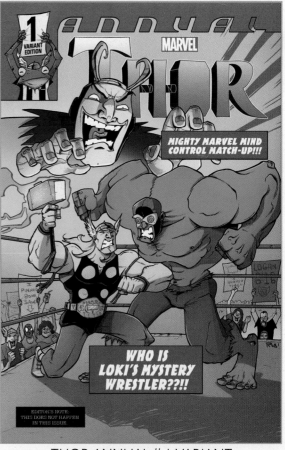

MARVEL AR AUGMENTED REALITY

MARVEL AUGMENTED REALITY (AR) ENHANCES AND CHANGES THE WAY YOU EXPERIENCE COMICS!

TO ACCESS THE FREE MARVEL AR CONTENT IN THIS BOOK*:

1. Locate the AR logo within the comic.
2. Go to Marvel.com/AR in your web browser.
3. Search by series title to find the corresponding AR.
4. Enjoy Marvel AR!

*All AR content that appears in this book has been archived and will be available only at Marvel.com/AR – no longer in the Marvel AR App. Content subject to change and availability.

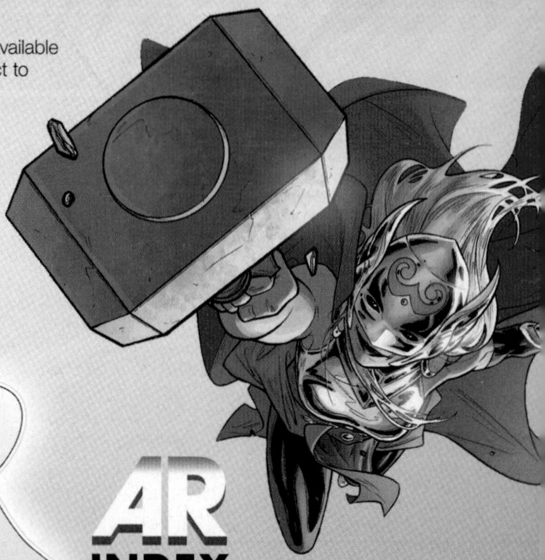

THOR AR INDEX